Contents

CW01498558

Handbook of Company Secretarial Administration

Handbook of Company Secretarial Administration

DAVID LINTOTT
BSc (Econ.), FCIS

SECOND EDITION

ICSA PUBLISHING · CAMBRIDGE

Published by ICSA Publishing Limited,
Fitzwilliam House, 32 Trumpington Street,
Cambridge CB2 1QY, England

First published 1986 as *Handbook of Company Secretarial Practice*
Second edition 1990
Second impression 1992
© ICSA Publishing Limited, 1986, 1990

British Library Cataloguing in Publication Data
Lintott, David
Handbook of company secretarial administration.–2nd ed.
1. Great Britain. Company secretaryship
I. Title II. Lintott, David. Handbook of company
secretarial practice
344.106664

ISBN 0-902197-92-4

Designed by Geoff Green
Typeset by Hands Fotoset, Leicester
Printed in Great Britain by BPCC Wheatons Ltd, Exeter

Foreword

The pace of change in company secretarial practice has been dramatic in recent years with ever increasing legislative demands being placed upon companies. In such a climate, it is essential that all who are affected by these developments understand clearly the practical implications and have access to a reliable information source.

Good company administration needs to be based upon principles of sound practice. In the pages that follow both newcomers to the field and qualified practitioners will find themselves being guided with ease and clarity on even the most complex aspects of the subject. In this regard, the Institute of Chartered Secretaries and Administrators is very willing, indeed, to lend its name to this work.

David Lintott has done a splendid job in fully updating the text of this handbook and has covered the many changes that have arisen since the first edition including the recent Companies Act 1989. David is a past Chairman of the Institute's Registrars' Group and formerly a member of its Law and Professional Services Committee.

He also has many years' experience as a practising company secretary, which he has carefully distilled into this excellent book and I commend it to every member, practitioner and student who seeks to attain a high degree of professionalism in company secretarial practice.

David Wright

David W R Wright FCIS FIPM MBIM
President of the Institute of Chartered Secretaries
and Administrators, 1990

Preface to the first edition

The object of this handbook is to prepare students for the company secretarial practice paper of the examination leading to membership of the Institute of Chartered Secretaries and Administrators. At the same time, it is hoped that it will serve as a quick and handy guide to anyone involved in the administration of companies. However, for the latter there can be no substitute for the manual *Company Secretarial Practice*, published by the Institute of Chartered Secretaries and Administrators, which is a comprehensive work published in loose-leaf form and kept fully up to date by periodic supplements. The Institute's manual also includes numerous precedents and secretarial practice notes for the detailed guidance of company secretaries. At various places in this handbook the reader in need of more detailed information is referred to the manual by reference to 'the Institute's manual'.

This present handbook, however, is intended to follow the tradition of a handbook first published in 1969 by A. Harding Boulton LLB, FCIS, which ran to three editions and was followed by a fourth edition in 1981 by Keith Walmsley LLB, FCIS, in collaboration with John Birds LLM. At the outset, therefore, it is fitting to pay tribute to the work of Harding Boulton and Keith Walmsley, whose works have provided generations of students for the Institute's examinations with practical advice on the company secretarial aspect of company administration.

At the same time, this new handbook must be seen not as a mere updating of previous editions but as a completely new work, rewritten and based on the Institute's manual to take account of the consolidated companies legislation which came into force on 1 July 1985 and which now governs the administration of companies (as referred to in the introduction). It also contains material not included in previous editions, reflecting the widening responsibilities of company secretaries in such fields as the administration of approved profit-sharing schemes, the latest developments in regard to share registration practice and transfer procedures, and the work of the securities industry.

Reference is made to the relevant legislation throughout the handbook, since anyone involved in the administration of companies should know the source of his authority and the location in the legislation which imposes the responsibility upon him. However, the emphasis throughout the handbook will be on practical application of company legislation and the work of the company secretary generally. The procedures described in this handbook are those applicable to companies registered in Great Britain, i.e. excluding Northern Ireland, where broadly similar practices are followed under the legislation and regulations applicable there, but which do not form part of the Institute's company secretarial practice syllabus.

The author would wish to express his grateful thanks to J. Wratten, Registrar of the British Petroleum Company, and currently chairman of the Institute's Registrars' Group, who kindly read the text of this handbook, as well as to Diane Brightman, who typed the manuscript and upon whom mini-cassettes fell like hailstones during the course of its production. In addition, the author thanks his wife in forgoing several months of his company during the first year of retirement in a new home on the Isle of Wight.

April 1986   DAVID LINTOTT

Preface to the second edition

Since the first edition of this handbook was published in April 1986 there has been no abatement in the number of changes regularly occurring in company secretarial practice as a result of new legislation, regulations, rules and practices promulgated by various authorities concerned with company administration.

New Acts have been brought into effect, e.g. the Insolvency Act 1986, the Financial Services Act 1986, the Company Directors' Disqualification Act 1986, and the recently enacted Companies Act 1989. Important changes in stamp duty came in with the Finance Acts 1986 and 1988 although it should be noted that the 1990 Budget proposes that most stamp duties are to be abolished when TAURUS, the dematerialised Stock Exchange settlement system currently in the process of development, is implemented, probably towards the end of 1991. The whole gamut of the securities industry was changed following 'Big Bang' on 27 October 1986, when The Stock Exchange prohibition on a person acting as both broker and jobber was removed. Accordingly, the chapters on share registration, the securities industry, receivers (now re-titled as 'Administration orders, receiverships and voluntary arrangements') and on winding-up have changed considerably. Furthermore, throughout the handbook amendments and additions have been introduced to reflect the up-to-date requirements of the new legislation, Regulations, Rules and modern procedures in company secretarial and share registration practice.

The opportunity has been taken to modify and slightly expand some parts of the text where this seemed desirable in the interests of clarity.

The author is gratified by the favourable reception of this handbook by students preparing for the company secretarial practice examination paper of the Institute of Chartered Secretaries and Administrators and hopes that this second edition will bring their knowledge up to date so as to cover the latest changes in the syllabus for this examination. It is also hoped that the company secretaries of smaller companies and others concerned with company administration may find the handbook a useful general guide to what is required of them; but it is emphasised that to be well equipped for his role the erudite company secretary will wish to acquire the Institute's manual, *Company Secretarial Practice*.

The author is indebted to former colleagues on the committee of the Institute's Registrars' Group, in particular, R. D. Gilbert MBE, currently chairman of the Group, B. P. Mould MBE, A. F. R. Watts and J. Wratten, who offered helpful suggestions on the content and text of this second and revised edition of the handbook. However, it should be made clear that responsibility for the text is the author's alone. Further, it could not have been produced without the assistance of the author's wife in patiently reading over the manuscript and proofs on numerous occasions during the production of the book.

May 1990   DAVID LINTOTT

Introduction

Company secretarial practice

The company secretary is the person principally concerned with the administration of companies; the art which he practises is known as company secretarial practice.

The term 'company secretary' is usually abbreviated merely to 'secretary', which does tend to cause confusion in many people's minds. This is unavoidable since there is no better title than 'secretary'; but it is inevitable that the uninitiated will be misled when someone holding the principal administrative post in a company describes himself as 'the secretary'. They will immediately think of someone who does the shorthand and typing in the company, although the role of that kind of secretary has rapidly expanded in recent years so that a company executive's secretary will deal with many administrative matters on his behalf, e.g. routine correspondence, travel arrangements, telephone calls and appointments. To avoid confusion, therefore, describe yourself as 'the company secretary' or perhaps 'the secretary of the company'.

This handbook, of course, is concerned with the practical duties and responsibilities of company secretaries and not secretaries of the other type. In particular, this handbook is concerned with the work of the secretaries of companies registered under the Companies Act 1985 (or the previous Companies Acts), which are required by law to have a person appointed as 'secretary'. Other types of organisation also employ secretaries as their principal administrative officers, for example professional bodies (like the Institute of Chartered Secretaries and Administrators), hospitals, public corporations, etc., the reason being that such organisations are usually controlled by a board of directors, a council or a body of governors, all of which find it necessary to have a secretary to be responsible for the overall administration of the body concerned, to take note of its decisions and to put them into effect. A secretary is often the person whom members of the public would first approach in order to bring a matter before such a body. In addition, where formal or legal documents need to be submitted to a company or an organisation, they would normally be addressed to the secretary. It might also become necessary to make some announcement concerning the activities of, or some development in, the work of the organisation, in which case the company secretary would often act as the company's or organisation's spokesman.

It should be emphasised that the company secretary will often be in possession of secret and confidential information which he acquires in the performance of his duties as secretary of the board of a registered company or of the governing body of other types of organisation mentioned above. Much of the information which the company secretary acquires will be unknown to other senior executives of the company or organisation; thus the position of company secretary is one of great responsibility and trust. Company secretarial practice can, therefore, take on another form as company *secret*arial practice.

Company secretarial practice and legislation

It has already been mentioned that company secretaries need to know where the source of their authority or their responsibility for acting in different situations can be found in legislation. The subjects of company secretarial practice and company law are, therefore, inextricably mixed and the student of company secretarial practice will have to devote a good deal of time to becoming acquainted with the legislation which affects him. It used to be necessary to take account of the provisions of a whole series of Companies Acts, i.e. Companies Act 1948, Companies Act 1967, Companies Act 1976, Companies Act 1980 and the Companies Act 1981. However, the position with regard to legislation has been simplified since most of the provisions of these Acts have been consolidated into the Companies Act 1985, which came into force on 1 July 1985, as now amended by the Companies Act 1989. (It should be mentioned here that throughout this handbook whenever reference is made to 'the Act' this is a reference to the Companies Act 1985, and whenever reference is made to a section number or a schedule without reference to any Act that reference is to the appropriate section or schedule of the Companies Act 1985 with a reference, where necessary, to provisions of the Companies Act 1989.)

As well as the Companies Act 1985 as amended by the Companies Act 1989, the following Acts also impinge on the work of the company secretary:

1. The Fair Trading Act 1973 (FTA).
2. The Company Securities (Insider Dealing) Act 1985 (IDA).

3. The Business Names Act 1985 (BNA).
4. The Companies Consolidation (Consequential Provisions) Act 1985 (CPA).
5. The Financial Services Act 1986 (FSA).
6. The Insolvency Act 1986 (IA).
7. The Company Directors' Disqualification Act 1986 (CDDA).

Further, the Income and Corporation Taxes Act 1988 (ICTA) is important in connection with employees' share schemes. As well as amending provisions in the Companies Act 1985 the Companies Act 1989 introduces some entirely new provisions. In the interests of brevity, where it is necessary to refer to a section or schedule number in any of the above Acts the reference will be preceded by one of the abbreviations shown in brackets after the full name of the Act. In the case of the Companies Act 1989 section and schedule numbers will be prefixed CA 1989.

Apart from the provisions of all these Acts, however, many rules and regulations covering company secretarial practice are laid down in what is known as subsidiary legislation. These comprise statutory instruments made under authority contained in the Acts concerned. The most important of these is Statutory Instrument No. 805 of 1985, The Companies (Tables A to F) Regulations 1985 as amended by Statutory Instrument No. 1052 of 1985, The Companies (Tables A to F) (Amendment) Regulations 1985. As will be explained later, these contain detailed regulations with regard to the internal administration of companies and are referred to as the Articles of Association. They apply to all companies except those which may have adopted special Articles of Association of their own and have excluded, in whole or in part, the regulations contained in The Companies (Tables A to F) Regulations 1985 (as amended). Any reference in this handbook to 'Table A', 'Table B', etc., is a reference to Table A, Table B, etc., contained in these Regulations. The Insolvency Rules 1986 (as amended by The Insolvency (Amendment) Rules of 1987 and 1989) are important in regard to Chapter 16 and references to these Rules in this chapter are preceded by the letters IR.

The company secretary will from time to time be required under the Act to submit certain information to the Registrar of Companies. The information has to be presented in the prescribed form as set out in Statutory Instrument No. 854 of 1985, The Companies (Forms) Regulations 1985, and Statutory Instrument No. 724 of 1985, The Companies (Registers and other Records) Regulations 1985. Since these Regulations were published amendments or changes in reference number of the prescribed forms have been brought about by amending or new Regulations which are mentioned at the appropriate places in this handbook, particularly in Chapter 10. Further, new Regulations concerning company forms may be expected to be published as a result of the Companies Act 1989. In this handbook references to a 'Companies Form No.' are references to the forms prescribed in the appropriate Regulations.

Apart from the Acts mentioned above and statutory instruments and Orders made under them, there are other rules and regulations with which companies must comply – laid down in The Stock Exchange's *Admission of Securities to Listing* (colloquially known as the 'Yellow Book'), *The City Code on Take-overs and Mergers* and *The Rules Governing Substantial Acquisitions of Shares* published by The Panel on Take-overs and Mergers. These are dealt with in Chapter 13 of this handbook.

It is again emphasised, however, that the purpose of this book is to guide students and others on the practical application of company legislation as it affects company secretarial practice, i.e. it is not a book on company law, which in any event is the subject of a separate paper in the Institute of Chartered Secretaries and Administrators' examinations.

Notes

1. References in this handbook to 'the Institute' are references to the Institute of Chartered Secretaries and Administrators.
2. References in this handbook to 'the Institute's manual' are references to *Company Secretarial Practice*.
3. References in this handbook to statutory instruments are cited as SI 1985/1052 which means Statutory Instrument No. 1052 of 1985.
4. References in this handbook to the 'Continuing Obligations' refer to the Continuing Obligations for Companies in the Yellow Book, Section 5, Chapter 2, which apply to companies listed on The Stock Exchange.
5. References in this handbook to The Stock Exchange are references to The International Stock Exchange of the United Kingdom and the Republic of Ireland ('ISE').

Special note on Companies Act 1989

This handbook has of necessity been written on the basis that by the time it is published many of the more important provisions of the Companies Act 1989 will have been brought into operation by various Commencement Orders and the publication of Rules and Regulations under the Act. The latest information available as to commencement dates, some of which are not relevant to matters covered in this handbook but are included so that readers may have complete information on the subject, is given below; but it should be noted that the timetable could be varied during the course of production of this handbook and even after its publication. Readers are, therefore, advised to check the position when reference is made in the text to the Companies Act 1989 provisions to ensure that the position as stated in the text has come into effect. Students will no doubt be advised by their lecturers and company secretaries should be aware of the latest position by their reading of the quality press and professional journals or, if they are unsure, by enquiry made of their company's solicitors.

Companies Act 1989

SUMMARY OF COMMENCEMENT DATES AS AT 8 MAY 1990
INDICATING MAIN COMMENCEMENT DATES, INCLUDING DATES
SPECIFIED IN FIRST FIVE COMMENCEMENT ORDERS
(INDICATED [1] TO [5] AS APPROPRIATE) OR DATES ESTIMATED
SO FAR BUT SUBJECT TO REVISION, INDICATING WHEN SOME
REGULATIONS WILL BE MADE AND ALSO SHOWING WHERE
APPROPRIATE THE RELEVANT STATUTORY INSTRUMENT
(INDICATED [A] TO [C]). THE COMMENCEMENT ORDERS AND
OTHER STATUTORY INSTRUMENTS ARE LISTED AT THE END OF
THIS TABLE TO WHICH REFERENCE SHOULD BE MADE FOR FULL
DETAILS AND FOR THE TRANSITIONAL ARRANGEMENTS.

Part I Accounts

Sections (all or part in force – see order) 1 (part), 2–6, 7 (part), 8–10, 11 (part), 13–22, 23 (Schedule 10, excluding para. 19)

1 April 1990, [4] and [2] subject to certain transitional provisions for financial years commencing prior to 23 December 1989 and certain other transitional and saving provisions. See also SIs [A] and [B]

Section 23 (in respect of Schedule 10 (para. 19))

1 August 1990, subject to certain transitional and saving provisions [4]

Paving provision in sections 1 and 15 to enable regulations to be made

1 March 1990 [2]

Regulations with respect to summary financial statements (section 15)

1 April 1990 [C]

Signing of defective accounts   September 1990
(section 7 new section 233(5) of CA
1985)

New civil procedure for defective   September 1990
accounts (section 12).

Civil penalties for late filing of   January 1991
accounts (section 11 new section
242a of CA 1985)

Part II Auditors

Sections (all or part in force – see   1 March 1990 [2]
order) 24, 30–33, 37–40, 41(1)(3)–
(6), 42–45, 47(1), 48(1) and (2),
49–54, Schedules 11, 12 and 14

Examinations regulations   June 1990

Fees regulations   June 1990

Register of auditors regulations   July 1990
with commencement of sections 35
and 36

Recognition of supervisory bodies   First quarter 1991
and full commencement of Part II

Part III Investigation powers

Section 75(2), (3) and (7)   25 January 1990 [1]

All other aspects (except in   21 February 1990 [2]
relation to Parts of the Act not yet
in force)

Part IV Registration of charges

All aspects   June 1991

Part V Other company law

Sections
  108–12 Ultra vires   November 1990
  113–17 Elective regime   1 April 1990 [4]
  118–24 Auditors   1 April 1990 [4]
  125–7 Company records   July 1990

Sections *cont.*

128	Partnership company (Table G)	January 1991
129	Membership of holding company	September 1990
130	Company seals	31 July 1990
131	Members' rights to damages	1 April 1990 [4]
132	Financial assistance for employees' share schemes	1 April 1990 [4]
133	Issue of redeemable shares	Not yet decided
134	Disclosure of interests in shares 134(1)(2)(3)(5) and (6)	31 May 1990 [5]
	134(4)	December 1990
	Regulations under 134 (5) and (6) to be made	December 1990
135	Restrictions on shares	November 1990
136	Company's registered office	1 April 1990 [4]
137	Insurance for directors, etc.	1 April 1990 [4]
138	Directors' loans	June 1990
139	Annual returns	October 1990
140	Floating charges (Scotland)	June 1991 (with Part IV)
141	Dissolution of company void	In force on Royal Assent (16 November 1989)
142	Deemed notice	November 1990
143	Rights of inspection	November 1990
144	Definition of subsidiary	September 1990
145	Minor amendments ● Schedule 19 ● Paras. 1,8,9,12,19 and 21	1 March 1990 [2]
	● Paras. 15–18	1 April 1990 [4]
	● Paras. 2–7	October 1990
	● Para. 11	November 1990
	● Paras. 13 and 14	July 1990
	● Para. 10	June 1990
	● Para. 20	To be decided

Part VI Mergers and related matters

Sections
146   Prior notice   1 April 1990 [2]
147–50
       ● Undertakings as
         alternative to
         merger reference
       ● Enforcement of
         undertakings   In force on Royal Assent
       ● Temporary restrictions   (16 November 1989)
         on share dealings
       ● Obtaining control by
         stages
151   False or misleading   1 April 1990 [2]
       information
152   Fees   1 March 1990 [2]
153   Other amendments   1 April 1990 [2]

Part VII Financial markets and insolvency

All sections   November 1990

Part VIII FSA amendments

All sections (192–206 except 192 in   15 March 1990 [3]
part, 193 in part, 201, 202 and 206
in part)
Remainder of 192, 193 and 206   To be decided
Sections
201   Compliance with   With Part VII
       international obligation   November 1990
202   Short-dated debentures   In force on Royal Assent
                                        (16 November 1989)

Part IX Transfer of securities

Section
207   (Commencement of   June 1990
       Order making power)

Part X Miscellaneous

Sections

208	Disqualification of directors (Scotland)	1 March 1990 [2]
209	Insider dealing	21 February 1990 [2]
210	Premium income	1 April 1990 [2]
211	Building Societies	
	211(1)	Not yet decided
	211(2)(3)	June 1990
212	Repeals	With relevant section of CA 1989
213 and 214	Provisions relating to Northern Ireland	21 February 1990 [2] so far as not already in force
215	Commencement and transitional provisions	As appropriate
216	Short title	25 January 1990 [1]

Commencement Orders made to 1 March 1990:
[1] SI 1990/98 made 24 January 1990
[2] SI 1990/142 made 31 January 1990
[3] SI 1990/354 made 26 February 1990
[4] SI 1990/355 made 26 February 1990
[5] SI 1990/713 made 23 March 1990

Other Statutory Instruments:
[A] SI 1990/438 made 5 March 1990 – The Companies (Unregistered Companies) (Amendment) Regulations 1990
[B] SI 1990/440 made 5 March 1990 – The Oversea Companies (Accounts) (Modifications and Exemptions) Order 1990
[C] SI 1990/515 made 7 March 1990 – The Companies (Summary Financial Statement) Regulations 1990

Special note on 1990 Budget

Reference is made throughout the text of this handbook to new proposals included in the 1990 Budget affecting stamp duty on shares, savings related share option schemes and employee share ownership plans. At the time of preparation of this handbook, however, the Finance Act 1990 had not yet been passed. Consequently readers are advised to verify the position, as stated in the text, relating to these matters after the Finance Act 1990 has been passed before taking action in reliance on the Budget proposals outlined in this book.

CHAPTER 1

Registration and re-registration of companies

Before you can begin to practise the art of company secretaryship, you need a company. It is appropriate, therefore, to consider first how companies come into being, and it is usually the secretary to be of the company who will be involved in its registration. Even if you are already the secretary of an established company subsidiary companies will have to be registered from time to time.

Registration is effected with an official of the Department of Trade and Industry, the Registrar of Companies. In the case of companies to be registered in England and Wales, the address of the Registrar is Companies House, Crown Way, Maindy, Cardiff CF4 3UZ; and in the case of companies to be registered in Scotland there is a separate Registrar, whose address is 102 George Street, Edinburgh EH2 3DJ.

Forms of incorporation

We are principally concerned with companies limited by shares, since this is the type of company most frequently encountered carrying on business in Great Britain. A form of partnership company has been introduced by CA 1989 s.128 which empowers the Secretary of State by regulations to prescribe a Table G containing Articles of Association appropriate for a partnership company which is a company limited by shares held to a substantial extent by or on behalf of its employees.

Apart from companies limited by shares there are other forms of incorporation which the company secretary needs to know about. These are the following:

1. Companies limited by guarantee, a form of incorporation mainly used by charitable or non-profit-making organisations.
2. Unlimited companies, which are used by professional practices and some special types of trading organisation where it is desired to obtain corporate status with perpetual succession. The advantage of

perpetual succession is that the company carries on in being notwithstanding the changes in the membership of the company that will inevitably occur from time to time.

Differences between companies limited by shares and those limited by guarantee

The main differences are that in the case of a company limited by guarantee, the following conditions apply:

1. Each member agrees to contribute to the assets of the company up to a certain amount if it should be wound up, e.g. £5.
2. Companies limited by guarantee may be classified as private companies only, unless they also have a share capital; but it should be noted that it is not now permissable for new companies to be formed or to become companies limited by a guarantee with a share capital (s.1(4)).
3. The Memorandum and Articles of the company must, as nearly as possible, be in the form set out in Table C or, if it is one of the companies limited by guarantee with a share capital, in the form set out in Table D.
4. The members of the company are those who were the original subscribers to the Memorandum of Association and any other persons whom the directors may approve for membership.
5. If the company is non-profit making it may be permitted to omit the word 'limited' from its name (ss.30 and 31). In such cases the company is also exempted from the provisions of ss.348, 349 and 350 with regard to publication of name (s.30(7)).
6. The company is, however, required to disclose on business letters and order forms that it is a limited company (s.351).
7. Companies permitted to omit the word 'limited' from their name need not submit a list of members with the annual return (s.30(7)).
8. It should be noted that by s.31 the Secretary of State may withdraw the exemptions if he considers that the company no longer complies with the provisions of s.30.

Differences between companies limited by shares and unlimited companies

1. As the title indicates, members of unlimited companies are liable for the company's liabilities without limit.
2. The Memorandum and Articles must, as nearly as possible, be in the form set out in Table E. Unlimited companies must always be private companies (s.1).

3. Any transfers of shares must be on the old 'common form' form of transfer, which has to be signed by both transferor and transferee, and not the form prescribed under the Stock Transfer Act 1963, which requires only the signature of the transferor. (The transferor is the person who wishes to pass on his shares to another person; the transferee is the person who wishes to be registered with such shares, thereby becoming a member of the company.)
4. Unlimited companies are exempt from filing accounts with the Registrar of Companies unless they are holding companies or the subsidiaries of limited companies.

Public companies and private companies

The former position was that private companies were those whose Articles of Association contained restrictions with regard to the transfer of their shares; any company not classified as a private company was a public company.

The definition of public and private companies is now as follows:

1. A public company is one limited by shares (or limited by guarantee with a share capital), complying with the following conditions:
   (a) the Memorandum of Association must state that the company is to be a public company;
   (b) the company must have been registered or re-registered as a public company on or after 22 December 1980.
2. A private company is a company that is not a public company.

Differences between public and private companies

1. The name of a public company must end with the words 'public limited company' or a permitted abbreviation or alternative in Welsh.
2. The Memorandum of Association must, as nearly as possible, be in the form set out in Table F.
3. The share capital of a public company which has been allotted must have a nominal value of not less than an authorised minimum, in 1989 £50,000.
4. The share capital which has been allotted must have at least 25 per cent of its nominal value paid up; if there is a share premium, 100 per cent of the premium must be paid up. (The share premium is any excess amount paid for a share over its nominal value.)
5. Private companies are prohibited from offering their shares or debentures to the public (s.81 and CPA s.7).
6. There are strict rules imposed on public companies to ensure that full value is given for any shares allotted (ss.99–116 and CPA s.9).

Although private companies need not have restrictions on transfers of shares in their Articles, some may wish to do so in view of (5) above.

Registration of companies generally

The addresses at which companies must lodge documents for registration have been given at the beginning of this chapter but it may be noted that companies to be registered in England and Wales may send their documents to Companies House at 55/71 City Road, London EC1Y 1BB instead of sending them to Cardiff.

The information which has to be filed with the Registrar of Companies is given on forms which are officially prescribed for the purpose and may be obtained from the Registrar or law stationers. On application for registration, Companies Form No. G10 'Statement of first directors and secretary and intended situation of registered office' would be filed with the Registrar and subsequent changes would be filed on Companies Form No. G288 'Notice of change of directors or secretaries or in their particulars'. The Registrar normally requires company documents and other documents lodged for registration to be printed and has issued guidance notes as to what is and what is not acceptable in order to meet this requirement (s.706 inserted by CA 1989 s.125(1)). The Registrar may also accept information otherwise than in legible form (s.707 inserted by CA 1989 s.125(2)).

Documents lodged with the Registrar must be suitable for publication and filing on the company's public file and clarity is therefore essential. A receipt should be obtained from the Registrar by handing in with the documents a duplicate copy of the covering letter which will be signed by the Registrar and returned to the person lodging the document.

Where it is necessary to submit an altered Memorandum and Articles of Association, the Registrar will accept, in the case of minor amendments, copies of the old document amended by typed slips permanently fixed on to the original with the old words obliterated. Manuscript amendments are not acceptable. If, however, the amendments are substantial, it will be necessary to submit a completely new printed Memorandum and Articles, unless it is possible to remove certain pages, replace them and then rebind the whole document. The alterations must be authenticated by the company's seal (if it has one) or official stamp.

Registration of private companies

These are the companies which are most commonly formed and they may subsequently become re-registered as public companies. It is appropriate, therefore, to consider the registration of private companies first, then to note the differences which apply in the registration of public companies. The first step is to find a suitable name for the company. An index of company names is kept by the Registrar of Companies and this must be checked to make sure that the proposed name will not be the same or too similar to the name of any existing company. The Registrar previously provided a name-checking service in advance of lodging documents for registration but this service is no longer available and care therefore needs to be taken. The name should not be one to which the Registrar, or other persons, are likely to take exception. In this connection the Registrar has issued *Notes for Guidance on Company Names* and *Notes on Sensitive Words and Expressions*, and these documents should be carefully studied prior to selecting a name. A new companies' incorporation starter pack is available from the Registrar.

When a name for the company has been selected, the following duly completed and executed documents must be sent to the New Companies Section, PO Box 717, Companies House, Cardiff CF4 3YA in order to secure the registration of a company:

1. Memorandum of Association. There must be at least two subscribers to the Memorandum, each of whom must agree to take at least one share in the company; the number of shares which each has agreed to take is shown against his name in the Memorandum. One witness must also sign against the name of each subscriber. A subscriber to the Memorandum need not necessarily be an individual; it may be a body corporate, in which case the Memorandum is signed by someone on its behalf, duly authorised. The Memorandum for a private company limited by shares must be as nearly as possible in the form contained in Table B.
2. Articles of Association. The Articles also need to be signed and duly witnessed.
3. The names of the first directors and secretary and intended place of the registered office of the company must be submitted on Companies Form No. G10 'Statement of first directors and secretary and intended situation of registered office'. This form incorporates a consent to be signed by the persons to become the first directors and secretary.
4. A solicitor engaged in the formation of the company or one of the directors or the secretary must swear a statutory declaration of compliance on Companies Form No. G12 'Statutory declaration of compliance with requirements on application for registration of a company'.
5. The formal approval of the name of the company (if required).

6. A cheque payable to the Registrar of Companies for the registration fee of £50.

If all is in order, the Registrar of Companies will issue a certificate of incorporation, bearing the date of incorporation and stating that the company is a private company. The certificate should be very carefully preserved since it may at some time be necessary to produce it. A private company may commence business as soon as it has become incorporated.

Registration of public companies

The documents to be sent to the Registrar of Companies for the formation of a public company are essentially the same as those set out above for a private company. However, the form of the Memorandum of Association must be, as nearly as possible, that contained in Table F, and the initial nominal share capital must not be less than the authorised minimum, in 1989 £50,000.

The minimum number of subscribers in a public company is the same as in the case of a private company, i.e. two. The Registrar's certificate of incorporation states that the company is a public company but a public company cannot immediately commence business on the issue of the certificate of incorporation or exercise any of its borrowing powers. The Registrar must first issue a certificate of compliance concerning the capital requirements of public companies and for this purpose Companies Form No. G117 'Application by a public company for certificate to commence business and statutory declaration in support' must be lodged with the Registrar. The statutory declaration includes confirmation that the nominal value of the authorised minimum share capital has been subscribed, giving details regarding the payment for the shares and certain other matters.

The issue of the certificate of entitlement to commence business by the Registrar of Companies means that the company can go ahead and carry on its business and exercise any of its borrowing powers. If a company should commence business or exercise borrowing powers before the issue of the certificate the company and any officer in default are liable to criminal penalties, although the transactions themselves are not affected. In such an event the Secretary of State may call upon the company to comply with the provisions of s.117 within 21 days and in the event of failure to do so any party to the transaction who has sustained loss or damage by such failure may claim against the directors, who are jointly and severally liable to indemnify him. If no certificate to commence business should be issued within one year of incorporation the Secretary of State, the company or any creditor or contributory of the company may petition the Court that the company be wound up.

Memorandum of Association

This must be in the relevant statutory form, i.e. Table B for private companies or Table F for public companies, although minor variations as circumstances may make necessary are acceptable. Tables B and F contain only a very short objects clause and this is usually replaced by a longer clause setting out the objects of the company. Some companies may wish to follow the alternative of adopting a very wide 'short form' objects clause stating that it may carry on business as a general commercial company; this would allow it to carry on any trade or business whatsoever and to do all such things incidental or conducive to the carrying on of any trade or business (s.3A inserted by CA 1989 s.110). In the case of a company limited by shares, the Memorandum includes the following clauses:

1. The company's name.
2. If the company is to be a public company, that it is a public company.
3. Situation of the registered office either in England and Wales or in Scotland.
4. The objects clause, as mentioned above.
5. That the liability of the members is limited.
6. The amount of the share capital of the company and its subdivision into shares of a fixed amount.

Any member of the company may request that a copy of the Memorandum and Articles be sent to him on payment of the prescribed fee. Any alterations which have been made to the Memorandum and Articles must be incorporated in the copies sent to the member, including copies of any resolutions which the company was required to file with the Registrar of Companies (ss.19, 20 and 380).

Companies' registered numbers

On incorporation every company is allocated a registered number by the Registrar of Companies, consisting of one or more sequences of figures or letters. The Registrar has power to change a company's registered number but for a period of three years following notification of a new registered number the company may use either the old number or the new one on business letters and order forms (s.705 inserted by CA 1989 Schedule 19, para. 14).

Name of company

This is stated in the first clause of the Memorandum. If it is a private company, it must terminate with the word 'Limited' or 'Ltd' and if a public company, the name must terminate with the words 'public limited company' or 'plc' or, if preferred 'Public Limited Company' or 'PLC'. Special provisions may apply if the registered office of the company is to be situated in Wales.

The company's name must be 'painted or affixed' outside every office or place of business and also engraved on the company's common seal if it has one. In addition it must appear on all business letters and other specified documents (ss.348–50). Additional requirements apply in the case of companies incorporated outside Great Britain which have a place of business (including a share registration office) in Great Britain (s.693) and the Secretary of State may require overseas companies to use a different name in Great Britain (s.694).

Control of company names

The Companies Act 1981 (which is consolidated into the Act) introduced a new system of control of company names. It has already been mentioned that there is no procedure for obtaining approval of a name in advance and it is for the persons forming the company to check the Company Registration Office's index of names. In particular it should be noted that:

1. A company will not be registered by the Registrar of Companies if the name would be 'the same as' an existing name on the index of names or where it does not bear the appropriate status, i.e. 'Limited' in the case of a private company or 'public limited company' (or an abbreviation) in the case of a public company. A name will not be registered if it would be offensive or constitute a criminal offence to use it (ss.26–9 and 714).
2. A name would not be approved if it gave the impression that the company was connected with the central or local government or contained an expression which may only be used with the approval of the Secretary of State (s.29 and BNA s.3).
3. Where a company has been registered with a name which is 'the same as' or 'too like' a name shown on the Company Registration Office's index, the company may be directed by the Secretary of State within 12 months of the registration to change its name within such period as he may specify (s.28(2)). This period is extended to five years of registration where the company has provided, for the purpose of registration, information which is misleading or which has not fulfilled assurances given at the time of registration (s.28(3)). At any time after registration the Secretary of State may direct a company to change its name within 6 weeks or such longer period as he may

allow where the company's name is so misleading in regard to the nature of its activities as to be likely to cause harm to the public (s.32).

4. There are detailed guidance notes on the provisions regarding new company names which may be obtained from the Registrar of Companies on request.

Change of name of company

A Special Resolution is required in order to change a company's name. The Notice of Meeting and Special Resolution could be in the following form:

Notice is hereby given that an Extraordinary General Meeting of the Company will be held at .... (place) at .... (time and date) to consider and, if thought fit, to pass the following resolution as a Special Resolution:

Resolution

THAT the name of the company be changed to .... Limited/ public limited company.

Upon the issue of a certificate of incorporation with the new name by the Registrar the change of name takes effect. It is possible to arrange that the change of name takes effect from some future date, in which case the resolution should incorporate the date on which the change is to take place and special arrangements made with the Registrar for his certificate to bear that date.

The detailed procedure for the change of name of a public company is as follows (it should be noted that some of the matters mentioned below would not be relevant in the case of private companies):

1. The proposed new name must be checked against the Company Registration Office's index of names and approval of the name obtained where required.
2. The directors should resolve to recommend that an Extraordinary General Meeting be convened to consider the Special Resolution to change the name, although this could be done as special business at an Annual General Meeting.
3. The directors should approve a circular explaining to members the reason for the proposed change of name and, in the case of an Extraordinary General Meeting, a notice would be sent to the members of the company as shown in the above example. The explanation would be included in the director's report if the change of name is to be approved at an Annual General Meeting.

4. In the case of a company listed on The Stock Exchange it would be necessary to send out with the notice of meeting a form of two-way proxy (Continuing Obligations, para. 37).

5. In addition, in the case of listed companies, four proof copies of the circular and proxy card would have to be submitted to The Stock Exchange through the company's stockbrokers, allowing sufficient time for the Exchange to approve these documents and, if necessary, resubmit them to The Stock Exchange with amendments that they may require. Six copies of the final documents must be sent to The Stock Exchange (Continuing Obligations, paras. 31 and 35).

6. Printed copies of the Special Resolution should be prepared for filing with the Registrar of Companies immediately following the meeting, certified by signature of the chairman, together with a fee of £40 (the fee for registration of a change of name). It is desirable that the resolution for change of name be sent to the Registrar separately from any other resolutions which may need to be registered in order to avoid delay. Four prints of the Special Resolution must also be sent to The Stock Exchange at the same time (Continuing Obligations, para. 35).

7. A certificate of incorporation on change of name is issued by the Registrar and the change of name has legal effect from the date of that certificate.

8. Steps must then be taken to see that the new name is painted or fixed outside the registered office and other places of business and elsewhere, such as on the company vehicles or on the packaging of its products.

9. The company's stationery must also be reprinted or, at least, overprinted with the new name where this is feasible. Where it is decided to make such preparations in advance, it is desirable not to incur any substantial expenditure in case the Registrar should raise any objections to the new name.

10. The directors at a board meeting must adopt a new common seal if the company has a seal as well as a new securities seal if the company has a seal and it uses a securities seal.

11. Banks and other organisations with which the company has dealings may require production of the certificate of incorporation on change of name certified by the secretary, although if an official copy of the certificate is required this can be obtained from the Registrar.

12. The Special Resolution must be attached to all copies of the Memorandum and Articles held in stock.

13. It is not necessary in this case to file a new copy of the Memorandum and Articles with the Registrar of Companies. However, all persons known to be in possession of a copy of the company's Memorandum

and Articles, e.g. the directors, auditors, solicitors, etc., should be sent a print of the Special Resolution to be attached to their copies.

14. If the Secretary of State should direct the change of name to take place, the same procedure as above applies except that the fee of £40 is not payable.

Business names

Where a company carries on business under a name which is not its corporate name, it is necessary to comply with the provisions of the Business Names Act 1985. These are as follows:

1. Although the controls on 'same' or 'too like' names do not apply in relation to business names, names implying connection with central or local government or containing certain words and expressions may only be used with the written approval of the Secretary of State (BNA ss.2 and 3). If the business name is used on business letters, written orders for goods, invoices, etc., the full name of the company must also be stated and an address given within Great Britain at which service of any document relating to the business will be effective (BNA s.4). Additional information must also be shown on business letters, as stated under 'Company letterheads' below.

2. The full name of the company must also be shown in all premises where the business is carried on under the business name so that customers or suppliers may refer to it, and the name must also be given immediately in writing to any person doing business with the company who may request it (BNA s.4).

Failure to comply with any of the above provisions renders any officer of the company responsible liable to criminal penalties and the company may suffer difficulties in enforcing contracts made under the business name where the provisions have not been complied with (BNA ss.4, 5 and 7).

Registered office

1. The Memorandum states the country within Great Britain in which the registered office is situated, with special provisions applying where the situation of the registered office is in Wales. As mentioned above, Companies Form No. G10, filed with the incorporation documents, states the address of the initial registered office. When the address is changed, notice must be given to the Registrar within 14 days of the change on Companies Form No. G287 'Notice of change in situation of registered office'. However, the registered

office of a company must be situated within the country specified in the Memorandum, so that a company registered in England and Wales may not alter the Memorandum to provide for a registered office to be situated in Scotland and the converse position applies in the case of companies registered in Scotland.

2. A company registered in Scotland, however, which carries on business in England and which may, therefore, become subject to Court proceedings in England, may have a document served on it at its principal place of business in England provided that a copy is sent to the company's registered office in Scotland by post.

3. An overseas company with a place of business in Great Britain must inform the Registrar of the name(s) and address(es) of one or more persons resident in Great Britain who may accept service of process and any notices required to be served on the company (s.691). The notice is sent on Companies Form No. G691 'Return and declaration delivered for registration by an overseas company', and notice of any change in the names or addresses of such persons must also be sent to the Registrar within 21 days of the change on Companies Form No. G692(1)(c) 'Return of alteration in the names or addresses of persons resident in Great Britain authorised to accept service on behalf of an overseas company'.

Company letterheads

1. The company's full name must be shown on all business letters and other documents as specified in s.349. The place of registration and the registered number of the company as shown on the certificate of incorporation must also be shown on business letters and order forms, together with the address of the registered office.

2. It is not necessary to show the amount of the share capital on business letters but if this is done the reference must be to the paid-up share capital.

3. The names of directors need not be shown on business letters but if it is desired to do so, then the names of all the directors must be stated and not just one. However, it would still be in order for a letter to be signed by a director with that title under his signature without showing the names of all the directors on the paper.

Objects clause in Memorandum of Association

As stated above, some companies' objects clauses in the Memorandum may be somewhat lengthy so as to include all the activities in which the company is likely to engage. This was because of the *ultra vires* rule but the Companies Act 1989 abolished this rule except for transactions between directors and connected persons. The position now is that if the company were to undertake an activity which was not included within the terms of its Memorandum, unconnected third parties dealing with the company in good faith would be protected even if aware that an act was beyond the directors' powers (ss.35, 35A and 35B inserted by CA 1989 s.108). The directors may, however, incur personal liability to the shareholders in authorising a transaction which exceeds their authority to bind the company where the parties to the transaction include a director of the company or of its holding company or a person connected with such a director or a company with which such a director is associated, as such transactions are void as between the company and any such party, unless ratified by the company (s.322A inserted by CA 1989 s.109).

Alteration of objects

A Special Resolution of the company is required to alter the objects clause in its Memorandum (s.4 inserted by CA 1989 s.110) which may be altered in any manner convenient to the company including the adoption of a 'short form' objects clause provided by s.3A inserted by CA 1989 s.110. The procedure for altering the objects clause of the Memorandum would be as follows:

1. The directors, at a board meeting, should resolve to convene an Extraordinary General Meeting of the company to consider the terms of the Special Resolution and to approve a circular to be sent to all members of the company explaining the alteration.
2. In the case of companies listed on The Stock Exchange, proof copies of the circular and of the two-way proxy card should be sent to the Exchange through the company's stockbrokers for approval (Continuing Obligations, para. 31).
3. Notice of meeting would then be sent out to all members of the company and information copies should be sent to debenture holders and those holding shares which do not entitle them to vote at meetings of the company.
4. A print of the Special Resolution should be prepared to be filed with the Registrar of Companies following signature by the chairman of the meeting. This certified copy must be sent to the Registrar within 15 days of the meeting.
5. Four prints of the resolution should be sent to The Stock Exchange if it is a listed company (Continuing Obligations, para. 35).
6. After 21 days following the meeting, during which time it is open for a proportion of the members or debenture holders to apply to the

Court for the alteration to the Memorandum to be cancelled, a printed copy of the altered Memorandum is to be filed with the Registrar of Companies within 15 days and a copy sent to The Stock Exchange if the company is listed (s.5).

7. If an application to the Court is made then the Registrar must be notified forthwith on Companies Form No. G6 'Notice of application to the Court for cancellation of alteration to the objects of a company'. If the Court confirms the alteration, a printed copy of the Memorandum, as altered, must be sent to the Registrar of Companies within 15 days or such longer period as the Court may allow (s.6).

8. It is then usual for the entire Memorandum and Articles to be reprinted incorporating the altered objects clause and including copies of the Special Resolution and of any Order of the Court, although it is possible for the existing copies held in stock to be suitably amended. Copies of the altered Memorandum should also be sent to the persons mentioned in (13) on pp10/11.

Other clauses in the Memorandum

1. If the company is to be a limited company, the Memorandum must state this fact, i.e. that the liability of the members is limited.

2. The amount of the share capital and its division into shares of a fixed amount should be stated in the Memorandum. The capital clause should be kept as brief as possible and the details of the division of share capital into classes of shares and the rights attaching to classes of shares is best dealt with in the Articles as, if any changes are to be made, it is easier to alter the Articles than to alter the Memorandum.

Companies with registered office in Wales

If the Memorandum of Association states that the registered office of the company is to be situated in Wales, the company may, if it wishes, have the Welsh equivalents of 'Limited' or 'public limited company' in its name. However, if the Welsh alternative is used, the fact that the company is limited must be stated in English on its letter paper, bill heads and other official documents and must also be included in a notice displayed at every place of business of the company.

The company's Memorandum and Articles of Association delivered to the Registrar of Companies prior to incorporation may be in the Welsh language but have to be accompanied by a translation into English, which must be certified as being a correct translation by a notary public or solicitor.

It is possible for a company registered in England to change its Memorandum to provide for its registered office to be situated in Wales, but not in Scotland. (It may then relodge its Memorandum and Articles in Welsh accompanied by a certified English translation.)

Any other documents which have to be submitted to the Registrar may also be in Welsh if accompanied by a certified English translation.

In the case of a company incorporated prior to the Companies Act 1985 the Memorandum may state that the registered office is to be situated in England or, if incorporated under the Companies Act 1985, in England and Wales. In either case, the company may have its registered office in Wales but the above provisions regarding documents in Welsh would not apply.

Articles of Association

The Articles of Association are the rules and regulations by which the internal affairs of the company are governed. They are to be printed and numbered into consecutive paragraphs and, in the case of the Articles registered at the time of the incorporation of the company, to be signed by the subscribers. A model set of Articles for companies limited by shares is contained in Table A. However, in the case of a company registered prior to the Companies Act 1985, the applicable Table A is that contained in the Act under which it was registered. However, these companies could bring themselves up to date by adopting the new Table A in the place of the old Table A Articles contained in the earlier Act by following the procedure for a change of Articles given below.

In the case of public companies, however, special Articles are normally drafted to replace Table A in its entirety and in the case of a company listed on The Stock Exchange the special Articles would have to comply with the requirements of The Stock Exchange set out in Section 9, Chapter 1 of the Yellow Book. The other alternative is to adopt certain of the Table A Articles but to exclude or modify the other ones. This practice is often followed in the case of private companies, including the subsidiaries of some public companies.

Alteration of Articles

The alteration of the Articles could be effected by amending the wording of one or more of the Articles, deleting certain Articles and adding new ones or adopting completely new Articles to take the place of the existing ones. In order to do this, a Special Resolution has to be passed and the procedure would be as follows:

1. The directors, at a board meeting, would resolve to recommend to members that the Articles be altered, to agree to the calling of an Extraordinary General Meeting to consider the Special Resolution, to approve a circular to members explaining the reasons for the alterations and, in the case of a company listed on The Stock Exchange, to approve a two-way proxy form (Continuing Obligations, para. 37).

2. All amendments in wording could be included in the resolution but if it was intended to adopt new Articles the circular would merely summarise the main provisions of the new Articles and state that a copy of the proposed new Articles was available for inspection either at the company's registered office or at the office of the company's solicitors from the time the notice was sent to members to the date of the meeting. Proof and final copies of the circular and proposed new Articles should be sent to The Stock Exchange for approval in the case of listed companies.

3. If a significant proportion of the shares are held by financial institutions, e.g. insurance companies and pension funds, confirmation that the proposed new Articles are acceptable should be sought from the relevant investment protection committee.

4. A print of the Special Resolution should be prepared for signature by the chairman following the meeting, to be filed with the Registrar of Companies.

5. A certified copy of the resolution has to be sent to the Registrar within 15 days of the meeting, together with a certified copy of the new Articles if completely new Articles have been adopted or a verified copy of the old Articles with the amendments inserted.

6. Four prints of the resolution and of the new or amended Articles should be sent to The Stock Exchange in the case of listed companies.

7. A reprint of the Memorandum and revised Articles incorporating a copy of the Special Resolution should be prepared or, alternatively, copies in stock should be suitably amended. Copies of the reprinted Memorandum and Articles or amended copies should be sent to directors of the company, its auditors, solicitors and others known to use copies of the Memorandum and Articles.

If only a minor amendment is to be made to the Articles the following would be a suitable form of wording to include in the notice of meeting:

To consider and if thought fit to pass the following resolution as a Special Resolution:

THAT the Articles of Association of the Company be altered by deleting in Article No. .... the words '....................................' and substituting therefor the words '..............................'

OR

THAT the Articles of Association of the Company be altered by substituting for the existing Article No. .... the following Article:

(Here give wording of the new Article)

If there are a number of changes, the Special Resolution could be as follows:

THAT the Articles of Association of the Company be altered as follows:

(Here list the several alterations required in a similar way to those stated above)

Where completely new Articles are to be adopted, the Special Resolution would read:

THAT the Regulations contained in the printed document submitted to this Meeting and, for the purpose of identification, signed by the Chairman hereof be approved and adopted as the Articles of Association of the Company in substitution for and to the exclusion of all existing Articles thereof.

The certification of the master copy would be dealt with by writing at the head of the first page:

This is the printed document referred to in a Special Resolution of ....
(name of company) considered at an Extraordinary General Meeting held on
....

Signed ....
Chairman of the Meeting

Re-registration of a private company as a public company

The general differences between private companies and public companies have already been mentioned. The procedure for re-registering a private company as a public company is as follows:

1. The directors, at a board meeting, resolve that an Extraordinary General Meeting be called to pass a Special Resolution that the company be re-registered as a public company, to alter the Memorandum of the company to state that the company is to be a public company and to make other amendments necessary to make the Memorandum and Articles conform with the requirements for the Memorandum and Articles of a public company. This includes changing the name of the company to end with the appropriate suffix, i.e. 'public limited company' or a permitted abbreviation or the Welsh alternative.
2. When the Special Resolution has been passed, an application is submitted to the Registrar of Companies on Companies Form No. G43(3) 'Application by a private company for re-registration as a

public company', signed by a director or the secretary, for re-registration of the company as a public company. The following documents have to accompany the application:

(a) a printed copy of the Memorandum and Articles as altered by the Special Resolution;

(b) a copy of a statement by the auditors of the company that in their opinion the company's relevant balance sheet shows that the amount of its net assets was not less than the aggregate of its called up share capital and undistributable reserves (s.43(3)(*b*)); the relevant balance sheet is one prepared at a date not more than 7 months before the application for re-registration;

(c) a copy of the relevant balance sheet itself, together with a copy of an unqualified auditors' report on it (s.43(3)(*c*));

(d) if shares have been allotted by the company between the relevant balance sheet date and the passing of the Special Resolution, a report with regard to the valuation of any asset in consideration for which the shares were allotted (s.44);

(e) a statutory declaration on Companies Form No. G43(3)(e) 'Declaration of compliance with requirements by a private company on application for re-registration as a public company' by a director or the secretary, certifying that the Special Resolution was duly passed, that the valuation of the allotted share capital is not less than the authorised minimum (in 1989 £50,000), that the consideration for any shares allotted between the relevant balance sheet date and the passing of the Special Resolution was adequate and that there had been no change in the company's financial position causing its net assets to be less than the aggregate of its called-up share capital and undistributable reserves.

3. The Registrar of Companies, if he approves the application, will issue a certificate of incorporation stating that the company is a public company; upon this happening any alterations to the Memorandum and Articles take effect.

4. Other matters would need to be dealt with as under the section 'Change of name of company' (pp9/11).

Re-registration of a public company as a private company

1. The directors, at a board meeting, resolve that an Extraordinary General Meeting be convened to pass a Special Resolution that the company be re-registered as a private company, altering the Memorandum so that it no longer states that the company is a public company and making such other alterations to the Memorandum and

Articles as are required, including a change of the name of the company deleting the suffix 'public limited company' or any abbreviation or alternative and substituting the word 'Limited'.

2. When the Special Resolution has been passed a copy must be sent to the Registrar of Companies within 15 days.

3. If holders of not less than 5 per cent of the issued share capital or a group of not less than 50 of the company members object to the change they may apply to the Court for cancellation of the Special Resolution within 28 days of its being passed (s.54(1)–(3)). If such an application is made the Registrar of Companies must be informed forthwith on Companies Form No. G54 'Notice of application made to the Court for the cancellation of a special resolution regarding re-registration' (s.54(4)). The Court will either cancel or confirm the resolution and a copy of the Court Order must be lodged with the Registrar within 15 days of the Order being made or such longer time as the Court may allow (s.54(5)–(7)). Assuming no application is made to the Court within 28 days of the passing of the Special Resolution, or if the Court makes an Order confirming the Special Resolution, application for re-registration is submitted to the Registrar of Companies on Companies Form No. G53 'Application by a public company for re-registration as a private company' signed by a director or the secretary, together with the following documents:
   (a) a printed copy of the Special Resolution;
   (b) a printed copy of the Memorandum and Articles as altered by the Special Resolution.

4. The Registrar of Companies will issue a certificate of incorporation appropriate to a company that is not a public company if he is satisfied that the application is valid; upon the issue of the certificate the alterations to the Memorandum and Articles take effect.

5. Other matters would need to be dealt with as under the section 'Change of name of company' (pp9/11).

The above procedure is for voluntary re-registration but it should be noted that a public company will be required by the Court to re-register before permitting a reduction of capital (under s.135) which would reduce the company's capital below the authorised minimum for a public company (in 1989 £50,000) (s.139). In these circumstances, the re-registration may be effected without passing the Special Resolution required in the case of voluntary re-registration and the Court would specify in the Order the amendments to be made to the Memorandum and Articles.

'Old' public companies

Under the Companies Act 1980 provisions were included requiring the re-registration of public companies, as previously defined, as public companies or private companies during a re-registration period which ended on 21 March 1982.

These companies were allowed the following concessions:

1. A 12-month period was allowed before the company's new name, ending with the appropriate suffix 'public limited company' or an abbreviation or alternative, had to be shown on its seal or business documents.
2. Three years were allowed following re-registration for the company's new name to be shown outside its places of business.

It should be noted, however, that these concessions only applied to re-registration under the initial provisions made for old public companies at the time of coming into force of the Companies Act 1980 and that that Act has now been repealed from 1 July 1985.

Re-registration of other types of company as public companies

Unlimited companies may be re-registered as public companies (ss.43–8 and 124). The procedure is similar to that in the case of the re-registration of a private company as a public company.

Joint stock companies (as defined by s.683) may also be re-registered as public companies limited by shares, the application for re-registration being made on Companies Form No. G680a 'Application by joint stock company for registration under Part XXII of the Companies Act 1985, and declaration and related documents' accompanied by a list of members on Companies Form No. G684 'Registration under Part XXII of the Companies Act 1985 list of members – existing joint stock company' and a statutory declaration on Companies Form No. G685 'Declaration on application by a joint stock company for registration as a public company'. Various documents have to be submitted with the application; particulars of these can be ascertained from ss.684 and 685.

Joint stock companies and certain other types of unregistered company may also be re-registered under Part XXII of the Act as private companies limited by shares, companies limited by guarantee or unlimited companies. Also, a limited company may re-register as an unlimited company (ss.49 and 50) and an unlimited company may re-register as a limited company (ss.51 and 52).

The detailed procedures for effecting the above changes are not covered in this handbook, however, since they are not common occurrences in the life of the company secretary. However, the procedures are set out in detail in the Institute's manual as well as in the Act.

CHAPTER 2

Capital

In this chapter we consider the main classes of securities issued by companies, the different sources of raising new capital, procedures for new issues of shares, renunciation of rights or entitlements to new shares and alterations of share capital.

We should first define the terms 'authorised capital', 'nominal capital' and 'issued capital'. The nominal capital of the company is the same as the authorised capital but the use of the word nominal gives a description of the face value (as opposed to market value on The Stock Exchange) of the authorised capital. In practice both authorised and nominal capital would be expressed in money terms.

In Chapter 1 it was noted that in the case of a company limited by shares the company's Memorandum of Association has a capital clause which states the amount of the share capital by which the company proposes to be registered and its division into shares of a fixed amount. The amount of share capital with which a company is initially registered (or the amount to which it may subsequently be increased) is the authorised or nominal capital of the company. Issued capital refers to that part of the company's total authorised or nominal capital which has been issued and taken up by the members of the company, having been issued either for cash or, as will be seen later, having been issued for a consideration other than cash.

There is another term which it is necessary to understand and that is the term 'paid-up' capital. This refers to the nominal amounts which have been paid up on the company's issued capital. Some examples will make the position clear. A company may be registered with a nominal capital of £500 comprising 1,000 shares of 50p each. The company's nominal capital is £500 but if only 500 of these shares have been issued then the issued capital is £250. If the shares are fully paid, the paid-up share capital will also be £250 but if the shares are issued only partly paid, i.e. 25p paid up on each share with another 25p to be paid on some subsequent date which the directors may determine in accordance with the Articles, the paid-up share capital would be £125.

Alteration of capital

The Act lays down procedures for the alteration of a company's share capital; the principal alteration which is met with in practice is that of an increase in the company's authorised (or nominal) capital. Other alterations occur, however; for example, consolidation of shares, subdivision of shares, conversion of shares into stock and vice versa, cancellation of unissued shares and reduction of capital. It is necessary that the power to make such alterations be contained in the company's Articles of Association but if the Articles do not contain such provision, they could be altered by the company in general meeting by Special Resolution so as to make possible the alteration in capital required. The company in general meeting passes an Ordinary Resolution to effect the desired change in capital unless the Articles require a Special Resolution; but a reduction of capital can only be done by a Special Resolution of the company and the alteration must also be confirmed by the Court (s.135). There is also a procedure in ss.425–30 for a company's capital to be reorganised under a scheme of arrangement.

Increase of authorised capital

Subject to provision in the Articles the authorised capital may be increased by an Ordinary Resolution. The following is the procedure to be adopted:

1. The directors, at a board meeting, resolve to recommend the proposed increase in capital, authorise the convening of an Extraordinary General Meeting to pass the Ordinary Resolution required and to approve a circular for issue to members explaining the reasons for the increase. The directors should also approve a form of two-way proxy; this is essential in the case of companies listed on The Stock Exchange (Continuing Obligations, para. 37). The Ordinary Resolution to increase the capital could, however, also be passed as special business at an Annual General Meeting of the company instead of at an Extraordinary General Meeting with an explanatory statement in the directors' report. In the case of listed companies, four copies of the proofs of the various documents must be submitted to The Stock Exchange for approval and six copies of the documents in their final form are required by the Exchange (Continuing Obligations, paras. 31 and 35).
2. A print of the Ordinary Resolution suitable for filing with the Registrar of Companies must also be prepared for signature by the chairman or the chairman of the meeting.

3. After the resolution has been passed a certified copy must be filed with the Registrar of Companies within 15 days with Companies Form No. G123 'Notice of increase in nominal capital'. It would also be usual to send a copy of the Memorandum of Association to the Registrar with the capital clause appropriately amended. In the case of a listed company four copies of the resolution and of the updated Memorandum, if one has been prepared, should be sent to The Stock Exchange (Continuing Obligations, para. 35).
4. A print of the resolution must be attached to all copies of the Memorandum of Association held in stock and sent to directors and others concerned with the administration of the company (e.g. the auditors) who are in possession of copies of the company's Memorandum and Articles.

Consolidation of shares

The share capital of a company may be consolidated if the Articles permit. Consolidation means that the shares of the company will be divided into shares of a larger nominal value, e.g. four shares of 25p each are to be consolidated into one share of £1 each.

Consolidation does not often arise but if a company has issued a large number of ordinary shares which are below the normal denominations of 25p, 50p or £1 it might be found convenient to consolidate the shares. However, many companies live happily with shares having a nominal value of 5p or 10p. The procedure is similar to that set out above in the case of an increase of authorised capital but certain additional matters have to be attended to, e.g. the Register of Members will have to be rewritten so as to show the holdings of each member in the new denomination.

It is not necessary in the case of consolidation to file with the Registrar of Companies a copy of the resolution passed at the general meeting if it is an Ordinary Resolution. However, Companies Form No. G122 'Notice of consolidation, division, sub-division, redemption or cancellation of shares, or conversion, re-conversion of stock into shares' must be sent to the Registrar within one month of the resolution being passed.

Some holdings of members will not consolidate into an exact number of shares in the new denomination so that it is necessary to sell fractions of shares in the new denomination on The Stock Exchange and deliver the proceeds to the members concerned. Where companies are listed on The Stock Exchange it is necessary to apply to the company's stockbrokers for the company's listing on the Exchange to be amended.

Share certificates may be called in for amendment but it would be more usual to send to members a notice that the consolidation has taken place and suggesting that the notice be kept with the member's share certificate(s) for information. An alternative would be to send out gummed slips to members requesting them to attach these to their share certificate(s).

Subdivision of shares

This is sometimes colloquially called a 'share-split'. Subject to provision in the Articles an Ordinary Resolution of the company in general meeting may be passed subdividing the company's shares into shares of a smaller nominal amount. Subdivision is often effected in the case of companies whose shares are listed on The Stock Exchange to make the shares more easily marketable, e.g. when the shares have risen to a very high value, described as 'heavy'. For example, if the company has £1 shares quoted on the market at £10 each, these could be subdivided into four shares of 25p each which would then carry a market value of just 250p each. If the shares are partly paid the proportion between the amount paid and unpaid would remain as before.

The procedure for effecting a subdivision of shares is similar to that for the consolidation of shares described above, except that fractions of shares cannot arise. Companies Form No. G122 must be sent to the Registrar of Companies within one month of the resolution.

Following a subdivision the Registrar of Members will have to be rewritten to show the number of shares held in the new denomination by each member. It would not be usual to call in share certificates for amendment unless the shares have distinguishing numbers.

Conversion of shares into stock

This is unlikely to be met with in practice since there are now no real advantages in having a company's capital in the form of stock rather than in the form of shares. Originally companies preferred to have stock rather than shares to avoid having to give each share a distinguishing number but under the Act distinguishing numbers may be dispensed with where shares are fully paid. Consequently, capital in the form of stock is only normally found in the case of companies which have been established for many years and where it is thought that the conversion of stock into shares might cause confusion or complications for stockholders.

The conversion of shares into stock may be effected by passing an Ordinary Resolution and the procedure is similar to that in the case of the consolidation of shares described above, except that fractions of shares do not arise in this case. The Ordinary Resolution would specify the units of stock which are transferable. Stock certificates are not called in for alteration but the holdings shown in the Registrar of Members will need to be amended. It should be noted, however, that stock cannot be issued directly, so that if at the present time a company's capital is in the form of stock and it is desired to increase the capital of the company, it must first be issued in the form of shares and an Ordinary Resolution passed converting the shares into stock. Companies Form No. G122 must be submitted to the Registrar of Companies.

Re-conversion of stock into shares

This is the reverse of the above and may be effected by an Ordinary Resolution of the company if the Articles so permit. Companies Form No. G122 must be submitted to the Registrar of Companies.

Cancellation of unissued shares

The cancellation of unissued shares, if permitted by the Articles, should not be confused with a reduction in the share capital, which requires the approval of the Court. The need for cancellation does not often arise but could occur following a scheme of arrangement or where the company has a class of shares none of which has been issued and which bear onerous conditions which the Memorandum of Association does not allow to be altered.

The cancellation of unissued shares may be effected by an Ordinary Resolution and the procedure is similar to that in the case of the consolidation of shares. Of course, in this case, amendment of the share certificates or of the company's listing on The Stock Exchange does not arise. Companies Form No. G122 must be submitted to the Registrar of Companies.

Reduction of capital

Subject to provision in the company's Articles and confirmation by the Court, a company may by Special Resolution reduce its capital. Confirmation by the Court is required in order to protect the interests of creditors and members, especially where different classes of shares are involved. The ways in which a company may reduce its capital are set out in s.135(2).

An application to the Court is necessary and it is desirable, therefore, to engage the company's legal advisers to settle the documentation (s.136). Generally, however, the secretarial procedures will be similar to those as in the case of a consolidation of shares, described above.

Since the secretary will be required to make an affidavit confirming that the appropriate procedural steps have been properly carried out, a detailed record should be kept of the actions taken. It is particularly important to record the dispatch of notices convening the Extraordinary General Meeting as regards time, date and place of posting. Other affidavits in support of the petition to the Court to reduce the capital may also be required. Under s.136 a creditor may object to the proposed reduction of capital and hence the need to ensure that the proper procedures have been followed.

When the reduction is confirmed by the Court a copy of the Court Order and approved minute showing the reduction of capital and its division into shares must be filed with the Registrar of Companies; the reduction will take effect from the date of such registration. A copy of the company's amended Memorandum of Association must be sent to the Registrar with the Court Order, a copy also being sent to The Stock Exchange if the company is listed. Although it is not usual the Court may require that the words 'and reduced' be added to the company's name for a certain period (s.137). If this is required by the Court the words 'and reduced' must also be added after the company's name on all business letters, the company's seal if it has one, etc.

In the case of a public company the Registrar will not register an order confirming a reduction of capital of a public company if this would bring the value of the allotted share capital below the authorised minimum for a public company (in 1989 £50,000) unless the Court directs otherwise or the company is first being re-registered as a private company (s.139). In the latter case, the Court may authorise the public company to be re-registered as private without it having to pass the Special Resolution normally required. The Court Order will also specify the alterations required to be made to the company's Memorandum and Articles to bring these into line with those of a private company. However, it is still necessary to apply to the Registrar to be re-registered as a private company; the special form to be used in these particular circumstances is Companies Form No. G139 'Application by a public company for re-registration as a private company following a Court Order reducing capital'.

Effect of alterations of capital on voting rights

The effect that the alteration may have on the existing voting rights of shareholders should be taken into account at the time an alteration of capital is made so that, if appropriate, suitable action may be taken so as to keep the voting rights between the different classes of shares in the same proportion as that which applied prior to the alteration. It may be necessary to hold meetings to obtain the consent of each class of shareholder.

Shares and stock

In what follows any references to shares should also be taken as including references to stock unless inappropriate in the context. As mentioned above, stock cannot be issued direct; the capital must first be issued in the form of shares and when fully paid may be converted into stock. There is no such thing as partly-paid stock. It is unnecessary for shares which are fully paid up and which carry equal rights with all other shares of the class to bear distinguishing numbers. Consequently, in practice distinguishing numbers are only met with in the case of shares which are not fully paid up, e.g. a 50p share of which only 25p is paid up.

Share premiums

A share premium is the amount of the issue price of a share in excess of its nominal value, e.g. in the case of a 25p share issued for £1.50, 25p is the nominal value and £1.25 is the premium. In a statement of a company's share capital only the nominal amount of the shares is included. The amount of any share premiums must be credited to a share premium account (s.130). This is a special form of capital reserve which can only be used for paying up unissued shares to be offered to members as fully paid shares, for writing off the company's preliminary expenses and for certain other purposes stated in s.130. However, the share premium account is treated as part of the company's paid up share capital and provisions applicable to the reduction of capital apply to this account (s.130). It should be noted, however, that ss.131 and 132 provide for a number of exemptions from the strict application of s.130 following a merger or reconstruction in cases where this is effected by an exchange of shares, and the company issuing its shares in exchange for shares in the other company issues its shares at a premium. For full details reference should be made to the Institute's manual.

Classes of shares

Although the Memorandum may set out the division of shares into different classes, with the respective rights of each of the classes being stated, this is not normally a desirable practice today. It is more usual for such matters to be included in the Articles of Association, which can be more easily altered, or in any resolution approving an increase in the capital of a company. The most common classes into which shares of a company may be divided are as follows:

1. Ordinary shares which rank after the preference shares as regards

dividends and return of capital but carry voting rights not normally given to holders of preference shares unless their preferential dividend is in arrears. These shares constitute the company's 'risk capital', i.e. each year the directors declare a dividend to be paid on the ordinary shares out of the profits of the company. If the company does well the dividends will be good and increase year by year, but if the company does badly the dividends may be reduced or even, in a very bad year, omitted entirely. The word 'ordinary' is commonly omitted from the description of the shares in the Memorandum and Articles of Association where a company only has one class of shares in issue. In some companies the risk capital is called 'deferred shares' or 'deferred stock'.

2. Ordinary shares which are non-voting shares, usually distinguished from the voting shares by calling them 'A' shares. Some companies have classes of ordinary shares which have restricted voting rights. In both cases, however, the shares otherwise have similar rights to those of the other ordinary shares as in (1) above.

3. Preference shares, which carry a preferential right to a fixed rate of dividend and, on a winding-up to return of capital with or without a premium, together with arrears of dividend. They constitute part of the company's share capital and repayment of capital on preference shares would rank ahead of repayment of capital on the ordinary shares (or the deferred shares or deferred stock) in a liquidation. The fixed rate of dividend is expressed as a percentage. Holders of preference shares get the same rate of dividend year in and year out unless in any year the profits of the company are insufficient to pay the preference dividends which, of course, take priority over payment of dividends on the ordinary shares.

4. Cumulative preference shares, which provide that if in any year the profits of the company are insufficient to pay the dividend on the preference shares the dividends not paid will be paid in subsequent years, together with the previous year's or years' dividend(s), when the company's fortunes improve. The payment of such arrears would rank ahead of payment of dividends on the ordinary shares.

5. Redeemable preference shares or cumulative redeemable preference shares, which will be redeemed by the company at their nominal or par value (i.e. the face value) at some stated date in the future. The amount of the repayment, however, is the actual nominal value of the shares, e.g. £1 preference shares would be redeemed at £1 per share notwithstanding that the market value of the shares on The Stock Exchange might be higher or lower than this amount.

6. Debentures and loan stocks, which are in effect loans to the company by investors who receive a fixed rate of interest on the debenture or

loan stock. They are mentioned here, although they are not a class of share, since they are frequently met with when considering a company's financial structure. Generally, debentures are secured loans on the assets of the company, whereas loan stocks are normally unsecured. Payment of the interest on debentures and loan stocks ranks ahead of the payment of preference dividends and ordinary dividends. They would also rank ahead of preference and ordinary shares in repayment of capital in a liquidation. It should be noted, however, that debentures and loan stocks do not form part of the company's capital, although quite often they are colloquially referred to as 'loan capital'. The company's capital is as stated in the capital clause in the Memorandum which is confined to the company's share capital which includes preference shares as well as ordinary shares.

Variation of rights attaching to a class of shares

Where a class of shares has special rights attached to it those rights may only be varied with the written consent of the holders of three-quarters in nominal value of the issued shares of that class or, if an Extraordinary Resolution is passed at a separate meeting of the holders of that class of shares to sanction the variation. The Articles of Association of the company may, however, contain provision regarding the variation of the rights, in which case the procedure in the Articles would be followed.

Holders of not less in the aggregate of 15 per cent of the issued shares of a class who did not consent to or vote in favour of the variation may apply to the Court for the variation to be cancelled within 21 days of the resolution consenting to the variation being passed. In this case the variation will not take effect until it is confirmed by the Court. The application may be made by one or more of these shareholders on behalf of those entitled to make the application. The Court will disallow the variation if it is satisfied that the variation would unfairly prejudice the holders concerned but if not so satisfied the Court will confirm the alteration (s.127). A copy of the Court Order must be filed with the Registrar within 15 days of it being made.

There are certain other provisions regarding the variation of class rights in s.125(4) and in the following subsections of that section. For example, in the case where the class rights are conferred by the Memorandum of Association, and the Articles adopted at the time of the original incorporation of the company contain provisions with regard to the variation of class rights, the class rights may only be varied by following the provisions in the Articles. If there are no such provisions the class rights can only be varied with the consent of all the members of the company and not just by the holders of the class of shares concerned (s.125(5)).

Shares may subsequently be allotted by a company with special rights attached to them which are not identical with those attaching to shares previously allotted. If such special rights are not stated in the Memorandum or Articles or in any agreement which has been filed with the Registrar, a statement of the special rights must be filed on Companies Form No. G128(1) 'Statement of rights attached to allotted shares' within one month of the date of allotment.

Membership

The subscribers to the Memorandum of Association are deemed to have agreed to become members of the company and on registration of the company their names should be entered in the Register of Members. A person may subsequently become a member by applying for new shares or by the transfer or transmission to him of shares already in issue and by his name being entered in the Register of Members. Such a person is not regarded as a member of the company until both of these requirements have been met.

A company should always have at least two members; any member of a company which carries on business for more than 6 months knowing it has only one member will be liable for the debts of the company contracted during the period when it only had one member. Care should be taken, therefore, when a company acquires a new subsidiary when the whole of the share capital of the acquired company is transferred to the purchasing company, to arrange for one other share to be transferred to another person to hold the share as a nominee of the holding company.

As long as there is no provision to the contrary in the Articles a legal person like a company may hold shares in a company as well as an individual. The Articles of some companies, however, exclude certain categories of person from membership, e.g. persons who are not able to give a declaration of British nationality. At the same time it is necessary to ensure that in the case of a registered company, for example, the company's Memorandum of Association, does not preclude the holding of shares in other companies.

However, an unincorporated body like a club or association not registered under the Act should not be accepted as a member of the company because it does not possess legal personality. If such a body wishes to hold shares they should be registered in the name of another individual or individuals or a person having a legal personality such as a bank nominee or a trustee company.

Similarly, the holder of an office should not be accepted as a member in that capacity unless it is an office created by statute, such as the Treasury Solicitor or the Accountant General. Some public officers are deemed to be legally a corporation, like the Public Trustee, and these may be registered as members of companies.

Shares should also not be registered in the name of an English partnership. They should be held in the names of two or more partners and no reference should be made in the Register of Members to the partnership. Scottish partnerships, however, have legal personality and may, therefore, be registered in the firm name as members of the company. Under s.128 of the CA 1989 provision is made for the Secretary of State by regulations to prescribe a Table G containing articles of association for a partnership company. At the time of writing this handbook it is not known whether such partnership companies may be registered shareholders. Shares in a company may be held by a number of persons in a joint account; some Articles of Association limit the number of persons who may be so registered. In the case of a company listed on The Stock Exchange the maximum number of joint holders is set at not fewer than four (Yellow Book, Section 9, Chapter 1, para. 1.3).

Unless a subsidiary company is acting only as personal representative or trustee without having any beneficial interest in the shares a subsidiary company is not permitted to be a member of its holding company. Schedule 2 provides detailed interpretation of references to 'beneficial interest' and the schedule makes special provision to enable a company's subsidiary company to act as trustee for a group employee share scheme or pension scheme. There is, however, no prohibition on the holding of shares by a subsidiary in its holding company if it held shares in the company which acquired it (which thereby became its holding company) prior to its becoming a subsidiary of that company; but in this case the subsidiary is not permitted to vote at meetings of the holding company. Of course, it would not be lawful for any further shares in the holding company to be allotted to such a subsidiary company, a situation which could arise if the holding company had a capitalisation issue.

Minors as members of a company

Since becoming a member of a company involves the assumption of liabilities in respect of the shares held it is not considered good practice to accept minors as members of a company in their own names; their responsibilities in respect of those liabilities would be voidable during the period of their minority. This is especially important where the shares may be partly paid, which imposes an obligation on the holders to pay further calls on the shares made by the directors. The Articles of Association may give express power to reject transfers in the name of minors but, if not, a right of rejection is conferred by the general law. Of course, it may only come to light subsequently that a registered holder of shares is a minor, in which case the company may subsequently repudiate the registration during the period of minority and restore the preceding holder as the holder of the shares. The Stock Exchange requires that the Articles of Association contain no restrictions on the transfer of fully-paid shares in the case of listed companies but it is maintained that the right of rejection would still exist under the general law. However, from a practical point of view, and especially in the case of listed companies, minors may well become members without the company's knowledge and in almost all cases no difficulty will be experienced by the company in this connection.

In Scotland, however, the law is different in this respect and reference should be made to the Institute's manual.

Application and allotment procedure

Where shares are to be allotted for cash it is first necessary to ensure compliance with the statutory requirements on the allotment of shares, which are outlined later in this chapter. These comprise the grant of authority to the directors by the company in general meeting to allot shares for cash, members' pre-emption rights and any pre-emption rights which may be set out in the Articles of Association. There are further considerations to apply where allotments are made by public companies under a public offer of shares (see Chapter 3).

Subject, therefore, to compliance with these statutory provisions, the required steps would be as follows:

1. It may be necessary for the authorised capital of the company to be increased because the present unissued authorised capital is insufficient to cover the proposed allotment.
2. The person wishing to subscribe for shares completes a form of application and returns it with the required payment.
3. A share certificate would then be prepared for each applicant on the company's printed share certificate forms. In the case of small companies, however, blank certificates for completion by hand may be obtained from law stationers.
4. The directors should pass a resolution to allot the shares to the persons applying for them, and if the company has a seal, authorise the sealing of the share certificates, and their issue to the applicants.
5. The share certificates after sealing, if appropriate, would be sent to the applicant informing him of the allotment. All these steps should be taken as soon as possible since until the applicant is notified that his application for shares has been accepted he is free to withdraw it.

6. The names of the persons allotted shares are then entered in the Register of Members of the company and they thereupon become members of the company.
7. Return of allotments on Companies Form No. G88(2) (Revised 1988) 'Return of allotments of shares' should be filed with the Registrar within one month of the date of allotment.

Shares allotted for non-cash consideration

In this case further considerations apply. There must be compliance with the statutory rules regarding payment for shares issued for a non-cash consideration, as described later in this chapter.

There is usually a formal contract entered into for the transfer of the non-cash consideration to the company and for the allotment by it of shares in consideration for the assets transferred. This formal contract should be approved by the board of directors. The agreement must be duly stamped and sent to the Registrar of Companies with the return of allotments accompanied by a certified copy of the agreement if the Registrar is to be requested to return the original agreement.

If there is no written contract particulars of the agreement must be set out on Companies Form No. G88(3) 'Particulars of a contract relating to shares allotted as fully or partly paid up otherwise than in cash', bearing the same stamp duty as would be payable on a written contract, and sent to the Registrar with the return of allotments.

Shares for a non-cash consideration may also be issued on a capitalisation of reserves the return of allotments being made on Companies Form No. G88(2) (Revised 1988) 'Return of allotments of shares' with the particulars of the contract on Companies Form No. 88(3), which in this case need not be stamped.

It will be seen that the issue of shares for a consideration other than cash involves certain formalities and expense and arrangements may be made for the transaction to be structured so as to constitute an allotment for cash.

Allotments by public companies

Special provisions apply in the case of issues of shares to the public by public companies. These are as follows:

1. An allotment cannot be made unless the amount stated in the prospectus as the minimum amount required to be raised has, in fact, been subscribed and the sum payable on application for the shares concerned has been received by the company.

2. There can be no allotment if the amount of capital offered for subscription is not fully subscribed, unless there is an express term in the offer that an allotment may be made notwithstanding that there has not been a full subscription. This applies both in the case of offers of shares for cash and offers of shares for a consideration other than cash.

If the above two requirements are not met the cash subscribed or other consideration paid must be returned to the applicants. Other procedural matters arising in connection with the allotment of shares pursuant to offers to the public are covered more fully in Chapter 3.

Nominee shareholding

These arise where the beneficial owner of shares does not wish to have them registered in his own name. The shares may be registered instead in the name of a nominee, usually one of the banks' nominee companies which include the word 'nominees' in their names. The beneficial owner of the shares has no contact with the company since the company has to address all communications to the registered shareholder, in this case to the nominee company. There must also be no reference in the company's Register of Members to the identity of the beneficial owner, since by s.360 a company is not permitted to recognise any trust affecting any of its shares.

This rule is not contravened, however, by a company accepting a body corporate as a shareholder with the word 'nominees' or 'trustees' in its name. At the same time, notwithstanding s.360, public companies are required to keep a register of persons who have a beneficial interest in 3 per cent or more of the company's share capital, which must be notified to the company within two days of the interest being acquired (ss.199(2) and 202 as amended by CA 1989 s.134). The company is entitled to make enquiry under s.212 of any registered shareholder, which may be a nominee or trustee company, as to the person or persons beneficially interested in the shares it holds (ss.198–213). Section 360 does not apply in Scotland.

A need for nominee shareholdings also arises in the case of wholly owned subsidiary companies. All the share capital of the subsidiary will be owned beneficially by the holding company and the subsidiary must have at least two shareholders. In practice, therefore, one or more of the shares in the subsidiary will be registered in the name of a nominee on behalf of the company. This requirement is often met by arranging for one share to be registered in the joint name of a director of the holding company as the first-named holder and the holding company as the second-named holder. The second shareholder, i.e. the holding company, would hold all the balance of the shares in the subsidiary company.

The nominee should provide a dividend mandate requesting that all dividends be paid to the holding company and should also execute a transfer of the shares, the name of the transferee and date being left blank so that if the director were to leave the company it would be possible for his nominee share to be transferred to another director who remained a director of the holding company. A short declaration of trust should also be executed by the director declaring that the share he holds is held by him as a nominee for the holding company and that he has no beneficial interest in it. An extended declaration of trust could also include the following provisions:

1. The director will pay any dividends on the shares as the company may direct.
2. The director will transfer or deal with the shares as the company may direct.
3. The director as nominee will vote at general meetings as the holding company shall direct, or execute proxies as the holding company may require, and that if any rights or options should be offered to him as holder of the nominee share, he will act in relation to the offer as the holding company may direct.

If the extended declaration of trust is executed there is no need for a blank transfer or dividend mandate. However, it may still be prudent to obtain a blank transfer already signed by the director in case he is dismissed by the company and is unwilling to cooperate in giving up his nominee shares.

Prohibition of financial assistance by company for acquisition of its own shares

Sections 151 and 154 render it unlawful for a company or any of its subsidiaries to give direct or indirect financial assistance for the purpose of acquisition of shares in the company. There is, however, a limited exception to this rule in the case of private companies. Financial assistance is very widely defined, including, for example, the giving of a guarantee or making a gift or a loan.

However, s.153 provides that the prohibition imposed by s.151 does not apply if the company's principal purpose was not to give assistance for the purchase or acquisition of its shares, if the giving of it was only an incidental part of some larger purpose of the company and if that assistance were given in good faith in the interests of the company.

There are certain other exemptions provided by s.153, e.g. dividend distribution, liquidation distribution, capitalisation share issues and arrangements sanctioned by the Court, and purchases by the company of its own shares under the provisions of s.162.

The ordinary business of the company may include the lending of money, in which case loans may be made for the acquisition of shares in the company.

A company may in addition provide money in connection with the acquisition of fully paid shares in the company or its holding company for the purpose of an employees' share scheme. Such schemes are fully described in Chapter 7. There are other exceptions as well and these are set out in detail in s.153. An amendment made to s.153(4)(b) by CA 1989 s.132 removes any doubts as to the legality of a company giving financial assistance for the purchase of its shares by an ESOP (see Chapter 7).

Section 155 provides a further exception in the case of private companies, where assistance may be given for the acquisition of shares in the company or shares in its holding company provided that the holding company is also a private company and that all the companies concerned are not subsidiaries of a public company. However, financial assistance by private companies may only be given if the company has net assets which are not thereby reduced or, if they are reduced, the financial assistance is provided out of distributable profits. A statutory declaration must be made by the directors of the private company in accordance with the terms of ss.155(6) and 156, which must be sent to the Registrar of Companies on Companies Form No. G155(6)a 'Declaration in relation to assistance for the acquisition of shares'. If the financial assistance is to be given by the company for the acquisition of shares in its holding company the directors of the holding company must also submit a statutory declaration to the Registrar of Companies on Companies Form No. G155(6)b 'Declaration by the directors of a holding company in relation to assistance for the acquisition of shares'. There is a detailed procedure to be followed which is fully described in the Institute's manual.

Statutory restrictions on allotment: authority for allotment

Relevant securities in a company may not be allotted unless the directors are authorised to do so by an Ordinary Resolution of the company or by the Articles of Association (s.80). The authority may be given in general terms or made subject to conditions and must state the maximum amount of the relevant securities that may be issued and specify the date on which the authority will expire – which must be not later than five years from the date of the resolution. An Ordinary Resolution for this purpose is now commonly included as part of the company's regular business at its

Annual General Meeting and when this is done the authority is given for one year only.

Relevant securities are defined in the Act as shares (other than those taken by subscribers to the Memorandum or allotted under an employees' share scheme) and securities giving a right to subscribe for, or convert into, shares of the company.

The authority to the directors to allot relevant securities may be revoked, varied or renewed by Ordinary Resolution even if the authority was given by a Special Resolution instead of the more usual Ordinary Resolution or if contained in the Articles of Association. A resolution renewing an earlier authority must also specify an expiry date within five years of the renewal resolution and state the amount of securities which may be allotted. Securities may be allotted after the expiry of the authority provided that the allotment is in pursuance of an offer or agreement made prior to the expiry of the authority. Section 380(4)(f) provides that a copy of a resolution giving authority to directors to allot relevant securities must be filed with the Registrar of Companies within 15 days after it is passed.

Statutory restrictions on allotment: pre-emption rights

It is quite common for the Articles of private companies to provide that where new shares are to be allotted they must first be offered to existing shareholders in proportion to their existing holdings. In the case of a listed company, The Stock Exchange requires that any new issues of shares for cash should first be offered to existing holders as in a rights issue. Pre-emption rights for existing shareholders in respect of the allotment of equity securities is now, however, provided by statute in ss.89–94 even though there may be no special provisions in the Articles of Association.

Equity securities are defined in the Act as relevant shares in the company, i.e. basically the ordinary share capital of the company on which the rate of dividend varies according to the profits of the company and which carry no preferential right in the repayment of the capital in the event of winding-up. Securities which may be converted into relevant shares (i.e. convertible loan stocks) are also included but the following are excluded:

1. Shares taken by subscribers to the Memorandum.
2. Shares which as regards dividends and capital carry right to participate only up to a specified amount in a distribution.
3. Shares held by a person acquired through an employees' share scheme or which are to be allotted in pursuance of such a scheme.

4. Shares allotted under a capitalisation issue.
5. Shares allotted wholly or partly paid otherwise than in cash.

It should be noted that any pre-emption rights contained in a company's Memorandum or Articles of Association take precedence over the statutory pre-emption rights. The requirement of the Act is that no equity securities may be allotted unless they have first been offered to the holders of all the relevant shares in the company in proportion to their existing shareholdings and this includes holders of any shares under an employees' share scheme (s.89). Section 90 lays down the detailed provisions with regard to the communication of the offer to the existing shareholders, who must be given a period of not less than 21 days in which to accept the offer. A record date to determine the holders entitled to receive the offer must be set within a period of 28 days before the date of the offer (s.94(7)). In the case of share warrants to bearer, the offer must be made by advertisement in the *London Gazette* or *Edinburgh Gazette* stating how copies of the offer may be received.

The company and every officer who knowingly permit an allotment of shares to be made in contravention of the statutory pre-emption provisions are jointly and severally liable to compensate any person who may suffer loss thereby.

Private companies may exclude the statutory provisions by provisions contained in their Memorandum and Articles which will prevail even if they are inconsistent with the statutory provisions.

It is also possible for both public and private companies to exclude the operation of the statutory pre-emption rights in s.89 if the directors obtain authority by a Special Resolution of the company passed at a general meeting or, alternatively, by a provision in the company's Articles (s.95). If the company's Articles do not already contain a provision to cover this an alteration to the Articles would be necessary and this would also require the approval of shareholders by a Special Resolution in a general meeting. In the case of a company listed on The Stock Exchange, the Continuing Obligations, para. 38, provide that unless shareholders in general meeting otherwise permit, or the company has a general authority to disapply pre-emption rights under s.95 granted not more than 15 months previously, a company must first offer securities having an equity element, to be issued for cash, to the existing equity shareholders of the company in proportion to their existing holdings. The statutory right for the disapplication of pre-emption rights is contained in s.95 and it is also quite common for the Special Resolution required by s.95, giving the directors power to disapply the Act's requirements with regard to pre-emption rights in regard to the allotment of securities up to a limit specified in the resolution, to be proposed as part of the regular business at the Annual General Meeting of a company.

The grant of the power to directors to disapply the pre-emption rights makes it possible for the company to make a rights issue of its shares and exclude or make such other arrangements as may be appropriate to resolve legal or practical problems, rendering it impossible to allot equity securities to all shareholders of the company in proportion to the respective numbers of shares held by them. This arises because in some countries (e.g. the United States) it would not be possible to offer the securities to residents of those countries without going through lengthy and costly procedures required by the legislation of the country concerned. The rights of the persons concerned would, whenever practicable, be sold for their benefit. Circumstances may also arise where the company might wish to make small allotments of equity shares for cash to persons other than existing shareholders.

The disapplication of the pre-emption rights would cease when the general authority of the directors to issue equity securities under s.80 lapsed. However, an offer made before the expiry of the authority to disapply the pre-emption rights would remain valid notwithstanding that the actual allotment did not take place until after that date.

Payment for shares: general requirements

There are two ways in which shares may be paid for:

1. In money or money's worth, including goodwill and knowhow.
2. By way of capitalisation of the company's existing reserves.

The following methods are, however, prohibited:

1. Payment for shares or any premium on them by a person undertaking to do work or perform services for the company or any other person (s.99).
2. The allotment of shares at a discount, i.e. at an issue price for a share below its nominal value (s.100). However, a company may pay commission as consideration for a person subscribing or procuring the subscription for shares in the company since this is not treated as a discount (ss.97 and 98).
3. Shares may not be allotted (other than under an employees' share scheme) unless at least one-quarter of their nominal value and the whole of their premium is paid up (s.101).
4. Public companies may not allot shares as fully or partly paid up (both as to their nominal value and any premium on the shares) if the consideration for the allotment includes an undertaking which is to

be, or may be, performed more than five years after the date of the allotment (s.102). If an allotment is made for a consideration which includes an undertaking to be performed within five years and the undertaking is not performed within that period the allottee of the shares becomes liable to pay the company an amount equal to the agreed price for the shares, which was to be treated as paid up by the undertaking, with interest.

5. Shares taken up by a subscriber to the Memorandum of Association must be paid for in cash, both as to nominal value and any premium (s.106).

Subsequent holders of shares may incur liability if any of the above provisions relating to the payment for shares are contravened (s.112).

Valuation of non-cash consideration

A public company is prohibited from allotting shares either fully or partly paid up as to nominal value or premium for a consideration other than cash unless the consideration has been valued by an appointed valuer within the 6 months previous to the allotment and a copy of the valuer's report has been sent to the proposed allottee of the shares (ss.103, 108 and 112). There is, however, exemption from this provision in the following cases:

1. Allotments of shares made in a take-over bid by way of share exchange if the offer is open to all holders of the class of shares concerned (s.103(3)–(5)).
2. Where the shares are allotted under a capitalisation issue by the capitalisation of reserves or sums standing to the credit of the profit and loss account (s.103(2)).

The valuation report must be made by an independent person who would be qualified to be an auditor of the company, unless he considers that it would be appropriate for some other person with the required knowledge and experience to make the report (provided that that person is not an officer or servant of the company).

The valuer's report must state the following:

1. The nominal value of the shares being allotted wholly or partly paid for a consideration other than cash.
2. The amount of any premium payable on the shares.
3. The consideration which he has valued and the method he has used to value it.
4. The amount of the nominal value of the shares and any premium treated as paid up for a consideration other than cash.

If the person appointed to make the valuation has appointed someone else to make it, the valuer's report must mention this and state:

1. The name of the other person with details of his knowledge and experience.
2. A description of the consideration that was valued by the other person and the method used to value it.

In both of the above cases the report must include a statement that the value of the consideration, together with any cash that may be payable, is not less than the amounts of the nominal value of, and premium on, the shares which are to be treated as paid up by the consideration of other than cash and that there has been no material change in its value since the date of the valuation.

A copy of the report must be sent to the Registrar of Companies when the return of allotments is filed.

The person making the report is entitled to call for such information from officers of the company as he may require and it is an offence for misleading or false information to be given to him. It is also an offence to contravene the above requirements for the allotment of shares for a non-cash consideration, including failure to send the allottee a copy of the report. The allottee will be liable to pay the company the amount equal to the nominal value and premium treated as paid up for a consideration other than cash on the shares allotted to him if he knew, or should have known, of the contravention. A subsequent holder of the shares, purchasing the shares for value without knowledge of the contravention, will not be liable and will also not be liable if the previous holder was not himself liable.

Acquisition of non-cash assets from subscribers or from certain shareholders

Special requirements apply if a public company proposes to acquire non-cash assets from a subscriber to the Memorandum of a company formed as a public company (or from any person who was a member of the company at the date of the re-registration of the company as a public company) within the period of two years from the date on which the company became entitled to commence business (or the date of re-registration) (ss.104, 105, 109 and 112). The requirements to be complied with are set out in s.104 and fall within the area of company law rather than of company secretarial practice; consequently, they are not dealt with in this handbook. Similarly, the following also falls within the field of company law: the imposition of penalties on the company (and any officer of the company) in the event of the default of any of the provisions described above relating to the payment for shares on allotment, the valuation of non-cash consideration before allotment of shares and the special provisions applicable in the case of acquisition of non-cash assets from subscribers to the Memorandum of a company formed as a public company (or from shareholders who were members of a company at the time of its re-registration as a public company), including the cases in which the Court may grant relief from such penalties.

Serious loss of capital

There is one other provision to be noted in connection with the capital of a public company. Section 142 provides that if the net assets of a public company become equal to one-half or less of its called-up share capital, the directors must call a meeting of the company within 28 days of the deficiency becoming known at which shareholders may consider what measures should be taken to deal with the situation.

Calls and instalments on shares

Calls on shares arise when shares have been issued on a partly paid instead of on a fully paid basis; but partly paid shares are not often met with in practice. Calls on partly-paid shares are made by a resolution of the directors under provisions contained in the company's Articles (e.g. Table A, Regulations 12–17); the resolution will specify the amount of the call, the due date for payment and where payment should be sent. Where shares are registered in two or more names the joint holders are jointly and severally liable for the calls. In the case of deceased shareholders the estate continues to be liable for outstanding calls unless the shares have been transferred into the personal names of the personal representatives in which case the personal representatives are personally liable. The company's Articles also make provision for action to be taken in the event of default of payment of a call (e.g. Table A, Regulations 18–22).

A general share registration point to note is that registration of transfers of shares on which a call is unpaid should not be accepted for registration since the liability for payment of the call remains with the holder of the shares who was registered on the date that the call was made.

It is necessary to draw a distinction between shares issued by companies as partly paid and the issue of new shares payable in instalments, as in some privatisation issues, where the procedure in the case of non-payment of the instalments as they fall due is different from the non-payment of calls made by the directors on partly-paid shares. In such cases the transfer may be registered through the TALISMAN system since the custodian bank handling the issue has other methods available to it to deal with the non-payment of instalments.

The procedure for dealing with the payment of a call made by the directors on partly-paid shares (i.e. other than the payment of predetermined instalments on shares) falls within the sphere of company secretarial practice and the following procedure should, therefore, be noted:

1. The directors pass the appropriate resolution making the call.
2. If the company is listed, The Stock Exchange should be sent a copy of the resolution and of the proposed call letter.
3. Bulk printing of the call letters is arranged, incorporating any amendments The Stock Exchange may require.
4. The call letters are prepared by the company by the appropriate means (e.g. the use of the company's computer) to be sent to the individual shareholders, specifying the number of shares and the total amount of the calls to be paid and the date and place of payment of the calls. Each call letter is serially numbered and a note of the issue of the call letters made in the Register of Members.
5. The call letters are dispatched to the shareholders when ready.
6. A receiving banker will usually have been appointed to receive the money for the calls and each day dockets detached from the call letters will be submitted to the company by the receiving bank.
7. After the final date for receipt of calls a reconciliation of the amounts received from the bank should be made and a list of unpaid calls agreed.
8. Reminder letters are sent out to the shareholders who have not paid the call stating that immediate payment must be made and that interest may be charged on the amount left outstanding.
9. If payment is still not received, say within the next 7 days, a further letter should be sent to the shareholders concerned warning them that unless the call is paid promptly the directors will consider the possibility of forfeiting the shares under the company's Articles.
10. The company's stockbrokers should be requested to arrange for the listing of the shares to be amended as regards the further amount called up if the company is listed on The Stock Exchange.
11. The partly-paid share certificates should be endorsed with the payment of the call and returned to the person lodging the certificate, i.e. the shareholder or an agent acting on behalf of the shareholder.
12. The accounts of the shareholders in the Register of Members should be noted with the payment of the call.

13. A note must be included in the company's balance sheet or annual return if at the time these documents are prepared there are any unpaid calls.

Instalments on shares

Although it is mentioned above that partly-paid shares are rare, payment for shares by instalments is frequently used in the case of an offer for sale of shares where the price is substantial, as in the case of some privatisation issues. It is usual in such cases for the shares, which may already be fully paid, to be held by a custodian bank which in turn offers the shares to the public for payment by instalments. In these cases non-payment of an instalment may result in the loss of the shares and the forfeiture procedure described below does not have to be followed. The terms of issue will provide for the payment of a first instalment on application and for a second instalment (and perhaps a third instalment) to be paid at a subsequent date (or dates) which are determined in advance, so that there is no need for the call to be formally made by the directors since information regarding the amount(s) of the instalment(s) and the due date(s) for payment are mentioned in the letter of acceptance sent to the shareholder on receipt of his application payment.

The shares may be sold by the holder of a letter of acceptance before payment of the second instalment by signing the form of renunciation on the back of the letter of acceptance. After about two months after dispatch of the letters of acceptance, however, holders become registered and the shares may then only be transferred by completion of a transfer form. A holder wishing to sell his shares must then return the completed transfer form to his stockbroker accompanied by the letter of acceptance.

The usual arrangement for the payment of the second instalment is for reminder notices to be sent out by the custodian bank about four weeks before the instalment is due setting out the procedures for payment and transfer of shares. An interim certificate is sent with the reminder notice which will be duly receipted and returned to the registered holder (or to his agent) by the receiving bank following payment. The procedure for the payment of a third instalment, if there is one, would be similar. After payment of the second (or third) instalment a fully-paid share certificate will be issued.

The letters of acceptance and interim certificates make it clear that in the event of the non-payment of any instalment the entitlement of the registered holder may be cancelled and the related shares sold. Instalments previously paid will be returned to the registered holder less expenses and any loss suffered by the custodian bank in disposing of the shares. It should be noted, therefore, that in such cases there is no need to go through the forfeiture procedure described below.

Forfeiture

If it should become necessary to forfeit shares, if the Articles so permit, because of non-payment of calls made by the directors on shares which may be offered by companies for subscription on a partly-paid basis, it is important to ensure strict compliance with the requirements of the company's Articles since if these are not followed the forfeiture could be declared invalid. The power is rarely exercised in practice; accordingly, it would be desirable to take legal advice before setting up forfeiture arrangements. When the shares have been forfeited the person concerned ceases to be a member of the company and the forfeiture should be entered in the Register of Members. Subject to the Articles a forfeiture of shares may be cancelled if the call should subsequently be received (with or without interest), assuming that at that time the shares have not been sold by the directors under the powers given to the company in its Articles of Association (e.g. Table A, Regulation 20). As a protection to the company where forfeited shares are sold, a statutory declaration on the lines set out in Table A, Regulation 22, should be sworn. It should be noted that forfeiture does not apply in the case of failure to pay instalments on shares (see above).

In the case of a public company special requirements are imposed by ss.146–9 where shares are forfeited or surrendered to the company in lieu of forfeiture under the company's Articles of Association for failure to pay calls. Under these provisions the company must cancel the shares and diminish the amount of its share capital by the nominal value of the shares if the forfeited or surrendered shares are not disposed of within three years of the forfeiture or surrender. Voting rights may not be exercised in respect of the forfeited or surrendered shares during this three-year period. If the cancellation should reduce the company's nominal capital below the authorised minimum for a public company (in 1989 £50,000) the company must apply for re-registration as a private company. In these circumstances the directors have power under s.147 to take steps to reduce the company's capital without complying with the special provisions laid down by the Act for doing this, i.e. a Special Resolution under s.135 to reduce share capital and application to the Court for approval under s.136. The company makes application to the Registrar of Companies to be re-registered as a private company on Companies Form No. G147 'Application by a public company for re-registration as a private company following cancellation of shares and reduction of nominal value of issued capital' accompanied by a copy of the altered Memorandum and Articles of Association.

It should be noted that a private company becoming re-registered as a public company, after having forfeited, surrendered or otherwise acquired any of its shares as stated above, must also comply with the above requirements within three years from the date of re-registration as a public company (s.148).

The following is the company secretarial procedure to be followed in connection with the forfeiture of shares:

1. A reminder letter is sent to the shareholder within 7 days of the due date for payment requesting that payment be made immediately and that interest may be charged from the due date for the payment.
2. A second reminder is sent out if no payment is received after 7 days.
3. If after a further period of 7 days the amount remains unpaid a final warning notice should be sent by recorded delivery requesting payment with interest not earlier than 14 days from the date of the notice and stating that in the event of non-payment by the specified date, the shares will be liable to be forfeited.
4. If the amounts continue to be unpaid the directors may pass a resolution without further notice which will include the names of the members and the numbers of shares held by each shareholder which are forfeited and giving authority to the directors to sell or re-issue the forfeited shares.
5. When the resolution has been passed a notification of the forfeiture should be sent by recorded delivery to the shareholders concerned requesting surrender of their share certificates or, if appropriate, allotment letters or letters of acceptance.
6. The accounts of each shareholder in the Register of Members whose shares have been forfeited should be debited and the appropriate shares placed to the credit of a 'forfeited shares' account.
7. The shares would then be sold (or re-issued), the forfeited shares account debited and the account of the purchaser of the shares in the Register of Members credited with the number of shares purchased.
8. A note should be made in the company's balance sheet or annual return of any forfeited shares remaining unissued at the time of preparation of the balance sheet or annual return.

Company's lien on its shares

As well as rights to forfeiture the Articles of most companies (e.g. Table A, Regulations 8–11) give the company a lien on its shares and on dividends payable thereon for all money due in respect of the shares. The lien would be enforced by sale of the member's shares after he had been given due notice of the debt owing to the company which remained unpaid, the notice being given in a similar manner to that described above in the case of forfeiture. If the amount realised by the sale exceeds the amount of debt the surplus must be paid to the shareholder upon the surrender of his share certificate. It should be noted, however, that in the case of a public company, certain liens are void (s.150).

Warrants and subscription rights

Warrants

A warrant is a document rather like a share certificate which entitles the holder to subscribe for equity capital in the company at some future date or dates at a price which is determined at the time of issue of the warrant. It should not be confused with a share warrant to bearer, which is a document evidencing title to shares already issued. Warrants to subscribe may be listed on The Stock Exchange and the company would normally have a register of holders of the warrants but the warrants do not form part of the company's capital and holders do not receive dividends or interest.

The Company's Articles of Association must permit the issue of warrants. They should not be confused with the rights to convert into ordinary shares attached to convertible loan stocks which cannot be bought or sold separately. Warrants may, however, be bought and sold on The Stock Exchange separately from other securities of the company. Warrants are often issued in connection with take-over offers in order to make the terms more attractive without immediate cost to the bidding company.

A register of holders is usually maintained in a form similar to that of the Register of Members and it will be necessary in the statement of the terms of issue to include the procedures regarding transfer of warrants, inspection of the register, requests for copies of the register and the dispatch of annual reports and accounts to warrant holders, although there are no statutory provisions covering these matters. *Ad valorem* stamp duty is payable on transfers of warrants in the same way as transfers of shares.

Subscription rights

Sometimes the issue of a loan stock includes an associated right to subscribe for shares in the company concerned. This is not the same as the conversion rights under a convertible loan stock, where the loan stock is surrendered in exchange for shares. With subscription rights the loan stock remains in issue and holders subscribe additional money in order to exercise their subscription rights. An alternative method of giving subscription rights is by the issue of option certificates. It will be seen that the exercise of subscription rights does not affect the company's register of loan stock holders, as it is in the case of a convertible loan stock where a person's holding of convertible loan stock would be reduced by the amount of stock which he converted into equity capital.

Exercise of subscription rights and warrants

The company secretarial procedure for the exercise of subscription rights and warrants is similar to that which is applicable in the case of convertible loan stock but there are additional matters requiring attention as follows:

1. The cash received for shares subscribed will be recorded and banked.
2. New loan stock certificates without the subscription rights should be prepared and sent out with the share certificates.
3. The register of holders of the loan stock should be divided into two parts, one part containing holders who still possess subscription rights exercisable at some future date and the other part containing the names of holders of loan stock to which subscription rights are no longer attached. If the loan stock is listed, there will necessarily be two prices on The Stock Exchange, i.e. one price for the stock which still has subscription rights attached and the other price for the stock on which the subscription rights have been exercised.
4. A return of allotments on Companies Form No. G88(2)(Revised 1988) should be prepared and sent to the Registrar of Companies.

In the case of the exercise of warrants to subscribe for shares a similar procedure will be followed as in the case of the exercise of subscription rights attached to loan stock but there is no need to issue new warrant certificates since once the right under it has been exercised it becomes dead. Balance certificates for warrants, however, may be required if the holder does not exercise the whole of his rights and some rights remain to be exercised at some future date.

Capitalisation issues

Capitalisation issues and the procedure for dealing with such issues by public companies are fully described in Chapter 3. Many of the requirements stated there do not apply to capitalisation issues by private companies. A private company may use a capitalisation issue in order to bring its allotted capital up to the statutory minimum required for re-registration as a public company (in 1989 £50,000).

The following are the procedural points to note in connection with a capitalisation issue by a private company:

1. The company must have power to make a capitalisation issue under its Articles.
2. There must be sufficient authorised but unissued capital to cover the issue – if not, the additional capital must be created by passing an Ordinary Resolution in a general meeting of the company.
3. The directors must have the authority to issue capital under s.80.
4. The capitalisation issue is sanctioned by passing an Ordinary Resolution at a general meeting.
5. The dispatch of renounceable letters of allotment (or renounceable certificates), dispatch of share certificates, submission of Companies Forms No. G88(2)(Revised 1988), the written agreement on Companies Form No. G88(3), to the Registrar of Companies, etc., then follow a similar procedure to that applicable in the case of capitalisation issues by public companies described in Chapter 3.

CHAPTER 3

Public issues

A public issue arises where a company decides to 'go public' and have its shares either listed on The Stock Exchange or quoted on the Unlisted Securities Market. It also covers the situation where a company which may already be listed on The Stock Exchange or quoted on the Unlisted Securities Market (USM – see p.58) may wish to raise additional capital by means of, for example, a rights issue under which members of the company may subscribe for additional shares in the company at a fixed price.

Public issues, however, are not merely confined to shares; consequently we will use the expression 'securities' in this chapter to include all types of shares, loan stock, debenture stock, etc.

As a member of the EC, the United Kingdom has to comply with EC directives relating to the admission of securities to official listing which require the appointment of a 'competent authority' to be responsible for compliance with the provisions of the directives. In order to comply with this requirement the Council of The Stock Exchange was nominated as 'the competent authority' by FSA s.142(6). The statutory provisions for an official listing of securities are contained in FSA Part IV and s.142(6) empowers The Stock Exchange, as the competent authority, to make listing rules for any of the purposes of those provisions. These rules are contained in The Stock Exchange publication *Admission of Securities to Listing* (colloquially known as the 'Yellow Book'), which is a loose-leaf book amended by official amendments published by The Stock Exchange from time to time. Before granting a listing for the issue of securities, particulars containing prescribed information must be approved by the Council of The Stock Exchange and be published.

It should be noted that FSA Part IV, i.e. the Yellow Book listing rules, applies only to securities already admitted or to be admitted to The Stock Exchange Official List and that these rules do not apply to unlisted securities to be quoted on the Unlisted Securities Market, which has its own booklet of regulations. In the case of the quotation of securities for unlisted companies the statutory prospectus requirements are contained in Schedule 3 of the 1985 Companies Act; but these will later be contained in FSA Part V when that Part is brought into force.

The function of The Stock Exchange

The Stock Exchange (full name The International Stock Exchange of the United Kingdom and the Republic of Ireland) is the place where an entrepreneur running his own business who wishes to sell all or part of it to the public may arrange for shares in his business to be admitted to the Official List in order that they may be bought and sold by investors generally. The entrepreneur will usually offer only part of the capital of his company for sale initially and retain a substantial shareholding himself. He will have to convince the sponsors to the issue of the soundness and favourable prospects for his company. When his shares have been admitted to the Official List the entrepreneur's company, in order to protect its prospective investors, must comply with the Continuing Obligations for Companies contained in the Yellow Book, Section 5, Chapter 2, other requirements of The Stock Exchange and relevant legislation, chiefly the Companies Act and the Financial Services Act. Generally, securities sold in this way are known as 'new issues' and are the means by which companies, including other public bodies such as governments and local authorities, raise capital by the issue of securities.

Types of public issues

Securities may be brought to the market on The Stock Exchange by various methods as follows:

Offers for subscription

Listing particulars are issued by the company under which the public is invited to subscribe for the securities which are allocated to successful applicants.

Offers for sale

In this case the securities to be offered to the public are acquired first by an issuing house (or by a firm of stockbrokers). These securities could be new securities allotted to the issuing house on an increase of capital or existing securities owned by the vendors of the business which are transferred to the issuing house or a combination of these two. The securities are then offered for sale to the public by the issuing house, which issues the listing particulars and invites applications. People wishing to subscribe for the shares complete an application form to be sent to the issuing house together with the money payable for the shares. Shares may be offered at a fixed price per share (the more usual method) or on a minimum tender price basis. Allotments may be scaled down if the issue is oversubscribed.

Placings

In this case securities are also subscribed or purchased by a firm of stockbrokers or issuing house but they are then 'placed', usually with various clients of the stockbrokers or issuing house, with a certain proportion being sold through the market. Consequently, the public is unable to apply directly in the case of a placing and The Stock Exchange might not permit a placing to be made if it considered that there would be a significant public demand for the securities. There are other restrictions imposed by The Stock Exchange on placings, e.g. a monetary limit (in 1989 £15 million) on placings of equities of companies applying for listing for the first time. This relaxation is allowed since it is difficult for companies to cover the expenses of full offers for sale for amounts below this.

Vendor consideration issues

Where a business or other assets are acquired by a company the consideration may comprise in whole or in part the issue of securities to the vendor, who in fact wants cash rather than securities in the purchasing company. The securities issued by the purchaser to the vendor are placed by the issuing house concerned with its clients, who pay for the shares in cash. The total cash received in this way is then paid to the vendor. Occasionally, arrangements may be made to claw back some of the securities which are then offered to existing shareholders to purchase at the same price as received by the vendor. The offer of shares in these circumstances should not be confused with a rights issue since the shareholder cannot sell the securities offered to him on The Stock Exchange for a premium as the offer is personal to the entitled holder.

Introductions

In this case the securities will already have been issued and already held by investors but the securities are to be listed on The Stock Exchange for the first time. There is thus no further issue of securities.

Rights issues

A rights issue is an invitation to existing holders of a company's securities to apply for additional securities in exchange for cash, the number of additional securities which they may apply for being allocated pro rata to their existing holdings e.g. in the case of shares, the rights issue may be in the form of one new share at a price, say, of 120p, for every four shares already held. The object of a rights issue is to enable the company to raise additional capital; existing shareholders then have the right either to increase their holdings by taking up the securities provisionally allotted to them or to renounce them and sell their rights on The Stock Exchange. Other investors purchasing the rights will then be responsible for paying for the new shares. Since companies wish to ensure that rights issues are fully subscribed, the rights issue price will normally be at some discount to the current market price of the shares. Consequently, when trading in the nil paid shares begins on The Stock Exchange they will attract a premium which existing shareholders will receive in exchange for the sale of their rights.

Open offers

In this case a company may offer additional securities for subscription by its holders but usually not in proportion to their existing holdings, i.e. shareholders may apply for as many additional shares as they wish to subscribe for. However, there will usually be a total limit on the number of new shares the company wishes to issue so that it may be necessary to scale down the allotments to the holders.

Capitalisation issues

In the case of capitalisation issues no new capital is raised by the company and the shareholder receives additional shares in proportion to his existing holding without payment, e.g. two new shares for every one already held – a 'two for one' capitalisation issue. A capitalisation issue usually takes place when the company wishes to bring its issued capital more into line with the scale of the company's activities and is effected by a capitalisation of the company's existing reserves or a balance standing to the credit of the company's profit and loss account. The new shares will be sent to members of the company, usually in the form of renounceable certificates. This enables existing shareholders who wish to keep the capitalisation issue shares to take no further action but merely to keep the certificate in a safe place; or, if they wish to sell the new shares on The Stock Exchange they can sign the form of renunciation on the back of the certificate and send it to their stockbrokers to effect the sale.

Using the example given above, since the price of the existing shares on The Stock Exchange will be adjusted to take account of the fact that whereas where there was previously only one share there are now three shares, it is incorrect to describe such issues as being a 'bonus', e.g. if the price before the issue was 300p, the price of the existing and the new shares will be around 100p. Nevertheless you will often come across the phrase 'bonus issue'; it is even used in the Companies Act 1985. Admittedly, however, the shares are issued free of charge.

Exchanges and conversions

This is merely the replacement of existing securities by new securities to be listed.

Options and warrants

New securities may be issued and listed following the exercise by option holders or warrant holders of rights to subscribe for new securities in cash.

Other issues

Apart from all the above methods of issuing securities there are other circumstances in which securities may be listed, for example, shares issued under an employees' share scheme. (Note: Where it is proposed to issue securities having an equity element, the pre-emption rights of existing holders must be considered and The Stock Exchange requirements also taken into account in the case of listed companies.)

The issue price

In the case of an offer for subscription or offer for sale the issue price is that at which the securities (usually ordinary shares) are to be offered to prospective investors and would usually be fixed by the company, the vendor or the sponsor, with advice from an issuing house. All applicants receiving shares under the offer will pay the same price; where the offer is for a very popular or attractive issue it may be oversubscribed, in which case allotments may have to be scaled down, that is to say, applicants may be allotted fewer shares than they have applied and paid for. Indeed, some small applications, if there is resort to a ballot, may be rejected altogether. A company would then have to return to the applicants application money in excess of that required to pay for the shares allotted.

Instead of making issues at a fixed price, which often leads to heavy oversubscription in the case of popular issues, applicants may be required to make an offer by tender with a minimum price specified. A tender is also suitable if the business of the company is unusual and it is difficult to assess an appropriate price for the shares.

In the case of a tender offer the issuing house invites applications for shares at a minimum tender price and the applicant for the securities states on his application form the amount which he is prepared to pay, either at the minimum price or above the minimum price. When all applications have been received, the vendors and its sponsors will agree a 'striking price' which will ensure a full subscription for all the shares to be issued. In this case it would be necessary to return the application money of those whose tenders were below the striking price. The striking price will usually be set at a level such that when dealings begin on The Stock Exchange the shares will change hands at a modest premium (i.e. the excess of the market price over the striking price).

Payment by instalments

Where the amount to be paid for the securities (usually shares) is fairly substantial the issue may be made on the basis that part of the issue price is paid on application with the balance becoming payable at a later date. This occasionally happens in the case of some privatisation issues, e.g. 100p payable on application for shares issued at a fixed price of 185p, with the balance of 85p to be paid as a second and final instalment at a later time. During the time when the shares have only 100p paid on them they are, of course, traded as partly paid shares.

In the case of a rights issue, however, the securities are normally issued nil paid and a period of at least 21 days is allowed for the holders of the securities to take up their rights by paying the amount due.

However, even after the payment date, the rights issue securities will still be traded on The Stock Exchange on a fully paid basis prior to their becoming registered in the names of the final holders. Thus, in the case of shares, for a total of 6 weeks following the original date of issue the shares may be traded on The Stock Exchange either nil paid or fully paid. Purchasers of the shares, either nil paid or fully paid, have to pay stamp duty reserve tax of 50p per £100 of the consideration money. Under the 1990 Budget proposals, however, this tax will be abolished when TAURUS is implemented, probably towards the end of 1991. At the end of the 6 weeks' period the shares will be registered in the names of the original holders if they have paid for their shares and have not sold them or into the names of the persons in whose names the shares have been renounced.

Payment by instalments may also very occasionally be used in the case of tender offers, especially government securities.

Underwriting

In order to ensure that an issue of securities is fully taken up at the agreed price it is usual for the vendor to arrange for the issue to be underwritten, usually by a merchant bank, which in exchange for a commission agrees to purchase (either at the issue price or at the minimum tender price in the case of a tender offer) any securities which are not taken up or to arrange for other institutions (called sub-underwriters) to do so. If a part of the issue is underwritten 'firm' the underwriters obtain an allocation of securities even if the issue is fully subscribed.

If the issue price is fixed very low, of course, then full subscription is almost inevitable and underwriting becomes unnecessary. This is known as a 'deep discounted' issue but such issues are in practice rare since the vendors of the securities usually wish to obtain the best price they can, having regard to market conditions generally.

Advisers to an issue

Public issues can become quite difficult operations when market conditions are volatile and it is essential that in this highly technical area the company should seek the cooperation of its advisers. The advisers whom the company should consult are as follows.

An issuing house

Issuing houses, merchant banks and other institutions who are members of the British Merchant Banking and Securities Houses Association are in the business of sponsoring capital issues and arranging for the sale of securities to the public. They advise on corporate finance matters, suggesting the form the issue should take, the timing of the issue, whether any capital reorganisation should precede it and the price that should be asked. The issuing houses have their reputation to keep up since there is keen competition in sponsoring new issues and they will, therefore, make very careful enquiries before agreeing to act. Their responsibilities in this connection are laid down in the Yellow Book, Section 1, Chapter 1, para. 5. Most companies usually retain the services of issuing houses on a longer-term basis, not merely when making a new issue, since various matters come up from time to time on which corporate financial advice is required, e.g. take-overs and mergers.

In order to resolve any difficulties companies or their advisers may experience in meeting Stock Exchange requirements either in connection with a new issue or in meeting continuing obligations of listed or USM companies, companies have direct access to the Exchange's primary markets division under arrangements set out in a Stock Exchange announcement dated July 1988 which is set out in full in the Institute's manual.

Stockbrokers

It is necessary for a company to appoint a firm of stockbrokers since any application to have securities listed on The Stock Exchange must be submitted to the Exchange through the broker. The stockbroker lodges the necessary documents, on behalf of the company, with the Exchange; he also is the channel for communication between the company or its advisers and The Stock Exchange. The requirements for an official listing on The Stock Exchange are set out in the Yellow Book, principally Sections 1, 2 and 3. Companies which have securities listed on The Stock Exchange are also required to comply with the Continuing Obligations for Companies set out in the Yellow Book, Section 5, Chapter 2.

A company wishing to make a new issue may do so at any time that the company and its stockbrokers consider most advantageous. Although the procedure under the Control of Borrowing Order under which the stockbroker had to arrange with the Government Broker for a place for the issue in the 'new issues queue' was abolished by the 1989 Budget, there now exists a voluntary arrangement for consultation between the stockbroker, the merchant banker handling the issue, The Stock Exchange and the Bank of England for issues in excess of £20 million to avoid clashes between competing issues.

Instead of using an issuing house, a company may arrange for its stockbrokers to act as sponsor and if a stockbroker acts instead of an issuing house he will also be subject to the responsibilities of sponsors as set out in the Yellow Book, Section 1, Chapter 1, para. 5.

Accountants

An accountants' report must be included in the listing particulars issued when securities are offered for subscription, and this report must comply with Section 4 of the Yellow Book. These 'reporting accountants' may be the company's usual auditors or some other and possibly larger firm suggested by the sponsor and reporting directly to it and to the company.

Solicitors

Unless the company's own solicitors are specialists in new issue work it will also be usual to appoint a specialist firm of solicitors to work with the company's own solicitors to assist in the preparation and checking of the issue documents to ensure strict compliance with all the requirements.

The Stock Exchange Unlisted Securities Market

The object of the Unlisted Securities Market (USM) is to provide a regulated market in securities which are not to be admitted to the Official List on The Stock Exchange. The USM was formed because it was considered that there were a number of smaller companies which would not find it attractive to meet the full conditions for official listing but which should, nevertheless, have the opportunity to raise finance through The Stock Exchange at an economic cost and subject to conditions with which they would have to comply, which were fewer than those required for a full listing but sufficient to ensure the adequate protection of investors and the maintenance of a fair and orderly market.

Two categories of company in particular may find a USM quotation attractive:

1. A company whose trading history is too short to meet the requirements for a full listing; even a company with no trading record at all may be still be admissible if the funds required to finance a project or product have been fully researched and costed.
2. Companies which are reluctant to have at least 25 per cent of their capital in public hands, which is a requirement for admission to the Official List. It should be noted that many companies entering the USM intend to obtain a full listing on The Stock Exchange when they have grown and are able to meet the requirements.

The regulations for quotation on the USM are contained in a separate booklet obtainable from the Quotations Department of The Stock Exchange.

Means of entering the USM

The usual methods by which securities can become traded on the USM are as follows:

1. A placing. This is the usual arrangement. Monetary limits are specified by The Stock Exchange from time to time, as quoted in the USM booklet.
2. Introduction. An established company whose securities are already spread in the hands of the public, and where no further securities are being issued, can be launched on The Stock Exchange by means of an introduction.
3. Offer for sale. This is a more expensive method in view of the advertising required, the handling of the receipt of applications from the public with payment for the shares, issue of letters of allotment, etc., and is the method to be adopted when neither an introduction

nor a placing is appropriate. The Stock Exchange would normally insist on an offer for sale if the amount to be raised exceeded £5 million.

Differences between the conditions for entry to the USM from the conditions for official listing

1. Only 10 per cent of the issued capital need be in public hands when dealing begins, whereas in the case of a listing at least 25 per cent must be in public hands (except in the case of marketings of a value of £2 million or less).
2. There are no restrictions as to the minimum size of company which may be launched on the USM but obviously it would be very expensive and impracticable for very small companies to enter the USM.
3. In the case of an application for quotation on the USM only a short newspaper advertisement is required, stating where copies of the prospectus may be obtained, the issue price, the amount of the company's authorised and issued capital and a statement to the effect that the detailed particulars are available in the Extel USM service. The reduced amount of advertising is a saving in cost to the company concerned because in the case of a full listing the full particulars must be published in at least two newspapers.
4. An accountants' report is not required in the case of an introduction.
5. Apart from the reduction in costs achieved by the above, the fees charged by The Stock Exchange for a USM quotation are also lower.
6. An offering on the USM is subject to the prospectus requirements of the Act which do not apply in the case of a listing which must comply with more onerous Stock Exchange requirements.
7. The Continuing Obligations for Companies in the Yellow Book, Section 5, do not apply to companies entering the USM. Instead they have to comply with broadly similar provisions covered by a general undertaking given by the company to The Stock Exchange.
8. The prospectus requirements are at present those set out in Schedule 3 pending the announcement of the commencement of the provisions in FSA Part V as amended by CA 1989 ss.198 and 199.

Effect of quotation on USM

Securities dealt in on the USM do not fall within the description 'listed on a recognised stock exchange', a Companies Act term, or 'listed in the official list of The Stock Exchange' or similar references in other legislation, the one exception being that securities dealt in on the USM are equated with listed securities for the purpose of Business Expansion Schemes under the ICTA, s.293, which means that they are excluded from such schemes.

The Stock Exchange Third Market

Below the USM The Stock Exchange used to have a market known as the Third Market for securities which did not qualify for listing or for quotation on the USM. No new companies are being admitted to the Third Market in 1990 at the end of which time it will be phased out. At the end of 1990 companies whose securities are quoted on the Third Market will either have to move up to a full listing or obtain a quotation on the USM. To assist them The Stock Exchange has reduced the period for which trading information must be available to three years in the case of a listing and to two years in the case of quotation on the USM. The securities of Third Market companies which do not qualify for listing or quotation on the USM at the end of 1990 will thereafter be dealt in under Stock Exchange Rule 535.2. The changes have been brought about by EC directive requirements.

Dealings in securities of companies or corporate bodies not listed on The Stock Exchange or quoted on the USM

As an alternative to listing on The Stock Exchange or quotation on the USM, securities may be dealt in under specific bargains between members of The Stock Exchange with the prior agreement of the Council of The Stock Exchange under Stock Exchange Rule 535. Further details of these specific bargains are given in Chapter 13.

Dealings in existing securities

We have seen that one of the objects in obtaining a listing for securities on The Stock Exchange or for the quotation of securities on the Unlisted Securities Market is that such securities may be freely traded by buying and selling. Dealings on The Stock Exchange are subject to the rules, regulations and usages of The Stock Exchange and the conduct of business rules of the Securities and Investments Board or one of its self-regulating organisations under the FSA. On becoming a holder of the securities concerned the investor becomes subject to the Articles of Association of the company in which he has invested. Further details on the methods of trading on The Stock Exchange are given in Chapter 13.

Securities that may be dealt in on The Stock Exchange

The following securities may be dealt in on The Stock Exchange:

1. Listed securities. These are securities of companies which have been admitted to listing on The Stock Exchange and are included in *The Stock Exchange Daily Official List* published by The Stock Exchange, which includes all the securities in respect of which listing has been granted and gives details of the last bargains transacted by members of The Stock Exchange in those securities.
2. Unlisted securities. These are securities of companies which have been accepted by The Stock Exchange for trading in the Unlisted Securities Market whose names are given at the back of the Official List in the USM appendix.
3. Securities of companies being traded in 1990 on the Third Market whose names are also given at the back of the Official List in the Third Market appendix.
4. Securities of certain other companies or corporate bodies incorporated in the United Kingdom or the Republic of Ireland where specific bargains may be made, with the permission of The Stock Exchange Council, under Stock Exchange Rule 535.2.
5. Certain other securities which have a quotation or listing on an overseas stock exchange or which may be traded by members of such an exchange.

Programme for a public issue of listed securities

The following is a brief resume of the procedure which would be followed when securities are to be listed on The Stock Exchange and brought to the market by an offer for sale. The full detailed programme for an offer for sale for shares, however, is contained in the Institute's manual.

The first step will be to hold a preliminary conference with the sponsor to consider the terms of the issue and the programme for its implementation, since no two issues are the same. The conference would be attended by the company's secretary and its accountant or finance director and another director, e.g. the chairman or managing director, with the company's advisers, i.e. its solicitors, auditors and stockbrokers. The sponsor of the issue will most probably be an issuing house, although this role could be taken on by a leading firm of stockbrokers. The listing particulars are extremely detailed and considerable care has to be exercised at this stage to ensure that the issue will be marketable, i.e. attractive to investors, and also that it will not contain any features which would make it unattractive to the institutional investor. The preliminary conference will have to decide on the following matters:

1.   The amount and nature of the capital to be issued.
2.   The approximate price at which the securities are to be offered. It should be noted, however, that the final price will not be decided until the last possible moment prior to the publication of the issue so that the price is reasonable in the light of the market conditions then obtaining.
3.   The type of issue, e.g. a public offer for sale, a placing or an introduction.
4.   What fees and commissions are to be paid.
5.   The timing of the issue. In the case of an issue of over £20 million, consultation should take place between the merchant bankers, The Stock Exchange and the Bank of England on a voluntary basis as regards the date of the issue.
6.   Any other details and general arrangements which need to be considered at this preliminary stage.

The representatives of the company must have the authority to proceed with the issue and have obtained any necessary consent from the existing shareholders.

Preparation of the listing particulars

The information given in the listing particulars is most important since it is on this information that the quality of the issue will be judged. The Stock Exchange's requirements as to the contents of the listing particulars are contained in the Yellow Book, Section 3. Briefly, these comprise the following:

1.   The names of the issuer, the persons responsible for the listing particulars, the auditors and other advisers.
2.   A description of the securities for which application for listing is being made.
3.   General information about the issuer and its capital, including the amount of working capital available.
4.   The activities of the issuer or group.
5.   Financial information concerning the issuer or group giving details of profits and losses for the last three years.
6.   Information about the management, e.g. names and addresses of directors and their other relevant business interests.
7.   The recent developments and prospects of the issuer or group.
8.   If the issue is of debt securities, additional information has to be given as stated in the Yellow Book, Section 3, Chapter 2, Part 8.

It will be quite normal for several drafts of the listing particulars to be prepared before all parties are satisfied that the information is complete and accurate, so that trading in the securities may take place with adequate information about the company concerned.

The need for secrecy at this stage cannot be overemphasised and to achieve this certain key details, such as the company's dividend and profit forecasts and the likely issue price, will be kept out of the printed drafts until the last moment.

Each copy of the listing particulars will contain the application form to be used under the offer for sale, although an application form may be issued without being accompanied by a copy of the listing particulars provided that the application form indicates where the listing particulars may be obtained or inspected.

The listing particulars must be published in at least two national daily newspapers, and in order to give wider publicity the company may also advertise abridged particulars of the issue in other newspapers and also in the financial press.

Function of the brokers to the issue

The main duties of the broker to the issue are as follows:

1. The Stock Exchange's approval of the listing particulars and other documents must be obtained through the company's broker, who will submit these to the Quotations Department of The Stock Exchange on the company's behalf both in draft form and later in the final form.
2. The broker must apply to The Stock Exchange for listing of the securities concerned.
3. If the issue is for more than £20 million the broker should consult informally with the merchant bankers, The Stock Exchange and the Bank of England to agree a convenient date for the issue to take place.
4. The broker will place a proportion of the sub-underwriting of the issue with his clients.
5. The broker will also advise the company on its obligations under The Stock Exchange's Continuing Obligations (Yellow Book, Section 5).

After an issue has been made, the company's broker continues to act as its link with The Stock Exhange.

Publicity

The opportunity of coming to the market should be taken by the company to improve its image in the eyes of the public. There are specialist firms available to provide valuable advice and services in the areas of public relations and financial advertising. Such publicity may help the company's share price and will also be of assistance to the company if it should later want to come to the market for additional capital.

The receiving bank

The leading clearing banks have specialist departments in the City of London in new issue work and it is usual for the completed applications plus cheques to be sent to the company's clearing bank new issue department. In the case of a large issue several receiving points may be provided. After totalling the applications and cheques the receiving bank reports the result of the issue to the company, following which the basis of allocation of the shares will be decided; the receiving bank will then send out letters of allotment to applicants who have been allotted shares, with letters of regret and returned cheques to the unsuccessful applicants. In the case of a small issue the issuing house or the company's registrars may perform the function of receiving bank.

The subscription lists

It is traditional for subscription lists to open at 10.00 a.m. on the date fixed for the receipt of applications; the subscription lists in the case of a successful issue will close very shortly afterwards, e.g. at 10.01 a.m., as the issue will have been oversubscribed. No applications can be considered after the lists have closed but all those received prior to the time of the closing of the subscription lists will be considered for an allocation.

Allotment and commencement of dealings

The receiving bank will prepare an analysis of all applications which are valid and send this as soon as possible after the lists have closed to the company. In the case of oversubscription an allotment committee must decide the basis on which the available shares are to be allotted to the public applicants after taking out the shares needed for preferential applicants, employees and existing shareholders in the company. In the event of heavy oversubscription necessitating a ballot some applicants will not receive shares. The receiving bank will also try to eliminate multiple applications (where one applicant has submitted a number of separate applications in the hope that some of these will be selected in the ballot for shares). In the case of privatisation issues multiple applications are usually illegal.

As soon as the basis of allotment has been decided, The Stock Exchange and the press should be informed of the date on which allotment letters, letters of regret and returned cheques will be posted to the applicants. This information is necessary in order for there to be a fair market in the shares when dealings commence. In the case of a very heavy oversubscription it may not be possible for all the allotment letters to be sent to successful applicants by the date on which it is agreed that dealings should commence on The Stock Exchange and, in this event, an applicant who considered that his application had been successful on the basis of the general information published and who sold his allocation on the first dealing day without having received his allotment letter, would do so at his own risk.

Rights issues

In the case of a rights issue the securities of a company are offered only to the existing holders of securities in the company, the amount of their entitlement to the rights being proportionate to their existing holdings. Most rights issues consist of the offer of new ordinary shares to the ordinary shareholders, but sometimes a rights issue takes the form of an offer of convertible or fixed interest loan stock and sometimes of warrants to the ordinary shareholders.

No new listing particulars need be published where the shares of the company are already listed and the rights issue will not increase the shares in issue by 10 per cent or more. Even in this case, however, the contents of the listing particulars are less extensive than they would be in the case of a completely new listing (Yellow Book, Section 3, Chapter 1, para. 3.1(b)). There are no advertising requirements in the case of a rights issue (Yellow Book, Section 2, Chapter 3, para. 3.2).

It is a requirement of The Stock Exchange that where a shareholder entitled to a rights issue (the provisional allottee) does not sell his rights and does not subscribe for his shares in the issue, his rights are aggregated with those of others who have not subscribed for the shares and these are sold on The Stock Exchange in nil paid form. The proceeds less expenses are then distributed to the provisional allottees by the company, although there is usually a provision that any small amounts, e.g. not exceeding £2, may be retained for the benefit of the company.

The announcement of a rights issue quite often coincides with the release of the company's preliminary results or half-year results. Dealings in rights issue shares are in nil paid form until the acceptance and payment date, after which they are dealt in fully paid form up to the date of renunciation.

A detailed programme for a rights issue is contained in the Institute's manual.

Capitalisation issues

In the case of a capitalisation issue new shares are issued to existing shareholders in fully paid form pro rata to their existing holdings. A capitalisation issue may be on the basis of the issue of one additional share for every four currently held, described as a 'one for four' issue. In this case, each shareholder would receive one new share for every four he already held. A capitalisation issue is sometimes called a 'bonus' or 'scrip' issue. The term bonus issue, however, is not a very good one, even though it is used in the Act, since the shareholder does not receive a bonus because following the capitalisation issue the value of each share will be revalued in line with the market price for the shares prevailing before the issue. For example, if four shares are worth £10, i.e. each share is valued on the market at 250p, following the issue the five shares will still be worth only £10 (subject, of course, to market conditions), so that the value of each share will be adjusted to 200p. Although the new shares issued in a capitalisation issue are identical to those already held, they might not rank for the company's current or next dividend. No new listing particulars need be published in the case of a capitalisation issue but The Stock Exchange requires that a circular should be sent by the company to its shareholders giving information, for example, as to the reasons for the issue and the dividend entitlement of the new shares.

As in the case of a rights issue the capitalisation issue shares may be renounced and sold by the shareholders (i.e. the provisional allottees), although if they do so they reduce their stake in the company. In the absence of any such action, however, the new shares will be formally registered in the names of the shareholders after the final date for renunciation. Instead of issuing letters of allotment to be replaced at a later date by share certificates, as in the case of a rights issue, the normal practice in the case of a capitalisation issue is to send out the entitlement to shareholders in the form of renounceable share certificates. These may then be renounced by the shareholders or, if they take no action, they will become definitive documents of title after the end of the renunciation period.

The term 'capitalisation' derives from the conversion into capital of amounts in the company's share premium account or a balance standing on the profit and loss account. These accounts are debited by the nominal value of the shares issued by way of the capitalisation issue. A capitalisation issue has the object of reducing the price of a company's share when it has become 'heavy'; it also brings the issued share capital of the company more into line with its net assets. Dealings in the new shares on The Stock Exchange normally begin on the first business day following the posting of the renounceable share certificates to shareholders, as in the case of a rights issue. Such posting should preferably be timed so that the documents are received on the first dealing day of a new Stock Exchange account.

A detailed programme for a capitalisation issue is contained in the Institute's manual.

CHAPTER 4

Register of Members

Forms of register

A public company with a large number of shareholders will keep its Register of Members on a computer. Where it does so the duties imposed by the Act on the company to allow inspection of, or the furnishing of a copy of, the Register or a relevant part are treated as a duty to allow such inspection, etc., in legible form (s.723 and SI 1985/724, The Companies (Registers and Other Records) Regulations 1985). In the case of smaller public companies, however, and private companies which do not have a large number of shareholders, the Register may be maintained on an accounting machine, by manual methods in a bound book incorporating other statutory registers as well or on loose-leaf printed sheets in a binder. The loose-leaf system will usually be found to be more convenient.

The statutory information to be kept in the Register of Members is contained in s.352 and is as follows:

1. The names and addresses of the members.
2. The date on which each person was registered as a member.
3. The date on which any person ceased to be a member

The first entry in an account and the last entry in a closed account is sufficient for the purposes of (2) and (3) above.

It is not usual to record the amount paid or agreed to be paid on the shares when all the shares in issue are fully paid. If the company's capital is in the form of stock it is usual to show the number of stock units held by each member, e.g. 400 stock units of 25p each, rather than £100 of stock. The accounts in the Register would, however, be headed 'Stock units of 25p'.

It is good company secretarial practice for the Register of Members not to include, in a form which may be identified, information which is not required to be included under the provisions of s.352, such as references to dividend mandates (which would include the name of the member's bank and account number) or powers of attorney. This non-statutory information is consequently suppressed on any copy of the Register made available for public inspection and where copies of the Register are supplied to any member or other person as required by s.356. The non-statutory information may be kept by the company separately. A Register of Members maintained without inclusion of non-statutory information is exempt from the provisions of the Data Protection Act 1984 since it is a requirement of the Companies Act to make the information available for public inspection.

The exemption would also extend to other registers which have to be made public under the Companies Act, e.g. the Register of Directors' Interests. Registration under the Data Protection Act will be required if the company keeps a list of the non-statutory information and other matters related to the field of share registration, e.g. the register of participants in an employees' share scheme, on its computer. It is also the practice of some companies, particularly private companies, to include the non-statutory information in the Register of Members rather than go to the expense of maintaining and referring to a separate record, bearing in mind that requests for inspection of the Register are rare in practice. It should be noted that registration under the Data Protection Act is not required if the Register of Members is not maintained on a computer, e.g. if a manual system is used, and this would also include a mechanised accounting machine system.

The entry in a Register of Members relating to a former member may be removed from the Register 20 years after the date on which he ceased to be a member (s.352(6)).

Location and inspection of Register of Members

The Register of Members must be kept at one of three places:

1. The registered office of the company.
2. Some other office of the company at which the work of making up the Register is done.
3. At the office of a person employed to make up the Register (e.g. a service registrar).

If the Register is not at all times kept at the registered office it is necessary to inform the Registrar of Companies of the place of its location and of any change in that place on Companies Form No. G353 'Notice of place where register of members is kept or of any change in that place'.

There are additional requirements if, as is quite common these days, the Register is kept on a computer in 'non-legible' form. In this case the above requirements are replaced by an obligation to notify the Registrar of Companies of a place at which it is possible to inspect a legible copy of the Register, and this notification must be sent on Companies Form No. G353a 'Notice of place for inspection of a register of members which is kept in a non-legible form, or of any change in that place'. Where a Register is changed from a legible to a non-legible form it is not necessary to send a notification if there has been no change in the place at which the Register may be inspected in legible form immediately prior to the change or if the place for inspection in legible form is at the registered office of the company.

The Register of Members must be kept in the country of registration, i.e. England and Wales or Scotland (s.353(1)). It is, however, legal for a company in England to appoint registrars in Scotland or vice versa, provided that the Register maintained at the registrar's office is treated as being a copy of the legal Register located in the country of registration.

A separate index of a Register of Members containing more than 50 accounts must be kept unless the Register itself is self-indexing (s.354).

Subject to the limited restriction referred to in s.356, and the period of 30 days in any year in which the Register may be closed under s.358, e.g. in connection with the preparation of a dividend payment, the Register must be open for inspection during business hours by any member of the company free of charge or by any other person on payment of the prescribed fee. Although the right of inspection does not include power to take copies of the Register it will probably be convenient for companies to allow people inspecting the Register to take notes since, if this is refused, the company may receive a request to supply a copy of all or part of the Register (s.356). As has been noted elsewhere in this handbook, however, most companies do not now take advantage of the power to close the Register in connection with dividend payments but follow the practice of establishing a 'record date' in order to determine the list of members entitled to receive a dividend.

Section 356 also imposes an obligation on companies to send within 10 days of the receipt of a request from any member or other person a copy of the Register or of any part thereof on payment of the prescribed fee. A request to send a copy of part of the Register often leads to difficulties of interpretation as in the following cases:

1. A list of members having the 100 largest holdings.
2. A list of members having registered addresses within a certain area.
3. A list of members whose surname begins with a certain letter.
4. A list of members holding, for example, over 10,000 shares each.

It does seem clear that a request for part of the Register containing the list of members whose surname begins with a particular letter (or letters) would fall within the statutory requirements of sending a copy of part of the Register, but it is open to doubt whether a request for a copy of a list of members involving the company in an analysis of its Register of Members would fall within the statutory requirements and the company may think it desirable to obtain legal advice. It would probably be more convenient to counter such a request by an offer to send a copy of the whole Register so that the person making the enquiry could carry out his own analysis. However, it is to be hoped that these uncertainties may be cleared up by regulations which the Secretary of State is empowered to make under CA 1989 s.143 as a result of consultations with interested parties to be made before the end of 1990. The regulations are also expected to cover the fees which companies may charge for inspection and copies of registers.

Closing the Register of Members

Section 358 provides that a company may close its Register of Members for a period not exceeding 30 days in any calendar year, although it is now fairly unusual for this power to be exercised as most companies prefer to rely on a 'record date' for determining dividend and other entitlements (e.g. in the case of a rights issue). During the period of closure the company need not accept transfers for registration and the rights provided by the Act to inspect the Register or to obtain copies of it are also suspended. The obligation continues, however, to certificate stock transfer forms by which the company represents that documents have been produced to it indicating a *prima facie* title to the shares in the transferor named in the transfer form (s.184). Such documents as changes of address and probates should continue to be registered whilst the register is closed.

The dates of closure of the Register, having been authorised by a directors' resolution, must be advertised in a newspaper circulating in the district in which the company's registered office is situated and, if the company is listed, The Stock Exchange should be separately advised of the dates of closure. The Stock Exchange should also be advised if the company adopts the simpler alternative of having a record date. This is usually done at the time when a dividend is announced.

Rectification of the Register of Members

Amendments to the Register of Members should, strictly speaking, only be made under the sanction of a Court Order for rectification of a Register (s.359). However, minor clerical slips in the Register may be altered shortly after the entries have been made on the authority of the company secretary or of the company's registrar to correct minor errors made by those lodging the documents for registration and subject to confirmation that there has been no sub-sale (i.e. that no change of beneficial ownership has taken place). In the case of a request to register a completely different name consideration should be given to whether the sanction of the Court is required. Extreme care is required in these cases and such requests should never be accepted if lodged by an individual. In all such cases full enquiry should be made before accepting the request for rectification as the procedure is open to abuse. In any event no request for rectification should be accepted if made more than three months from the date of registration or if a dividend has been paid on the shares. Requests for such rectification should be made to the company on the TALISMAN form 'Request for rectification/no sub-sale declaration'. Some companies charge a fee for making such corrections.

Branch registers

A company may establish an 'overseas branch register' of members resident in territories in which it transacts business (s.362). Part I of Schedule 14 of the Act lists those countries in which overseas branch registers may be kept. Part II of Schedule 14 gives the general provisions to be followed with respect to overseas branch registers.

The Registrar of Companies must be informed when any overseas branch register is established or discontinued on Companies Form No. G362 'Notice of place where an overseas branch register is kept, of any change in that place, or of discontinuance of any such register'. As in the case of the principal register, the overseas branch register may also be kept in non-legible form in which case the Registrar must be informed of the place of inspection in legible form on Companies Form No. G362a 'Notice of place of inspection of an overseas branch register which is kept in non-legible form or of any change in that place'.

The maintenance of an overseas branch register makes it more convenient to record dealings in the company's shares in the territory concerned, registered in the names of members resident in that country. Such transfers are not, of course, liable to UK *ad valorem* stamp duty (which in any event will be abolished under the 1990 Budget proposals when TAURUS is implemented) but may be subject to any local requirements. A branch register contains only the names and addresses of shareholders with a registered address in the territory in question and the company is not concerned with making enquiries as to the residential status of members. A duplicate of the branch register must be kept at the same place as the principal register and be open to inspection in a similar manner to the principal register.

If a member who is on the principal register wishes to have his shares registered in the overseas branch register he should complete a form of request in duplicate and send it to the company with his share certificate, stating the name of the overseas branch register in which he wishes his holding to be registered. The entry relating to the member will then be deleted in the principal register and his share certificate cancelled. The company will prepare a schedule of such requests and send them to the person responsible in the territory concerned for maintaining the overseas branch register. The holding will then be recorded in the overseas branch register and a new certificate prepared which will be clearly marked to indicate that the shares are registered in the overseas branch register. Certificates of companies which have a common seal will be sealed with the company's official seal for use abroad in the relevant territory (s.39 as amended by CA 1989 Schedule 17, para. 2). The reverse procedures will be followed in the case of a member whose shares registered in the overseas branch register wishing to have his shares registered in the company's principal register.

Share certificates

The preparation of share certificates should be undertaken with due regard to the importance of accuracy and security, since the issue of a share certificate (or stock certificate of a company whose ordinary capital is in the form of stock units) under the common seal of the company (or a securities seal under s.40 as amended by CA 1989 Schedule 17, para. 3) is *prima facie* evidence of the title of the member to the shares or stock (s.186 as substituted by CA 1989 Schedule 17, para. 5); the company is estopped from denying the title of the person named in the certificate unless it has been sealed without the company's authority, which would render it void as a forgery and not binding on the company. Similar protection is given in the case of certificates not under seal where the company does not have one under the provisions of s.36A(3) inserted by CA 1989 s.130 if they are signed in accordance with the provisions of s.36A(4). The liability of the company in respect of the issue of certificates would usually be covered under the terms of the company's forged transfer insurance policy.

Most of the larger and/or listed companies have their share certificates specially printed since the certificates will be prepared as part of the normal computer routine for the maintenance of the Register of Members, although occasionally a mechanised or manual method may be used. Blank certificate forms are, however, obtainable from law stationers for small private companies who do not issue many share certificates.

Certificates should contain the following information:

1. The serial number of the certificate.
2. The company's number.
3. The name(s) of the registered holder(s).
4. The description of the shares or stock to which the certificate relates and the number of shares or amount of stock the certificates represents and, in the case of stock units, the number and denomination of the units.
5. The extent to which the shares are paid up which will, of course, normally be fully paid.
6. The date of the certificate.

In the case of companies listed on The Stock Exchange there are further requirements to be met as set out in the Yellow Book, Section 9, Chapter 4. These include a statement as to the authority under which the company is constituted (e.g. 'Incorporated under the Companies Act 1948' (or in the case of more recently incorporated companies, under the Companies Act 1985) or the country of incorporation in the case of an overseas company, and the company's registered number, if any. The certificates of listed companies should show the number of shares or amount of stock twice, once in figures and again in words, each word being contained in a box relating to millions, hundreds of thousands, tens of thousands, thousands, hundreds, tens and units.

The registered holder(s) must be given their full name(s) (and titles) on their certificates. Some companies include decorations and professional qualifications but this is not essential. In the case of a corporate holder, e.g. a company, the full name should be shown without abbreviations, except those which are recognised such as 'plc' rather than the full expression 'public limited company' (s.27). It is quite common nowadays for addresses of holders not to be shown on certificates; this makes it unnecessary to amend a certificate in the event of a change of address. If the address is shown, however, the full address as recorded in the Register of Members must be stated. In the case of joint holders only the address of the first-named holder need be given. If the absence of an address should pose any question of identity of a shareholder the matter can be resolved by referring to the certificate numbers recorded in the Register of Members and the serial numbers of the certificates held.

The share certificates should be sealed with the company's common seal if it has one, although many companies which have a seal have adopted a securities seal (s.40 as amended by CA 1989 Schedule 17, para. 3) to be used for sealing share certificates and other documents evidencing title to securities of the company. The securities seal is useful if the company's Register of Members is maintained by an outside firm of service registrars, which can be supplied with a copy of the securities seal for sealing certificates issued by them. This avoids the necessity of the registrars having to send the certificates to the company to be sealed with the common seal. It is also usual for Articles of Association to provide that the board may pass a resolution to the effect that signatures on certificates relating to securities need not be autographic, may be affixed to certificates by a mechanical means, may be printed on the certificates or that certificates need not be signed at all. It is the more usual practice today to provide that certificates need not be signed at all but this is permissible, of course, only in the case of certificates which have been sealed by a company's common seal or by a securities seal since s.36A inserted by CA 1989 s.130 provides that the execution of a document by a company which does not have a seal must be signed by a director and the secretary or by two directors.

Issue of certificates

Share certificates must be ready for delivery within two months after allotment or after the date on which the transfer is lodged with the company or its registrars for registration (s.185). However, in the case of companies listed on The Stock Exchange, the Continuing Obligations, para. 28 provides that certificates must be issued without charge within one month of the date of expiration of any right of renunciation or within 14 days of the lodgement of transfers. Some changes in the law governing the issue of certificates are to be expected following the introduction of TAURUS (see Chapter 5) under the wide powers given to the Secretary of State to make regulations under CA 1989 s.207.

A member may request the company to issue a number of separate certificates covering his total holding and this request may be acceded to if the company's Articles so permit. This is subject to payment of any fee that the directors may determine for the issue of several certificates other than the first, which has to be issued free of charge (e.g. Table A, Regulation 6). A worn out certificate may be replaced on payment of a small fee but no fee may be charged if the company is listed (Yellow Book, Section 9, Chapter 1, para. 2.2).

Lost certificates

There is a recognised company secretarial procedure to be followed if a member reports the loss of a certificate relating to securities of a company. This is as follows:

1. The member should be requested to make a further thorough and careful search for the certificate and then to inform the company whether or not the certificate has been found.

2. If it is confirmed that the certificate still cannot be found (or it has been clearly established that the certificate has been destroyed), the member must give an indemnity to the company covering the issue of a duplicate certificate. The indemnity must be given in the form approved by the Institute of Chartered Secretaries and Administrators, a copy of which is to be found in the Institute's manual. The indemnity has to carry the guarantee of a bank, insurance company or guarantee society. However, some companies may be prepared to dispense with the guarantee if the number and/or value of the securities comprised by the lost certificate is very small. At the same time companies must take into account the fact that a small shareholding may rise in value substantially over the years; consequently, the company is undertaking an open ended liability in issuing a duplicate certificate without the protection of a guarantee. Sometimes a certificate is lost in transit between the member's stockbroker (or other agent) and the member's home address or his bank (if he has given instructions to the broker to send certificates to his bank) and in these circumstances most companies would accept an indemnity from the stockbroker or agent. However, the indemnity should still be guaranteed by a bank, insurance company or guarantee society unless the agent is itself one of these bodies.

3. When the company or its registrars receive the indemnity, the duplicate certificate, which must be clearly marked as a duplicate copy, will be prepared and issued subject to the payment of any fee required. However, no fee may be charged by a company for the issue of a duplicate certificate if it is listed on The Stock Exchange (Yellow Book, Section 9, Chapter 1, para. 2.2).

4. The issue of the duplicate certificate should be noted in the Register of Members and on a stop list.

Bearer share warrants

Form of warrants

The issue of bearer share warrants by English companies is not often met with in practice, although it is very common on the Continent for shares to be issued in bearer form. A company may issue bearer share warrants in respect of any fully paid shares if authorised by its Articles (s.188). Where the company has a common seal, they are issued under seal and entitle the bearer of the certificate to the number of shares stated on the warrant. Consequently, they are negotiable instruments, which means that the title to the shares represented by the warrants may be passed to another holder by mere delivery of the warrant to that other person.

Strict security measures thus need to be observed in connection with warrants and precautions taken against possible forgery. Not unnaturally, The Stock Exchange lays down stringent requirements in connection with bearer share warrants ('bearer securities') which are contained in the Yellow Book, Section 9, Chapter 4, para. 2. One of these is that warrants must be printed by security printers from engraved plates on special paper with a distinctive water mark, thereby rendering forgery more difficult.

To enable dividends and other entitlements under bearer share warrants to be claimed, a supply of numbered coupons is attached to each warrant, together with a talon which may be exchanged for a further supply of coupons when all the numbered coupons or the original warrant have been used up.

There are special requirements concerning the payment of stamp duty on bearer share warrants laid down in the Finance Act 1963, ss.59–61, as amended. Consequently, companies proposing to issue share warrants to bearer would be well advised to consult the Inland Revenue on the stamp duty procedure. However, it should be noted that the stamp duty charges on bearer share warrants will be abolished under the 1990 Budget proposals when TAURUS is implemented, probably towards the end of 1991.

Registers

It is not possible to maintain a Register of Members who hold share warrants to bearer since the company will be unaware of the holders from time to time. This is because, as noted above, the warrants can be passed from hand to hand, thereby transferring title to the new holder of the warrant. However, it is usual for a company to maintain the following registers for its information:

1. A stock register recording the number of warrants printed and issued and the numbers of those surrendered for cancellation, e.g. by a holder wishing to exchange his bearer warrants for registered shares.
2. A coupon register in which the coupons lodged for the payment of dividends are recorded.

It is also desirable for companies to keep a file of applications for share warrants to be issued in exchange for registered shares and vice versa, kept in numerical order and suitably cross referenced to the stock register.

Issue of bearer warrants in exchange for registered shares

The following company secretarial procedure is suggested for the issue of bearer warrants in exchange for registered shares:

1. An application form supplied by the company should be completed and lodged with the company, together with the certificate for the registered shares and accompanied by any fee payable. The applicant will also have to pay the stamp duty (until it is abolished under the 1990 Budget proposals with the implementation of TAURUS, probably towards the end of 1991) when assessed.

2. The application should be acknowledged by sending a receipt to the member, which he will exchange in due course for the share warrants.

3. The application form should be given a serial number and carefully checked. A check should also be made to ensure that there is no restraint or other entry on a stop list relating to the registered shares.

4. The share warrant should be prepared and an appropriate entry made in the stock register, the certificate for the registered shares being cancelled.

5. The coupons on the warrants relating to any dividends which have already been declared and paid should be detached from the share warrants and cancelled.

6. The share warrants must be submitted to the Inland Revenue Stamp Office with evidence of the market value of the shares to which the warrants relate in order that the stamp duty payable (until it is abolished – see item 1 above) may be ascertained.

7. A board resolution should be passed authorising the sealing and issue of the share warrants.

8. The applicant's account in the Register of Members should be debited with the number of shares for which share warrants have been issued in exchange and, if the complete holding of registered shares of the applicant has been exchanged, his name should be struck out from the Register of Members (s.355(1)). The following particulars should also be in the Register of Members:
    (a) the fact of the issue of the warrants;
    (b) a statement of the shares included in the warrants;
    (c) the date of issue of the warrant.

9. For control purposes the number of shares for which warrants have been issued should be credited to a register of 'share warrants to bearer issued'. This will make it possible to reconcile the number of shares comprised in share warrants and the number of registered shares to the total number of shares of the company in issue.

10. The warrants should then be dispatched by registered post to the applicants in exchange for the receipt previously issued. In the case of a limited company, Continuing Obligations, para. 30 requires that the warrants be dispatched within 14 days of the registered certificates being deposited with the company.

11.   The serial number of the warrants issued should be entered in the coupon register.

Exchange of bearer warrants for registered shares

Subject to authority in the Articles the holder of a share warrant to bearer may, upon surrendering the warrant, request to have his name entered in the Register of Members in respect of the shares to which the warrant relates. The following company secretarial procedure should be followed in this case:

1.   A form of application supplied by the company to exchange share warrants to bearer for registered shares should be completed by the applicant and lodged, with the share warrants, with the company.
2.   The warrants should be checked against those listed on the application form and be acknowledged.
3.   The share warrants should be cancelled and marked in the stock register as having been surrendered, with a corresponding entry being made in the coupon register. It must, however, be verified that all the coupons numbered for dividends following the most recent dividend are still attached to the warrants. If there are any missing coupons relating to these dividends a certificate for the registered shares should not be issued until the holder of the warrant surrenders the coupons concerned (he may have detached the coupons from the warrant to keep them in a separate place) or he provides an indemnity with regard to the missing coupons. Failure to do this may result in the company being liable to pay dividends both on the coupons and on the registered shares.
4.   A share certificate should be prepared and a resolution passed by the board approving the sealing (if the company has a common seal or a securities seal) and issue of the certificate for the registered shares.
5.   The member's name should be entered in the Register of Members, showing the number of shares now registered in his name, and the company's register 'share warrants to bearer issued' should be debited in respect of such shares.
6.   After sealing, if appropriate, the share certificate will be issued to the member. In the case of a company listed on The Stock Exchange the certificate must be issued within 14 days of the deposit of the warrants (Continuing Obligations, para. 30).

Payment of dividends on bearer share warrants

It is usual to advertise in a newspaper that a dividend has become payable and give instructions as to the place at which the dividend will be paid on presentation of the appropriately numbered coupons. Places of payment will not necessarily be restricted to the United Kingdom and newspaper advertisements must be inserted in any country in which the company undertakes to make payment of dividends. It is to be noted that by their very nature share warrants to bearer are likely to be held internationally. A person who holds a number of warrants should complete a listing form giving details of the coupons surrendered for payment of the dividends.

The procedure for payment of dividends is as follows:

1. Each coupon should be checked to make sure that it bears the correct number relating to the dividend in question and that the total number of coupons agrees with the listing form.
2. The coupons would be marked off in the appropriate dividend column of the coupon register.
3. The surrendered coupons should be cancelled and filed numerically.
4. The payment to the person lodging the coupon should be made by way of cheque or dividend warrant, together with the tax credit certificate.

Quite often the company's bankers deal with the collection of coupons and payment of dividends, in which case two copies of the listing form should be lodged with the bank, which should send one copy with the coupons to the company for checking before the bank is authorised to make the payment.

Issue of further coupons

Shortly before the payment of the last coupon on the original share warrant becomes payable new sheets of coupons should be ordered from security printers. Here again security is most important; the requirements for the issue of further coupons on the bearer shares of companies listed on The Stock Exchange are laid down in the Yellow Book, Section 9, Chapter 4, para. 2. The new coupons should also be serially numbered following on from the number of the last coupon attached to the original bearer share warrant, so that no confusion may arise if some of the coupons attached to the original warrants should not be lodged for payment until some time after the new set of coupons have come into use.

When advertising in the newspaper the surrender of the final coupon on the original warrant for the payment of a dividend, instructions should also be given that on surrender of the talon attached to the share warrant a further supply of coupons will be issued. Entries should be made in the coupon register of the issue of a further supply of coupons against the surrender of talons; the supply of new coupons will also have attached to it a talon to be exchanged in due course for a further supply of dividend coupons.

Further points of procedure

The following additional points arise in connection with share warrants to bearer:

1. Since it is not possible to send a copy of the report and accounts and notice of Annual General Meeting to holders of share warrants to bearer since the names and addresses of the holders are unknown to the company, the notice of general meetings must be published by advertisement in one or more newspapers in the United Kingdom and in countries overseas where dividend payment offices are maintained. This procedure would have to follow any provisions contained in the company's Articles, and, in the case of a company listed on The Stock Exchange, the Continuing Obligations. The advertisement must contain instructions as to how the holders of share warrants to bearer may vote at the general meeting, either in person or by proxy. The usual arrangement is that the holders must deposit their warrants with the company three days before the meeting, although some Articles provide that if the holder has lodged his warrants with a bank or some other agent of repute for safe custody, the confirmation of the bank or agent that he holds the warrants in respect of a certain person may be accepted by the company instead of the deposit of the warrants with the company itself. An authority is then issued to the person depositing the warrants entitling him to attend the particular meeting in question and to vote in respect of a specified number of shares.

2. Advertisements must also be placed in appropriate newspapers if the company makes a rights issue or a capitalisation issue. The usual procedure would be for the notice to state that the holders may claim their entitlements by surrendering the next available coupon attached to their warrants at the offices at which payment of dividends is made on the surrender of coupons. It would be usual to impose a time limit for the claiming of rights by surrendering of the coupon. In the case of a rights issue a statement should appear in the advertisement that if coupons are not submitted by a given date, the entitlements represented by them will be sold and the net proceeds paid out against the surrender of the coupon after the final date stated in the advertisement for claiming entitlement to the issue. However, in the case of a capitalisation issue authority should be contained in the company's Articles, or given by a resolution of the shareholders in general meeting, to sell capitalisation issue shares entitlements of the non-claimants. Arrangements would need to be made to pay the proceeds to entitled holders who may later submit a claim.

3. The summary of issued share capital on the draft of the new Companies Form No. A363 'Annual return of a company' does not include provision for information to be given regarding share warrants to bearer. However, in the case of persons who during the year have either exchanged registered shares for bearer shares, or exchanged bearer shares for registered shares, the current position will be reflected in the list of members submitted with the annual return, e.g. those who have exchanged registered shares for share warrants will be treated as having ceased to be members.

Lost share warrants

Extreme caution is obviously necessary if the company should receive an application for the issue of a duplicate share warrant to bearer to replace one that has been lost or destroyed. In all such cases, therefore, a full indemnity should be insisted upon from a bank, insurance company or guarantee society and a statutory declaration made by the applicant that the warrant has been destroyed or lost beyond recovery. In the case of listed companies The Stock Exchange requires that a new share warrant shall not be issued to replace one that has been lost unless the company is satisfied beyond reasonable doubt that the original has in fact been destroyed (Yellow Book, Section 9, Chapter 1, para. 2.3).

Designation of accounts

A company's Articles of Association may provide that designated accounts be accepted in the Register of Members but otherwise there is no obligation on the company to divide an account in this way. Designations are usually recorded by a letter or letters of the alphabet, by a number, or by a combination of both, e.g. 'ABC Nominees Ltd, XY/497 A/C'. However, the use of designations makes life easier for banks and nominee or trustee companies, which may have shares registered in their names that they hold for various clients as the beneficial owners. In the case of a listed company, however, para. 29 of the Continuing Obligations requires that designated accounts must be arranged if requested by the holders of securities.

A request for the designation or redesignation of an account should be submitted to the company on the form approved for the purpose by the Institute of Chartered Secretaries and Administrators and The Stock Exchange, a copy of which is included in the Institute's manual. It should be signed by the holder or by all the holders, if more than one, and lodged with the company or its registrar accompanied by the appropriate share certificate. This certificate will then be cancelled and replaced by a new certificate bearing the designation on its face. Although companies, including some listed companies, may make a charge for each designated account opened it may be preferred not to make a charge where the account is to be divided into a number of separate designated accounts if the number is not unreasonable. Quite often an account will be designated from the outset by the inclusion of a designation on the TALISMAN bought transfer or a letter or request received from the executors or administrators of a deceased shareholder.

Joint accounts

A limit may be placed on the number of holders in a joint account by the company's Articles of Association but the number of holders is commonly limited to four and, in the case of securities of listed companies, a company's Articles of Association must not limit the number of joint holders to less than four persons (Yellow Book, Section 9, Chapter 1, para. 1.3).

A number of company secretarial points should be noted in connection with joint accounts and the following suggestions are made subject to the provisions of the company's Articles of Association:

1. A request may be received to divide a joint account into two or more separate accounts with the names of the joint holders listed in a different order for each account, rather than have the account split into a number of designated accounts with the names of the joint holders remaining in the same order. Requests of this sort may be accepted provided that the request is signed by all the holders of the shares concerned and that the request also confirms that no sub-sale or disposition of the shares has been involved. In this case no stock transfer form need be signed. The share certificates must, of course, be sent in with the request in order that new certificates may be prepared for the separate holdings with the joint holders' names shown in a different order. Such accounts can, however, lead to misunderstandings and mistakes in dealing with the accounts and many companies insist that the matter should be dealt with by designation of the separate accounts rather than by changing the order of names.

2. It may also be requested that the names in a joint account should stand in a different order. Here again the request should be signed by all the holders and include a confirmation that no sub-sale or disposition of the shares is involved, and be accompanied by the share certificate for the issue of a new certificate with the names of the holders in the revised order. No stock transfer form need be signed.

3. It is usual for notices and other communications (including dividends where not mandated) to be sent to the first-named holder in a joint account but a company's Articles of Association may permit it to comply with a request signed by all the holders in a joint account for notices and other communications to be sent to one of the other holders rather than to the first-named holder. An Article in the form of Regulation 112 of Table A would not prevent a company from accepting such a request. However, if it is desired to send dividends to one of the other holders instead of to the first-named holder, a dividend mandate should be completed, signed by all the holders, and sent to the company. This is what has been described elsewhere in this handbook as 'a third party mandate'. An alternative method of dealing with the matter would be merely to change the order of names in the joint account so that the person to whom it was desired to send notices, other communications and dividends would stand as the first-named in the account. Administrative complications can arise, however, in dealing with requests such as these, and many companies would refuse to accept them.

4. What is important is that the full names of all the holders in a joint account should be entered both in the Register of Members and on the share certificates and, subject to (3) above, all formal communications should be addressed only to the first-named holder, with the initials of the other holders included on the communication for the purpose of identification by the first-named holder.

CHAPTER 5

Share registration

The shares in companies subject to the Act are transferable as personal property in the manner provided by the Articles of Association (s.182 (1)). A proper instrument of transfer must be completed and delivered to the company unless the shares may have been transmitted by operation of law (s.183). Companies' Articles in this respect are frequently based on Table A, Regulations 23–31.

The form of transfer for fully paid registered securities of companies limited by shares within the meaning of the Act is governed by the Stock Transfer Act 1963 which provides that a transferor's signature need not be witnessed, that a transferee need not sign (an important reason why the 1963 Act applies only to fully paid securities) and that transfers need not be executed under seal unless the transferor is a body corporate having a common seal.

Guidance on points of procedure under the system in force since the passing of the 1963 Act are laid down in the *Guide to the New Transfer System* which was published in 1963, an extract from which is published in the Institute's manual.

Private transactions

In the case of a private transaction in the shares of both private and public companies a member wishing to dispose of his holding (i.e. the transferor) will complete a stock transfer form in the form contained in Schedule 1 to the 1963 Act and pass this to the purchaser (i.e. the transferee) with the relative share certificate or certificates, in exchange for the agreed price. The transferee should then enter his name and address as transferee on the transfer, date it and have it stamped at an Inland Revenue Stamp Office. The transfer and share certificate(s) should then be lodged with the company for registration. The transferee does not have to sign the stock transfer form.

The following procedure should be adopted by the company on receipt of the transfer:

1. Details of the transferor and shareholding transferred should agree with the share certificate and with the account in the Register of Members.
2. If the company has several classes of shares in issue it should be checked that the shares transferred are fully and correctly described.
3. If the shares are partly paid it should be checked that the amount shown as paid up on each share on the share certificate has been correctly entered on the transfer; if the company has recently called up a further amount on the shares the transfer should not be accepted until due payment of the call (unless the call has previously been paid). It should be noted that in the case of partly-paid shares a transfer should be in the old common form of transfer in general use prior to the 1963 Act, which also had to be executed by the transferee. In the case of partly-paid shares, the shares will have distinguishing numbers and it should be checked that the numbers stated on the transfer are the same as the numbers stated on the share certificate.
4. It must be checked that the share certificate is the original and that no duplicate certificate has been issued and is still outstanding. If a duplicate has been issued, this must also be surrendered to the company prior to registration.
5. The execution of the transfer by the transferor (or by his attorney) should be checked and it may be desirable to obtain confirmation of the authenticity of the signature of the transferor since the transfer has been lodged with the company by a private individual. Under the *Guide to the New Transfer System* the stamp of the agent acting for the transferor acts as a warranty as to the genuineness of the execution by the transferor, but this protection is not available to the company in the case of transfers lodged by private individuals. If the shares are partly paid it should be checked that the transfer has also been signed by the transferee.
6. It must be checked that the company's registration records do not indicate that there is any lien or restraint on a transfer of the shares.
7. It should be checked that the transfer has been duly stamped by the Inland Revenue's impressed stamp and that the amount of the *ad valorem* stamp duty paid shown on the stamp (i.e. 50p per £100 or part thereof) is the correct amount for the consideration stated on the transfer. However, it should be noted that under the 1990 Budget proposals *ad valorem* stamp duty will be abolished on the implementation of TAURUS, probably towards the end of 1991.

8. Subject to all the above matters being in order, the share certificate(s) should be cancelled and a new certificate prepared in the name of the transferee. Where only part of the holding covered by a certificate is being transferred, a balance certificate should be prepared in the name of the transferor. The cancelled certificate(s) should be endorsed with details of how the shares have been dealt with.

9. The transfer should be approved by the company's board and authority given for the new certificate to be sealed, if the company has a common seal or the special securities seal described in the preceding chapter, after checking that the transfer does not contravene any pre-emption rights in the company's Articles. A check should also be made to ensure that there is no other reason why the transfer should not be registered (e.g. an infant, or person of unsound mind). If the directors resolve to refuse registration for any reason, the transferee must be informed within two months of lodgement of the transfer.

10. The name of the transferee will be entered in the Register of Members crediting the number of shares transferred to him, and the transferor's account in the Register should be debited with the number of shares transferred.

11. The transfer and cancelled share certificate(s) should be filed.

12. The new certificate should be sent to the transferee, after it has been sealed, if the company has a common seal or a securities seal, if the transferee lodged the transfer personally, or to any agent who may have lodged it with the company on his behalf. If there is a balance certificate this should be sent direct to the transferor or his agent. Section 185 provides that certificates should be ready within two months from the date on which the transfer is lodged, although it should be noted that the law in this respect may change following the introduction of TAURUS (see below).

Non-market transactions

These are transactions in which The Stock Exchange is not involved and which do not relate to a sale or other disposition for value. This occurs in the case of the distribution of deceased estates or other trustee holdings among beneficiaries. One of the more common types of non-market transaction is the transfer of trustee holdings on a change of trustees. Forms in the form set out in Schedule 1 to the 1963 Act are invariably used in the case of non-market transactions, regardless of the number of individual transferees. Since such transfers do not have to be signed by the transferee and are not, therefore, generally seen by the transferees prior to registration with the company, care must be taken to ensure that the particulars of the transferees are correct. The transfers must agree with existing holdings of shares in the company, including any designation that may be applied to the account. Alterations on transfers must be initialled by the transferor.

Usually an agent will be employed by the transferor, e.g. solicitor or bank, and the agent will place his rubber stamp in the box alongside the signatures of the transferor(s) to warrant the genuineness of the execution of the transfer. The agent may also have to have the transfer stamped by the Inland Revenue, making any declarations necessary where nominal stamp duty is involved or signature of an appropriate certificate where the transfer is exempt from stamp duty and does not have to be submitted to the Inland Revenue. (Nominal stamp duty will be abolished under the 1990 Budget proposals on the implementation of TAURUS, probably towards the end of 1991, but for further details of the position applicable until then, see the section below on stamp duty on private and non-market transactions).

Usually the same agent who acts for the transferor(s) will lodge the transfer for registration into the name(s) of the transferee(s) and he will, therefore, also place a copy of his rubber stamp in the appropriate box at the foot of the form; but if another agent is acting for the transferee(s), it will be his stamp which will appear in that box.

On receipt of the transfer for registration by the company in respect of non-market transactions the procedure set out above for private transactions should be followed. However, in the case of non-market transactions, particular attention should be paid to the points outlined below.

Regarding the transferor(s)

1. If the holding is in joint names the transferor(s) should be shown in the same order on the transfer as they appear on the certificate and in the Register of Members, since it often happens in the case of trustee holdings that there will be other holdings on the Register in the same names but in a different order.

2. If the account is designated it should be checked that the correct designation appears on the transfer; otherwise the wrong account in the Register might be debited.

3. The transfer should deal with only one holding in the Register, i.e. there must be separate transfers if the same persons are concerned with other holdings with names in a different order or bearing different designations.

4. A transferor should be described as an executor or administrator only if he remains on the company's Register in that capacity.

5. Except in the unlikely event that the Articles of Association permit a single transfer to cover more than one class of share a transfer should deal with only one class of share.

6. As mentioned above in the case of private transactions consideration should be given to whether the transfer has been properly executed by the transferor(s). Many companies take the view that the genuineness of the signatures of the transferor(s) should be verified by making enquiries from an independent source. Where a transfer is lodged by a professional adviser, that adviser should confirm in writing the validity of the transferor's signature. However, the view is sometimes held that seeking such confirmation might be considered contrary to the spirit of the Stock Transfer Act 1963 under which signatures of transferees are no longer automatically supplied to companies. On the other hand, the contrary view is also supportable, since on the stock transfer form prescribed in Schedule 1 of the 1963 Act the stamp of any agent of the transferor must be placed alongside the transferor's signature, the agent having satisfied himself as to the genuineness of the execution of the transfer.

7. Provided that only a short time has elapsed following the death of a holder of securities and that no grant of representation has been registered with the company, a transfer may be accepted for registration if otherwise in order.

8. A transfer signed by an attorney, however, must not be accepted for registration if it is known that the holder has died since the power of attorney is revoked by the death of the donor (i.e. the shareholder) of the power.

9. A transfer executed by the mark of the registered holder may be accepted if it has been witnessed by two persons, one being a medical practitioner, solicitor, minister of religion or other person of public standing, to the effect that the transfer has been read to the transferor and understood by him. In Scotland, however, notarial execution is required in these cases.

10. A transfer may be registered up to the last moment prior to the company going into liquidation (unless the Articles stipulate otherwise), provided that the transfer is bona fide in that the transferor retains no interest in the shares.

Regarding the transferee(s)

1. The transferee(s) must be either individuals or corporate bodies without qualification as to any representative or trustee capacity in which they hold the shares.

2. Unincorporated bodies such as partnerships (in England and Wales) or clubs are not acceptable. The registration should be in the names of one or more members of the club or one or more of the partners.

3. Transfers to the holder of an office can only be accepted if the office is of an official or public nature, e.g. the Accountant General of the Supreme Court, or where the office is created by a statute as a corporation sole separate from the person holding that office, e.g. the Public Trustee.

4. Where a number of transferees are to be registered it should be checked that the number does not exceed any limits laid down by the Articles.

5. Holdings may be registered with designations, and companies listed on The Stock Exchange are bound to register designations without limit (Continuing Obligations, para. 29). Unlisted companies, however, may impose a limit on the number of designated accounts they will accept.

Stamp duty on private and non-market transactions

It should be noted that what follows in this section on stamp duty is based on the current position but that this will change under the 1990 Budget proposals when stamp duties on these transactions will be abolished on the implementation of TAURUS, probably towards the end of 1991.

It has already been mentioned that on receipt, transfers should be checked to ensure they have been duly stamped. The current rate of *ad valorem* stamp duty is 50p per £100 or part of £100 of the consideration.

Transfers operating as gift *inter vivos* executed on and after 1 May 1987 are exempt from stamp duty and do not have to be submitted to the Inland Revenue. However, the appropriate certificate must appear on the document as specified in the Stamp Duty (Exempt Instruments) Regulations 1987. Where the certificate is not signed by the transferor, the grantor or a solicitor, e.g. it is signed by an agent such as a bank or a stockbroker, the agent must confirm that he is authorised to sign and that he has knowledge of the facts of the transaction.

There are several other types of transactions falling within an exempt category and these are listed in the Regulations mentioned in the preceding paragraph. Before accepting such transfers, and transfers operating as gifts *inter vivos*, for registration the company or its registrars should ensure that the appropriate certificate is endorsed on the transfer form or other document.

Transfers to Stock Exchange market makers in the ordinary course of business are also exempt from stamp duty but these must carry the Inland

Revenue supplementary stamp denoting that they are not chargeable to duty under Section 81 of the Finance Act 1986.

Transfers and re-transfers of securities used as security for a loan and between beneficial owners and nominees are still, however, liable to a fixed duty of 50p.

It is important to remember that the person responsible for maintaining the company's Register of Members (e.g. the secretary or the company's registrar) is legally responsible for ensuring that all transfers accepted for registration are properly stamped or correctly certified as exempt. There is, however, no need for the secretary or the registrar to ascertain if the consideration is in accordance with the market value. He only has to ensure that the stamp duty is correct according to the consideration stated on the transfer. Adjudication should be requested in any case where the transfer appears not to have been properly stamped. The Inland Revenue's adjudication is evidenced by an impressed adjudication stamp in addition to the impressed stamps representing any duty paid. It should be noted that the rubber stamp of the Inland Revenue marking officer is not evidence of adjudication.

It should also be noted that there is an arrangement between the United Kingdom and Eire to accept each other's stamps on transfers signed in either country.

Stock Exchange transactions

Most transfers presented for registration in the case of listed companies will relate to transactions on The Stock Exchange and all such dealings in the registered shares or debentures of listed companies are settled through the TALISMAN system (TALISMAN's full name is Transfer Accounting Lodgement for Investors and Stock MANagement for Jobbers). A detailed description of this settlement system is contained in *A Guide for Institutional and other Large Investors'* published by The Stock Exchange. The detailed operation of the system as it affects the Register of Members, is set out in the *TALISMAN Registrars' Service Description* published by The Stock Exchange, and which is made available to the secretary or registrar of listed companies. For the purpose of the following description we will confine ourselves to the shares of a company, although other registered securities listed on The Stock Exchange can be settled through the TALISMAN system.

The basis of the TALISMAN system is that all sold stock is transferred from the seller into a 'pool' in the name of SEPON Limited, forming a single holding of the shares in the course of settlement (SEPON's full name is Stock Exchange Pool Nominees). The purchasers receive their shares by transfer out of the SEPON Limited account. The SEPON pool account is managed by The Stock Exchange Settlement Centre (the 'Centre'). The Centre maintains separate records for each market maker dealing in the company's shares. The term 'jobber' as given above in the full name of TALISMAN fell out of use following the 'Big Bang' on 27 October 1986 and was replaced by the term market maker or, where a broker acts as a principal in a stock as well as agent, the term broker/ dealer. A broker selling shares on behalf of a client sends him a TALISMAN sold transfer for signature, which the client returns to the selling broker with his share certificate. The TALISMAN sold transfer and certificate are passed by the selling broker to the Centre. Here they are checked for good delivery and are then passed by the Centre to the registrar of the company for registration into the account of SEPON Limited. Upon such registration the legal title passes to SEPON Limited.

On account day (also called settlement day) the shares are transferred by the Centre to the market maker's trading account and the selling broker will receive payment from the Centre on the market maker's behalf. 'Apportionment' then takes place, i.e. the stock in the market maker's trading account is allocated to his sold bargains in the 'shapes' in which they are dealt. 'Shapes' means the number of shares dealt in by each transaction.

Following apportionment the stock is held to the order of the various buyers and the Centre then prepares TALISMAN bought transfers to transfer the stock from the SEPON Limited account into the names of the various buyers. These TALISMAN bought transfers are then lodged with the company or its registrar for registration. Once the bought transfer is registered by the company or the registrar the legal title passes from SEPON Limited to the buyer and the company or its registrar prepares a new certificate which is sent to the Centre for onward transmission to the purchaser's broker.

The following points concerning the TALISMAN system should be carefully noted:

1. Since all TALISMAN sold transfers have SEPON Limited pre-printed as the transferee, for reasons of security registrars should reject any TALISMAN sold transfer which is not received directly from the Centre or if any alteration has been made to the transferee details.
2. The Centre may not have been informed of the names of all the buyers at the time the TALISMAN bought transfers have to be prepared. In this case the Centre will complete the TALISMAN bought transfers with a standby nominee name which the purchaser's broker will previously have supplied to the Centre. Institutional investors may also use standby nominee names who maintain numbered stock deposit accounts with the Centre.

3. Prior to the establishment of the TALISMAN system institutional investors paid for stock purchased only after receipt of the relevant stock. In order to receive payment from institutional investors the Centre prepares a document called a stock note which identifies the bargain and specifies the registration details and contains an undertaking by The Stock Exchange that a transfer from SEPON Limited to the persons named will be lodged for registration. Brokers pass these stock notes to their clients in return for payment. However, stock notes do not constitute good delivery with the Centre against recent sales. Consequently, where stock has been sold by a recent purchaser and he has not received the relevant certificate from the company or its registrar, the client should make arrangements with the broker for the relevant TALISMAN transfer to be certificated by the company or its registrar.

4. TALISMAN bought transfers do not have Inland Revenue impressed stamps on them for the amount of stamp duty payable since all stamp duty is collected centrally under the terms of a composition agreement between the Inland Revenue and The Stock Exchange in accordance with the Finance Act 1976, s.127. However, the amount of stamp duty payable on the TALISMAN bought transfer is stated on the transfer and the secretary or registrar is still responsible for ensuring that this information is shown on the transfer before it is registered. He is not required, however, to check that the amount of stamp duty shown on the transfer is correct having regard to the recent price of the shares or stock transferred. As mentioned above, however, stamp duty will be abolished under the 1990 Budget proposals when TAURUS is implemented, probably towards the end of 1991.

5. With regard to the settlement of dividend and other claims, the company should strike a balance on the record date for a dividend (or entitlement to a rights or capitalisation issue) on the account of SEPON Limited and the Centre informed of this balance. The schedules supplied daily by the Centre to registrars include provision for this balance to be stated. Apart from this, the company is not directly involved in the settlement of such claims.

Registration of TALISMAN transfers

The following points of procedure should be noted with regard to registering TALISMAN bought or sold transfers:

1. There is a space at the top of the transfer forms for the company to attach a sticker or rubber stamp with boxes to facilitate the recording of the various procedural steps necessary in processing the transfer.

2. In the case of transfers of shares out of the name of a corporate body the TALISMAN sold transfer must be completed under the corporate body's seal in accordance with its Articles or other regulations governing use of the seal. Companies quite often request an extract from the corporate body's Articles or other regulations at the time the corporate body originally becomes a member in order to facilitate verification that the seal has been properly used when a sale takes place. It should be noted, however, that companies registered under the Companies Acts may opt not to have a seal under the provisions of s.36A(3) inserted by CA 1989 s.130.

3. In the case of fully paid shares of listed companies, The Stock Exchange requires provision in the company's Articles that such shares shall be free of any restriction on the right of transfer. A company is, however, entitled to refuse to register a transfer where it is known that the transferee is an infant under English law or other person with a legal disability, and this does not conflict with The Stock Exchange requirements since such right of refusal is given by the general law.

4. Transfers are entered in the Register of Members, debiting the transferor's account and crediting the new or existing account in the name of the transferee. The entries must be made in the Register even if it is known that the shares have immediately been transferred again. Where a transfer results in a nil balance in the transferor's account that account should be removed to the closed accounts section of the Register.

5. A new certificate is then prepared in the name of the transferee(s) and it is important to note that a certificate must be prepared covering every transfer registered, even though it may be known that the shares have been sold or otherwise transferred. These certificates would cover the certification by the company or its registrar of TALISMAN sold transfers before the certificates were due to be sent out. Certificates are not prepared in respect of transfers into the name of SEPON Limited.

6. It is quite a frequent practice for companies where the registration procedure is manual to arrange for batches of new certificates to be audited against the relevant TALISMAN sold transfers, the audit being carried out either within the share registration department, by an auditor from the company's accounts department or by an external auditor. In the case of mechanical or computer controlled systems such audit may be considered to be unnecessary.

7. The company's Articles of Association will state how share certificates are to be issued and it is now unusual for certificates to be

signed autographically. Articles may provide, however, that the signatures may be impressed mechanically, in which case there must be an adequate security system controlling the use of the machine under which such signatures are applied to the certificates. However, if the company has a common seal or a securities seal, all certificates should be sealed (s.40 as amended by CA 1989 Schedule 17, para. 3 and s.186 as substituted by CA 1989 Schedule 17, para. 5). It is common practice for the Articles to authorise the affixing of the seal without attesting signatures.

8. In the case of listed companies, certificates must be available for delivery within 14 days of the lodgement of the transfer with the company or its registrar (Continuing Obligations, para. 28).

9. Those certificates which require to be cancelled immediately because of the certification of TALISMAN sold transfers (see (5) above) should be withdrawn and the remainder issued to The Stock Exchange Centre for dispatch to the buying brokers. The certificates for each broker should be collated and labelled with the broker's name and number. If certificates are sent out by post, ordinary letter post may be used but a record of dispatches should be kept.

10. Cancelled share certificates and transfers which have been registered should be filed in a suitable numerical sequence so as to facilitate future reference. It is more likely that future reference to the transfers rather than to the cancelled share certificates may be needed; it would be convenient, therefore, for cancelled certificates to be boxed up separately and labelled with the dates appropriate to them.

Forged transfers

Private and non-market transactions

No rights can pass to any transferee under a forged transfer, even if he acted in good faith and had received a share certificate from the company before the forgery was discovered. When the forgery is discovered the purported transferor whose signature has been forged is entitled to be put back on the Register of Members as the owner of his shares. It is the company's responsibility to provide these shares together with any dividends or other entitlements which he may have missed. The transferee receiving the shares under the forged transfer may have transferred the shares for valuable consideration to a third party without knowledge of the forgery. In this event the company is liable in damages to that third party for any loss he may have suffered, in addition to the liability of the company to restore the name of the defrauded transferor to the Register of Members. Where the third party relies on a sealed certificate issued to him by a company which has a common seal or a securities seal it is estopped from denying the validity of certificates which have been sealed (s.186 as substituted by CA 1989 Schedule 17, para. 5). Since under the provisions of s.36A(4) inserted by CA 1989 s.130 a document signed in accordance with that subsection has the same effect as if executed under the company's common seal (which also includes an official seal for securities under s.40 as amended by CA 1989 Schedule 17, para. 3), there is similar protection for unsealed certificates issued by companies which do not have a common seal under the provisions of s.36A(3) inserted by CA 1989 s.130. However, it is to be expected that a company which issues many share certificates will wish to continue to have a seal so that certificates may be sealed as a precaution against forgery of signatures on unsealed certificates. A further convenience is that companies may make provision in their Articles for sealed certificates not to be signed.

A company would have a right of action against the person lodging the forged transfer since by lodging it he implies that it is genuine. Even so, the company and its officers are not absolved from exercising due care in connection with the registration of transfers. At some time, however, a company may incur liability in respect of a forged transfer and under the Forged Transfer Acts 1891 and 1892 a company may pay compensation out of its funds for any loss arising from a forged transfer.

It is, however, more usual for companies to have a forged transfer insurance policy, either with an insurance company or with Lloyd's, to cover this risk. These policies generally cover documents lodged for registration, dividend warrants, etc., the forgery of which could involve the company in liabilities. In selecting a policy care should be taken to ascertain whether it covers fraud or forgery whenever it took place or only those occurring during the period of insurance.

Stock Exchange transactions

The above applies equally in the case of listed companies but a difference does arise under the TALISMAN system. It has already been stated that no certificates are issued on the account of SEPON Limited so that estoppel cannot arise in that connection against the company. Consequently, The Stock Exchange has made its own arrangements for the protection of listed companies in respect of liabilities arising out of forgery. This protects companies in respect of TALISMAN documents lodged for registration; thus problems for the company which might arise because of the broker responsible for lodging the original forged transfer having gone out of business are avoided.

TAURUS

Background

Details of the introduction of a central dematerialised electronic share settlement system which will automate the way in which securities are transferred from one holder to another were published by The International Stock Exchange in March 1990 in a document entitled 'PROJECT TAURUS – A Prospectus for Settlement in the 1990s'. TAURUS, or Transfer and Automated Registration of Uncertificated Stock to give it its full name, will form a completely new method of equity settlement and share registration. A dematerialised system is one which does not require the issue of physical securities in the form of share or stock certificates. Shareholders will be able to hold their stocks and shares in the securities equivalent of a bank account. It will also do away with the need for stock transfer forms thus permitting the introduction of a computer-driven ownership system for stocks and shares instead of the current paper-driven system. TAURUS is expected to cover UK and Irish equities, and corporate loan stocks. In this description of TAURUS, however, for the sake of simplicity, we will refer only to shares. When the system is running there will be a new same day trade confirmation system to replace the present overnight matching of bargains described in the section on the mechanics of dealing on The Stock Exchange in Chapter 13 on the securities industry.

The need for TAURUS is self-evident. It will be recalled that in the period of high activity on The Stock Exchange in the summer of 1987, the very large volumes of paper caused severe problems in brokers' back offices and it became apparent that to maintain the status of London as an international capital market a new transfer system was needed based on a computerised accounting system.

Under TAURUS companies will still maintain consolidated records of their shareholders although the precise legal status of these records is yet to be defined. Even though investors will not have documents of title in the form of share certificates they will continue to enjoy the benefits of direct share ownership. Their shares will, however, be held for them in dematerialised form within the company account or they may choose an account controller to hold them. In order that the company's registrar may maintain a consolidated record of the members of the company, information regarding the shares held by each account controller will be confirmed to the company on a daily or other agreed basis.

The description of TAURUS which follows is based on the information given in the March 1990 prospectus but it should be noted that there are several areas where no final decisions have been taken and that some aspects of the system as described below could change before TAURUS is implemented as a result of discussions still proceeding at the time of preparation of this handbook.

Objectives and benefits of TAURUS

The main objective of TAURUS is to assist participants in the market while at the same time safeguarding the interests of listed companies and their shareholders. It is also an objective to provide companies with at least the same level of shareholder information as at present. The benefits of TAURUS will be as follows:

1. The elimination of expensive and high risk paper will reduce the problems referred to above when there are significant and sudden increases in trading volumes at times of high volatility in the market.
2. Make settlement procedures more cost effective by the elimination of share certificates and transfer forms thus reducing the amount of administration as ownership will be transferred by book entry electronically thereby eliminating much of the work of creating, transferring, controlling, reconciling and the safeguarding of valuable documents of title.
3. The elimination of paper will shorten the settlement cycle and permit the introduction of a rolling settlement system as described in the section below on implementation.
4. It will no longer be necessary for private investors to safeguard their share certificates and pay indemnity fees when they lose them.
5. Investors currently on companies' registers remaining within a company account will notice little difference while those whose securities are held in a bank or brokers' nominee name can retain the benefits of these arrangements by choosing a commercial account controller to manage their holdings.
6. The consolidated records of membership held by companies are expected to be more up to date than under the present system even though some information will only be provided monthly. That information, however, and other information provided daily to companies' registrars, is intended to ensure that they are no worse off as regards shareholder information as they are at present and in some cases registrars could have a more comprehensive record of their companies' shareholders.

Investors

The existing Register of Members has a legal status under the Companies Acts being the legal record of a company's ownership. This register is usually maintained in computer form, either by a bank or company offering share registration services, or by an in-house company registrar. When an investor's name is added to the Register of Members, he is issued with a certificate for his stock or shares.

Under TAURUS, the dematerialised holdings of investors will be maintained by bodies known as account controllers who will manage holdings of shares on behalf of investors. The TAURUS operator will reconcile daily with account controllers and registrars. The legal position of the lists of investors held by account controllers under TAURUS at the time of preparing this handbook is being examined by working parties under the chairmanship of the Department of Trade and Industry (DTI) and consequently what is set out below could change as a result of these discussions.

The term 'investor' means one of the following names held directly on an account controller's settled records:

1. A single nominee where account controllers hold only one name, i.e. the nominee's name.
2. Multiple or designated nominees where account controllers hold either a number of nominee names or a single nominee name with multiple designations.
3. Individuals where account controllers hold the names of individuals, either as sole holder or as joint holders.
4. Individuals and nominees where account controllers hold the names of some individuals and some nominees.

Investors, i.e. names held on an account controller's records, will be recognised as having legal ownership of their shares. Beneficial owners may continue to hold their shares in a nominee name if they so wish and in this case the nominee is the legal owner of the shares. Accordingly, the term 'investor' refers to the legal owner of the shares, either an individual (or joint individuals) or the nominee of beneficial owner(s).

As at present, where an investor's name is a nominee, the company may issue a Section 212 notice to ascertain the name(s) of the beneficial owner(s).

It has been mentioned above that some aspects of the TAURUS system described in the March 1990 prospectus could change as a result of discussions still proceeding at the time of preparation of this handbook. One area where the position has already changed from the prospectus description is in regard to the legal concept of membership of a company.

The current proposal concerning this now under discussion with the DTI is as described in this section on investors and in the section below on the Register of Members. When an investor buys shares the holding will be entered in the records of his account controller and at that time the legal title to the shares passes to him and he becomes entitled to all the rights and benefits appertaining to his holding. In due course, under the arrangements described below in the section on the Register of Members, the company's registrar will be advised of the investor's details so that he may update the consolidated record (i.e. Register of Members) which he maintains and, at that time, the investor becomes a member of the company. Similarly, when an investor sells shares, his legal title to the shares ceases as soon as his holding is removed from the account controller's records. Assuming that he sold all his shares, the selling investor would cease to be a member of the company on the next occasion that investors' details are notified to the registrar to update the consolidated Register of Members. Additions and subtractions from holdings are treated in the same way.

TAURUS accounts

Under TAURUS there will be various types of account in which shares may be held as follows:

1. The market settlement account comprising the existing SEPON account to be used by the TAURUS operator to hold shares on behalf of market makers and shares in the course of settlement.
2. Commercial accounts where it is likely that financial institutions, banks and trust companies etc., and stockbroking firms, will wish to become account controllers running commercial accounts (commercial account controllers). They will be paid for their services directly or indirectly by the investor for whom they act. Commercial accounts will be subdivided according to the way in which they provide listed companies with the information they require to fulfil their legal, regulatory and management requirements. There will be:
    (a) designated accounts whose controllers will advise company registrars electronically via TAURUS of the identity of buyers and sellers of the company's shares on a daily basis, of changes to standing details of investors and of any off-market transactions. Registrars thus have a continuous record of investors in designated accounts;
    (b) undesignated accounts whose controllers will provide company registrars electronically via TAURUS with an up-to-date portion of the registers they maintain on a monthly basis.

(An organisation may control more than one account and each one may be designated or undesignated).

3. Company accounts funded by the company run by a company account controller. Investors who do not wish their holdings to be maintained in a commercial account will be added to the records of a company account. In this case, the identity of the investors will be reported directly to the registrar by the company account controller. The company will determine the relationship between the company account controller and itself or its registrar but initially the company account controller and the registrar may be the same body or person.

The account controllers will hold and manage investors' shares in dematerialised form and will act as the channel of communication between the investor, the market and the company's registrar. The TAURUS operator will specify the conditions under which account controllers may function.

To protect investors, security features will be built into TAURUS to ensure the safe operation of the system, e.g. to prevent the unauthorised transfer of stock out of an investor's name.

The Register of Members

The form of the company's register will be somewhat different from its present form as each commercial account controller and each company account controller will be responsible for a portion of the register containing the records of its investors. The company account controller will be responsible for monitoring and authorising movements into and out of its own account, while the commercial account controllers, through the TAURUS operator, will do the same for the commercial accounts. As already noted, the name of an investor on an account controller's records represents his legal title to the shares of the company which he holds.

Registrars will receive details of investors from commercial account controllers via TAURUS either daily in the case of designated accounts or, in the case of undesignated accounts, monthly in the form of an updated copy of their portion of the register. However, if required, arrangements could be made between account controllers and registrars for major movements within undesignated accounts to be reported daily.

Companies will be able to communicate directly with their members. The records used by the company to determine who its members are will be compiled by the registrar from information supplied by commercial account controllers via TAURUS or directly by the company account controller. This will enable the registrar to prepare a consolidated record, i.e. Register of Members, at least at monthly intervals. The investors become members of the company when the consolidated register is prepared. As members of the company they become entitled to receive the company's report and accounts, interim or quarterly statements, dividends, the right to vote at meetings and eligible for shareholder 'perks'.

The registrar will be able to update his records and keep a consolidated Register of Members from the details of the investors which are advised to him. Where the investor holds his shares in the company account details of movements as a result of market purchases and sales will be advised by the TAURUS operator to the company account controller. Such movements will be in and out of the market settlement account (i.e. the existing SEPON account). Changes to investors' holdings which occur as a result of transactions not effected through The Stock Exchange (i.e. off-market transactions) and changes in the standing details of investors will be advised to the company account controller either directly by the investor or by an intermediary instructed by him.

The details of market movements as a result of purchases and sales where the investor holds his shares in a designated account will be advised to the registrar by the TAURUS operator. Off-market movements and changes in standing details will be advised by the account controller to the registrar via the TAURUS operator. Any communications received by registrars direct from investors who hold their shares in a designated account should be referred to the account controller for authentication. As already noted, undesignated account controllers supply the registrar with a replacement register via the TAURUS operator at monthly intervals or more frequently by request.

It is again emphasised, however, that the concept of the Register of Members under TAURUS is still under discussion with the DTI at the time of preparation of this handbook and the final outcome could be different from that described here.

Listed Companies' Access Service

It has already been noted that under TAURUS a portion of the register of members is kept by account controllers. Companies require information about their members, however, to fulfil legal obligations, to comply with regulations of The Stock Exchange or for management information purposes, e.g. for dividend payments, the dispatch of the report and accounts with proxy cards, the annual or extraordinary general meetings, the annual return, half-yearly or quarterly statements, etc. Accordingly, TAURUS will provide an access service to provide such information from commercial account controllers to companies through their registrars. The service will be called the Listed Companies Access Service (LCAS).

Company account controllers maintain details of investors who use company accounts to hold their shares which will presumably be communicated directly to registrars by the company account controllers and consequently company accounts will not be included in the access service.

Information concerning transferors and transferees of a company's shares held in a designated account for both market and off-market transactions are supplied by designated account controllers for each transaction and changes in investors' standing details, e.g. name and address, are supplied daily. Registrars thus have a continuous record of investors in designated accounts. Undesignated account controllers supply a full list of current investors monthly.

The registrar is, therefore, able to amalgamate information from three sources, i.e. company account controllers, designated account controllers and undesignated account controllers, to compile a consolidated register of members to enable the company to meet its legal and management requirements. The object of LCAS, however, is for TAURUS to provide additional information to registrars as follows:

1. Daily account balances for each commercial account so as to monitor significant changes in account totals. (The register will, of course, already be aware of company account balances which are not maintained by TAURUS).
2. Details of market bargains and information concerning off-market transactions settled through TAURUS.

LCAS will ensure the continuation of the company/shareholder link whenever required by companies to enable them to meet statutory and other obligations or when, because of some special purpose or situation arising, there is a need for full details of its members to be supplied more frequently than the normal TAURUS system provides.

Investor documentation

With the introduction of TAURUS and the elimination of share certificates and physical forms of transfer some investors may still wish to have evidence of their shareholdings, and also perhaps confirmation of share sales. Those investors who have holdings of shares in a commercial account should be able to arrange with their account controller to be sent periodic statements, the form and frequency of which can be agreed by the investor with his account controller.

There are two categories of investors using a company account:

1. Those who use a stockbroker's portfolio management service.
2. Those who independently manage their own shareholdings.

The first category will probably agree to documentary evidence of holdings being sent by the company account controller to the investor's stockbroker. Details of the holdings will be entered in the records of the broker's portfolio management system, regular statements of which can be sent to the investor in such form and at such intervals as may be agreed.

Those in the second category who manage their own holdings in a company account will require physical evidence of acquisitions, disposals or of other changes in their shareholdings. A statement will be issued by the company account controller to each such investor whenever their shareholding changes, e.g. purchases, sales, capitalisation issues, etc., or if the investor advises the company account controller of changes of name and address, etc.

When a sale is to be made, the selling broker will use his judgement as to whether he requires sight of the statement before he deals.

Market settlement

The March 1990 TAURUS prospectus gives detailed information concerning the market settlement procedures to be followed by The Stock Exchange, the TAURUS operator, stockbrokers, account controllers and custodians when TAURUS is implemented. A description of these procedures has not been included in this discussion of TAURUS as they are beyond the scope of this handbook.

It may be noted, however, that when TAURUS is implemented it is likely that participants in the Institutional Net Settlement Service will become account controllers and that those who are not members of The Stock Exchange will settle monies through that Service which will become part of the TAURUS payment service.

Also, in the case of off-market transactions, account controllers will be able to make movements through TAURUS either free or against payment.

Reconciliation

The smooth running of TAURUS will depend on an effective reconciliation service and the comparison processes will as far as possible be automated with only manual intervention required to resolve queries. It will be necessary each day for the TAURUS operator and the registrar to agree the aggregate total of all commercial accounts including the market settlement account (currently SEPON). Individual account balances will be advised to the registrar daily. Also, every day, the TAURUS operator will advise each account controller of its total holding and they will be required to confirm their agreement of this holding within a specified time. Each designated account controller will also at regular intervals supply the registrar, through the TAURUS operator, with a list of investors and their details so that the registrar may check these against his records and take any action required to correct differences.

Stock dividends, benefits and situations

Dividends
Dividends and other cash benefits may be paid directly to investors or mandated to their banks. Those investors who hold their stock in a commercial account may receive such monies via the account controller under arrangements likely to be included in their client agreement with their account controller.

To determine entitlement to dividends, the registrar takes record date information from the undesignated account controllers to be amalgamated with information previously supplied by the designated and company account controllers. Dividends to be distributed to investors via commercial account controllers will be paid in total to the TAURUS operator to be distributed to the individual account controllers on the due payment date to be paid through the TAURUS payment procedures. Under this procedure, the account controllers will be responsible for issuing the dividend tax vouchers to the investors. In the case of designated accounts, the registrar will provide details of the payments due to the investors to be passed to the designated account controllers.

Stock benefits
Stock benefits (e.g. rights or capitalisation issues) will be distributed through account controllers. In the case of a rights issue:

1. On the day that it is announced (i.e. the 'impact day') all major holders will be identified by the company, underwriting arranged and the approximate number of holders counted. Usually this will be from the last full record of members of the company, i.e. the consolidated register compiled from the last monthly breakout supplied by TAURUS.
2. On impact day a full breakout as at the record date for the issue will be requested from the undesignated account controllers via the TAURUS operator. Registrars will have to ensure that all changes advised by the TAURUS operator in respect of designated and company accounts dated prior to the record date have been processed in order to strike the record date balance.
3. As soon as possible after the record date, allotment advices will be dispatched by the registrar to investors on the register as at the record

date including investors within undesignated accounts. The allotment advice will contain similar information to the current rights issue allotment letter but it will not be, as at present, a document of title. The allotment advices of investors holding shares in commercial accounts will include wording telling them to get in contact with their account controller.

4. Simultaneously, the TAURUS accounts will be credited with the nil paid shares as follows:

    (a) undesignated accounts: the number of shares required for the total of each account is credited and reported to the account controller via the TAURUS operator without regard to the number of shares required by each individual investor, i.e. it is left to the controller to do this allocation;

    (b) designated accounts: the new shares are allocated to the account of the individual investor and reported to the account controller via the TAURUS operator both at investor and total level. The report gives details of the number of shares and cash fractions, where applicable, calculated for each investor, with the total for the account;

    (c) company account: the new shares are allocated to the account of the individual investor and held on the records of the company account controller.

Dealings in the rights issue shares take place in nil paid form. Details of settled transactions and off-market movements relating to designated and company account controllers will be passed electronically to the registrar daily up to and including the last day for the apportionment of the shares. Registrars will have to update their registers to record these changes before call payments are validated.

Commercial account controllers will advise the TAURUS operator prior to the last time for acceptance of the shares on which they wish to pay the call. Undesignated account controllers will simply advise the quantity of shares on which the call is to be paid but the designated account controllers will also advise the details of each individual investor as well as the quantity of shares on which the call is to be paid. The TAURUS operator, after amalgamating the quantities advised, and checking that this is equal to or less than the total quantity held in each account, will charge each account controller with the total call due.

The TAURUS operator will advise the registrar of the shares to be taken up as follows:

1. Undesignated accounts: one figure for each account.

2. Designated accounts: one figure for each investor with a total for each account.

The TAURUS operator will also advise the receiving bank of the total number of shares to be taken up and will pay the call due.

Investors holding shares in a company account will pay the call directly to the receiving bank using an acceptance advice as evidence of their entitlement. Facilities to enable recent purchasers to pay the call are being developed.

Nil paid shares on which the call has been paid will be transformed into fully paid shares and nil paid shares on which the call has not been paid will be lapsed.

Stock situations

Stock situations arise in cases where shares are replaced by other shares (or a combination of shares and/or other securities and cash) as in the case of take-overs. It is usual in all such cases for the offeror company to ask the registrar of the target company for a copy of the consolidated record (or register of members) which under TAURUS combines details of shares held by commercial account controllers and the company account controller. The registrar will probably provide the last complete consolidated record, i.e. as at the last LCAS breakout or he may request a new LCAS breakout.

The offeror will send out the offer documents to the investors containing an acceptance card. This will include the same information as on the current form of acceptance and transfer but may be used by the investor to communicate with the account controller, the acceptance card containing wording telling him to get in contact with his account controller. As the take-over bid proceeds, further *ad hoc* LCAS breakouts may be requested to ascertain the most up-to-date record of investors.

Investors who hold their stock with a commercial account controller will make their wishes in regard to the bid known to their account controllers who will advise the TAURUS operator of the shares on which they wish to accept the offer. Undesignated account controllers will merely advise the quantity of shares wishing to accept the offer but the designated account controllers will also advise details of the individual investors. The shares which have accepted the offer are moved by the TAURUS operator to an 'assented' security code so that movement of such shares may be frozen.

The TAURUS operator will pass details of the investors in a designated account who have accepted the offer to the merchant bank acting for the offeror. Undesignated account controllers will provide details of investors who have accepted following a request from the merchant bank, the information being provided via TAURUS on an LCAS breakout. Investors who hold their shares on the company account pass their acceptances directly to the merchant bank using their shareholder advice as evidence of their holding.

Voting and shareholder perks

Voting
A consolidated record (Register of Members) is compiled from the regular or an *ad hoc* LCAS breakout to be used by the company to post the annual report and accounts, notice of meeting and proxy cards to investors. The proxy cards are returned direct to the company to be validated against the consolidated record produced two days before the meeting. In the case of purchases of shares by a new investor where they are added to the investor's account too late for a proxy card to be received from the company, the relevant account controller will provide the investor with a letter of representation enabling him to attend, speak and vote at the meeting. However, discussions with the DTI were proceeding at the time of preparation of this handbook on having a record date for general meetings to allow a sufficient time before meetings to obviate the need for letters of representation.

Shareholder perks
Documents giving entitlement to shareholder perks, or perks in kind, will be sent direct by the company to the investor. Where there is a qualifying period for eligibility, undesignated account controllers will be responsible for advising the company of their investors' eligibility.

Collateral

To enable investors to use their shares as collateral for a loan, arrangements will be made for the shares to be moved to an account nominated by the lender by an off-market transaction. The lenders will either hold the shares in the investors' names or substitute their own nominee name.

The legal framework of TAURUS

Before Taurus can be introduced changes in company legislation are required and the CA 1989 s.207 gives the Secretary of State power to make these changes by regulations which are currently being drafted. The regulations will have to cover, as already mentioned above, the form of the Register of Members, arrangements for the inspection of the register by shareholders and members of the public as well as the removal of the need for share transfers and the legal obligation requiring companies to issue share certificates to shareholders. The latter may require the agreement of shareholders in general meeting to alter companies' Articles of Association unless this is avoided by provisions in the regulations governing the legal framework of TAURUS empowering companies to act in accordance with the regulations notwithstanding anything to the contrary contained in their Articles. In addition, the implications of the FSA have to be considered. The position of persons holding shares under deeds will also have to be covered permitting them to hold shares in dematerialised form.

Implementation

The above brief description of TAURUS based on the March 1990 prospectus issued by The Stock Exchange must still be regarded as tentative pending the publication of more detailed user documentation which The Stock Exchange hopes to make available towards the end of 1990. The Secretary of State's regulations may also be available by then. The initial implementation is unlikely to be until towards the end of 1991 and will probably be on a phased basis perhaps beginning with the institutions.

It should also be noted that in connection with TAURUS The Stock Exchange is planning to abolish the two-week account system for settlement of bargains and replace it by a five-day settlement cycle or 'rolling' settlement account. At the time of preparation of this handbook, it seems that dematerialisation will have to preceed the rolling account settlement but this could change. The period for rolling settlement will probably be five days initially followed by a move to three day settlement in due course. The rolling settlement system reduces the time between dealing and settlement, reduces the exposure to risk that settlement may not take place and evens out the work flow.

When the system has been fully developed and is in operation, all who are engaged in company secretarial and share registration work will need to be as familiar with the methods of operating TAURUS as they are at present with TALISMAN.

Transmission of shares

Shares are a type of personal property and transmission of shares may be defined as the devolution of those shares to another party by operation of law instead of by the normal method of share transfer arising from the voluntary act of the shareholder. Transmission also arises upon death or bankruptcy or upon a member becoming of unsound mind and the subject of an Order of the Court of Protection.

Registration of documents

Differences between English and Scottish practice

There are substantial differences between the law of England and the law of Scotland on matters of private company law. For instance, there are major differences between probates and letters of administration granted by an English court and confirmations granted by a Scottish court. A grant of probate or letters of administration in England generally establishes the right of the executor or administrator to deal with the whole of the estate. In the case of a Scottish confirmation, however, the executor is only given power to deal with such part of the estate to which he has been confirmed; other assets not included in the confirmation may be the subject of a further grant to the executor or of a grant to other persons. However, by the Administration of Estates Act 1971 a company registered in England and Wales or in Northern Ireland may register a confirmation issued in Scotland without further formality. Some documents issued by the English courts are acceptable in Scotland, although in some cases validation by a Scottish court is required. In all other cases, however, documents issued by English courts are totally unacceptable in Scotland either because the situation dealt with by the English document cannot arise under Scottish law or because there is no analogous Scottish legal process.

Apart from confirmations some documents issued by Scottish courts are acceptable in England. In some cases validation by an English court may be required, while other Scottish documents are unacceptable in England for reasons similar to those applying in Scotland, i.e. the analogous situation cannot arise in England. One particular example to note in the case of shares is that in Scotland there is a rule which permits a majority of the holders in a joint account to sign a transfer for the shares registered in their names when registered as trustees, whereas in England all the holders would be required to sign a transfer of the shares without reference to their trustee capacity.

Documents issued by other jurisdictions

Orders or documents issued by Courts outside England and Wales and Scotland are not acceptable for registration either by English or Scottish companies and consequently should not be accorded any recognition. It is possible for such orders to be validated for use here but if there are no such procedures a fresh English or Scottish order must be obtained. Court orders should be read very carefully since some may operate themselves to effect a transfer of shares into a new name or names, whereas others merely empower a named person or persons to effect transfers which must then be completed in accordance with the Companies Acts and with the company's Articles of Association.

General points regarding documents

The following general points should be noted in relation to documents received for registration:

1. Any person lodging the document with the company is deemed to represent to the company that the document is genuine.
2. Where only a small shareholding is involved some relaxation of the strict requirements may be accepted if the person lodging the document is of appropriate repute, e.g. bank, solicitor, chartered secretary, accountant.
3. The Stock Exchange has introduced a document service to facilitate the registration of documents and the avoidance of delays (further details of the service are given later in this chapter).
4. The particular shareholding must be clearly and precisely identified and include the full name and address of the shareholder as registered. In the case of joint holdings the names in the documents should be in the same order as they appear in the Register of Members. If there is any discrepancy between the names in the document and the names in the Register a declaration of identity should be obtained before registration of the document. Such discrepancies would include documents stating fewer or more forenames than those appearing in the Register or where the forenames may be in a different order or spelt differently from those in the Register.
5. Section 360 of the Act precludes a company registered in England and Wales from noting in the Register any nominee or trustee capacity in which registered shareholders hold their shares. However, this does not preclude the use of designations.
6. It may be necessary to make endorsements or alterations to existing share certificates, in which case the endorsement should be signed and marked with an official stamp so as to prevent unauthorised alterations or endorsements being made.
7. If authorised by the Articles of Association a fee may be charged for the registration of documents but, in the case of listed companies, no fees may be charged (Continuing Obligations, para 27).

Recording of documents

In the following description of procedures reference is made only to 'shares' and 'shareholdings' but the procedures indicated apply to any class of shares, stock, debentures, loan stocks or other securities of a company. Where reference is made to a document register this may comprise a loose-leaf or bound register in which the relevant information is extracted or summarised from the document being registered.

However, it is quite common for the register to comprise photocopies of the documents lodged, thereby avoiding the requirement to make extracts which could involve clerical errors; further, in the event of a query, reference to a photocopy of the original document would be more useful as evidence of its contents.

Probates

Grants of probate are issued by the High Court in England to the person or persons named in a will of a deceased person as his executor(s). It is usual for probate to be granted to all the executors (or surviving executors named in the will), although one or more may renounce probate or reserve power to prove subsequently, in which case a further grant known as a double probate would be issued. Where a sole surviving executor dies before the estate is completely distributed and without himself having named an executor by will, application should be made to the Court by a person or persons interested in the original estate for the grant of letters of administration *de bonis non*. However, where a deceased sole or surviving executor has named an executor in his own will, then upon such an executor obtaining a grant of probate to the estate of the deceased executor, he is entitled to continue executorship of the original estate. This is known as the 'chain of representation'.

A probate includes a copy of the will and is issued over an impressed seal of the High Court. In order to speed up the process of administration of the estate, executors or their advisers may obtain additional office copies of the grant of probate, bearing an impressed seal of the Court which does not include a copy of the will but does include the names of the persons authorised to deal with the estate. These 'office copies' are extremely useful where the deceased held shares in a number of companies and it is desired to avoid delay in registering the probate with those companies.

In the case of grants of probate issued overseas, in the Commonwealth or in the Republic of South Africa, the Court will reseal grants of probate and companies should only accept such grants for registration which have been resealed. Grants of probate issued in Northern Ireland and confirmations issued in Scotland do not require to be resealed in England. A separate English grant of probate must be obtained, however, in the case of the Isle of Man, Channel Islands and the Republic of Ireland, since probates issued in these countries cannot be resealed in England.

The procedure for registering probates by companies or their registrars is as follows:

1. Check that there is complete identity between the deceased named in the probate and the registered shareholder. This will be facilitated if the relevant share certificates are submitted with the probate. Should there be any doubts as to whether the probate relates to a shareholder a declaration of identity should be obtained from the person lodging the document, who would usually be the solicitor acting for the estate, or from the bank at which the account of the deceased executor was held.
2. Record the names of the executors named in the probate in the document register.
3. Record in the Register of Members the date of death and the date of registration of probate with the name(s) and address(es) of the executor(s) named in the probate and with the word 'deceased' added after the name of the deceased shareholder. The account should not be removed to another place in the Register as legally the deceased remains a registered shareholder.
4. Endorse the share certificate with the fact and date of death, the date of registration of probate and the name(s) and address(es) of the executor(s) and validate the endorsement by the company's registration stamp.
5. The registration stamp should be impressed on the back of the probate which should then be returned to the person who lodged it with the company, together with the endorsed share certificate. It is useful to include a new dividend mandate form for completion by the executors since the mandate lodged by the shareholder would have been revoked by his death.
6. It is also usual to send with the returned documents a form known as a letter of request which the executors can complete in order that the shareholding may be registered in their names. This is helpful to the company as it is then no longer concerned with the 'chain of representation' if any of the named executors should die before the shares are sold or transferred to a beneficiary. A letter of request need not be sent if the person lodging the transfer indicated that the shareholding was to be disposed of by transfer.
7. The person lodging the letter of request should be requested to send in the share certificate if it was not lodged with the probate.
8. Registration of a double probate should be accepted only if the original executors are still registered in their representative capacity, i.e. if they have not been registered in their own names following submission of a letter of request.

9. Communications from the company would be sent to the first-named executor.

Letters of administration

These are also granted by the High Court, appointing a person or persons to administer the estate of a person who died without having made a valid will.

Grants of administration also bear the impressed stamp of the High Court and sealed office copies may also be obtained to facilitate registration with a number of companies.

As regards the Commonwealth, Isle of Man, Channel Islands, Republic of Ireland and foreign probates, the points made above regarding probates originating in those countries apply equally to grants of letters of administration.

The procedure for registering letters of administration is also similar to that set out in the case of probates, administrators taking the place of the executors.

There are a number of different forms of grant of letters of administration and entries in the Register of Members and endorsements on certificates should indicate the exact form of the grant. Usually a letter of request for the administrator(s) to be personally registered as holder(s) of shares is appropriate only in the case of a grant of letters of administration with the will annexed, issued by the High Court in cases where the deceased left a will but did not name any executor, where the executor may have predeceased the shareholder or the executor has renounced probate.

Confirmation

This is the Scottish document issued by the Sheriff Court having similar effect to an English probate or letters of administration, and the procedure for registration by companies in England and Wales is the same as in the case of probates set out above. It is granted to the executors named in the will, who are termed 'executors nominate'; but if there are no surviving executors or if the deceased left no will the Court makes a grant to a person or persons to administer the estate who are termed 'executors dative' (called administrators in England). The chief difference to note between English probates and letters of administration is that the Scottish confirmation has annexed to it an inventory of the deceased's property to which the executors have been confirmed and they may only deal with the property listed. Consequently, companies must check that the list includes the securities of the company to be dealt with by the executors. If not included they can be added by the Court. Extracts are issued, to assist companies and others, under the seal of the Court and signed by the Clerk. Reference should be made to the Institute's manual for guidance as to the procedure to be followed where a sole or surviving executor dies before the estate has been completely administered as Scottish practice here is quite different from that in England.

Bona vacantia

If a person dies domiciled in England and Wales without having made a will and no persons remain with the lawful rights of succession which apply in such cases, the High Court will issue a grant of administration (known as *bona vacantia*) appointing the Treasury Solicitor or officers of the Duchy of Lancaster or the Duke of Cornwall to adminster the estate. The procedure for registration is the same as in the case of a probate. In such cases it would be usual for the shareholding to be disposed of forthwith and consequently no letter of request would be issued. The appropriate Scottish document is *ultimus haeres* and in this case the Queen's and Lord Treasurer's Remembrancer takes possession of the estate.

Small estates

There is no statutory definition of a small estate in relation to shareholdings in companies but many companies permit concessionary procedures where the total estate does not exceed £5,000 in value. Many companies are prepared to dispense with the formalities of obtaining a full probate or confirmation where the total value does not justify the expense of obtaining a grant of representation from the Court. However, some risk is involved and some companies may specify a lower limit such as £1,500 or £500.

Applications to waive such formalities are normally considered individually and if it is decided that it would be appropriate in the circumstances to dispense with the formalities the personal representative or beneficiary should be required to submit the following:

1. The death certificate.
2. A statutory declaration as to the identity of the person claiming to deal with the shareholding and of his entitlement to deal with it.
3. A letter from the Capital Taxes Office confirming that on the information supplied to it, no liability to inheritance tax arises in connection with the holding.
4. The share certificate(s).
5. A letter of indemnity under which the applicant undertakes to indemnify the company if any liability on the company should arise by permitting the concessionary procedure and also undertaking to obtain and produce a formal grant of probate, confirmation or letters of administration should the company require this at any time.

Occasionally it may be appropriate to dispense with the production of a letter from the Capital Taxes Office where the applicant is an elderly widow or widower because of difficulties which the applicant would experience in providing the necessary information to the Capital Taxes Office to obtain the letter. If this concession should be granted a paragraph concerning the absence of liability to inheritance tax should be included in the indemnity referred to above. Care is needed because the reason why the estate is only a small one may be that the deceased made substantial gifts in his lifetime so that no liability to inheritance tax would arise on his death.

If the deceased holder was resident abroad the documents to be submitted to the company would, of course, be different; these are set out in the Institute's manual.

Letters of request

These are addressed to the company by executors or administrators of a deceased shareholder and request the company to enter their names in the Register of Members as the holders of the shares held by the deceased. The letter may be registered by the company only if a grant of representation in respect of the deceased shareholder has already been registered, appointing the persons who signed the letter of request as the executors or administrators of the deceased's estate. The letter must be signed by all the executors and administrators but their signatures need not be witnessed. The executor or administrator may be a body corporate, in which case a letter must be executed under its seal unless an officer of the company has authority to execute such documents, in which case the authority under which it is signed should be produced to the company.

When a letter of request is received, the procedure for registering it is similar to that which applies in the case of non-market transfers, considered earlier in this chapter.

Death of a holder in joint account

If shares are registered in the names of two or more joint shareholders, upon the death of one of the holders the shares remain registered in the name(s) of the surviving holder or holders and no executors or administrators are involved. All that the company requires is the production of the certificate of death of the joint holder, which should be the original although some companies will accept photocopies if they are lodged by a person of professional standing. This does not, however, apply in Scotland where any photocopy must be authenticated by signature of the District or Assistant Registrar or, alternatively, the death may be proved by a decree of the Court of Session.

A grant of probate or grant of letters of administration or confirmation to the estate of the deceased joint holder may be submitted instead of a death certificate and this is equally acceptable as evidence of the death. Upon receipt of a death certificate or other evidence of death of a joint holder, the following procedure should be adopted:

1. The company or its registrar would carefully check that there was complete identity between the person named in the certificate and the registered shareholder, obtaining a declaration of identity in the event of any doubt.
2. The particulars of the document (i.e. death certificate, probate or confirmation) would be recorded in the document register.
3. The fact and date of death and date of registration would be entered in the Register of Members, deleting in the account the name and address of the deceased joint holder. If the deceased joint holder was the first-named in the account, then the person who was second-named in the account will become the first-named holder, involving transfer of the account to a different part of the Register of Members.
4. The share certificate should be appropriately endorsed, validated by the company's registration stamp and returned to the shareholder accompanied by the document submitted to prove death. If the latter was a probate or confirmation, it should be endorsed as registered as 'proof of death only'.
5. Dividends would continue to be paid on the holding in accordance with any existing mandate unless the surviving shareholder(s) execute a new mandate.
6. If there was no dividend mandate in force, dividends would be paid to the first-named survivor in the account, to whom all communications would also be addressed.

Change of name of shareholder
Changes of name can arise in a number of ways:

1. A person may alter his name with or without formality. Provided there is no fraudulent intent, this is quite lawful, but before registering the change of name the shareholder should be asked to provide a statutory declaration as to the change of name or a declaration of identity by some independent person of public standing.
2. By execution of a deed poll duly stamped, or a copy of the *London Gazette* or the *Edinburgh Gazette* containing the advertisement of the deed poll.
3. By marriage in the case of a female shareholder. In this case the marriage certificate provides the necessary evidence. The original

should be requested but some companies may accept photocopies of certificates if lodged by a person of professional standing. In Scotland, however, the photocopy must be authenticated by signature of the District or Assistant Registrar. A shareholder may have personal reasons for not wishing to submit her marriage certificate and in this case a statutory declaration is an acceptable alternative.

4. Grant of an honour such as the conferment of a knighthood may involve a change of name and this may be proved by a copy of the *London Gazette* containing the grant of the honour.

5. Where the shareholder is a company the certificate of incorporation on change of name (or a certified photocopy) should be produced for registration.

6. In the case of companies which are shareholders a change of name may occur where a company re-registers under the Act as a public company or a private company. In this case the certificate of incorporation on re-registration (or a certified photocopy) issued by the Registrar of Companies is acceptable evidence of the change of the company's name.

On receiving evidence of change of name for registration the procedure to record the change by the company or by its registrar should be as follows:

1. Check that there is complete identity between the document (which should be accompanied by the share certificate(s)) and the registered shareholding and obtain a declaration of identity by a person of public standing in the event of any doubt.

2. Enter details in the document register.

3. Make appropriate entries, including date, in the Register of Members and move account to new position in Register if necessary.

4. Endorse the share certificate(s) validated by the company's registration stamp and return it or them to the shareholder.

5. If thought desirable, issue a new dividend mandate form for completion.

Change of address of shareholder

Changes of address notified by a shareholder should generally be signed personally by the shareholder. If the notification is by way of a printed card this should be returned for signature if it has not been signed. Some companies, however, are prepared to accept notifications of change of address given on behalf of a shareholder by his bank, solicitor or stockbroker. A notification of change of address purported to be given by a member of the shareholder's family should never be accepted. Ideally, notifications of change of address should give both the old and the new addresses as this facilitates identification.

Upon receipt of an acceptable notification of change of address the change should be noted in the Register of Members and the company's records suitably amended for the purposes of future communications with the shareholder. Most companies no longer issue an acknowledgement of notifications of change of address unless this is requested, nor are share certificates generally amended to show a change of address. It is in any case modern practice not to give addresses on share certificates.

Powers of attorney

A power of attorney is an appointment by an individual or body corporate of a person or persons to act on his or its behalf to the extent and for the time specified in the power. Such appointments are usually made when the person granting the power is going to be absent abroad for some considerable period or is facing a long illness or just because he wishes to free himself from dealing with matters of routine.

The Powers of Attorney Act 1971, Schedule 1 sets out a short form of general power of attorney and this may conveniently be used to confer wide powers on the attorney. This form is most suitable for use by individuals as it is short and simple. A person may lodge a do-it-yourself power of attorney which is neither executed under seal, nor witnessed by an independent person and with wording not in accordance with the Powers of Attorney Act, 1971, Schedule 1. Such a power of attorney should not be accepted for registration.

Powers of attorney granted by bodies corporate would generally be in more extended form, setting out in detail the precise extent of the powers granted. This would also apply in Scotland as the short form of general power of attorney under the 1971 Act is not available for powers created in Scotland.

It is advisable for the power of attorney to be executed under seal since the attorney himself may have to execute documents under seal on behalf of the principal, i.e. the 'donor' of the power. Since 26 March 1985 it has not been necessary for powers of attorney to be stamped by the Inland Revenue but powers executed before this date should be stamped with 50p duty. The signature of the principal on the power of attorney should, however, be witnessed; one witness is needed in the case of powers executed in England and Wales and two if executed in Scotland. Powers given by bodies corporate must be under their seal. A power of attorney given by a company should be under its common seal if it has one. When completed abroad powers of attorney require notarial attestation or consular legalisation.

It often happens that the person granting a power of attorney is unable to execute it by reason of physical infirmity. In this case the power may be signed and sealed by some other person in the presence of two other persons as witnesses, who must also sign the document. Companies may register copies of powers of attorney instead of the original if they are copies certified by the principal or by a solicitor or stockbroker. The certificate should certify that the copy is a true and complete copy of the original. Powers of attorney are sometimes expressed to be irrevocable for a period of one year, after which the power of attorney may be revoked by the donor of the power. The power is automatically revoked on the donor's death. The Powers of Attorney Act 1971 gives some protection to companies which have registered powers of attorney in relation to a shareholder, since it provides that where a power has been revoked and a person without knowledge of revocation deals with the donee of the power, the transaction shall be as valid as if the power had continued in existence. This applies only in England and Wales.

Where the power of attorney is not in the general simple form provided by the Powers of Attorney Act 1971 the company should read it carefully before acting on the power of attorney to ensure that the action to be taken is within the powers set out. Companies will be particularly concerned with the provisions in the power regarding the purchase and sale of investments, receipt of dividends, interest or capital monies, attendance and voting at meetings and completion of such documents as may be issued in connection with the shareholding. When executing documents, it is usual for the attorney to sign as, e.g. 'A. B., attorney of C.D.' or 'C.D., by his attorney A.B.'.

An attorney may not delegate his powers or appoint a substitute unless the power granted to him specifically provides for this. It is emphasised that the law governing powers of attorney is wide and complex and in cases of doubt reference should be made to the more detailed information given in the Institute's manual or to the publication *Powers of Attorney and Other Instruments Conferring Authority* also published by the Institute.

The following procedure should be followed when a power of attorney is received by a company or its registrar for registration:

1. The document must be either the original power, bearing 50p impressed stamp if it was executed before 26 March 1985 or an authenticated copy as mentioned above.
2. It should be checked that there is complete identity between the donor of the power and either a registered shareholder or a person in the course of acquiring shares for registration, evidenced by a 1963 Act stock transfer form, a TALISMAN bought transfer, a renounced allotment letter or a renounced certificate lodged for registration.

3. A photocopy of the complete power should be made for the company's records.
4. The execution, continued validity, scope and the general interpretation of the power should be scrutinised extremely carefully.
5. It should be noted whether the power appoints more than one person as the attorneys; if it does it should be checked whether the appointment is joint, in which case all the attorneys must act together, or whether it is joint and several, when any of the attorneys may act individually.
6. It should be checked whether the power affects the registered address of the shareholding or manner of payment of dividends. If there are no changes in these respects the registered address remains as before, as do any instructions with regard to the payment of dividends.
7. The company's registration stamp should be affixed to the power and returned to the sender.
8. It is not now normal to send a protective notice to the donor of the power informing him that the power of attorney has been received and that it will be assumed to be in order and registered unless he notifies the company otherwise. Such a protective notice should, however, be sent where the person executing the power by the direction of the donor because of physical infirmity is himself the attorney appointed by the power.
9. Every time a document executed by the attorney is lodged with the company, the validity of the particular transaction should be verified by reference to the copy of the power of attorney held by the company.

If the power of attorney is revoked or lapses the company's copy should be marked accordingly and moved to a separate file for lapsed powers of attorney.

No entry need be made in the Register of Members regarding the registration of a power of attorney nor should any alteration be made in the heading of the relevant account in the Register of Members.

Enduring Powers of Attorney Act 1985

The above act (EPA) came into force on 10 March 1986 and applies to England and Wales only. The operation of the Act is governed by Regulations and Rules which are contained in The Enduring Powers of Attorney (Prescribed Form) Regulations 1986 (SI 1986/126) and The Court of Protection (Enduring Powers of Attorney) Rules 1986 (SI 1986/127). For powers executed after 1 November 1987 the prescribed form is contained in The Enduring Powers of Attorney (Prescribed Form)

Regulations 1987 (SI 1987/1612) although powers executed before 1 July 1988 in the form prescribed by SI 1986/126 (revoked by SI 1987/1612) continue to be valid.

Under the EPA individuals may give a power of attorney in the form prescribed in the appropriate Regulations which will continue in force even if the donor should become mentally incapable, subject to the power being registered with the Court of Protection. If the power is in the prescribed form, the following further points arise:

1. The company may act on the power even though not registered by the Court of Protection if it is unaware that the donor has become mentally incapable. This protection derives from the Powers of Attorney Act 1971, s.5(2).
2. The company may not act on the power if it is aware that the donor has become mentally incapable but no application has been made to the Court of Protection for registration of the power.
3. The company may act on the power if it is aware that the donor has become mentally incapable and has evidence produced to it that an application for registration has been made to the Court of Protection, even though the registration has not been completed. The EPA gives certain powers of maintenance and for the prevention of loss to the estate of the donor of the power. It also gives statutory protection to a company acting under a power governed by the EPA provided that it is not aware of any irregularity in the exercise of the powers by the attorney.
4. The company may act on the power if it has documentary evidence of the registration of the power with the Court of Protection. The documentary evidence which the company should require to see are Court office copies of the fact of registration by the Court of Protection. The company is protected in this instance if there should be any irregularity concerning the power or if it should have been revoked by the Court provided that the company is unaware of the irregularity or the revocation.

(Note: The above is only a very rough and brief outline of the legislation, and companies or their registrars may consider it prudent to obtain legal advice before dealing with powers created under the EPA if they have not had previous experience of these provisions. It has already been ruled by the Court that the appointment by a person (i.e. the donor of the power) already suffering from a degree of mental illness and, therefore, unable to manage his or her affairs, is valid if the person making the appointment was aware of what he or she was doing.)

Other documents

A company may be concerned with the registration of numerous other documents apart from those most frequently encountered, described above. Such documents may include the following:

1. Court of Protection orders: made when a person becomes of unsound mind and appoints a person to act on his behalf and deal with his affairs.
2. Bankruptcy orders: these have the effect of vesting the property in shares in a trustee for the benefit of the shareholder's creditors (in Scotland these are Acts and Warrants appointing a trustee in bankruptcy).
3. Charging orders: which attach a shareholding for the benefit of a judgement creditor (called letters of arrestment in Scotland, which may not be registered by English companies).
4. Garnishee orders: orders of the Court attaching debts (including dividends and interest on securities) for the benefit of a judgement creditor (no Scottish equivalent).
5. Stop notices: official notices given under the rules of Court restraining the transfer of specified shareholdings (no Scottish equivalent).
6. Injunction or restraining orders: made by a Court pursuant to a previous stop notice restraining the transfer of a specified shareholding (the Scottish document is an interdict, which may not be registered by English companies).
7. Vesting orders: made by the Court for removing a person from the Register of Members and the substitution or addition of different person(s), usually where a trustee neglects or refuses to act. The equivalent Scottish document, order for removal of a trustee or appointing a new trustee, may not be registered by English companies.
8. Vesting pursuant to statute: vesting shares in different name(s) under authority contained in an Act of Parliament or a statutory instrument.
9. Court orders for rectification of the Register of Members under s.359 – removal of person(s) from the Register and the substitution or addition of other person(s). An order made by a Scottish Court for rectification of the Register of Members may not be registered by English companies.
10. Restrictions on shares imposed by Department of Trade and Industry under ss.210, 216 or 445.
11. Appointment of receivers or receivers and managers.

12. Appointment of liquidators.

Further details of the effect of these other documents and how they are dealt with by the company or its registrar (including information on some other documents issued only in Scotland) are contained in the Institute's manual. Generally, however, the action to be taken by the company or its registrar is as follows: to check that there is complete identity between the document, the person(s) concerned and the shareholding(s); to make an appropriate entry in the Register of Members; and to take such other action needed to ensure compliance with the terms of the document, as set out in the Institute's manual.

The document service

It will be noted from the above that time-consuming and expensive delays may occur when such documents as probates and powers of attorney have to be registered with a company or its registrar where a person holds shares in a large number of companies, even though a reasonable supply of office copies of probates may have been obtained.

Accordingly, a document service was introduced by The Stock Exchange in January 1985 which was developed in liaison with the Institute's Registrars' Group to facilitate the registration of the following documents:

1. English probates
2. Letters of administration.
3. Powers of attorney.
4. Death certificates
5. Deed polls.
6. Marriage certificates
7. Certificates of incorporation on change of name.
8. Memorandum and Articles of Association.

Under the service, certified copies of such legal documents are prepared for dispatch to companies or their registrars. The service, which is intended to operate on the basis of a 24-hour turnround, also covers the deposit of associated stock into TALISMAN, certification where necessary of associated stock transfer forms for non-TALISMAN transactions and the surrender, where appropriate, of certificates to registrars for replacement or endorsement.

Stockbrokers are required to submit to The Stock Exchange Centre the original or a Court-sealed copy of the document, a correctly completed document advice form for each company registrar to whom a copy of the document is to be sent, and the associated certificates and transfers.

The Centre checks the authenticity of the documents and produces photocopies, which are certified as true copies and dispatched to companies or registrars for registration. They would then act upon the document received from the Centre in exactly the same way as if they had had an original or certified true copy of the document lodged with them direct.

In order to protect companies or registrars, member firms of The Stock Exchange are required to do the following:

1. Undertake to submit the actual document to any company or registrar who may require sight of it.
2. Indemnify the company and registrar against any loss or liability that may arise from the information provided in the document advice.
3. Ensure that the document advice is completed correctly and that the indemnity section is signed only by an authorised signatory of the firm of stockbrokers.

The name and address of the original agent to whom queries regarding missing certificates may be referred, e.g. a solicitor dealing with the deceased's estate, should always be stated on the document advice form since it would save time if registrars were able to communicate with the original agents instead of having to do this via the firm of stockbrokers.

CHAPTER 6

Dividends

The arrangements for the payment of dividends on a company's shares or interest on its debentures and loan stocks is an important aspect of company secretarial practice and responsibility for these arrangement lies with the company secretary's department or with its registrar. Before dealing with the procedures to be followed and the related documents used, consideration needs to be given to the statutory powers and restrictions imposed on companies by the Act in regard to making distributions, as defined in the Act.

There is an implied power for trading companies to distribute their profits to the members subject to any limitations included in the Memorandum and Articles of Association or the prior rights, e.g. the payment of interest on debentures and loan stocks, and subject also to the provisions of the Act and the general law. In the case of shares (both ordinary shares and preference shares) the distributions are made in the form of dividends which are expressed as a specified amount of money per share – or per unit of stock in the case of companies whose ordinary capital is in the form of stock. Occasionally the dividend may be expressed as a percentage of the paid-up nominal value of the capital. In some older companies the provisions regarding the declaration of dividends are contained in the Memorandum, but it is the modern practice for the provisions governing the distribution of profits and the declaration of dividends to be included in the company's Articles.

In the case of a company with different classes of shares the Articles will provide for the priority of dividend payments, e.g. the fixed rate of dividend on the preference shares must be paid before any dividend is paid on the ordinary shares. Unless there are provisions to the contrary the preference dividends are presumed to be cumulative, which means that if in any year the profits of the company are insufficient to pay the fixed preference dividends, the entitlement will be carried forward to the next year or following years when the company may be in a position to make the payment. Some companies have participating preference

126

shares, which may be cumulative or non-cumulative; these shares give entitlement to a specified share in the profits related to the level of dividends paid on the ordinary shares, in addition to the fixed annual preferential dividend.

Table A, Regulations 102 and 103, provide that the company may declare dividends by Ordinary Resolution and that interim dividends may be paid by the directors subject to the provisions of the Act.

Restrictions on distributions under the Act

There are limits imposed on the company's power of distribution set out in ss.263–78. The Articles of some companies may also contain other provisions restricting sums out of which dividends may be paid, in which case the provisions of the Articles apply notwithstanding the provisions of the Act. A general summary of the restrictions imposed by the Act is as follows:

1. The cardinal rule is that private and public companies may only make distributions out of 'profits available for the purpose'. This means accumulated realised profits, so far as not previously utilised by a distribution or capitalisation, less accumulated realised losses so far as these have not previously been written off in a reduction or re-organisation of capital (s.263(1)–(3)). No distinction is made between capital profits and losses and revenue profits (s.280(3)) but, of course, dividends may only be paid out of profits realised on capital transactions and not out of capital itself.

2. 'Distributions' include all distributions whether or not in cash but do not include capitalisation issues of shares, the redemption or purchase of shares under the provisions of Chapter VII of Part V of the Act, formal reductions of share capital or distribution of assets to members on a winding-up (s.263).

3. There are provisions in the Act regarding the distinction between realised and unrealised profits; e.g. where depreciation provisions are written back on a revaluation, this is treated as giving rise to a realised profit (s.275(2)). If the directors are unable to ascertain whether a profit made prior to 22 December 1980 is a realised or an unrealised profit, they may treat the profit as realised or any loss as unrealised (s.263(5)).

4. Although there is no obligation to disclose in the company's audited accounts the extent to which reserves and/or retained profit are distributable, it is desirable that some internal record be kept and that the company's position in this respect on 22 December 1980 be agreed with the company's auditors.

5. There is an additional restriction in the case of a public company which may make a distribution only if at the time of the distribution the amount of its net assets is not less than the aggregate of its called up share capital and undistributable reserves and provided this position will remain the same after the distribution is made. The detailed provisions in this respect are contained in s.264.

6. In order to ascertain whether a distribution may be lawfully made under these provisions reference is made to the relevant accounts of the company, i.e. usually its latest audited annual accounts adjusted for any distributions made since those accounts were prepared. If, on the basis of these accounts, the proposed distribution would not be justified, reference may also be made to interim accounts which, if the company is a public company, must comply with s.272 and have been filed with the Registrar of Companies. Such accounts need not, however, be audited. In the case of a newly incorporated company, reference may be made to the initial accounts (s.273).

7. If the auditors have given a qualified report on the relevant accounts they must also make a statement in writing as to whether their reasons for giving a qualified report are material in determining whether the proposed distribution may be made, and a copy of the statement must have been laid before the company in general meeting (s.271). In the case of special category accounts, i.e. accounts of banking, shipping and insurance companies prepared under Schedule 9, a copy of the auditors' statement must also be filed with the Registrar of Companies with the relevant accounts. There are in addition special provisions applicable in the case of investment companies (ss.265 and 266) and insurance companies carrying on long-term insurance business (s.268).

Final and interim dividends

Table A, Regulation 102, and most companies' Articles of Association, provide for dividends to be declared by the company in general meeting by Ordinary Resolution, the amount not to exceed that recommended by the directors. These dividends are usually known as final dividends and are paid after the accounts for the year concerned have been laid before the company in general meeting. Table A, Regulation 103 and most companies' Articles also provide for the directors to pay, i.e. declare, interim dividends without the approval of the company in general meeting. The interim dividend is declared and paid between the general meetings of a company and is usually paid out of the profits for the first half year, although interim dividends may be declared and paid at any time during the year. American companies usually pay quarterly dividends and there is at least one British company with a large number of American shareholders which has adopted this practice.

Payment generally

Many factors need to be considered by a company when paying a dividend, e.g. the rights or needs of its own shareholders, the tax implications, arrangements with banks through which dividends are to be paid, requirements of The Stock Exchange, and the effect on the postal authorities if the number of warrants to be posted direct to shareholders is considerable. It used to be fairly simple for a company to pay dividends, prepare cheques and post them to shareholders with a letter explaining how the dividend was calculated, the letter serving as a tax voucher, and this is a procedure still adopted by some private companies. In the case of listed companies, however, with a large number of shareholders, the banking system provides services which can cope quickly and efficiently with the much larger number of dividend and other payments.

Mandates

Form and completion

It is to be expected that most shareholders will have bank accounts; consequently shareholders are encouraged to lodge mandates with the company authorising it to pay dividends on their shares direct to their individual bank accounts. In order that the company and the bank may receive all the details required to effect payment in this way, the Institute has prepared a standard form of dividend mandate known as 'Request for payment of interest or dividends'. The dividend mandate is the authority from the shareholder to the company to pay dividends becoming due to a specified branch of a specified bank. The mandate incorporates an authority to send dividends to a new branch of the bank if the company receives notice from a bank that the shareholder's bank account has been transferred to another branch. Mandates instructing that payment be made to a particular account at a bank should not be accepted since the company has no control over the destination of the dividend once it has been received by the bank. Companies should also not accept mandates limited to particular specified shareholdings, e.g. dividends on ordinary shares to be paid to one bank and dividends on a preference shareholding to be paid to another, since this could cause confusion in the event of changes of branch. The shareholder's objective in this respect should be achieved by applying a designation to one account in the company's Register of Members, i.e. a specified number or identifying letters to one of the accounts in the Register of Members, the shareholder signing a separate dividend mandate for each holding.

Dividend mandates should be signed by the shareholder; if there are joint holders, the dividend mandate should be signed by all the joint holders. In the case of a corporate body the mandate may be signed by an official who should state his office. In the case of administrators, attorneys, executors, etc., or any other person acting on behalf of the shareholder, the authority under which they sign the dividend mandate must be registered with the company.

Routeing of mandates

Companies should not receive mandates direct from shareholders and any mandates so received should be returned to the shareholder with a request that it is lodged with the company by the shareholder's bank. The submission of the mandate through the bank, authenticated by the stamp of the branch of the bank on the mandate form, ensures that the mandate contains the correct address and title of the branch, the branch's sorting code number and the account number to which the dividend is to be credited. Companies should also make sure that they receive mandates on the accepted standard form of mandate approved by the Institute.

The bank sorting code number consists of three groups of two figures separated by dashes. The first two figures indicate the bank concerned and the other two groups indicate the branch of the bank concerned. These figures are also shown on the bank's cheques. The use of bank sorting code numbers, associated with the bank customer's personal account number, facilitates the electronic sorting processes in the credit-clearing system. The reason for the submission of mandates through banks to the company is that the Committee of London Clearing Bankers and the Committee of Scottish Clearing Bankers, as well as the Trustee Savings Bank, accept full liability in respect of the customers' bank account numbers shown on the dividend mandate form and bearing the stamp of the bank. It is for this reason that mandates should never be accepted direct from shareholders, even if they know their bank's sorting code number and their own individual account number.

The sorting code and a customer's account number are used in connection with the payment of dividends under the bulk distribution system, which is described more fully below. Occasionally it may be necessary to send individual warrants direct to other banks and in such cases, the numbers should also be given on the individual warrants to ensure that the dividend reaches its correct destination.

Registration of mandates

It is not usual to send acknowledgements to shareholders when dividend mandates are received from their banks, especially in the case of the larger companies. The shareholder will be aware that his instructions have been received by the crediting of the next dividend to his bank account.

Dividend mandates must be recorded when received by the company and, although it may be convenient to record this information in the Register of Members, it should be omitted from any Register of Members which is kept for inspection by the public. Companies still using address plates must prepare a new plate giving the branch title, address, shareholder's name, bank account number and sorting code number of the bank to which the dividend is to be sent. The majority of companies, however, will have a computer system in use, in which case the mandate instructions are processed as input to the computer records and the computer would print the warrants for each shareholder with the required information. If the company uses the bulk payment system, however, one warrant only is issued and sent to a designated central office of each bank.

When notification is received from a female shareholder that she has married it is desirable for a company to obtain confirmation from her of any existing mandate instruction because, as a result of the marriage, the shareholder may have changed her address and/or her bank. This is not necessary, however, in the case of a mere change of name, e.g. the grant of a title.

The lodgement of a power of attorney with the company does not affect the payment of dividends in accordance with any existing mandate unless the attorney has been given specific authority under the power to give a dividend mandate himself, in which case he may request the company to pay the dividends either to himself or to a bank.

It saves the company time and money if shareholders agree to mandate their dividends to a bank. To encourage them to do this some companies include a form of mandate on the back of the dividend warrants sent out direct to the shareholders whose dividends are not mandated. This is not a very satisfactory procedure, however, and the best plan is to send out the normal approved mandate form with the dividend warrants from time to time with an explanatory note setting out the advantages to the shareholder and to the company of mandating dividends, and informing the shareholder that if he does wish to mandate his dividends in future, he should complete the form and send it to his bank for onward transmission to the company in the usual way.

Non-bank mandates

These are sometimes known as third party mandates, where for personal reasons a shareholder may wish his dividends to be paid to some other person instead of to a bank, e.g. a firm of solicitors or accountants or a building society. They are, however, not frequently received. Table A, Regulation 106, and most common forms of Articles of Association, do not contain any provision for a company to refuse to accept a dividend mandate no matter in whose favour it may be given.

Revocation and lapsing of mandates

A mandate may be revoked at any time by the shareholder giving notice in writing to the company. It also lapses automatically upon the death of the shareholder, when the company should withhold payment of further dividends until the appointment of executors or administrators has been registered. It would then be in order for the company to accept instructions from the personal representative for the payment of dividends. If one of the holders in a joint account should die the dividend mandate continues to apply. There may, however, be a separate account in the name(s) of the survivor(s), in which case the accounts would normally be merged in the Register of Members. On the other hand, if on the accounts in question there were mandates in favour of different banks or branches the company would need to seek further instructions before merging the accounts. If it is desired to keep the two accounts separate so that the accounts may have different mandates applicable to them it will be necessary to designate one of the accounts, since the accounts will both be in the same names. It should be noted that a bankruptcy or protection order (or in Scotland the appointment of a *curator bonis* or judicial factor) does not, of itself, terminate a dividend mandate, although the receiver, trustee, curator or factor may give his own instructions which will supersede those on the original mandate.

In the case of a small company with few shareholders the closing of an account in the Register of Members does not involve the lapse of the dividend mandate, which would be revived if the account were to be re-opened. However, it is impracticable to follow this procedure in the case of large companies since the accounts in question will be moved to a closed section of the Register, either by the removal of the account cards or appropriate computer input instructions. Consequently, if a new account should be opened, fresh dividend instructions should be obtained.

Change of branch notice

The issue of change of branch notices by banks to companies (or to their registrars) in which their customers have shareholdings is convenient for the customer who transfers his account to another branch of the same bank. The issue of such a notice also enables the bank to notify the company in the event of the removal of the branch to a new address and the customer consequently wishes to transfer his account to another branch which is more convenient. It is usual for a company to receive change of branch notices shortly after the payment of a dividend since the payment of the dividend to the old branch will bring to light the need for a change. It has already been noted that the standard form of dividend mandate already includes the shareholder's authority for the bank to notify the company or its registrars of another branch to which the dividends are to be sent and there is a standard form for a change of branch notice agreed between the banks and the Institute. The existing branch prepares and signs the notice, which is then passed on to the new branch, which inserts and verifies the details of its sorting code number and account number of the customer. The notice is then stamped by the bank in confirmation of this information and forwarded to the company to be recorded, as in the case of an original mandate form.

Like the ordinary dividend mandate, the change of branch notice applies to all shares and stocks of any class which are currently registered or may in future be registered in the name(s) of the shareholder(s) concerned. A change of branch notice limited to a particular holding or class of shares or stocks should not be accepted by a company, although the existing holding may be mentioned for reference and identification purposes. It should be noted that a change of branch notice may not be used if the customer transfers his account to a different bank altogether, as this would be outside the authority given in the original mandate by shareholder to the company. In the event of a shareholder changing his bank he should be given a new mandate for completion. A change of branch notice should not be accepted if it is not possible to identify the notice with the original mandate given by the shareholder. The procedure for recording an acceptable bank change of branch notice on receipt by the company is the same as that which applies in the case of an original mandate.

Banks' bulk distribution system/automated credit clearing

The use of this system by companies for the payment of dividends on shares and interest on their loan stocks involves the issue of one warrant (i.e. a cheque) by a company to a designated central office of each of the major banks covering the total amount of the dividends and/or interest payable to those shareholders who are customers of that bank and who have given mandates in favour of branches of that bank. It is, however, necessary to prepare individual tax vouchers for each shareholder in respect of each payment and these are sent by the company to the bank with a schedule listing all the payments to be made by that bank. The schedule will show the sorting code number (and perhaps also the title of the branch concerned), the names of the shareholders/stockholders, the amounts of dividend or interest to be paid to them and the total of the amounts listed. This should, of course, agree with the total of the individual tax vouchers sent to the bank. The banks require that the schedule and tax vouchers should be lodged with at least 7 working days before the dividend payment date to allow them time in which to make the arrangements for shareholders'/stockholders' accounts at the branches to be credited on the payment date.

The central office of each bank distributes the individual tax vouchers to the branches concerned and these are in due course sent to the customer with his bank statement or, perhaps, to the customer's tax adviser if this has been requested by the customer. It will be appreciated that banks have to handle an enormous volume of these tax vouchers and they have consequently introduced a mechanical sorting process. To facilitate this the tax vouchers must be prepared in a particular way with regard to the information to be shown and the position of the information on the vouchers. Accordingly, a standard type of tax voucher has been introduced which companies or their registrars are required to use and which is known as 'Standard 32' (see below).

Bulk distribution of dividends and interest payments through the bank is advantageous to companies in that it reduces postage and stationery costs for the envelopes in which individual dividend warrants and accompanying tax vouchers have to be sent to each individual shareholder/stockholder. Putting thousands of warrants into envelopes and stamping or franking the envelopes takes up a considerable amount of time. There is a further saving to the company in that the number of paid warrants to be checked against dividend/interest lists or bank statements is considerably reduced. There is also a reduction in the number of warrants which may go astray, e.g. because the shareholder/ stockholder has changed his address and has not notified the company or its registrar, although his bank account would, perhaps, have remained unchanged. The advantages to the shareholder/stockholder are that the risk of loss of the dividend or interest warrant in the post is reduced and the amount of his dividend or interest payment will be credited to his bank account on the due date for payment without the need for him to go to his bank in order to pay in the warrant.

There is one possible disadvantage to companies: since the cheque for the total dividend or interest payment payable to each bank has to be dispatched to the bank 7 days prior to the actual payment date the company may suffer loss of bank interest if the amount is debited to the company's bank account upon receipt by the banks. However, it will usually be possible to avoid this if appropriate funding arrangements are made with the company's bankers.

An alternative system for the bulk distribution of dividends to banks to that described above is to make the dividend payments through the banks' electronic payment system which is used by some companies; banks now tend to prefer this system. However, in this case the company must send the tax vouchers by post to each shareholder and the cost of this nullifies to some extent the convenience of the electronic payments system from the company's point of view.

Dividend warrants

Regulation 106 of Table A provides that dividends may be paid by cheque, usually called a warrant in most companies' Articles, and that these may be posted to shareholders.

There is a standard form of dividend/interest warrant and related tax voucher which has been agreed by all parties concerned, including the Institute, the banks and The Stock Exchange. It is Standard 32, *Dividend and Interest Warrants and Related Tax Vouchers*, published by the Association for Payment Clearing Services (APACS) and it is obtainable from APACS at 14 Finsbury Square, London EC2A 1BR.

The Stock Exchange requires that, in the case of limited securities, the full identifying code should be printed in a box 'Securities Code' to be located as close as possible to the top right hand corner of the tax voucher. Security code numbers are published against the names of companies in The Stock Exchange Daily Official List. The Stock Exchange has special requirements in the case of warrants and tax vouchers for convertible loan stocks or stocks carrying subscription rights.

Because of the large number of shareholders and the increase in the number of warrants to be issued it is now usual for warrants to bear printed facsimile signatures of the persons authorised by the company to sign them. In this case the banks require an indemnity from the company to protect them against the issue of unauthorised warrants. The banks also require the indemnity to cover the issue of warrants showing the amount in figures only instead of in both words and figures.

Tax vouchers

The tax voucher is a statement and explanation to the shareholder or stockholder which shows the number of shares (or the amount of stock) on which payment has been made, the tax credit (in the case of a dividend payment) or the income tax deducted (in the case of an interest payment), and the net amount payable. Tax vouchers for interest payments also show the gross amount payable. The tax voucher includes a certificate by the secretary to the effect that the tax credit or the income tax deducted will be accounted for to the Inland Revenue. The tax voucher should conform to Standard 32 mentioned above if the company uses the banks' bulk distribution system and automated credit clearing. APACS and the banks are very willing to assist in ensuring that the correct information is included on the voucher and that there are no problems with regard to the reading of the vouchers by the banks' electronic equipment.

Some countries have double taxation agreements with the United Kingdom and residents of those countries who are holders of debentures or loan stocks of UK companies may receive their interest payments without deduction of income tax at the basic rate or under deduction of tax at a reduced rate. Non-resident holders of equity capital (i.e. ordinary shares) may in some cases also receive their dividend payments with the tax credit appropriate to a dividend subject to UK withholding tax instead of the normal UK tax credit.

The authority for payment of interest and dividends to such non-resident shareholders or stockholders is issued by the Inland Revenue; companies should therefore not make special arrangements (including the preparation of amended or special tax vouchers) until the authority is received from the Inland Revenue, which will identify the shareholder's/stockholder's account precisely and set out the reduced rate of tax to be applied or the rate of tax credit to be allowed.

The use of machinery

The use of addressing machines with stencils or plates for the preparation of dividend warrants is decreasing as more and more companies make use of a computer. Accounting machines may also be used for the purpose of payment of dividends and interest, with punch card systems as well; but, here again, the use of such methods is becoming less widespread.

Continuous stationery is widely used for the preparation of warrants and tax vouchers; after going through the printing machine these are passed through another machine which separates the individual warrants and attached tax vouchers and removes the perforated edges. Machines are also available for inserting the separated warrants and vouchers into envelopes. The use of continuous stationery will most frequently be found in the case of companies which use a computer for their dividend run. When the Register of Members has been brought up to date, as at the record date for the payment of the dividend, the rate of dividend is put into the computer, which is programmed to produce the warrants, tax vouchers and a payment list, at the same time storing the totals of the numbers of shares, the amount of tax credits and the amount payable.

Payment procedure

The payment of a dividend needs to be very carefully planned and it is of great assistance if, in advance of the payment of each dividend, a control statement is prepared setting out all the various steps which have to take place so as to ensure that nothing is overlooked. In preparing a control statement, the following points should be remembered:

1. In the case of listed companies, the Continuing Obligations, para. 6, requires that the Exchange be informed of the date of any board meetings at which a declaration or recommendation of a dividend is to be considered. It is helpful if this information is sent to The Stock Exchange at least 10 days prior to the date of the board meeting so that it may be published. Immediately after the board meeting at which a dividend is declared or recommended, The Stock Exchange should be informed. The announcement of the dividend will usually be accompanied by the company's half-yearly report or preliminary figures for the year, and this would be sent to The Stock Exchange at the same time. The contents to be included in the half-yearly report or preliminary profits statement are given in the Continuing Obligations, para. 25.

    Announcements of dividends should follow The Stock Exchange's recommended record dates, a list of which is published every year for the guidance of companies. Adherence to these recommended dates facilitates The Stock Exchange's dividends claims procedure, enabling the shares to be dealt in on The Stock Exchange in ex-dividend form at the earliest possible date after the announcement. This reduces the number of dividend claims which have to be made against the seller of shares who may have sold his shares xd (i.e. ex-dividend), but whose shares are still registered in his name on the company's record date (see below) for the payment of the dividend. It is also helpful to include in the announcement the actual date of payment of the dividend.

    In the case of dividends on preference shares and interest payments on debentures and loan stocks which fall due for payment on fixed dates each year, The Stock Exchange should be advised of the record date for each payment.

2. Some companies close their Register of Members for the maximum permissible period of 30 days in any one year (s.358) in order to prepare lists of dividend or interest payments. The dates of the closing and opening of the Register should be published. This

procedure, however, has a major disadvantage in that, although staff can concentrate on preparation for payment of the dividend, there is a backlog of transfers lodged for registration during the period when the Register is closed until it is re-opened. It is more usual these days, therefore, to use a record date. Under this procedure all transfers received prior to the record date are posted to the Register of Members, the Register is then balanced and the dividend list drawn up. Transfers may continue to be registered after the record date but no dividends will, of course, be paid on the shares registered by those transfers.

In the case of listed companies where shares are registered through the TALISMAN system, The Stock Exchange transfer office should be notified of the balance registered in the name of SEPON Limited at the record date on the next SEPON advice completed after that date.

Table A, Regulation 106, and most companies' Articles, provide that in the case of joint holders of shares the company is legally bound to pay the dividend to the first-named shareholder in the joint account.

The company need not concern itself if at the time of the record date a shareholder had disposed of all or part of his holding and the transfer has not been registered by the record date in favour of the purchaser of the transferor's shares. As mentioned above the company is bound to pay the dividend to the registered shareholder at the record date, and it is the responsibility of the purchaser's stockbrokers to claim the dividend from the seller. This is accomplished by claims between the stockbrokers concerned, usually through the TALISMAN system. Since the tax voucher for the dividend will have gone to the seller of the shares together with the dividend payment, the purchaser's stockbrokers, when they receive the dividend, will provide the purchaser with their own form of certificate giving the tax credit deducted from the dividend or the amount of income tax deducted from an interest payment on debenture or loan stock, which is acceptable to the Inland Revenue. Claims only arise if the shareholder has purchased his shares cum dividend; no claim arises if the shareholder purchased his shares ex-dividend since the amount of the dividend would have been taken into account by adjustment of the share price on The Stock Exchange on the first day on which the shares were quoted ex-dividend. In this case the dividend belongs to the seller, who may retain the dividend on receiving it although he has sold his shares. The schedule of dates, referred to above, should be adhered to so as to minimise claims.

If a transaction in shares is effected outside The Stock Exchange, the right to any current or pending dividend will have to be settled between the parties concerned. This is of no concern to the company, who will pay the dividend to the registered holder on the record date.

3. The draft of the dividend warrant and tax voucher should be prepared in good time to allow for any corrections necessary to the proof. The bulk order for printing can be given to the printers when the rate of dividend is known. At the time of the Budget it is necessary to bear in mind the possibility of a change in the basic rate of income tax. When part of the dividend will be distributed through the banks' bulk payment system a separate supply of tax vouchers should be ordered in the form of Standard 32. It is usual for warrants to be serially numbered and also for each dividend payment to be given its own identifying number. This assists in reconciling different dividend accounts. If there are several classes of stock on which dividends are to be paid it is a good idea to use different coloured paper for each class of security. If the information relating to the amount of dividend and the tax credit (or gross and net interest payments in the case of debentures and loan stocks) has to be inserted by hand and the company has a large number of shareholders with, e.g. 100 or 500 shares each, it could save work if a supply of warrants for these holdings were to be printed with the relevant information already inserted. Arrangements should also be made to keep in stock a supply of unnumbered warrants and vouchers to use when warrants or vouchers are damaged or mislaid or lost in the post and have to be replaced.

4. An adequate supply of dividend sheets and window envelopes should be kept and, in view of the fact that the size of dividend warrants and tax vouchers is standard, it will be economical to lay in a substantial stock of envelopes which can be used over the next few years.

5. Postage costs may be saved by using special facilities provided by the Post Office for bulk posting.

6. Arrangements should be made to ensure that all transfers, transmission documents, probates, confirmations, letters of administration, marriage certificates, changes of address, dividend mandates, etc., received up to the close of business on the record date are duly processed so that the dividends or interest payments may be correctly dispatched. It should also be checked whether there are any stop notices or other restraints on dividends; if so, the relevant payments must be withheld.

7. The dividend sheets should be run off either using addressograph plates or the other machinery in use for the purpose. If it is possible to programme the printing machinery on a selective basis it may be

desirable to omit the addresses from the dividend sheets in order to save space. In the case of a computerised system the dividend record sheets and completed warrants will be produced simultaneously.

8. With a manual system each shareholder's holding has to be entered on the dividend sheets with the amount of dividend and tax credit alongside his name. The overall total of the number of shares on which the dividend is paid should agree with the company's issued capital and the columns relating to the tax credits and net dividends balanced to the total amount of the payment. It will, of course, be necessary to round off net payments resulting in odd fractions of a penny but the total of the dividends to be paid should not exceed the total cost of the dividend when calculated by reference to the company's issued capital. In the case of a manual system the warrants and vouchers will need to be fully addressed from plates or stencils for dispatch. The information on the warrants and vouchers should agree with that shown on the dividend sheets and, to make sure that they have been accurately completed, the warrants should be totalled and agreed with the totals on the dividend sheets.

9. If the banks' bulk distribution system is being used a separate series of the dividend sheets should be prepared relating to each bank and tax vouchers should be prepared for each item on these lists. A cheque for the total amount for each bank as shown on the dividend list for the bank concerned, together with the tax vouchers for customers of that bank, would be sent with the lists to the head office address of the bank designated for the receipt of these documents. A list of bank sorting code numbers, titles and postal addresses of each branch of banks in the United Kingdom, and the designated head office addresses to which the lists, dividend and interest tax vouchers and cheques should be forwarded for transmission through the clearing banks' bulk distribution system is given in the *Directory of Sorting Code Numbers* published by Thomas Skinner Directories which also publishes the *Bankers' Almanack and Year Book*. The documents should be received by the bank at least 7 working days before the payment date.

10. In the case of warrants sent direct to shareholders who have not mandated their dividends, each one should be signed. The signature may be applied either autographically (i.e. handwritten) or with a machine-affixed facsimile signature which involves passing each warrant through a machine for the signature to be applied. As already mentioned earlier in this chapter, however, in the case of most large companies, the signatures will be preprinted on the warrants, usually in facsimile form. If, following the record date, documents other than transfers and transmissions have been

received appointing personal representatives of a deceased shareholder, change of name on marriage, etc., the shareholder's warrant should be withdrawn and endorsed appropriately prior to dispatch. It may also be possible to deal with some changes of address or the receipt of bank mandates before dispatch of the warrants. There may be other queries in relation to a holding, e.g. the advice of a death in respect of which the grant of probate has not yet been received by the company with the names and addresses of the executors or administrators. In these circumstances the warrants concerned should be withdrawn and retained until lodgement of probate or letters of administration. If it is known that the shareholder's previous dividend warrant has remained uncashed a reminder letter about the uncashed warrant could be sent with the new dividend warrant although, since possibly 6 months will have elapsed since the dispatch of the first warrant, it may be necessary to request a shareholder to return the warrant to the company or to the registrar for re-dating. It may be found that a number of earlier warrants have remained unpaid, despite the reminder, and in this case it would be advisable to withdraw and retain further warrants until the matter of the shareholder's whereabouts can be clarified. However, it is necessary to observe the provisions of the company's Articles of Association with regard to the dispatch of dividend warrants which may prohibit this. In the case of listed companies, the Yellow Book, Section 9, Chapter 1, para. 15.1 provides that where companies take power in their Articles to cease sending dividend warrants by post because warrants have been returned undelivered or left uncashed the power will not be exercised until such warrants have been returned or left uncashed on two consecutive occasions.

11. Although some companies only maintain one dividend account it is convenient to ask the bank to open a separate account for each dividend designated with the title and the identifying number of the dividend payment, and for the total amount of the dividend to be credited to this account on the payment date by transfer from the company's current or deposit account. Of course, the bank should already have had instructions informing it of the persons appointed by board resolution to open and operate banking accounts in the name of the company. If only one dividend account is maintained, i.e. in respect of the current dividend in course of payment, it will be necessary to open an unclaimed dividend account to which would be transferred any amounts which remained unclaimed at the time of funding the dividend account to pay a new dividend. Even if more than one dividend account is maintained it would be undesirable to

leave separate dividend accounts open indefinitely and balances on earlier separate dividend accounts may be transferred to an unclaimed dividend account when the quantity of old warrants being presented for payment on specific dividend accounts becomes reduced to a trickle.

12.   Putting warrants in envelopes is a tedious chore for many companies, although this may be assisted by special machines which will seal and frank the envelopes. The envelopes should be dispatched in time to be received by shareholders on the payment date, the date of posting being dependent on whether the company uses first class or second class post for sending out dividend warrants.

13.   Inevitably a number of envelopes containing warrants will be returned by the Post Office as undeliverable, usually because the shareholder has not notified the company of a change of address or advised the company after the warrants were sent. Efforts should be made to trace the new address of these shareholders by making enquiries of the bank at which warrants for previous dividends were paid in or, if it is the first dividend sent to a new shareholder, through the stockbroker who acted for the purchaser. On TALISMAN transactions the stockbroker acting for the purchaser is shown on the TALISMAN bought transfer.

Some warrants may be returned because the shareholder has died and these should be retained until probate or letters of administration are received in the case of a sole shareholder, or the death certificate relating to a shareholder who was the first-named in a joint account. These warrants may then be appropriately endorsed and, if necessary re-dated and reissued to the persons entitled to receive them.

In the case of the banks' bulk distribution system some of the tax vouchers may be returned by the banks with cheques in refund of the dividends represented by the vouchers returned because the shareholders concerned have died or have closed their account with the bank. These refund cheques should be paid into the current dividend account if the dividend is still in course of payment, the appropriate earlier dividend account or into the unclaimed dividend account if the money for that dividend has been transferred to that account. Efforts should then be made to try to trace the shareholders concerned.

14.   After the payment date batches of paid warrants, accompanied by a bank statement, will be received from the bank. The paid warrants should be checked against the bank account and the dividend lists so that eventually a list of outstanding uncashed warrants can be

prepared, the total of such warrants agreeing with the bank balance. Now that the banks use electronic sorting equipment it is possible for the warrants to be sorted into numerical order, providing details of the outstanding warrants and the balance of the dividend account. This greatly facilitates the work in the company.

Unclaimed dividends

When dividends are paid direct to shareholders the warrants may occasionally go astray in the post, e.g. because of incorrect addresses. Some shareholders do not bank their warrants immediately they receive them and this sometimes results in the warrant being mislaid in the shareholder's home. Outstanding unpaid dividend warrants are a nuisance to the company and it is usual for companies to indicate on the warrants that unless they are paid within 6 months they will have to be returned to the company for re-dating.

Accordingly, about a month before the expiration of the 6-month period, it is a good idea to write to shareholders who have not yet banked their dividend warrants to remind them to do so, in the hope that they will then pay them into their bank account; if they do, these warrants may then be debited against the current dividend account before that account is closed and the balance on the account transferred to the unclaimed dividend account when the new dividend is to be paid. Of course, as mentioned above, some companies may keep previous dividend accounts open for some time before transferring balances to unclaimed dividend accounts; but it is still desirable to remind shareholders to pay in their dividend since failure to act on the reminder may serve as a warning to the company that the shareholder may have changed his address.

This first reminder could be followed by the issue of a further reminder notice with the next dividend payment sent out to the shareholder, to the effect that the previous warrant is still unpaid and requesting that it be returned for re-dating if more than 6 months have elapsed. If the shareholder should indicate that the warrant has been lost, a duplicate will be issued against signature of a simple form of indemnity or, if the dividend is not of a large amount, by signing an undertaking. The difference between the indemnity and an undertaking is that in the case of an indemnity the shareholder undertakes to indemnify the company against any losses which it may incur as a result of the issue of a duplicate warrant; in the case of the undertaking the shareholder merely agrees to return to the company for cancellation the original warrant if it should ever be found. Before the issue of a duplicate warrant payment of the original warrant should be stopped at the bank and an appropriate note made on the dividend sheets. If it is found that the shareholder has died the usual procedure followed on receipt of notice of death of a shareholder should be followed, i.e. the dividend withheld until probate, letters of administration or confirmation is lodged.

It is in the company's interests to clear outstanding dividends as quickly as possible since the queries arising may result in a need to alter the Register of Members and it is desirable for this to be kept as up to date as possible. Similarly, prompt action should be taken in the event of the return as undeliverable of copies of the company's report and accounts sent to shareholders. At least two dividend warrants should be sent to shareholders before action is taken to withhold the dispatch of further warrants and, indeed, in the case of listed companies, The Stock Exchange requires that dividend warrants should not be withheld unless two consecutive dividend payments have been returned as undeliverable or left uncashed. It is necessary, however, to have the appropriate authority in the company's Articles since if the company's Articles follow Table A, Regulation 106, it could be argued that the company has no right to withhold the dispatch of dividend warrants to shareholders. Clearly, from the security point of view, it is unwise to continue to send out dividend warrants when it is known that they will not be received by the shareholder or, if received, will not be acted upon by him. Moreover, if the reason for the non-delivery of the dividend warrant is that the shareholder has changed his address, the new occupier at the old address will be subject to considerable annoyance by the continuing receipt of money for the previous occupier. The annoyance will be increased if the new occupier has returned the dividend warrant to the company with a covering letter from himself to the effect that the shareholder has moved.

Dividends become statute barred (in England) under the Limitation Act 1980 after 12 years from the date of declaration, although some courts have held that the period may be 6 years. In the case of Scotland, the Prescription and Limitation (Scotland) Act 1973 applies and the limitation period is 5 years after the date of declaration. However, most companies do not dispute dividend payments, since the publication in the company's accounts of the unclaimed dividends may be held to be an acknowledgement of the debt by the company – which means that the limitation periods start afresh each time an entry is made in the accounts.

In order to deal with this matter, therefore, The Stock Exchange is agreeable to listed companies including in their Articles of Association the following powers:

1. To forfeit dividends which have not been claimed for 12 years or more after the date of declaration.
2. To sell shares of untraceable shareholders, the company retaining the

net sale proceeds of the shares pending the possible receipt of claims from the shareholders concerned.

To meet The Stock Exchange's requirements in this respect, however, the Articles must stipulate the following:

1. During a period of 12 years at least three dividends in respect of the shares in question have become payable and no dividend during that period has been claimed.
2. On expiry of the 12 years the company gives notice by advertisement in two national newspapers of its intention to sell the shares and notifies the Quotations Department of The Stock Exchange of that intention (Yellow Book, Section 9, Chapter 1, para. 15.2).

Of course, once the shares have been sold, no further dividends have to be paid on them.

In order to effect the transfer of the shares sold the directors authorise a person to execute the TALISMAN sold transfer on behalf of the untraced member; it is also desirable for the secretary to make a statutory declaration that the provisions of the Articles have been satisfied. The action taken will then be conclusive and binding on the member.

Duplicate tax vouchers

It has already been noted that companies are required to issue with every dividend or interest warrant a voucher relating to the tax credit or tax deducted applicable to the payment. Shareholders who are entitled to reclaim the tax credit or tax deducted sometimes find, when preparing their tax repayment claims, that they have mislaid the tax vouchers which they are required to submit in support of their claims; consequently, they ask the company to issue duplicates. Duplicate tax vouchers may be issued without an indemnity but they should be clearly marked duplicate, and some companies make a nominal charge for the issue of duplicate tax vouchers. Requests for duplicate tax vouchers may also be received from a shareholder's accountant or other taxation adviser.

Scrip dividends

Some companies allow shareholders to elect whether to receive dividends in the form of shares instead of in cash. This is effected by the issue of fully paid shares to equity shareholders in lieu of cash dividends, but authority to do this but must be contained in the company's Articles. The advantage to the shareholder is that he is able to build up his shareholding in the company without incurring brokerage expenses and (until they are abolished under the 1990 Budget proposals when TAURUS is implemented, probably towards the end of 1991) stamp duty expenses; the advantage to the company is that the money which would be distributed in cash as dividends is retained in the business for the benefit of the company and the company also saves advance corporation tax on dividends which are not paid in cash. However, the value of the shares issued is still taxed as a distribution of income in the same way as a cash dividend, which means that the shareholder must be provided with a tax voucher. Many companies now follow the practice of offering scrip dividends which is popular with some shareholders.

The procedure for dealing with a scrip dividend is as follows:

1. Ensure that the company's Articles give power to the board to offer shareholders the right to elect to receive new ordinary shares in the company instead of receiving a dividend in cash. If not, the company's articles may be altered by a Special Resolution at a general meeting to give this power.
2. At a general meeting of the company (usually the Annual General Meeting) the authority of the shareholders should be sought by an Ordinary Resolution for the board to offer shareholders the right to elect to receive new ordinary shares instead of cash for all or any part of any interim and final dividends for the financial period of the company ending on the next accounting date.
3. When the board declare an interim dividend or recommend a final dividend on the company's shares it should also resolve to make the offer of new shares to shareholders as an alternative to the cash dividend, subject, of course, in the case of the final dividend, to that dividend being approved by shareholders at the annual general meeting.
4. Entitlement to the alternative scrip dividend instead of a cash dividend will be to those shareholders on the company's Register of Members on the record date for the dividend.
5. The price of the new shares will be determined by taking the average of the middle market quotations for the company's shares derived from *The Stock Exchange Daily Official List* for the five business days commencing on the date when the company's shares were first quoted ex-dividend on The Stock Exchange.
6. A circular letter is prepared to be sent to shareholders giving the price of the new shares determined as above and explaining the action they should take if they wish to receive new shares instead of the whole or any part of the cash dividend to which they are entitled. It would be stated in the circular that shareholders who do not wish to elect to receive any new shares need not take any action and that

their dividend will be paid in cash in the usual way on the payment date.

7. A form of election, which must be signed by the shareholder(s), is prepared to accompany the circular letter and these will be run through the company's or the company's registrar's computer system giving the following information in appropriate boxes:
    (a) number of shares held on dividend record date;
    (b) maximum number of shares on which election may be made (this number will be an exact multiple of the number of shares required to be elected to receive one new share);
    (c) number of shares on which the dividend will be paid in cash if the maximum number of shares is elected as in (b) above (i.e. the balance of the shares being less than the multiple required for one new share);
    (d) the maximum number of new shares to be issued if the maximum number of shares is elected as in (b) above;
    (e) the number of shares which the shareholder wishes to elect for new shares if he wishes to elect fewer than the maximum in (b) above.

8. Special dividend warrants will be prepared with boxes to show the number of elected shares and the number of non-elected shares on which the normal full cash dividend will be paid. On these dividend warrants the pence per share, tax credit and amount payable boxes will be as usual.

9. Shares elected for the scrip dividend may receive a nominal dividend of 0.01p per share once in each year, paid on the occasion of either the interim or the final dividend, in order to preserve the wider range investment status of the company's shares under the Trustee Investments Act 1961. The payment of a nominal dividend on the elected shares also serves the purpose of ensuring that shareholders who elect to receive shares instead of the full cash dividend will, as nearly as practicable, receive the same value as if they had received the full cash dividend.

10. New share certificates will be prepared for each shareholder for the number of shares issued in lieu of cash dividend. These certificates should have a counterfoil attached showing information as to the number of shares on which a valid share election was made, number of new shares allotted, total cash equivalent of new shares allotted (i.e. the cash dividend multiplied by the number of shares elected) and the notional tax (i.e. what would have been the tax credit if the dividend on the elected shares had been paid in cash). This information is to assist shareholders in preparing their income tax returns. The counterfoil should also state the number of shares on

which the full cash dividend is being paid for which a separate tax counterfoil with the dividend warrant attached will be received as in item 8 above. It is usual to attach to the counterfoil sent with share certificates an explanatory note explaining how the figures in the counterfoil have been determined. (Note: Each shareholder would thus receive two tax counterfoils as in (8) and (10) above, unless his holding amounted to an exact multiple of the number of shares required for the issue of a new share in lieu of the cash dividend so that no cash dividend was payable to that shareholder, except on the occasion when a nominal dividend had to be paid).

11. A sum equal to the aggregate nominal amount of the new ordinary shares allotted pursuant to the elections for new shares made by shareholders will be capitalised out of any amount standing to the credit of any reserve or fund (including the profit and loss account), as determined by the directors.

12. Application will be made to The Stock Exchange for the new shares issued as scrip dividends to be listed.

It is usual for companies offering scrip dividends to notify shareholders on the occasion of each dividend payment of the terms on which scrip dividends may be elected for that particular dividend. This is because the terms depend upon the rate of dividend and the price of the company's shares at the time in question. This also gives shareholders the opportunity of deciding on each occasion whether or not they wish to receive that particular dividend in the form of shares rather than in cash. This does not arise, of course, in the case of those shareholders who have given the company continuing scrip dividend mandates.

Some companies have introduced scrip dividend mandates. If the shareholder signs a scrip dividend mandate, all his future dividends (except for any part of his dividend which is paid in cash in respect of any balance of his holding of shares which does not make up the multiple required for a new share) will be in the form of shares until he cancels the mandate. However, a company may adopt an alternative procedure where shareholders have given scrip dividend mandates, of carrying forward to the next dividend payment any balance of the cash dividend on shares which are insufficient in number to make up the multiple required for a new share, to be added to the amount of the next dividend payment and the total is then used for the purpose of the scrip dividend on that occasion, any balance of cash then arising again being carried forward. The company secretarial procedure described above for the implementation of a scrip dividend scheme would have to be appropriately modified in the case of shareholders who had signed scrip dividend mandates.

In the case of shareholders who have also signed ordinary dividend mandates for their dividends to be paid into a bank, the payment made to the bank would comprise the cash dividend on the balance of their shareholding which did not add up to the multiple required for the allocation of a new share under the scrip dividend scheme or the amount of nominal dividend paid on elected shares of 0.01p per share in order to preserve trustee status under the Trustee Investments Act 1961. Thus bank mandates still operate for the purpose of any residue of dividend which has to be paid in cash irrespective of whether or not the shareholder has signed a scrip dividend mandate.

When prices on The Stock Exchange are volatile some companies may afford protection to their shareholders by providing that all share elections will be automatically withdrawn if by the date on which elections have to be received by the company the price of the company's shares has fallen to the extent that the market value of the shares received is substantially less than the cash dividend forgone. Some companies may propose a specific amount for this purpose, e.g. a fall of 15 per cent or more in the company's share price.

Dividend re-investment schemes

These should not be confused with scrip dividend schemes described above. Under these schemes a shareholder signs a mandate to the effect that all dividends on his shares in future be paid to the company or its registrar to be used in the purchase of additional shares in the company on the stock market and added to his existing holding. The shares are purchased as a single transaction on the day the dividend is paid at the current market price, taking advantage of the lower dealing costs involved in a bulk purchase, although the shareholder will have to pay stamp duty on the transaction with a minimum of 50p. However, this charge will not be payable when it is abolished under the 1990 Budget proposals to be brought in with the implementation of TAURUS, probably towards the end of 1991. A few weeks after each purchase particulars of the transaction are sent to the shareholder with a certificate for the additional shares purchased which are added to his holding and a tax voucher for the dividend paid. Any balance of dividend which is insufficient to buy one new share is carried forward in the shareholder's dividend re-investment account and added to the next dividend paid. This scheme is not often used by commercial companies but it is popular with investment trust companies in connection with regular savings schemes. It should be noted, however, that under these schemes there is no saving of advance corporation tax for the company and that the shares are purchased on the stock market and are not new shares issued by the company. There is thus no dilution of the company's share capital but at the same time the cash saved on the dividends which are not paid in cash is not retained in the company for its benefit as in the case of a scrip dividend scheme.

Waivers of dividends

Shareholders with substantial holdings, particularly directors of small companies, may elect to waive future dividend payments by signing a form of waiver under seal which, to be effective, must be received by the company prior to the declaration or payment of an interim dividend or the approval by shareholders of a recommended final dividend. In the case of listed companies, it is a requirement of The Stock Exchange that particulars of waivers be given in the company's annual report unless the amount(s) are minor and some payment has been made on each share during the relevant calendar year in order not to prejudice the status of the shares under the Trustee Investments Act 1961 (Continuing Obligations, para. 21(o)).

Where a listing is sought on The Stock Exchange disclosure of any waiver(s) of dividends must be made in the listing particulars and it must also be reported upon by the auditors in their report accompanying the listing particulars.

CHAPTER 7

Profit-sharing and share option schemes

Employees' share schemes

It has already been noted that a company is permitted to provide financial assistance for the purchase of its own shares in connection with an employees' share scheme. The power must be exercised by the company in good faith, and in the interests of the company (s.153 as amended by CA 1989 s.132). Employees' share schemes are defined in s.743 as schemes for encouraging or facilitating the holding of shares or debentures in a company by or for the benefit of the following:

1. The bona fide employees or former employees of the company, the company's subsidiary or holding company or a subsidiary of the company's holding company.
2. The wives, husbands, widows, widowers or children or step-children under the age of 18 of such employees or former employees.

The adoption of a scheme in the case of listed companies (or subsidiaries of listed companies) must be approved by an Ordinary Resolution of the shareholders (Yellow Book, Section 1, Chapter 3, para. 9). There are five types of scheme currently in use, four of which enjoy taxation concessions. These are as follows:

1. Profit-sharing schemes approved under ICTA s.186. Under these schemes funds are allocated by the company which are used to buy shares in the company, to be held on trust for employees within prescribed limits and for prescribed periods.
2. Savings related share option schemes approved under ICTA s.185. Under these schemes options are granted for the future purchase of shares at a price being not less than 80 per cent of the value of the shares at the date of grant of the options, the purchase money for these shares being provided under a Save As You Earn (SAYE) contract with either the Department for National Savings or a

151

building society. Prior to the Finance Act 1989, the price had to be not less than 90 per cent of the value of the shares at the date of grant of the options. Under the 1990 Budget proposals the banks will be able to offer SAYE contracts which may also be used in conjunction with these schemes.

3. Selective share option schemes also approved under ICTA s.185 under which options may be granted for the future purchase of shares at a price not manifestly less than the current price at the date of grant of the options.

4. Employee share ownership plans (ESOPs) under the Finance Act 1989 as amended by the 1990 Budget proposals, but also called employee share ownership trusts (ESOTs).

5. Unapproved share option schemes.

In view of the taxation concessions involved, the company's professional advisers and the Inland Revenue should be consulted at an early stage when the introduction of any of these schemes is under consideration.

The administration of these schemes usually devolves upon the company secretary and it is necessary, therefore, to consider how such schemes are approved and how they are administered.

Profit-sharing schemes

The main feature of these schemes is that the company determines each year a percentage of its profits to be allocated to the profit-sharing scheme for the purchase of shares in the company for the employees. On the basis of case law the amount paid by the company for this purpose is tax deductible for Corporation Tax.

Usually the company will create more shares for the purpose of the scheme, as agreed by the shareholders when the scheme was approved by them at a general meeting, instead of purchasing existing shares on The Stock Exchange. The annual limit for the amount of shares that may be given to employees under approved profit-sharing schemes has been increased by the Finance Act 1989 to £2,000 or 10 per cent of salary up to a maximum of £6,000.

The shares which are acquired for each employee are registered in the names of the trustees of the scheme and the law requires that the shares be held in trust for a minimum period of two years; under normal conditions employees cannot sell or otherwise dispose of their shares during that period. The trustees of a profit-sharing scheme may be a professional firm of trustees independent of the company.

Staff profit-sharing schemes were brought into effect by provisions in the Finance Act 1978 and Schedule 9 of that Act as amended but these provisions are now contained in ICTA principally ss.185, 186, Parts I, II, V, VI of Schedule 9 and Schedule 10 of that Act. This description of profit-sharing schemes is based on the law in force following amendments made by the Finance Act 1989. The schemes enjoy favourable tax treatment, as will be seen later, and they were introduced by the government to encourage the creation of employee shareholders who would then have the opportunity to participate in the profits of the company in which they worked. The company will first decide who shall be eligible to join the scheme. These may be full-time employees in the service of the company who have completed a continuous period of service for two years on the last day of the close of the company's financial year. Employees should be required to sign a form of acceptance to participate in the scheme in which they agree to be bound by its rules.

The amount of money to be allocated by the company to the scheme each year will be decided by the company in the light of its performance but there is an upper limit of 5 per cent of the profits that can be allocated to such schemes, which is set by the investment committees of the Association of British Insurers and the National Association of Pension Funds Limited, representing the interests of institutional investors and pension funds. The amount of profit allocated is then announced to the staff by means of notices or circulars to each employee eligible to participate in the scheme, informing him or her of the amount of money which constitutes their individual profit share.

The total amount of the profit share allocated to the scheme is paid by the company to trustees, who use the money to purchase shares in the company. As already mentioned new shares are usually created by the company for the purpose of the scheme and in order to meet the requirements of the legislation the share price is calculated by taking the range of prices quoted in *The Stock Exchange Daily Official List* over the three dealing days immediately following the announcement of the company's results for the year. On each of the three days one-quarter of the range between the bid and offer prices as published in the Official List is added to the bid price and the average of that amount over the three days is deemed to be the price at which shares can be issued to employees in the scheme. This price will be recorded as the initial market value of the shares issued to employees under the scheme. The following is an example as to how the cost of the shares allocated to the scheme is calculated:

Day No.	Bid	Offer	Plus 25% of range	Total
1	325p	345p	5p	330p
2	326p	346p	5p	331p
3	324p	344p	5p	329p

Average price over the three dealing days as described above equals 330p. (Note: the bid price is the price at which shares may be sold and the offer price is the price at which shares may be bought by investors on The Stock Exchange.)

In order to ascertain how much each employee will receive we will assume that the company's after tax profits amount to £10 million and that the company decides to allocate 3.5 per cent of this amount to its profit-sharing fund, i.e. £350,000. This sum of money is transferred to the trustees of the scheme to form the profit-sharing fund. The appropriation rate has then to be determined; this is the percentage of aggregate qualifying remuneration of all the employees eligible to participate in the scheme which the profit-sharing fund represents. This appropriation rate is then applied to each individual employee's qualifying remuneration to calculate his individual profit share in money terms. If the appropriation rate is 3.3 per cent and an employee's qualifying remuneration is £10,000, his individual profit share will amount to £330. Based on the share price of 330p, that employee would receive 100 shares in the scheme. Usually, however the allocation will not work out to an exact amount and the number of shares allocated to each employee will be rounded down and the excess money retained in the profit-sharing fund until the next appropriation date, i.e. the date on which shares are appropriated to participants in respect of an accounting period of the company. The locked in value for tax purposes of the 100 shares allocated to the employee in this instance will be £330.

A letter should be sent to each employee informing him of his profit share, to be followed in due course by a share appropriation statement giving the employee information under the following headings: the allotment number, the appropriation date, the number of shares allocated, the locked in value for tax purposes and the release date, i.e. the date on which the shares will automatically be released into the possession of the employee without any income tax liability. The release date is five years after the appropriation date.

The shares of each employee must be retained in the scheme for at least two years (the retention period) but if the employee then decides to have the shares transferred into his own name, either to keep them registered directly in his own name as an investment or to sell them, he will have to pay income tax on the locked in value. The amount of income tax that an employee will pay depends on the number of years that have elapsed from the date on which the shares were first allocated to him. The amount of income tax payable is determined by the table below:

Date of disposal after appropriation date	The percentage of the locked in value for tax purposes (or of the share proceeds if smaller) charged to income tax ('the appropriate percentage')
2 years or over, but less than 4 years	100%
4 years or over, but less than 5 years	75%
5 years or over	Nil

There is, however, provision that in the case of employees leaving the company before the release date as a result of injury, disability, redundancy or retirement, the shares may be transferred or sold even if the two-year retention period has not expired; the amount of income tax payable if the employee wishes to have the shares transferred into his name before the expiry of five years after the appropriation date in these circumstances is calculated on 50 per cent of the locked in value. An employee leaving service can still leave his shares with the trustees until the release date if he prefers to do this. If an employee resigns, however, the usual conditions of the scheme relating to income tax payable as in the table above continue to apply.

If the employee dies all the shares held by the trustees for the employee are released and his personal representatives can decide whether to sell the shares or transfer them to the deceased employee's estate. In either case no income tax is payable and no capital gains tax is payable on any rise in value of the shares up to the date of death.

The employee receives dividends on his shares while they are registered in the names of the trustees just as in the case of an ordinary shareholder; he is also sent copies of the company's annual report and accounts and interim statements. As he is not a shareholder, however, he cannot attend the company's Annual General Meeting. Nevertheless, in order to enable the participant to exercise his voting rights he will be issued with a proxy card on which he can direct the trustees as to how he would wish the votes represented by his shares in the scheme to be applied in the event of a poll being demanded on any resolution at a general meeting. If the company has a large number of employees in the scheme, it may wish to take advantage of s.251 inserted by CA 1989 s.15 and send a copy of a summary financial statement to each participant instead of the full annual report and accounts, subject to the right of any participant to request a copy of the full report and accounts if desired.

It should be noted that although there are special income tax provisions applicable on the sale of shares prior to the release date and that there is no income tax liability at all if shares are sold after the release date, there is a liability to capital gains tax on any increase in value of the shares over the locked in value for tax purposes when shares are sold if the total gains in a tax year exceed the annual capital gains tax exemption limit (£5,000 in 1990/1).

Variations of profit-sharing schemes

Some companies adopt a different type of sheme, i.e. not based on a yearly profit share for each participant for the purchase of shares. One of these is an arrangement under which the trustees use the participant's own money to buy shares in the company. The company then allocates more shares of equal value at no cost to the employee. Alternatively, the participant may transfer into the scheme shares he already owns. Shares bought with the participant's own money or shares he transfers into the scheme are called investment shares; shares provided by the company are called additional shares. Both the investment and the additional shares must be left with the company for two years, after which the investment shares may be sold if the employee wishes and, of course, no income tax is payable on the investment shares since these were purchased with his own money or were shares he already owned. The additional shares, however, are subject to the income tax rules previously described if sold before the release date. There is a liability to capital gains tax on both the investment and the additional shares if the capital gains tax exemption limit is exceeded.

Savings related share option schemes

Savings related share option schemes were introduced by provisions in the Finance Act 1980 as amended but these provisions are now contained in ICTA, principally ss.185, 187 and Parts I, II and III of Schedule 9 of that Act. This description of savings related share option schemes is based on the law in force following the Finance Act 1989. Under these schemes, a monthly paid employee may save any amount from £10 up to £150 per month and weekly paid employee anything from £2.50 per week up to £37.50 per week, under a 5- or 7-year Save As You Earn (SAYE) contract either with the Department for National Savings or with a building society. Under the 1990 Budget proposals the banks will be able to offer SAYE contracts for the purpose of these schemes. A company setting up a scheme may decide to restrict the savings related contract either to the Department for National Savings, a bank or to a building society, or give the employee the choice of deciding which he would prefer.

In the case of a monthly paid employee, a minimum total of 60 payments must be made, i.e. one per month for 5 years, at the end of which a tax free bonus is added to the amount saved. The bonus, currently equal to 14 monthly payments, is free of all tax and is guaranteed no matter what may happen to the level of interest rates during the period of the SAYE contract. In the case of the 7-year contract the bonus is equal to 28 monthly instalments. The bonus does not have to be declared on income tax returns. It is thus possible at the outset to determine how much the employee will have available at the end of the 5 years (or 7 years). In the case of an employee saving £40 per month, therefore, the amount saved after 60 payments will be £2,400 which, with the 5 year bonus, makes a total of £2,960.

The option to convert this amount into shares of the company arises after the 60 monthly payments have been made but the price at which the shares will be allocated is determined at the time the contract is started. The subscription price of shares under SAYE share schemes is an amount equal to not less than 80 per cent of the middle market price on the dealing day last preceding the grant of the options, ascertained from *The Stock Exchange Daily Official List*. If, therefore, at the time of commencement of the contract the price of the company's shares on the stock market is 300p, the option price will be 20 per cent less than that, i.e. 240p. This amount may be divided into the total value of the contract, plus bonus of £2,960, giving a share entitlement of 1,233 costing £2,959.20. Thus at the end of the contract period the employee could have 1,233 shares registered in his name with the balance of 80p returned to him in cash.

If the company's share price has risen during the 5-year period of the contract the employee will have made a profit on his savings contract if he should then decide to sell the shares, although it is hoped that many employees will decide to retain those shares as long-term investments in the company in which they work. There is no income tax payable by the employee either on the cost of the shares allocated at the time of the commencement of the savings contract or on the value of the shares on the completion of the 5-year savings contract. However, if the employee should sell his shares, he will be subject to capital gains tax on the excess of the amount of the proceeds received over the allocation price of the shares, i.e. in our example £2,959.20.

At the end of the 5-year period the employee is not bound to convert the proceeds from the savings contract into shares and he obviously would not wish to do this if the price of the shares has fallen during the period of the savings contract. In this event he would have the choice of withdrawing his savings and bonus in cash or leaving the money in the savings contract for a further two years, in which case the amount of the bonus would be doubled. Some companies allow their employees at the start of the savings contract to decide in advance whether they wish to have a 5-year savings contract or a 7-year savings contract with the doubled bonus. In the latter case the number of shares over which options were granted would, of course, be increased but the employee would not be able to exercise his option until the 7 years had elapsed. On the completion of the savings contract the employee may also elect not to use all the cash in the contract to purchase shares. He may decide to use part of it to purchase shares and to take the balance in cash.

Unlike the case of the profit-sharing schemes described above, the employee does not become a shareholder until he exercises his option at the end of 5 or 7 years and he is consequently not actually a shareholder during that time and therefore does not receive dividends. However, the company may send him annual reports (or the summary financial statements under s.251 inserted by CA 1989 s.15) and interim statements so that he may see how the company is progressing. The option to convert the savings plus bonus into shares must be exercised within 6 months of the end of the contract. There are also special provisions in the case of employees reaching retirement date or leaving the company as a result of injury, disability or redundancy. In this case the 5-year rule does not apply and the employee will have 6 months after leaving the company to use the amount of money saved up to his date of leaving plus the interest it has earned to purchase shares in the company at the price determined at the date the contract commenced.

If the employee should die during the currency of the savings contract his personal representatives have 12 months in which to decide whether to use the money saved up to date of death, including interest, to exercise the options and take the company's shares for the deceased employee's estate. If death should occur during the 6-month period after completion of the contract, which is the time allowed to the employee in which to exercise his option, the personal representatives will have one year from the date of completion of the contract to decide whether they wish to exercise the option to buy shares.

It should be noted that although capital gains tax would be payable if the employee sold his shares on completion of the contract and the amount realised was greater than the acquisition cost of the shares, there is an exemption limit up to which capital gains may be realised (£5,000 in 1990/1) which is not subject to capital gains tax. Unless, therefore, the employee had other shareholdings which he sold so that his capital gains exceeded the exemption limit he would not normally have to pay capital gains tax on the excess proceeds from selling the shares acquired under the SAYE contract.

Selective share option schemes

Share option schemes under which companies could grant options on its shares on a selective basis with tax incentives for their higher paid employees were brought into effect by provisions in the Finance Act 1984 and Schedule 10 of that Act as amended. These provisions are now contained in ICTA, principally, ss. 185, 187 and Parts I, II, IV and VI of Schedule 9 of that Act. The description that follows is based on the law currently in force following the Finance Act 1989.

There is no liability to income tax under these schemes; the option holder is liable only to capital gains tax as and when he disposes of his shares if this exceeds the capital gains tax exemption limit for the year in which disposal takes place. Under these schemes options may be granted to such full-time employees (including executive directors) of the company or of its participating subsidiaries as the board of the company may select. The options are granted within 6 weeks following the preliminary announcement to The Stock Exchange of the company's results for the preceding financial year or half year.

The price at which the shares under option are acquired (known as the subscription price) is the higher of its nominal value or the price calculated in accordance with s.150(3) of the Capital Gains Tax Act 1979. This will usually be the bid price plus one-quarter of the difference between the bid and offer prices quoted in *The Stock Exchange Daily Official List* on the dealing day immediately prior to the date on which the options are offered.

On the grant of options some companies' schemes require participants to pay an option price for the grant of the options (e.g. 1 per cent of the subscription price payable for the shares under option) and this amount is treated as part of the subscription price for the shares if and when the options are exercised. The scheme may provide that the option price is or is not refundable in the event of the options not being exercised.

One particular feature of these schemes is that, unlike the profit-sharing schemes and the SAYE share option schemes described above, a company may operate a scheme under ICTA Schedule 9 on the basis that it may select the directors and employees who may participate in it. It is for this reason that these schemes are likely to be operated by companies for their higher paid executives and directors. In the case of the other two schemes mentioned above they must be open to all, although the company may set a minimum period of service before employees may become participants.

An Inland Revenue approved selective share option scheme provides that the total gain on shares over which options are granted, that is the difference between the amount paid for the shares when the option is exercised and the proceeds received on eventual disposal, are chargeable only to capital gains tax. No income tax is payable on the proceeds and thus these schemes are extremely beneficial in the case of higher paid company executives and directors.

Since 6 April 1988 capital gains tax is calculated by reference to the individual's marginal rate of income tax, i.e. in 1990/91 at the rate of 25 per cent or 40 per cent. However, if the total gains realised on the sale of option scheme shares and on any other Stock Exchange transactions the participant may make, do not exceed £5,000 in 1990/1, the whole gain will be free of capital gains tax. Where there are gains in excess of £5,000 these are added to the individual's income chargeable to income tax to determine the rate of capital gains tax payable.

If the scheme is to receive the favourable tax treatment mentioned above it must be approved by the Inland Revenue and meet the requirements set out in ICTA Schedule 9. In this connection, the particular points to note are as follows:

1. Participants must be full-time directors or qualifying employees, i.e. a director who works for the company at least 25 hours a week or an employee who works for the company at least 20 hours a week, and at the time the participant obtains or exercises his rights he must not have had a material interest in the company within the preceding 12 months if the company is a close company for corporation tax purposes. The material interest tests have been changed by the Finance Act 1989 making it easier for some companies to set up, and for their employees to participate in, employee share schemes.

2. The market value of the shares over which options are granted when added to the market value of options over shares granted under any other approved share option scheme (other than an unapproved scheme or an approved SAYE scheme) must not exceed:
   (a) four times the employee's annual relevant emoluments (i.e. payments liable to deduction of tax under PAYE); or
   (b) £100,000.

3. The scheme shares must:
   (a) form part of the ordinary share capital of the company or of a company which has control of the company granting the option;
   (b) be quoted on a recognised stock exchange;
   (c) be shares in a company which is not under the control of another company;
   (d) be fully paid up, not redeemable and not subject to any restrictions other than those which apply to all shares of the same class. (This restriction does not apply, however, to restrictions on the acquisition and dealing in the company's shares imposed on

senior executives and directors under company rules complying with The Stock Exchange's *Model Code for Securities Transactions by Directors of Listed Companies* contained in the Continuing Obligations, para. 45.)

4. Although the exercise of an option is not subject to a company's rules based on the *Model Code,* the sale of shares by the director or executive would be subject to these rules.

5. The rights obtained under this scheme must be non-transferable, although if the participant dies the options may be exercised within one year of the date of his death by his personal representatives; if the exercise is within 10 years of the date of grant of the options, the exemption from income tax still applies.

6. The price of the options must be stated at the time the options are granted and the price must not be manifestly less than the market value of the shares at that time.

7. The options must be exercised between 3 and 10 years from the date of grant, and the option holder must not exercise within 3 years of the date of his last exercise of an option under the scheme or any options obtained under any other approved selective system, ignoring any other exercise occurring on the same day. The effect of this is that during the 3- to 10-year period in which options may be exercised the exercise may take place on three occasions only if the tax benefits are to be obtained.

8. A scheme may provide that the option holder may exercise options obtained under it after ceasing to be a director or employee of the company. Company rules often limit this to leaving as a result of ill health, redundancy, or retirement and impose a time limit in which to exercise options of 12 months from the date of ceasing to be a director or employee.

In framing the rules of the scheme it will be useful to include a provision whereby it may be amended by the directors to secure or maintain approval of the scheme by the Inland Revenue under ICTA Schedule 9. This will mean that if some minor technical alteration to the scheme is needed as a result of any amendment to the requirements for approval, the directors may implement such minor variations without having to obtain the sanction of shareholders in general meeting. Subject to this, however, it should be provided that any amendments to the advantage of employees or participants (e.g. if the Inland Revenue maximum limit were to be raised so that the number of options over shares granted to participants could be increased) should not be made without the prior approval of the shareholders. This is important because the shareholders should have some control over the number of options which may be granted to its executives and directors. Moreover, the investment committees of the Association of British Insurers and the National Association of Pension Funds Limited impose limits of their own in order to secure their support for the approval of the scheme in general meeting.

Employee share ownership plans

Employee share ownership plans (ESOPs), also called employee share ownership trusts (ESOTs), qualify for new tax reliefs introduced by the Finance Act 1989 as amended by the 1990 Budget proposals. These are typically employee benefit trusts funded by the company or externally linked to a share participation scheme for the benefit of the company's employees. Companies may claim corporation tax relief on payments made to trustees of these plans but in order to qualify for this relief all beneficiaries in these special trusts must be employees and they must all benefit on similar terms. The trust must have UK resident trustees (because they could incur a tax liability if certain conditions are not met) and be independent of the company. One trustee must be a trust corporation, solicitor or a member of some other approved professional body but the majority of the trustees must be employees of the company chosen by the employees although directors may be trustees provided that they are in the minority.

ESOPs are not entirely new but until the Finance Act 1989 there was some doubt whether contributions made by companies to finance such trusts were eligible for corporation tax relief. This relief is now provided by statute in that Act. Also the substitution of a new s.153(4)(*b*) made by CA 1989 s.132 removes any doubt as to the legality of a company giving financial assistance for the purchase of its shares by an ESOP.

The main features of ESOPs are as follows:

1. The trust is set up by the company which may borrow money from the company or a financial institution. The company is permitted to lend money to the trust as a result of the substitution of a new s.153(4)(*b*) made by s.132 of CA 1989.
2. The funds are used to acquire an equity stake in the company, either new shares or by purchases in the market.
3. The shares are distributed to employees over a number of years (maximum 7) via an approved or unapproved share scheme.
4. As shares are distributed the trust can repay the loan from the contributions made to the trust by the company. Dividends on shares held by the trust pending distribution to employees may be used to pay interest on the loan.
5. The trustees may incur a tax liability if they make non-qualifying distributions of shares or if shares are held by the trust for more than 7 years.

The above complications and possible potential tax liability on the trustees are seen as disadvantages of ESOPs compared with profit-sharing schemes approved by the Inland Revenue under ICTA and, as at the date of writing this handbook, it appears that no companies have set up ESOPs under the Finance Act 1989. However, some companies may be encouraged to set up ESOPs as a result of a change announced in the 1990 Budget whereby owners of shares in unquoted companies may sell their shares to an ESOP and defer any capital gains tax liability on the sale of the shares by investing the proceeds in replacement assets which are also subject to capital gains tax until there is a disposal of the replacement assets. To qualify for this relief the ESOP must have a 10 per cent stake in the company within 12 months of the sale of the shares and the vendors must acquire the replacement assets within 6 months of the sale of their shares to the ESOP or the 10 per cent condition being satisfied if that is later. As this is a Budget proposal, reference should be made to the Finance Act 1990 when it is published in case there should be any change in these provisions.

Unapproved share option schemes

The statutory provisions covering these schemes are set out in ICTA ss.135 and 136. Briefly, there will be a charge to income tax on the gain arising from the exercise of an option (not on the grant of the option) on any increase in value less any consideration paid for the option. If, however, the option is exercisable only after 7 years there will be an income tax liability on the value of the option at the time of its grant. In this case, however, the amount of tax charged may be deducted from any income tax that may be payable when the option is exercised. When the shares have been acquired following the exercise of the option there may be a capital gains tax liability on the eventual sale of the shares.

Unapproved schemes may become more popular in particular circumstances when a company wishes to reward very senior employees above the limits set for approved schemes now that the top rate of income tax is limited to 40 per cent.

Duties of company secretary or registrar

Profit-sharing schemes

In the case of these schemes it would be usual for the company secretary or for the company's registrar to maintain a register of the participants in the profit-sharing scheme which would be updated year by year on the grant of further allocated shares to the employees. In carrying out this function, however, the company secretary or the registrar will be acting as an agent for the trustees of the profit-sharing scheme, whose responsibility it is to maintain such records. Such a register must also be kept by the company or by its registrar in order that the annual and half-yearly dividends may be paid to the participants by the company and for the dispatch of the annual report and accounts (or summary financial statements) and interim statements to the participants. The trustees of a profit-sharing scheme may be a specialist or professional firm of trustees unconnected with the company.

Another function of the company in respect of these schemes is to deduct the PAYE tax which may be payable in the event of employees selling their entitlements within the period after the end of the retention period and prior to the release date. If a participant wishes to sell some or all of his shares during this period the trustees will sell the shares on the stock market and receive the proceeds from the brokers for the shares sold. Assuming that the shares have risen in value and that the proceeds are, therefore, in excess of the locked in value for tax purposes, the proceeds will then be divided by the trustees between: that amount which is not subject to assessment to PAYE tax, i.e. the profit realised on the shares, being the total proceeds of the sale less the locked in value for tax purposes; and the amount which is so assessable, i.e. the locked in value for tax purposes.

The trustees will send a cheque to the participant for the amount of profit, i.e. the amount which is not subject to PAYE tax, and a separate cheque to the company for the part of the proceeds representing the original cost of the allocation, i.e. the locked in value for tax purposes. The company can then arrange for the appropriate PAYE tax to be deducted and then remit the balance of that part of the proceeds to the employee through the normal payroll arrangements.

Calculation of income tax under profit-sharing schemes

As already noted, the cost of the shares allocated to a participant each year is called the locked in value of the shares and these values are used to determine the tax liability if the shares are sold before the release date. Thus, if 100 shares were allocated in Year 1 at 330p, the locked in value is £330. If these shares were sold after four years but less than five years at a price of 600p, the tax liability would be calculated as follows:

Shares sold	Locked in value	Sale value of shares	Sale proceeds total
100	£330	600p	100 × 600p = £600

(This is a simplified example as in an actual case the cost of brokerage would be deducted from the sale proceeds.)

Income tax is then charged on £247.50 (75 per cent of £330) and if tax is paid at the basic rate of 25 per cent the tax payable would be £61.87.

A cheque for the profit, £600 − £330, i.e. £270, plus the amount of the proceeds not subject to tax, i.e. £82.50 (total £352.50), would be sent direct by the trustees to the participant. The part of the proceeds subject to tax, i.e. £247.50, would be sent by the trustees to the company, which would deduct the £61.87 tax and remit the balance £247.50 − £61.87, i.e. £185.63, to the participant through the payroll.

If at the time the first sale takes place a number of yearly allocations have been made to the employee, the sales are dealt with on a first in, first out basis.

SAYE share option schemes

In this case the company secretary or its registrar will need to maintain individual records of all SAYE contracts taken out by employees, listing them by name, stating whether they are 5-year or 7-year contracts, the number of options which have been granted and the price at which they were granted. Arrangements will have to be made for the monthly contributions of the participants to be deducted from their salaries and remitted by the company either to the Director for National Savings, to the bank or to the building society. The company will also have to issue option certificates to the participants.

On conclusion of the savings period the company will obtain payment from the Department for National Savings, the bank or the building society in order to pay for the shares which are to be issued to the participant, assuming that he has, in fact, elected to receive shares by signing the statement on the back of the option certificate. As already mentioned the participant has the choice of whether to use the proceeds of his savings contract to acquire the shares in the company for which he was granted options or to receive the amount in cash. He may also exercise the options in whole or in part.

It should be noted that in the case of these schemes the records maintained by the company do not constitute a register of shares held by the option holders since in fact they do not acquire their shares until they exercise their option at the conclusion of the savings period. Consequently, no dividends fall to be paid on the shares under option and there is no requirement to send out copies of the report and accounts (or summary financial statements) and interim statements to option holders.

Selective share option schemes

As in the case of the SAYE share option schemes it will be necessary for the company or its registrar to maintain a list of persons to whom options have been granted under the scheme, the date of grant and a note of the period during which the options may be exercisable. This list will also record the receipt from the grantee of the option price, if any, for the options granted.

Option certificates must be issued to participants following the grant of options and the receipt from them of the amount due for the option price, if any.

When options are exercised the participants endorse their option certificate to the effect that they wish to exercise the option and return it to the company with the subscription price payable (or the balance of the subscription price less the option price) for the number of shares for which they wish to exercise options. The company will then prepare a share certificate and send it to the participant; he may then either sell the shares on The Stock Exchange or retain them as an investment in the company.

As in the case of SAYE share option schemes it is not necessary to keep a register of option holders in a form similar to that of the company's ordinary Register of Members because option holders, until they exercise their option, are not entitled to receive dividends from the company (unless the scheme so provides) or to receive copies of the company's report and accounts (or summary financial statements) and interim statements.

Adjustments to share option schemes

It should be noted that both in the case of SAYE share option schemes and selective share option schemes adjustments will be necessary in the event of any capitalisation or rights issue or any consolidation, subdivision or reduction in the capital of the company. Such adjustments will affect the number of shares over which options have been granted and the price of the options. It is usual in such cases for the company to request its auditors to determine what adjustment would in their opinion be fair and reasonable. In particular it should be provided that the aggregate amount payable on the exercise of an option should not be increased and that the subscription price for a share should not be reduced below its nominal value. Any such adjustments should not be made without the prior approval of the Board of Inland Revenue.

When the adjustments have been determined by the auditors and agreed by the company and approved by the Inland Revenue, a notice of the adjustments should be sent out to the option holders. The company may also call in the option certificates for endorsement or replacement.

Adjustments to profit-sharing schemes

In the case of profit-sharing schemes a capitalisation issue will increase the number of shares per participant, which will be deemed to have been appropriated to the participant on the day when the original holding was appropriated to him. Where a rights issue takes place the participant will be given the opportunity to direct the trustees either to subscribe for the rights with cash provided by the participant or to dispose of the rights. In the latter case the proceeds will be treated under the scheme as a capital receipt to which special taxation rates apply if it arises before the release date, since it is treated as a part disposal taxable at the appropriate percentage. However, there is a tax free allowance for capital receipts of £20 for each year in which shares are appropriated to a participant with an overall maximum of £100.

Other adjustments will be required in the event of any consolidation, subdivision or reduction in the capital of the company; but all of these are rare occurrences.

Take-over of companies with employee share schemes

It is possible for employees with share options in the scheme of a company which is being taken over by another company to release their options under the scheme in consideration of the grant of equivalent share options in the acquiring company (ICTA Schedule 9, para. 15). The rules of the scheme should provide for this eventuality. It overcomes the problem in the case of savings related share option schemes where the early exercise of options, or in the case of selective option schemes where if options are exercised in less than three years from the date of grant, or within three years of a previous tax exempt exercise, there is an income tax liability for the option holders on any gain arising from the exercise.

Pre-flotation share option schemes

Under certain circumstances share options in companies may be granted to directors and executives 6 to 12 months before the company is to be floated on The Stock Exchange. These can lead to substantial gains by the option holders when the company comes to the market.

CHAPTER 8

Directors

Appointment

It has already been seen that the first directors of a company are those whose names are entered on Companies Form No. G10 'Statement of first directors and secretary and intended situation of registered office' on the incorporation of a company.

Subsequent appointments as directors are governed by the provisions of the company's Articles of Association. These usually provide that the board itself may fill any casual vacancies or appoint additional directors up to the maximum number permitted by the Articles. However, elections or re-elections of directors following retirement by rotation or removal of directors must be approved by the company in general meeting (Table A, Regulations 73–80). It should be noted that at the company's first Annual General Meeting all the directors retire from office and have to be re-elected by the shareholders at the meeting.

A casual vacancy is one arising from the death or resignation of a director. The procedure for appointing a director to fill a casual vacancy is as follows (it having first been established that the person concerned is willing to be appointed a director of the company, since his consent will have to be formally confirmed by his signing a consent to act section on Companies Form No. G288 'Notice of change of directors or secretaries or in their particulars' which has to be sent to the Registrar of Companies):

1. If the company is listed on The Stock Exchange, The Stock Exchange should be notified of the appointment.
2. If desired an appropriate press announcement should be sent to leading newspapers or through the company's press agents, if it employs such agents.
3. The secretary should write to the newly appointed director confirming that the board has appointed him as a director and dealing with the following matters:

(a) ask the director for his personal particulars, including date of birth, which are required to complete Companies Form No. G288 and so as to make the necessary entry in the Register of Directors and Secretaries (s.288), also asking him to sign the consent section on Companies Form No. G288. The date of birth is required for all directors and not just those subject to s.293 (s.289 as amended by CA 1989 Schedule 19, para. 2(2)(*b*));

(b) ask the director for a copy of his specimen signature, to be sent to the company's bank if the director is likely to be involved in signing cheques on the company's behalf;

(c) inform the director of any share qualification which he must acquire under the Articles and the time allowed in which to do this;

(d) inform the director of his obligations to disclose his interests in shares and debentures of the company (s.324) and ask him to provide the necessary information regarding such interests so as to make the relevant entry in the Register of Directors' Share and Debenture Interests;

(e) invite the director to give a general notice of his interests in contracts with the company (s.317);

(f) give the director the dates of forthcoming board meetings so that he may mark his diary;

(g) enquire how the director wishes his emoluments to be paid, e.g. sent to his home address or paid direct into his bank account, including information regarding his PAYE coding and National Insurance contributions (if he is already paying the maximum contributions in connection with another employment, he should obtain and submit to the company a certificate of exemption from contributions);

(h) general information about the business of the company should be sent to the newly appointed director, together with copies of the Memorandum and Articles, reports and accounts for recent years and interim reports and circulars. If the company has debenture stocks or loan stocks in issue, a copy of the trust deeds should be sent to the director for his information;

(i) if the company is listed on The Stock Exchange send to the director a copy of the company's rules for securities transactions based on the *Model Code* (Yellow Book, Continuing Obligations, para. 45) and ask him to acknowledge receipt.

4. When the director provides the above information the necessary entries in the Register of Directors and Secretaries and in the Register of Directors' Share and Debenture Interests should be made and the completed Companies Form No. G288 sent to the

Registrar of Companies within 14 days of the date of appointment. Other matters may need to be attended to, if necessary, depending on the circumstances: e.g. informing the bank of the director's appointment and enclosing his specimen signature and, if necessary, note that the director is required by a certain date to have acquired his share qualification.

5. It should be noted that Table A does not contain any provision requiring directors to obtain a share qualification and this is not usually required by modern forms of Articles where Table A is not followed. However, it is usual for a director to wish to have some share interest in the company of which he is a director and, in this event, a notice of his interests must be included in the company's report and accounts each year. Where a director is not required to have a share qualification it is usual for the Articles to provide that the director may receive notice of, and attend and speak at, general meetings of the company since, as a non-shareholder, he would not otherwise have such power except where he may be the chairman of the meeting and the Articles give him a casting vote when there is an equality of votes.

6. If the company has in force an insurance policy covering directors and officers of the company against liabilities they may incur in carrying out their duties the insurance company should be notified of the appointment of a new director (s.310 as amended by CA 1989 s.137).

Remuneration

The amount of remuneration that may be paid to directors is normally included as a total overall amount in the company's Articles, and where it is desired to increase the amount available for payment to directors as remuneration the appropriate Article must be amended by the company in general meeting. If the directors are to be paid expenses in addition to remuneration, provision for this should also be made in the Articles. The same applies where the chairman, deputy or vice-chairmen are to be paid additional remuneration.

The amount payable each year by way of remuneration to directors must be disclosed in the company's accounts. Similarly, where directors have waived any of their fees, the amount waived must also be stated in the company's accounts (s.231 and Schedule 5, Part V).

Contracts of employment

A contract for a director that is not determinable within a period of five years must be approved by the shareholders in general meeting (s.319). Shareholders' approval may be given by an Ordinary Resolution passed at a general meeting provided that a written memorandum setting out the terms of the proposed agreement is available for inspection by members of the company at the registered office for not less than a period of 15 days prior to the date of the meeting. Companies are required to keep copies of directors' service contracts available for inspection by members at the registered office of the company at all times.

Managing directors and other executive directors

The appointment of directors to be managing or executive directors is usually governed by provisions contained in the Articles, giving the directors power to appoint such directors, to determine the terms of their appointment and remuneration and to delegate to them such powers of the board as may be desired (Table A, Regulation 84). Since the office of managing director is normally a full-time executive appointment it is good practice for this appointment to be governed by a formal service agreement so that the remuneration and other benefits associated with the appointment may be made clear of all doubt. The agreement should also contain any restraints that may be attached to the appointment relating to confidentiality, with some control over the director's activity in the event of his leaving the service of the company. The contracts of directors who also hold salaried executive positions with the company should specify whether the remuneration stated in the contract is exclusive or inclusive of directors' fees.

In the case of a smaller company the terms of appointment could be set out in the minutes of the board appointing the director and a letter sent to him containing a copy of the minute and asking for his acceptance in writing of the proposed appointment.

The Articles normally give the board of directors power to revoke any appointment of a managing director subject to the terms of any agreement which he has with the company. The appointment would also cease if the director ceased to be a director of the company for any reason.

Alternate directors

There is no provision in the Act authorising a director to appoint an alternate to act on his behalf in his absence, so alternates may only be appointed if the Articles specifically provide for this. Regulations 65–9 of Table A make provision for a director to appoint another director to be his alternate, or he may appoint any other person as his alternate subject to that person being approved by the board of directors.

Alternate directors are included in the definition of director in s.741 and their particulars should be entered in the Register of Directors and Secretaries and filed with the Registrar of Companies on Companies Form No. G288. They are subject to the same rules as regards disclosure of interests in shares and debentures of the company and transactions with the company. Their names must also be shown on letterheads if it is company practice to show the names of directors on these. It should be particularly noted that the alternate director may only act in the absence of the appointing director – it is not a complete assignment by the director of his office under s.308.

Special types of director

Some companies' Articles provide for the board to appoint persons to offices with word 'director' as part of their title, e.g. divisional director, associate director. Such a person is not a director within the meaning of s.741. Such persons are not entitled to attend board meetings and are not subject to the statutory responsibilities and liabilities of a director, provided that they do not represent themselves as being directors in their dealings with third parties. It is clearly misleading to appoint officials with the word director in their title when they are not actually subject to the legal duties of a director. However, the practice is sometimes followed by companies in order to give an added measure of status to senior executives which facilitates their dealings with customers and suppliers, especially if the company has substantial dealings in overseas territories.

Local boards are also sometimes formed by companies under provisions contained in their Articles. These persons are not full directors for the purposes of the Act

Retirement

The Articles of Association normally provide for the retirement of directors (Table A, Regulations 73–6), there being no general requirements in the Act itself for directors to retire by rotation at Annual General Meetings.

It is usual for the Articles to provide that a person appointed a director by the board to fill a casual vacancy, or to be an additional director, must be elected at the next following Annual General Meeting of the company. Such retirements and elections are not taken into account in determining the directors who are to retire by rotation at that Meeting (Table A, Regulation 79). If the company is a listed company, the Yellow Book, Section 9, Chapter 1, para. 4.2, requires that the Articles contain provision for directors appointed to fill casual vacancies or persons appointed additional directors, to hold office only until the next following Annual General Meeting when they will be eligible for re-election. In the case of additional directors, any maximum number of directors specified in the Articles must not, of course, be exceeded.

The procedure to be followed for the retirement of directors by rotation depends on the wording of the Articles but, based on the Table A provisions, it is as follows:

1. At the first Annual General Meeting of the company all the directors must retire and be elected by the company in general meeting.

2. After this one-third of the directors for the time being or, where the number is not an exact multiple of three, the number nearest one-third, retire from office. Directors who are retiring because of having been appointed since the last Annual General Meeting and directors excluded from the retirement by rotation provision, like managing directors, are not taken into account for this purpose. Some companies' Articles are slightly different from Table A in providing that the number of directors to retire by rotation shall be one-third of the directors for the time being or, if their number is not three or a multiple of three, then the number nearest to but not exceeding one-third shall retire. An example will make the position clear. In the case of a board of directors consisting of eight directors, under the Table A provisions three directors would retire but under the alternative Articles only two directors would retire by rotation.

3. The directors to retire at any Annual General Meeting are those who have been longest in office since their last election; as between persons who became directors on the same day, those to retire (unless they otherwise agree among themselves) shall be determined by lot.

4. Directors retiring by rotation are eligible for re-election but the company in general meeting may elect some other person to take that director's place provided that the provisions of Table A, Regulation 76, are followed.

5. Section 292 provides that in the case of a public company, the Resolutions at a general meeting for the appointment or reappointment of directors must be voted on individually unless the meeting first agrees unanimously that the appointments or reappointments may be made by a single Resolution.

Vacation of office

The office of director may be vacated by his death or under a provision in the Articles of Association of the company. Vacation of office may also arise under statute as follows:

1. If the director has not obtained any required share qualification within two months of the appointment or, if obtained, he subsequently disposes of his share qualification (s.291).
2. In the case of a company subject to s.293, where the director reaches the relevant age limit when the office of director would be vacated at the conclusion of the next following Annual General Meeting, subject to possible re-election.
3. If the director becomes bankrupt, unless the court permits him to continue in office (CDDA s.11).
4. If the director is disqualified from being a director by Court Order (CDDA ss.1–6 as amended by CA 1989 Schedule 10, Part II, para. 35 and CDDA Schedule 1 as similarly amended). A register of such disqualification orders is maintained by the Secretary of State for inspection by the public (CDDA s.18).

Under the Articles further methods of vacating office may be specified as follows:

1. In the event of the director resigning, the resignation will usually take effect from the date on which his letter of resignation is received by the company unless it states some subsequent date on which the resignation is to become effective. Resignation does not need to be accepted by the board to be effective unless the Articles otherwise provide.
2. If the director is absent from board meetings for some specified period (often 6 months) without leave of absence given by the board. In order to monitor the operation of any such Article, therefore, the secretary should arrange for the board to grant leave of absence where it is known that the director is likely to be absent for a period exceeding 6 months, e.g. because of overseas travel on the company's business or long illness.
3. If a receiving order is made against a director or he compounds with his creditors generally.
4. If an Order is made by the Court on grounds of mental disorder.
5. If the director is removed from office, e.g. by a notice signed by all his co-directors.

Retirement on attaining age limit

Section 293, which applies to both public companies and to the subsidiaries of public companies, provides that a director who has attained the age of 70 is required to vacate office at the conclusion of the next succeeding Annual General Meeting unless the company's Articles of Association provide otherwise. Where such a person is to be appointed or re-elected a director, special notice must be given to the company of the necessary Resolution, stating the age of the person concerned.

The reappointment of a director under these provisions does not affect the normal retirement by rotation so that should someone else be appointed in his place, that person would be subject to retirement by rotation at the same time as the outgoing director who has reached the age of 70 would have retired.

Where a person is appointed a director on attaining the age of 70 he will retire by rotation in the normal way and it is not necessary for him to be re-elected in the intervening years. Special notice, of course, must be given when he comes up again for re-election following retirement by rotation.

A managing director who is not, therefore, subject to retirement by rotation must be re-elected on attaining the age of 70, unless the Articles provide otherwise but thereafter need not be re-elected whilst holding the office of managing director.

Removal of directors

Sections 303 and 304 provide that the company may remove a director at any time by Ordinary Resolution regardless of anything to the contrary in the Articles or in any agreement with the director. Removal, however, does not deprive the director of any right he may have to compensation or damages payable in respect of the termination of his appointment as a director.

Special notice must be given to the company of the intention to propose such a resolution, a copy of which must be sent to the director concerned to give him the opportunity to make representations in writing to the company and to request that these be circulated to the members.

Where such special notice is received by the company, care must be taken to ensure that the requirements of ss.303 and 304 are strictly complied with and it may be advisable to obtain legal advice as to the precise procedure. A resolution could be proposed at the next following Annual General Meeting but could also be dealt with at an Extraordinary General Meeting provided that the special notice was given to the company within the time limit specified in s.379.

Articles of Association may not exclude the provisions of ss.303 and 304 and may make further provision for removal of directors.

A number of administrative matters must be dealt with when a director ceases to hold office for whatever reason:

1. The Stock Exchange must be notified if the company is a listed company.

2. A press release could be issued if desired.
3. The company's bank should be informed if the director was an authorised cheque-signing signatory.
4. The date of ceasing to be a director must be recorded in the Register of Directors and Secretaries and the Register of Directors' Share and Debenture Interests. A notice on Companies Form No. G288 should be sent to the Registrar of Companies within 14 days of the date of vacation of office.
5. Any fees for the period to the date of cessation of office should be paid to the director or, if he is deceased, to his personal representatives and the Inland Revenue informed of the cessation of fees.
6. The name of the director should be removed from letterheads if it is the practice to show the directors' names on these.

Defective appointment of directors

It should be noted that s.285 provides that if it is found that the appointment of a director was defective in any way, any earlier acts made by the person concerned acting as a director remain valid, for the protection of third parties. It may be thought desirable, where the defect is discovered after a long period has elapsed, for a Special Resolution or Ordinary Resolution to be passed by the company in general meeting to give retrospective validation to the acts of the person whose appointment as a director was defective.

Duties and responsibilities of directors generally

The extent of the authority of the board of directors will depend on the provisions of the company's Articles of Association, but the board is generally responsible for the management of the business of the company. Table A, Regulation 70, for example, provides that the directors are empowered to exercise all the powers of the company subject to the provisions of the Act and the company's Memorandum and Articles. It should be particularly noted, however, that some Articles provide specific provisions and restrictions regarding the exercise by the directors of powers to borrow money for the purposes of the company.

Directors may be liable to penalties if they fail to ensure that the company fulfils its statutory duties, although it would be a defence if they had reasonable grounds to believe that a competent and reliable person was charged with the duty of ensuring compliance with these provisions. Since the secretary is generally the person responsible for the performance of most of the duties imposed by the Act the directors must ensure that he is competent and reliable.

Duties and responsibilities

The provisions of the CDDA should be carefully noted t
particularly as regards the disqualification of directors o
companies and the personal liability of directors guilty o
trading.

Duties and responsibilities of directors in relation to accou..s

The directors of every company have a statutory duty to prepare accounts (ss.226–7 inserted by CA 1989 ss.4–5) which must be laid before the company in general meeting (s.241 inserted by CA 1989 s.11), except private companies which have made an election not to do so and which has not been contested by a member or auditor of the company (ss.252–3 inserted by CA 1989 s.16). The directors of both public and private companies are, however, required to deliver a copy of the accounts to the Registrar of Companies (ss.242–242A inserted by CA 1989 s.11) but unlimited companies are exempt from this requirement (s.254 inserted by CA 1989 s.17). A person who is a director of a company immediately before the expiry of the period allowed for laying accounts before the company in general meeting and delivering a copy to the Registrar of Companies is subject to a penalty specified in Schedule 24 for non-compliance with this duty, although the director may raise a defence that he took all reasonable steps to secure compliance (s.241(3)–(4) and s.242(4)–(5) inserted by CA 1989 s.11).

The accounts of a company have to be prepared in respect of a period known as an accounting reference period ending on an accounting reference date. A company must notify the Registrar of Companies of its chosen accounting reference date within 9 months of incorporation but if not so notified, a company incorporated before the commencement of Part I of the Companies Act 1989 is deemed to have an accounting reference period ending on 31 March, and in the case of a company incorporated after the commencement of that Part, the last day of the month in which the anniversary of incorporation falls (s.224 inserted by CA 1989 s.3). The notification is made on Companies Form No. G224 'Notice of accounting reference date (to be delivered within 9 months of incorporation)'. The concept of accounting reference periods was brought into effect by the Companies Act 1976 (now consolidated in the Companies Act 1985 as amended by CA 1989) and existing companies at the time of the provision coming into effect under the 1976 Act were given a certain period of time in which to notify the Registrar of Companies of the date selected as the date for the end of the company's accounting reference period, failing which the period would be deemed to end on 31 March.

There is provision in the Act for a company to alter its accounting reference period during the course of an accounting reference period

Directors

(s.225 inserted by CA 1989 s.3) by notice to the Registrar of Companies on Companies Form No. G225(1) 'Notice of new accounting reference date given during the course of an accounting reference period'. In the case of a company which is a subsidiary company or holding company of another company, notice of a new accounting reference date, to coincide with the accounting reference date of that other company, may be given after the end of an accounting reference period to the Registrar of Companies on Companies Form No. G225(2) 'Notice of new accounting reference date given after the end of an accounting reference period by a holding or subsidiary company or by a company subject to an administration order', provided that the period allowed for laying and delivering accounts in relation to the previous accounting reference period has not already expired at the time when the notice is given (s.225(5) inserted by CA 1989 s.3).

In the case of a public company it is the duty of the directors to ensure that the accounts are both laid before a general meeting and delivered to the Registrar of Companies within 7 months after the end of the accounting reference period (10 months in the case of a private company (s.244 inserted by CA 1989 s.11)). In the case of companies having business overseas, which may delay the receipt of accounting information to enable the company to prepare its accounts, the directors may give notice to the Registrar of Companies claiming an extension of the period allowed for laying and delivering accounts by three months (s.244(3) inserted by CA 1989 s.11), the notice being given to the Registrar on Companies Form No. G242 'Notice of claim to extension of period allowed for laying and delivering accounts – overseas business or interests'.

It should be noted that the responsibility for preparing accounts and laying them before the company in general meeting lies with those who are directors of the company at the expiry of the time allowed, but that the company shares responsibility where there is delay in filing the accounts with the Registrar of Companies. The directors are responsible if the content and the format of the accounts do not comply with the requirements of the Act (ss.245–245A–C inserted by CA 1989 s.12). Accordingly, it is a specific requirement that the company's board must formally approve the company's annual accounts and a director must sign the balance sheet on behalf of the board. The copy of the company's balance sheet delivered to the Registrar of Companies must be signed manually by a director (s.233 inserted by CA 1989 s.7). In practice the director would also sign the consolidated balance sheet although, in law, he is only required to sign the balance sheet of each individual company of which he is a director. The copies of the balance sheet laid before the company in general meeting and any other copies issued or circulated must state the name of the person who signed it on behalf of the board.

It is a common practice for companies to publish extracts from their annual accounts, or half-yearly or quartely statements, in newspapers as company advertising to promote the company's image. Under FSA s.57 'investment advertising' requires approval by an authorised person before publication. There is a Department of Trade and Industry guidance note published in July 1988 which states that such publication would be exempt from FSA s.57 unless the extracts chosen for publication taken out of context would be misleading. Reference should be made to the DTI Note before publication to make sure that the proposed advertisement is exempt from FSA s.57.

Companies listed on The Stock Exchange may send summary financial statements, containing information required by regulations made by the Secretary of State to shareholders instead of the full accounts which have to be prepared under the Act. However, the full accounts must be sent to any shareholders who request them (s.251 inserted by CA 1989 s.15).

In this chapter we are concerned with the duties and responsibilities of the directors. Further provisions of the Act relating to accounts, e.g. circulation and publication of accounts, content of accounts, the accounting exemptions for small and medium-sized companies, the auditors' report, disclosure rules for transactions with directors, loans to directors, accounts of overseas, listed and unregistered companies, which include the additional requirements regarding the content of accounts laid down by The Stock Exchange for listed companies, are outside the scope of this handbook. However, it should be mentioned that the Companies Act 1989 contains revised provisions for the content of accounts generally and group accounts in particular (including an expanded definition of 'subsidiary undertaking' so as to consolidate the accounts of less directly controlled companies) which must be prepared in accordance with Schedule 4A inserted by CA 1989 Schedule 2.

Directors' report

The directors are, however, responsible for preparing a directors' report to be attached to every balance sheet, sending it to members and debenture holders, laying it before a general meeting of the company and delivering it to the Registrar of Companies (ss.234–234A inserted by CA 1989 s.8 and ss.241–242–242A inserted by CA 1989 s.11)

Section 234A inserted by CA 1989 s.8 provides that the directors' report must be formally approved by the company's board and signed on its behalf by a director or by the secretary of the company and that every copy of the report laid before the company in general meeting, or otherwise circulated or published, shall state the name of the person who signed it. The copy of the report sent to the Registrar of Companies must be a manually signed copy. There is no requirement to deliver to the Registrar a copy of the directors' report in the case of unlimited companies (s.254 inserted by CA 1989 s.17) or small and medium-sized companies (CA 1989 Schedule 6, Part I, para. 4).

It is appropriate, therefore, to consider in a handbook of company secretarial practice the content of directors' reports for which the directors have responsibility.

It should first be noted that the content of the report depends on whether the accounts are on the Schedule 4 or the Schedule 9 basis. However, Schedule 9 applies only to the accounts of banking and insurance and companies, called 'special category accounts'. Accordingly, we will consider first the content of directors' reports on the Schedule 4 basis and note the difference for Schedule 9 accounts later. The matters to be included in directors' reports are specified in s.234 inserted by CA 1989 s.8 and Schedule 7 as amended by CA 1989 Schedule 5, the principal ones being as follows:

1. The principal activities of the company and of its subsidiary undertakings and of any significant changes therein (s.234 inserted by CA 1989 s.8).
2. A fair review of the development of the business of the company and of its subsidiary undertakings during the year and the position at the end of it (s.234 *ibid.*).
3. Details of any important events since the year end to which the accounts relate and an indication of the likely future development of the business, including a note of the company's activities in research and development (Schedule 7, Part I, para. 6).
4. The amount of the recommended dividend (s.234 *ibid.*).
5. The amount that it is proposed to carry to reserves (s.234 *ibid.*).
6. Significant changes in fixed assets (Schedule 7, Part I, para. 1(1) as amended by CA 1989 Schedule 5, para. 2(1)).
7. If the directors consider that the attention of members should be drawn to it, any difference in the market value of interests in land over the book value at the year end (Schedule 7, Part I, para. 1(2)).
8. The names of all persons who were directors of the company at any time during the financial year (s.234 *ibid.*).
9. Directors' interests in shares or debentures of the company, both at the beginning (or in the case of a new director on his appointment) and at the end of the year, and the grant or exercise of any right to subscribe for shares or debentures in the company during the financial year. If preferred, these details may be given instead in notes to the accounts (Schedule 7, Part I, para. 2 as substituted by CA 1989 Schedule 5, para. 3).

10. If the company has during the financial year purchased or maintained insurance for liabilities incurred by its directors in carrying out their duties a statement of that fact (Schedule 7, Part I, para. 5A inserted by CA 1989 s.137(2)).

11. Donations by the company for charitable or political purposes if they exceed £200 (Schedule 7, Part I, paras. 3–5). Wholly owned subsidiary companies of companies incorporated in Great Britain are exempt from this requirement and money given for charitable purposes outside Great Britain may also be omitted.

12. Details of the acquisition by the company or its nominees of its own shares or of shares made subject to a lien or charge (Schedule 7, Part II).

13. A statement of the company's policy in giving full and fair consideration to applicants for employment who are disabled, continuing the employment of those who become disabled whilst employed by the company, and for the training and development of disabled employees (Schedule 7, Part III). This provision applies to companies with an average of more than 250 employees in each week during the financial year, excluding those who work wholly or mainly outside the United Kingdom. In the case of a group of companies, the number of employees in each company in the group need not be aggregated for this purpose as regards the holding company's accounts.

14. A note of the action taken by the company during the year to introduce, maintain or develop arrangements to keep employees systematically provided with information of matters of concern to them as employees; consulting the employees or their representatives regularly so that their views can be taken into account by the company in making decisions likely to affect their interests; encouraging the involvement of employees in the company's performance, e.g. through an employees' shares scheme or by some other means in order that employees may be aware, equally with the company, of the financial and economic factors affecting the company's performance (Schedule 7, Part V). This provision also applies to companies having the number of employees specified in (13) above.

(Note: Schedule 7, Part IV, requiring the directors' report to contain information concerning arrangements in force for securing the health and safety at work of employees and for protecting other persons arising out of the activities at work of employees, had not yet been brought into effect at the end of 1989. If and when it is, it will be by a statutory instrument made under the Health and Safety at Work Act 1974.)

CA 1989 Schedule 7 makes considerable amendments to the special accounting provisions for banking and insurance companies contained in Schedule 9 which should be carefully noted by those concerned with the administration of such companies. Additional matters are required to be stated in directors' reports of such companies (Schedule 10 as substituted by CA 1989 Schedule 8). These are principally as follows:

1. Details of shares or debentures issued, the reason for making the issue, the classes of shares or debentures issued and the consideration received for the issue.
2. Where the company carries on business of two or more classes which, in the opinion of the directors, differ substantially from each other a statement of the proportions of turnover and profit or loss dividend among those classes.
3. Average number of employees and aggregate remuneration paid, excluding persons working wholly or mainly outside the United Kingdom. This information is not required if the average number of employees is less than 100 or in the case of a wholly owned subsidiary of a company incorporated in Great Britain.

Interests in contracts

Where a director is directly or indirectly interested in a contract or a proposed contract with the company he must declare the nature of his interest at a meeting of the directors. Table A, Regulation 94, imposes restrictions on a director in voting on a matter in which he is personally interested. The type of interest relevant for this purpose is extremely widely defined and would include contracts by the company with any other company of which the director was also a director. However, if the director's interest in a contract arises merely because he is a shareholder in another company which is a party to the contract, this could be considered to be immaterial and not require disclosure if the shareholding was very small, e.g. less than 5 per cent of the voting capital.

Section 317(3) provides a useful procedure for a director to give general notice of his interests. The form of this notice could be as follows:

To the directors, ... Limited/plc

Pursuant to Section 317(3) Companies Act 1985, I give notice that I am to be regarded as interested in any contract which may, after the date hereof, be made with any of the under-mentioned companies and firms:

Name of company or firm   *Nature of interest*

A board minute appropriate to that notice would read as follows:

There was produced and read to the meeting a notice dated ....
19.... given by .... pursuant to Section 317(3) Companies Act 1985.

Material transactions between the company and its directors must be disclosed in the company's accounts. There are limitations imposed by the Act on substantial property transactions by companies with their directors; such transactions require the prior approval of members in general meeting if the value of the property exceeds the lesser of £50,000 or 10 per cent of the company's net assets but no approval is required if the value is less than £1,000 (ss.320 and 321).

In the case of listed companies, The Stock Exchange normally requires that transactions between directors and the company are the subject of a circular to shareholders and submitted to the company in general meeting (Yellow Book, Section 6, Chapter 1, para. 6.1).

Loans to directors

Prohibitions on a company making loans to directors (or giving similar financial assistance) are imposed by ss.330–44.

Except as mentioned below, a company may not make loans to its directors or to directors of its holding company nor may it give guarantees or other securities for such loans. However, a loan which is outstanding when a person is appointed a director does not come within the prohibitions contained in the Act; any additional advances would come within the prohibitions.

Further restrictions apply in the case of public companies and to companies that are members of groups containing a public company. Quasi-loans to directors of such companies are prohibited, as well as loans and quasi-loans to persons connected with such directors. A quasi-loan is a transaction under which one party pays a sum for someone else or agrees to reimburse expenditure incurred by someone else on the terms that that person will reimburse the person making the payment or where the circumstances give rise to a liability on that person to reimburse the payer.

A director's 'connected persons' are his spouse, children under 18 years of age, partners, any company of which he has at least 20 per cent control or the trustees or any settlement for the benefit of such persons. A company is also prohibited from entering into 'credit transactions' as creditor for the benefit of a director or person connected with him (e.g. hire purchase or leasing agreements).

The exceptions which apply to a company making loans or quasi-loans to directors or persons connected with them are strictly limited and are as follows:

1. A quasi-loan is permissible provided that the amount concerned does not exceed £5,000 and is repayable within two months (s.332(1)(b) as amended by CA 1989 s.138).

2. A credit transaction for an amount not exceeding £5,000 is permitted, as is a transaction entered into in the ordinary course of the company's business, provided that the value of the transaction and the terms on which it is made are not more favourable than those which would be offered to a person of similar financial status unconnected with the company (s.335).
3. An advance of up to £10,000 may be made to a director to enable him to meet expenditure incurred for the purpose of the company or to enable him properly to perform his duties, provided that prior approval is given in general meeting or approval is given at the next following Annual General Meeting, failing which the advance must be repaid within the following 6 months (s.337).
4. Special exemptions apply for loans made by money lending companies (including banks) in the ordinary course of their business where the limit is £100,000 (s.338 as amended by CA 1989 s.138).

Without prejudice to the foregoing exemptions there is no prohibition on the making of a loan to a director of the company concerned or of its holding company if the aggregate of the loans made by the company to the director does not exceed £5,000 (s.334 as amended by CA 1989 s.138). However, the loan must still be disclosed in the statutory accounts.

The provisions prohibiting loans to directors contained in the Act are extremely complex and reference should always be made to the detailed legislation in the Act and, if thought desirable, legal advice taken.

Interests in shares and debentures

A director must notify the company of his interests in the shares and debentures of the company and of its holding company and subsidiary companies, and of changes in those interests (s.324 and Schedule 13, Parts I–III). The notification must be given within five days (excluding Saturday, Sundays and bank holidays) of the occurrence of the event affecting such interests. The information which must be given is as follows:

1. Particulars of the interests which subsist on the date of his appointment as a director.
2. Details of subsequent acquisitions or disposals by him giving price paid or received.
3. Details of the assignment of any right granted by the company to subscribe for shares or debentures, giving the consideration received. (This will include renunciation of rights for shares or debentures provisionally allotted on a renounceable allotment letter in a rights issue.)

4. Details of the grant by any other company within the group of a right to subscribe for its shares or debentures, the exercise of any such right or the assignment thereof, giving particulars of the consideration received in the case of an assignment.
5. A director is not required to give notice at the time of the original grant of a right to subscribe for shares or debentures or of its exercise since the company will be aware of the details and should enter them in the Register of Directors' Share and Debenture Interests.
6. A listed company must inform The Stock Exchange of any notification received from its directors immediately and the information may be published by The Stock Exchange (s.329).
7. The interests of the spouse of a director (assuming the spouse is not a director in his or her own right) are aggregated with the interests of the director, as are the interests of directors' children under the age of 18 if not themselves directors.

The interests disclosable under these provisions are widely defined in Schedule 13, Part I, and include, for example, the interests held by a body corporate if the director controls or exercises one-third or more of the voting power at general meetings of the body corporate concerned.

Statutory Instrument No. 802 of 1985 provides various exemptions from disclosure or notification. These include the following:

1. No disclosure is required of interests in shares or debentures of any person in his capacity as trustee or personal representative of any trust or estate of which the Public Trustee is also a trustee (other than as custodian trustee) or a personal representative.
2. No disclosure is required of an interest of a person in his capacity as trustee or as a beneficiary under a trust relating exclusively to a retirement benefits scheme or superannuation fund, provided it is an approved scheme or fund for the purposes of the income tax legislation.
3. Notification need not be made to a company which is the wholly owned subsidiary of a company incorporated outside Great Britain of interests in the shares or debentures of the foreign holding company.
4. Notification need also not be made of an interest of a director of a wholly owned subsidiary, who is also a director of its holding company, in the shares and debentures of the holding company and any other group company (being a wholly owned subsidiary), provided that the holding company is itself required to keep a Register of Directors' Share and Debenture Interests. This exemption is very useful in simplifying the secretarial administration of groups of companies as it often happens that directors of subsidiaries are also directors of the holding company and have interests in the holding company's shares.

It should be noted that no disclosure is required in respect of shares in a wholly owned subsidiary which are held by a director as a bare nominee for the holding company (Schedule 13, Part I, para. 10). If, however, although it is probably unlikely, the director of a subsidiary also holds shares in his own right in the subsidiary company, the subsidiary company would be required to keep a Register of Directors' Share and Debenture Interests and include the director's interest in that Register.

If a director has interests (including family interests) in shares or debentures in a variety of different capacities he may merely disclose his total interest provided that he separately discloses his interests in the various classes of shares or debentures or he may disclose each interest separately, showing the nature and extent of the interest where applicable and may require the company to record that information in the Register of Directors' Share and Debenture Interests. In the case of listed companies, however, the Continuing Obligations require the statement of directors' interests in the share capital to be distinguished between beneficial and non-beneficial interests (Continuing Obligations, para. 21 (h)). However, the director can request that this information not be recorded in the Register of Directors' Share and Debenture Interests, he having provided it solely for the purpose of The Stock Exchange requirement.

A director has a defence, however, for non-disclosure of any interests of which he may be unaware – for example, if the director is separated from his wife and is unaware of her acquisitions or disposals of shares in the company where her husband is a director.

Some companies provide their directors with a supply of forms on which they may notify their interests in shares or debentures. The advantage of this is that it ensures that all the necessary items of information are included.

Insider dealing

The Companies Securities (Insider Dealing) Act 1985 makes insider dealing a serious criminal offence (IDA s.8). It is important that directors are aware of the provisions of this Act since they are the most likely persons to be in possession of unpublished price-sensitive information in relation to the company. However, apart from directors, other persons such as employees of the company or advisers to the company are also covered by the legislation.

An individual who is, or at any time during the preceding 6 months has been, knowingly connected with the company may not deal in the securities of the company on a recognised stock exchange or other securities market if he has information by virtue of his being connected with the company which he knows to be unpublished price-sensitive information in relation to those securities (IDA s.1). A person is connected with a company if he is a director of the company or of a related company, or an officer or employee of that company or related company, or occupies a position involving a professional or business relationship between himself (or his employer or a company of which he is a director) and the first company or related company (IDA s.9).

Unpublished price-sensitive information is information relating to specific matters of concern directly or indirectly to the company, i.e. information not of a general nature which is not generally known to persons who are accustomed or likely to deal in those securities but which, if it were generally known to them would be likely to affect the price of those securities (IDA s.10).

The provisions also cover the abuse of inside information by a person who knowingly obtains (directly or indirectly) inside information from a person connected with the company concerned (IDA s.1(3) and (4)).

There are, however, provisions containing exemptions for transactions which are effected otherwise than with a view to the making of a profit or the avoidance of a loss and for bona fide transactions by trustees (IDA s.3).

It should be emphasised that the provisions contained in the IDA are lengthy and complex and many companies issue detailed notes of guidance for their directors and senior executives.

The Stock Exchange Model Code

Continuing Obligations, para. 45, requires a listed company to adopt rules governing dealings by directors in the listed securities of the company in terms which are not less exacting than those laid down in The Stock Exchange *Model Code for Securities Transactions by Directors of Listed Companies*, which is contained in the Yellow Book after the Continuing Obligations for Companies in Section 5, Chapter 2. The code provides that directors must not deal in the securities of the company concerned on considerations of a short-term nature and, in particular, provides that directors may not generally deal in the securities of the company in the two-month period preceding the announcement of the annual results and half-year results. Further such dealings may not take place prior to the announcement of matters of an exceptional nature which are likely to affect the share price in the stock market.

The Code also provides that directors shall not deal in the securities of the company at any time without first notifying the chairman (or other director(s) appointed for the purpose) and receiving an acknowledgement. In his own case, the chairman should first notify the board at a board meeting or the other director(s) appointed for the purpose and receive acknowledgement.

As part of good company secretarial practice, therefore, the secretary should establish the necessary procedure for recording the receipt of such notifications and issue of acknowledgements.

It has already been noted that under the provisions of s.329, any dealings by directors of companies whose shares or debentures are listed on a recognised stock exchange in the shares or debentures of the company must be notified immediately to The Stock Exchange, which may publish the information. In addition, the secretary should ensure that a list be tabled at board meetings of directors' dealings in the securities of the company since the date of the last list or, alternatively, provide that the Register of Directors' Share and Debenture Interests is available for inspection by other directors at each board meeting.

CHAPTER 9

Debentures and loan stocks

The directors have implied power to borrow money on behalf of the company under their general powers to manage the business of the company, subject to the provisions of the Act and the Memorandum and Articles of the company (Table A, Regulation 70). However, the Articles of some companies are more specific and impose restrictions on the amounts that may be borrowed by the directors and it is necessary for the company in general meeting to alter the appropriate Article if it is considered desirable that the directors' borrowing powers should be increased. A common provision in the Articles is that the amount for the time being remaining undischarged of moneys borrowed or secured on the undertaking and property of the company (apart from temporary loans obtained by way of overdraft from the company's bankers) shall not, without the previous sanction of the company in general meeting, exceed the nominal amount of the share capital of the company for the time being issued. If the company's Articles contain an article restricting the directors' borrowing powers it must be carefully followed, since if they were to borrow in excess of the limit specified they might find themselves personally liable. The position of third parties acting in good faith would not, however, be affected by any restriction imposing a limit on the directors' powers to borrow on behalf of the company. In the case of large public companies wishing to borrow a substantial sum of money on a sterling security (i.e. more than £20 million) arrangements should be made for consultation to take place between the merchant bank handling the issue, The Stock Exchange and the Bank of England as to the date of the issue. This is a voluntary system to avoid clashes in regard to timing between competing issues.

The ways in which the company may borrow money may be in the form of debentures of various types, unsecured loan stocks and convertible loan stocks, apart from borrowing from the bank by way of overdraft for the company's day to day business.

Types of debenture

Section 744 defines a debenture as a debenture stock, bonds and any other securities of the company, whether constituting a charge on the assets of the company or not. In effect a debenture is a document which creates a debt or acknowledges a debt and it may, therefore, be an unsecured promise to pay or a promise to pay secured by a mortgage or a charge over the property of the company.

Occasionally debentures may be issued in bearer form similar to the share warrants to bearer which may be issued in respect of shares. Arrangements for the payment of interest on bearer debentures are similar to those which apply in the case of the payment of dividends on bearer shares. In practice, the issue of bearer debentures by companies is rare. Eurocurrency securities, however, will often be in this form.

The more common method is to issue a series of debentures in registered form, and the conditions relating to interest, redemption or security will be printed on the reverse of each debenture issued. Registered debentures may be transferable on stock transfer forms under the Stock Transfer Act 1963 and such transfers are exempt from stamp duty (with a few exceptions). However, the exemption from stamp duty will be irrelevant when it is abolished under the 1990 Budget proposals to be brought in on the implementation of TAURUS, probably towards the end of 1991. When a debenture or one of a series of debentures is transferred, the name and address of the new holder are endorsed on the debenture itself by the company. If the company keeps a Register of Debenture Holders, the transfer should be recorded in the Register, and if it creates a charge over the undertaking or any property of the company, an entry should be made in the company's Register of Charges (s.411 inserted by CA 1989 s.101). Registered debentures are normally issued only in the case of private companies, although a public company may issue such a debenture to its bank by way of security for a loan.

Public companies normally issue their debentures in the form of debenture stock secured on the company's assets and constituted by a trust deed between the company and a corporate trustee, e.g. an insurance company or a trust company. Where debenture stock is not secured by a charge over the undertaking of property of the company, it is described as 'unsecured loan stock'. The use of the word 'unsecured' is a requirement of The Stock Exchange for listed companies (Yellow Book, Section 9, Chapter 2, para. 6.1). Unsecured loan stock is usually constituted by a trust deed in the same way as in the case of secured debenture stock, which is usually called 'mortgage debenture stock'. Debenture stock traded on The Stock Exchange is transferable through the TALISMAN system using TALISMAN bought and sold transfers.

Secured debentures

The security for a mortgage debenture may be either fixed or floating or a combination of the two. Fixed charges are equivalent to mortgages and the company is restricted in dealing with the asset or assets charged without the prior consent of the debenture holder or of the trustee for the debenture stock. The difference in the case of a floating charge is that this extends over the whole of the undertaking of the company and is not restricted to particular assets. This enables the company to deal with its assets in the ordinary course of its business. It is possible for a fixed charge to be given over an asset which is already the subject of a floating charge and this would then take priority over the floating charge, although it would be usual to expect the terms of issue of a debenture creating a floating charge to prohibit the company from doing this.

A floating charge crystallises and becomes a fixed charge if an event should happen which allows the debenture holders or the trustee to take possession of the security or to appoint a receiver. The circumstances in which this may happen will be specified in the debenture or the trust deed. Usually, of course, one of these circumstances will be the non-payment of interest within a specified time from the due date or if a resolution should be passed to wind up the company. Subject to the rights of preferential creditors specified in s.614 and Schedule 19, the debenture holders have priority, to the extent of the security held, over the ordinary and other secured creditors on the crystallisation of a floating charge. The Secretary of State has power to make regulations to require notice to be given to the Registrar of Companies of the occurrence of events affecting a floating charge which has been registered with the Registrar or of the taking of any action in exercise of powers conferred by a fixed or floating charge (s.410 inserted by CA 1989 s.100). Notice of the appointment of a receiver or manager of a company's property must also be notified to the Registrar within 7 days of the appointment (s.409 inserted by CA 1989 s.100).

Particulars of a charge to secure any issue of debentures in Great Britain must be registered with the Registrar of Companies within 21 days of the creation of the charge (s.398(1) inserted by CA 1989 s.95). Further, the company must deliver to the Registrar particulars in the prescribed form of the date on which any debentures of the issue were taken up, and of the amount of the issue taken up, and to do so within 21 days after the date on which they were taken up (s.408 inserted by CA 1989 S.100).

Particulars of charges registered with the Registrar must be entered in the company's own Register of Charges (s.411(2) inserted by CA 1989 s.101). The provisions with regard to the registration of company charges generally are contained in ss.395–420 inserted by CA 1989 ss.92–104.

It is not necessary to send to the Registrar with the particulars the original or a copy of the charge document so he will not check the particulars, although he may reject particulars which he considers to be unregistrable. Copies of instruments creating or evidencing a charge over the company's property, brief particulars of which are included in the company's Register of Charges, must be kept at the company's registered office (s.411(1) inserted by CA 1989 s.101) and be available for inspection by any creditor or member of the company without fee or by any other person on payment of such fee as may be prescribed (s.412 inserted by CA 1989 s.101). It is obviously important to the debenture holders that the particulars of a charge created by an issue of debentures is registered with the Registrar of Companies, since a charge is void unless particulars are filed with the Registrar within 21 days of its creation (s.399(1) inserted by CA 1989 s.95). It is usual, therefore, for the trustee for the debenture holders to attend to the registration under the authority contained in s.398 inserted by CA 1989 s.95 which provides that registration of a charge may be effected on the application of any person interested in it.

Special provisions exist in regard to the registration of charges on property in Great Britain created by overseas companies which have registered a place of business in Great Britain under s.691. These are contained in sections 703A–N inserted by CA 1989 Schedule 15 (CA 1989 s.105). In the case of an overseas company copies of instruments creating or evidencing a charge over property of the company situated in Great Britain, and the company's Register of Charges, has to be kept at its principal place of business (s.703J inserted by CA 1989 Schedule 15).

It should be noted that under the provisions of s.413 inserted by CA 1989 s.102 the Secretary of State may by regulations make further provisions relating to charges of any description but at the date of prepration of this handbook no such regulations have been made.

Issue of debenture stock

What has been said in this handbook in relation to public issues of shares applies equally in the case of a public issue of debenture stock and, subject to the provisions of the trust deed, arrangements for the transfer, payment of interest, meetings of holders etc., will also be similar. There are Stock Exchange requirements to be met if the debenture stock is to be listed on The Stock Exchange and the necessary regulations regarding prospectuses, trust deeds, certificates, etc., may be found in the Yellow Book, Section 9, Chapters 2 and 4.

A trust deed to secure the issue of debenture stock will usually cover the following matters:

1. Details of the stock, terms of issue, payment of principal and interest, any conversion rights and stock certificates.
2. The provisions constituting the charges of assets of the company in favour of the trustee, stipulating the events on which the security becomes enforceable.
3. Trustees' powers to concur with the company in dealings with the charged assets.
4. Covenants by the company in relation to its business and to the charged assets.
5. The trustees' remuneration.
6. Where a floating charge is constituted, a prohibition on the issue of any other security ranking ahead of the stock without the consent of the holder.
7. Schedules to the trust deed containing the form of stock certificate, the detailed conditions of redemption in whole or in part by drawings or purchase and of any conversion rights, regulations with the regard to the Register of Holders, provisions governing the transfer and transmission of the stock, and regulations governing meetings of holders of the stock.

If the debenture stock is listed the reverse of the certificate will have printed on it a summary of the conditions rather than the full conditions, unless this is prohibited by the trust deed. The holder of debenture stock is entitled to be supplied with a copy of the trust deed at his request on payment of a fee (s.191 as amended by CA 1989 Schedule 24).

Unsecured loan stock

A loan stock which is unsecured obviously carries a higher risk for investors and to compensate for this it is usually necessary for such stocks to bear a higher rate of interest than would be appropriate if the stock were a secured debenture stock. Sometimes it is also necessary to offer options in the form of a right to convert the stock into equity shares of the company at certain dates in the future (i.e. convertible loan stock) in a ratio determined at the time of issue of the stock or, alternatively, a right to subscribe for equity shares at a future date in a ratio and price determined at the time of issue. With regard to the latter, i.e. subscription rights attached to unsecured loan stock, it should be noted that the loan stock continues in existence after the holder has exercised the subscription rights to which he is entitled; in the case of a convertible loan stock, which is described more fully below, the exercise of the holder of his right to convert into ordinary shares extinguishes his holding of the convertible loan stock to the extent that it is exercised.

The trust deed constituting unsecured loan stock will usually cover the following matters:

1. Details of the terms of issue, payment of principal and interest and any conversion or subscription rights which may be attached to the stock.
2. Restrictions on issuing further unsecured loan stock.
3. Restrictions on further borrowing
4. Restrictions on disposal of the business or specified assets.
5. A covenant by the company to maintain sufficient equity capital to satisfy any conversion or subscription rights, further issues of equity capital and in regard to the business generally.
6. Events in which the whole of the stock becomes immediately payable (e.g. default in payment of interest or ceasing to carry on business).
7. The trustees' remuneration
8. Schedules will be attached to the trust deed containing the form of stock certificate, the detailed conditions for redemption in whole or in part by drawings or purchase and of any conversion or subscription rights, regulations regarding the Register of Holders of the stock, arrangements for transfer and transmission of the stock, and regulations governing meetings of holders of the stock.

If the loan stock is listed, a summary of the conditions may, instead of the full conditions, be printed on the reverse of the certificate, provided that the trust deed does not prohibit this. The holder of the stock is entitled to be supplied with a copy of the trust deed at his request on payment of a fee (s.191 as amended by CA 1989 Schedule 24).

Convertible loan stock

Convertible loan stock is a form of unsecured loan stock which includes provision for the stock to be converted into equity shares at ratios determined at the time of issue of the stock, and there is a requirement for the company to give the stock-holders notice of their right to exercise the conversion rights in every year in which the right exists. For example, each £100 nominal of convertible loan stock may be converted into ordinary shares during specified conversion periods as follows:

On conversion in 1994 – 166 ordinary shares
On conversion in 1995 – 160 ordinary shares
On conversion in 1996 – 154 ordinary shares
On conversion in 1997 – 148 ordinary shares

The secretary or the company's registrar will be concerned with the proper procedure for dealing with applications from holders to exercise their conversion rights. The following is a summary of the procedure which should be followed:

1. Send a circular letter just prior to each conversion date in each year to those holders of the loan stock who have not yet converted, reminding them of the opportunity to convert into ordinary shares, enclosing a form of nomination and acceptance to convert or instructing them that if they wish to convert they should complete the form already printed on the reverse of the convertible loan stock certificate. If the company is a listed company, proof prints of the documents should be submitted to The Stock Exchange for approval.

2. Unless the board has delegated its powers, submit the documents to be approved by the board.

3. Order the final prints of the circular letter and form of nomination and acceptance, sending them to the holders of the loan stock who have not yet converted into ordinary shares.

4. On receipt of loan stock certificates from holders, check that the form of acceptance to convert or the notice of conversion on the back has been properly completed and is accompanied by a completed form of nomination and acceptance if the holder has nominated another person to receive the allotment of shares.

5. In order to keep control over the necessary steps to be taken a record sheet should be prepared for each holder who has lodged a notice of conversion, showing his name and address, the amount of stock to be converted, the number and date of the stock certificate lodged, any balance of convertible loan stock remaining which is not being converted, the name and address of any other person who he has nominated to receive the ordinary shares arising from the conversion, the name and address of any agent to whom the new share certificate and any balance certificate for unconverted loan stock is to be sent, the number of shares to be allotted as a result of the conversion and whether there are any fractions of £1 of loan stock remaining to be redeemed at par.

6. The daily running total of stock lodged for conversion should be maintained, showing the total number of shares to be allotted and the fractions (if any) of loan stock to be redeemed at par.

7. When the last day for the receipt of notice of conversion has passed, The Stock Exchange (if the stock is listed), the trustee for the holders of loan stock and the press should be notified of the amount of stock converted and the number of ordinary shares to be allotted.

8. The new share certificates should be prepared, together with any balance certificates for unconverted loan stock and cheques drawn

for any amounts for fractions of £1 of loan stock to be redeemed at par. The serial numbers of the new share certificates and the balance certificates for unconverted loan stock should be entered on the record sheet.

9. If the shares of the company are listed on The Stock Exchange application should be made for the new shares to be listed.

10. The board or an allotment committee of the directors should formally allot the shares to the holders of the loan stock who have converted, or to their nominees if they have nominated another person to receive the shares arising out of the conversion, the certificates relating to the loan stock converted should be cancelled; the share certificates and balance certificates should be sealed if the company has a common seal or a securities seal; and the certificates should be sent with any remittance for fractions of £1 of loan stock which have been redeemed.

11. The necessary entries should be made in the Register of Members, recording the holdings of ordinary shares by those who have converted, and entries also made in the register of loan stock holders from the information contained on the record sheets.

12. One month after the allotment a return of allotments should be delivered to the Registrar of Companies on Form No. G88(2) (Revised 1988) together with Form No. G88(3).

Redemption of debentures

Although debentures may be reissued (s.193), this is unusual and in practice debentures and debenture stock are redeemable not later than a fixed future date. The title of the stock will give the date of redemption, e.g. '10.5% Mortgate Debenture Stock 1995/99', in which case the whole of the stock outstanding would be redeemable between specific dates in 1995 and 1999, usually at par but possibly with a small premium.

The company should give notice of its intention to redeem the stock to every holder. The money for the redemption may come from a new issue of securities, out of profits or out of a combination of the two. Where redemption is out of profits of the company the proceeds will usually have come from a sinking fund or similar arrangement. It is not unusual for the trust deed to provide for partial redemptions of the stock during the course of its life in advance of the final redemption date by making annual drawings or by making market purchases at prices not exceeding those laid down in the trust deed.

The procedure for the redemption of loan stocks and debentures which are redeemable through the operation of a sinking fund is similar to the procedure for the redemption of redeemable shares issued by the company under the provisions of ss.159–61. Where debentures or debenture stock, secured by a registered charge over the company's property or any part of it, are redeemed or converted in whole or in part, a memorandum of satisfaction that the property ceases to be affected by the registered charge may be filed for registration with the Registrar of Companies in the prescribed form signed by or on behalf of the company and the chargee (s.403 inserted by CA 1989 s.98). On registration of the memorandum the Registrar will send a copy of it to the chargee and to the company and to any other person interested in the charge. Although this procedure is not obligatory under the section which provides that such a memorandum may be delivered, it is, however, in the best interests of the company for charges to be deleted from the public register immediately they are satisfied in whole or in part so as to avoid misleading any banks or other creditors who would otherwise form an unduly adverse view of the company's credit. It will also be necessary to make the appropriate entries in the company's own Register of Charges.

Issue of redeemable shares

Redeemable shares, or shares which are liable to be redeemed at the option either of the company or of the shareholder, may, if so authorised by its Articles of Association, be issued by a company limited by shares or limited by guarantee and having a share capital (ss.159–61). The provisions of ss.159–61 supersede those contained in the 1948 Act relating to the issue of redeemable preference shares, and any such shares issued by a company before 15 June 1982 are redeemable in accordance with the provisions of Chapter VII of the Act (s.180(1) and (2)). Redeemable shares may be issued by a company only if the following conditions are satisfied:

1. There must be provision in the company's Articles authorising it to issue redeemable shares.
2. At the time of issue of redeemable shares the company must have other shares which are not redeemable.
3. Redeemable shares may not be redeemed unless they are fully paid.
4. The terms of redemption must provide for payment on redemption.
5. The redemption money must come only out of distributable profits or out of the proceeds of a fresh issue of shares made for the purpose. Private companies, however, subject to certain conditions, may make redemption out of capital.
6. Shares which have been redeemed must be cancelled on redemption,

and the amount of the issued share capital (not the authorised share capital) is diminished by the nominal value of the shares redeemed. If a company is about to redeem any shares, it may issue shares up to the nominal amount of the shares to be redeemed as if those shares had never been issued. Where redemption takes place wholly or partly out of distributable profits, a transfer must be made to the company's capital redemption reserve.

Capital redemption reserve

Where redemption or purchase of shares is effected out of the company's distributable profits the nominal value of the shares so redeemed or purchased must be transferred to the company's capital redemption reserve. If part of the redemption or purchase money comes from the proceeds of a fresh issue of shares the amount transferred to the capital redemption reserve is the aggregate value of the proceeds of the new issue less the nominal value of the shares redeemed or purchased (s.170). The capital redemption reserve is treated as part of the capital of the company but it may be used in connection with allotting fully paid shares to members under a capitalisation issue.

A capital redemption reserve fund established under the repealed provisions of the Companies Act 1948 covering the redemption of redeemable preference shares now constitutes the company's capital redemption reserve under the Act (s.180(3)).

Premium on redemption of shares

Any premium over the nominal value payable on redemption of redeemable shares must normally be paid out of the company's distributable profits (s.160(1)(b)). If, however, the redeemable shares were issued at a premium, the premium payable on redemption may be paid from the proceeds of a fresh issue of shares made for the purpose of the redemption up to an amount equal to: the aggregate of the premiums received by the company on the issue of the shares redeemed; or the current amount of the company's share premium account (including any sum transferred to that account in respect of premiums on the new shares), whichever is the less.

In this case, the company's share premium account must be reduced by the amount of the premium paid on the redemption out of the proceeds of the fresh issue (s.160(2)). As an exception to this rule, however, any premium payable on the redemption of redeemable preference shares issued under the repealed provisions of the Companies Act 1948 may be paid out of the share premium account (s.180(1) and (2)).

Drawings of redeemable shares

A company' Articles may require shares to be redeemed by a specified date and it is usual to establish a sinking fund for this purpose. The fund is normally operated by annual drawings of shares to be redeemed at the redemption price or by purchases on the market if they can be bought there at a lower price. If making market purchases, this should be done prior to the date on which the annual drawing would normally take place. It is much easier for the company to meet its target for annual redemptions by making market purchases; the arrangements for making drawings are complicated and more costly since, in order to ensure impartiality, it is usual to arrange for the drawing to be supervised by two or more professional persons such as a solicitor, a chartered accountant or a notary public. Of course, if the price of shares in the market to be redeemed is higher in the market than the redemption price, it is appropriate to effect the annual instalment of redemption by a drawing.

Where purchases are made on the market the company's brokers are instructed to purchase the number of shares required for the annual instalment of redemption. However, if the price is favourable on the market there is nothing to stop the company from continuing to make market purchases at prices lower than the redemption price to cover future annual instalments of redemption.

As indicated above the procedure for a formal drawing is both complicated and tedious; but it is nevertheless an important part of company secretarial practice in case a company secretary should ever be involved in making arrangements for a drawing of redeemable shares. The following is a summary of the procedural points which arise:

1. Lists should be prepared in triplicate of the shareholders and their holdings, balanced up to date to the record date for the drawing.
2. Complete groups of, say, 100 or 1,000 shares each, depending on the size of the issue, subject to the drawing, should be allocated progressive numbers. Holdings of less than the group figure of 100 or 1,000, as well as odd amounts of holdings over the group figure, should be aggregated into composite groups and also numbered.
3. Tickets individually numbered corresponding to the total number of groups of shareholdings should be prepared and thoroughly mixed in a suitable container. An example will help to make this numbering procedure clear. Assuming that it is proposed to break down the entire issue into blocks of 1,000 shares, a shareholder with 5,000 shares will be allocated group numbers 1–5, a shareholder with 10,000 shares will be allocated group numbers 6–15, a shareholder with 5,600 shares will be allocated group numbers

16–20 and his additional 600 shares will be carried forward to the pool of excess shares, and a shareholder with 900 shares will have the whole of his holding transferred to the pool of excess shares. It will be seen that there are now 1,500 excess shares so that 1,000 of these will constitute a composite group with number 21, leaving 500 excess shares. The group numbers allocated to each shareholder should be entered on the list which has been prepared under (1) above.

4. The date and place of drawing must be arranged and the requirements of the Articles must be observed in regard to the manner in which the drawing is to be made, e.g. in the presence of a notary public or solicitor.

5. If the shares are listed, The Stock Exchange should be advised of the date of drawing, the record date for the drawing, the number of shares to be drawn and the redemption price.

6. The following documents should be prepared:
   (a) a formal notice to be sent to shareholders whose shares have been drawn for redemption, stating that the necessary payment authority and discharge form will be sent in due course;
   (b) a circular letter to be sent to shareholders whose shares have been drawn for redemption, giving details of the procedure for redemption and enclosing the form of payment authority and discharge form to be returned with the appropriate share certificate(s). The letter would explain that if the shares being redeemed are only part of the holding, and the shareholder cannot give certificate(s) covering the exact number, he should send certificate(s) to the nearest number over the number of shares drawn for redemption and that a balance certificate for the excess (i.e. the shares not redeemed) will be sent to him. It will also explain that no further dividends will be paid on the shares redeemed;
   (c) a payment advice with attached cheque.
   (The documents will have blanks for the insertion of the names and addresses of the shareholders, the number of shares, the amount of payment, etc.)

7. It is desirable that the drawing should be made in the presence of at least three persons. One, e.g. a notary public or a solicitor, will draw the numbered tickets from the container, the two other persons each having a list of the shareholders on which they will mark the numbers drawn against the relative holding. The tickets drawn should be kept in a separate box from which will be prepared a master list of the holdings which have been drawn for redemption. The last ticket drawn will usually represent a fractional number of

shares so as to complete the drawing to the exact sinking fund redemption instalment and if this ticket applies to a composite group, the Articles usually authorise the person in charge of the drawing to determine the holding to which it is to apply. The person in charge of the drawing, e.g. notary public or solicitor, will prepare a formal list of the holders and holdings drawn and deliver it to the company.

8. After the drawing, The Stock Exchange should be advised that it has taken place, mentioning the number of shares which are still in issue which will remain listed on The Stock Exchange.

9. The formal notices prepared under (6a) above will be then sent to the shareholders whose holdings have been drawn for redemption, informing them of the fact and that a further circular and letter of authority will be sent to them in due course informing them of the procedure to be followed in order to secure the proceeds of the redemption. This will normally take place some two or three months after the actual date of drawing.

10. It is, of course, no longer possible to transfer the shares which have been drawn for redemption, and brokers instructed to sell shares should ascertain from the list posted in The Stock Exchange that they have not been drawn for redemption.

11. About three weeks before the date on which the payment of the redemption monies is due, the circular letter prepared under (6b) above will be sent to the shareholders concerned detailing the procedure and enclosing the forms of payment authority and discharge to be signed by them and returned to the company with the certificate(s). All joint holders should sign the form of authority and corporate shareholders, if they have a seal, would execute the form of authority under seal. Cheques for the redemption payments will be prepared so as to be available when the forms of authority are received back from the shareholders.

12. A redemption account will be opened with the company's bankers and the necessary funds transferred to the account to cover the cheques to be issued.

13. When forms of authority are received from the shareholders they should be checked to ensure that they have been properly completed and, if the certificate(s) lodged is(are) for more than the number of shares being redeemed, balance certificates should be prepared for issue to the shareholder.

14. Before dispatching cheques, the payment advices prepared under (6c) above should be checked against the official drawing list and the cheques should be sent out so as to arrive on the due redemption date.

15. Reminders should be sent to shareholders who have not returned their forms.
16. The shareholders' accounts in the Register of Members should be debited with the number of shares redeemed and if the redemption closes the shareholder's account completely, the account should be transferred to the closed accounts section of the Register.
17. The secretary should formally report to the board the completion of the redemption following the annual drawing for the sinking fund purpose.
18. A notice of the redemption should be sent to the Registrar of Companies on Companies Form No. G122 'Notice of consolidation, division, sub-division, redemption or cancellation of shares, or conversion, re-conversion of stock into shares' within one month of the redemption.
19. If the shares redeemed are preference shares, they will remain entitled to any dividend for the half year ending on the redemption date and warrants should be prepared for the payment of the preference dividend to be dispatched to the holders in the ordinary way. Payment of the preference dividend should be dealt with quite separately from the payment of the redemption money.
20. If the company is a listed company and the shares are redeemed at a premium over the nominal value, the amount paid on redemption which exceeds the original issue price will be treated as a taxable distribution; the company should therefore issue a tax voucher to cover the amount of such distribution.

Further information with regard to the procedure for drawing redeemable shares will be found in the Institute's manual, together with specimens of the various documents issued in connection with a drawing.

Purchase of redeemable shares

The following is a summary of the procedure to be followed where the necessary shares to cover the sinking fund redemption instalment have been purchased on the market:

1. The company should carefully check the contract notes received from its brokers in respect of the shares purchased.
2. If the shares are listed, The Stock Exchange should be advised of the number purchased and the number remaining outstanding.
3. Unless settlement of the shares is through the TALISMAN system, the brokers will have prepared standard forms of discharge in respect of the purchase price, to be signed by the shareholders concerned. If settlement is through the TALISMAN system, the shareholder will

have signed a TALISMAN sold transfer in the name of SEPON Limited 'A' account and the form of discharge will then be executed by SEPON Limited. However, the brokers should inform the company of the names of the shareholders concerned without delay in case there are any queries, e.g. lost certificates, or the holding being covered by a stop notice or other restraint.

4. The company secretary will arrange to pay the brokers for the shares purchased on the relevant settlement date against the contract notes.

5. Forms of discharge and certificates when received from the brokers should be carefully checked.

6. The shares may have been purchased cum dividend, in which case the holdings concerned must be withdrawn from the dividend list, since no dividend will be paid on them. If the shares have been purchased ex dividend, however, no special action is necessary and the shareholders who have sold their shares will be entitled to the dividend in the usual way.

7. The accounts of the relevant shareholders in the Register of Members should be debited with the shares purchased, which should be transferred to a redemption account in which is recorded the sinking fund redemption date on which the shares will be utilised for the redemption instalment.

8. The points of procedure in respect of drawings of redeemable shares in paragraphs (17) and (18) (p.202) will also apply.

It should be noted that, whilst the above procedure is described as a 'purchase' of redeemable shares, the operation is, in fact, another form of redemption of shares.

Procedure for redemption of loan stocks and debentures

The procedure for the redemption of loan stocks and debentures through the operation of a sinking fund is similar to that described above in respect of the drawings of redeemable shares and purchase of redeemable shares. Debentures and loan stocks may be redeemed by annual drawings or by purchases on the market in order to meet the sinking fund requirements.

Purchase of own shares

A company may purchase its own shares which were not issued as redeemable shares provided that the purchase is authorised by the company's Articles of Association (s.162). There are, however, certain procedural requirements to be followed, as indicated below. Generally, however, the administrative procedures are similar to those applying when a company purchases its redeemable shares on the market.

The provisions relating to the purchase by a company of its own shares were introduced by the Companies Act 1981 and are now consolidated in the Act. It will be advisable for a company contemplating purchasing its own shares to take legal advice before embarking on the exercise. One of the points which arises is that if the amount paid by the company for the purchase of its shares exceeds the issue price of the shares, on general principles the excess would be treated as a distribution by the company taxable as income in the hands of the vendor and a tax voucher should be issued in respect of the excess. The company would also be required to account for advance corporation tax. Section 219 of ICTA, however, contains a provision to the effect that if the company is not a listed company or the subsidiary of a listed company, the excess will not be treated as an income distribution but be treated as part of the capital proceeds of the sale of the shares. Advance clearance that a proposed purchase will be treated in this way can be obtained from the Inland Revenue but it is recommended that, since the conditions are complicated, the company's taxation advisers should be consulted before taking any action in this respect (ICTA s.225).

Procedure for off-market purchases

Sections 163 and 164 contain detailed and stringent requirements for off-market purchases by a company of its own shares. Off-market purchases would be either of the following:

1. Purchases made other than on a recognised stock exchange.
2. Where the shares are purchased on a recognised stock exchange but are not subject to a marketing arrangement on that stock exchange, i.e. (a) the shares are not listed on that stock exchange; or (b) if the company may, without prior permission, effect individual transactions on that stock exchange without time limit as to the time during which those facilities are to be available (e.g. the Unlisted Securities Market (see pp.58–60)).

It is necessary to comply with the following procedural steps:

1. A Special Resolution of the company must authorise the terms of the proposed contract of purchase before the company enters into the contract. The purchase may also be made under a contingent purchase whereby a company may become entitled or obliged to purchase its own shares provided that this also has been previously authorised by Special Resolution. Authorities may be varied,

revoked or renewed by a Special Resolution. However, in the case of a public company, the Special Resolution confirming or renewing authority for a company to purchase its own shares must specify a date for its expiry, which must be not later than 18 months from the date of passing the Special Resolution.

2. The Special Resolution will not be effective, however, unless a copy of the proposed contract of purchase (or a written memorandum of its terms if it is not in writing) is made available for inspection by members of the company at the company's registered office for not less than 15 days ending with the date of the meeting at which the resolution is passed and is also available for inspection at the meeting itself. The memorandum must include the names of the members holding the shares to which the contract relates. If it is the contract itself which is available for inspection it must have annexed to it a written memorandum specifying the names if they do not appear in the contract itself. Similar arrangements must be made in the case of the variation of an existing contract, which also has to be approved by a Special Resolution.

3. A member of the company holding shares covered by the proposed contract may not vote on the Special Resolution if his votes would determine whether the resolution was passed or not by the requisite 75 per cent majority of the members attending and voting at the meeting. The resolution will be ineffective if this provision is contravened.

A company may not enter into an agreement to release its rights under a contract to make an off-market purchase of its shares approved under the above procedure unless the release agreement is also approved by Special Resolution.

Procedure for market purchases

The Act's conditions in respect of market purchases by a company of its own shares are less stringent than those which are applicable in the case of off-market purchases. It should be noted, however, that in the case of listed companies The Stock Exchange has issued its own rules governing the purchase by a company of its own shares on The Stock Exchange, a copy of which is reproduced in the Institute's manual. The Stock Exchange circular covers notifications to be made to The Stock Exchange, the contents of circulars to shareholders, the position with regard to convertible securities, warrants and options to subscribe for ordinary shares, purchases of 5 per cent or more of the company's shares, notification to The Stock Exchange of purchases, information to be given in the directors' report of the company, and the application of The Stock

Exchange's *Model Code for Securities Transactions by Directors of Listed Companies*, i.e. the company should not purchase shares at any time when the directors would not be free to do so on their own account under the *Model Code*.

A market purchase is one made on a recognised stock exchange other than an off-market purchase (s.163(3)). In the case of market purchases the purchase must be authorised by an Ordinary Resolution of members and the resolution may give a general authority to purchase a company's own shares or limit the authority to a particular class or description of shares. It may also be either unconditional or conditional. However, the resolution must specify the maximum number of shares authorised to be acquired and give the maximum and minimum prices which may be paid. The resolution must also specify a date not later than 18 months from the date of passing the resolution on which the authority will expire. The resolution may be so worded that, provided the contract is concluded before the end of the time limit, the execution of the contract, i.e. the delivery of the shares concerned, may take place after the expiry of the authority.

The Ordinary Resolution conferring, varying, revoking or renewing authority to make a market purchase of the company's own shares must be filed with the Registrar of Companies within 15 days of it being passed and must also be included in copies of the company's Memorandum and Articles issued subsequently (s.380).

The possible need to send tax vouchers to the vendors of the shares purchased should not be overlooked, but before doing so The Stock Exchange should be consulted in the case of transactions on The Stock Exchange.

Further procedural requirements

Any payment a company may make in consideration of acquiring a right to purchase its own shares, e.g. under a contingent purchase agreement, or to vary an approved contract to make off-market purchases, or to release it of any of its obligations to purchase its own shares, must be made out of the company's distributable profits (s.168).

Companies Form No. G169 'Return by a company purchasing its own shares' must be filed with the Registrar of Companies within 28 days of the delivery of the shares purchased by the company (s.169). The return includes information as to the number, class and nominal value of the shares purchased, the date of delivery to the company and, in the case of a public company, the aggregate amount paid by the company for the shares to which the return relates together with the maximum and minimum prices paid.

A copy of a contract to purchase the company's own shares (and a copy of any variation of it), or a memorandum of the terms if it is not in writing, must be kept at the registered office of the company from the conclusion of the contract until the end of a period of 10 years commencing with the date on which the purchase of all the shares under the contract was completed. This document must be kept open for inspection by any member without charge and, in the case of a public company, it may be inspected by any other person also without charge (s.169).

Redemption or purchases by private companies out of capital

Purchases by a company of its own shares as described above may only be made out of distributable profits or the proceeds of a fresh issue of shares. In the case of private companies, however, ss.171–7 provide a procedure to effect purchases or redemptions of shares out of capital. Very stringent and complicated additional procedures have to be complied with in this case and it should be noted that ss.504, 507 and 519 deal with the liability of past shareholders and directors in the event of the winding-up of the company where a payment has been made out of capital for redemption or purchase of any of the company's own shares.

The amount of the payment which may be made out of capital is strictly defined and is called in s.171 the 'permissible capital payment for the shares' which is such amount as, taken together with any available profits of the company and the proceeds of any fresh issue of shares made for the purposes of the redemption or purchase, is equal to the price of redemption or purchase. The effect of the permissible capital payment on the company's capital redemption reserve, share premium account, fully paid share capital, any amount representing unrealised profits of the company and the company's revaluation reserve, as defined in Schedule 4, Part II, para. 34, as amended by CA 1989 Schedule 24, are outside the scope of a practical handbook on company secretarial practice and information about this should be sought from the Institute's manual. Generally, however, it may be said that the object of the permissible capital payment for the shares is to ensure that no payment is made out of capital unless any retained profits or other distributable reserves of the company have been applied first for the purchase of shares or exhausted in other ways.

The procedural steps to be followed in the case of the purchase by a private company of its own shares out of capital are covered in s.173, and the company secretary should be aware of the practical steps which have to be followed:

1. A statutory declaration must be made by the directors on Companies Form No. G173 'Declaration in relation to the redemption or purchase of shares out of capital', which specifies the amount of the permissible capital payment for the shares. The form also incorporates a statement by the directors that, having made a full enquiry into the affairs of the company, they have formed the opinion that once the payment out of capital has been made, there is no ground on which the company would then be unable to pay its debts, having regard to any contingent or prospective liabilities of the company which may exist and that, in the year following the payment, the company will be able to carry on its business as a going concern and pay its debts as they fall due.

2. An auditors' report must be attached to the statutory declaration confirming that:
    (a) the auditors have enquired into the company's state of affairs;
    (b) the amount specified in the declaration as the permissible capital payment for the shares has been properly determined in accordance with ss.171–5;
    (c) they do not consider that any opinion expressed by the directors in the declaration is unreasonable.

3. A Special Resolution of the company must be passed on or within one week of the statutory declaration, approving the proposed payment out of capital, and copies of the statutory declaration must be available for inspection by members of the company at the meeting at which the resolution is passed. A member whose shares are the subject of the Special Resolution may not vote on the resolution.

4. Publicity must be given to the proposed payment out of capital in the following manner:
    (a) within one week of the passing of the Special Resolution, a public notice must be published in the *London Gazette* or *Edinburgh Gazette*, together with a notice in a national newspaper or a notice in writing to each of the creditors of the company stating that the company has approved a payment out of capital for the purpose of acquiring its own shares by redemption or purchase;
    (b) also within one week of the passing of the Special Resolution, copies of the statutory declaration and auditors' report must be filed with the Registrar of Companies, to be received by him not later than the date on which the public notice is given.

5. From the date of the public notice to the end of the fifth week following the date on which the Special Resolution was passed, the statutory declaration and auditors' report must be kept at the company's registered office and be open for inspection by any member or creditor of the company without charge.

6. Payment out of capital must be made within the period commencing 5 weeks after the date of passing the Special Resolution and terminating 7 weeks after the date of the Special Resolution.

7. Up to the end of the fifth week following the date of passing the Special Resolution, any member of the company (other than a member who voted in favour of the resolution) and any creditor may apply to the Court for the resolution to be cancelled (s.176). If such an application is made notice must be given to the Registrar of Companies immediately on Companies Form No. G176 'Notice of application to the Court for the cancellation of a resolution for the redemption or purchase of shares out of capital'. On the making of a Court Order a copy must be filed with the Registrar within 15 days of it being made or a longer period if the Court allows (s.176(3)). The Court has wide powers in considering any such application and may alter or extend the date or period specified in the resolution or in the Act. It may also direct any necessary alterations to be made to the company's Memorandum and Articles, which will then have the same effect as if passed by a Special Resolution of the company. If the Court makes alterations to the Memorandum and Articles the company must obtain the Court's permission before making further alterations which would be in breach of the Court's requirements (s.177).

Section 504 provides that, if the company should be wound up within one year of a payment for shares out of capital, personal liability may attach to the directors and to the shareholders who sold the shares to the company.

Failure to redeem or purchase shares

A company failing to redeem or purchase its shares under an agreement will not be liable to pay damages if other remedies could be available to the shareholder concerned (s.178). Section 178 also covers the position if at the commencement of the winding-up of the company any shares have not been redeemed or purchased pursuant to the Special Resolution.

CHAPTER 10

The secretary

No handbook on company secretarial practice would be complete without considering the nature of the office of the company secretary and setting out his duties with regard to statutory registers, forms which the company is required to submit to the Registrar of Companies and his responsibilities in relation to meetings and minute books. The secretary is also responsible for the custody of the company's seal and is empowered to authenticate any document requiring authentication by the company. All these functions may be regarded as the 'compliance' duties of the company secretary.

The office of secretary

Section 283 provides that every company must have a secretary and that a sole director may not also be the secretary. The section also stipulates that a corporate body may be appointed secretary provided that, in the case of a company with a sole director, he is not also the sole director of the body corporate appointed secretary. Although a partnership may be appointed secretary in the name of the firm, this has effect in England and Wales as an appointment of all the partners as joint secretaries. In Scotland, where partnerships have corporate status, the firm may be appointed secretary in its own right. Subsection (3) of s.283 provides for the appointment of deputy or assistant secretaries who may act in the office of secretary if the office is vacant or there is no secretary capable of acting. As well as the statutory requirements in s.283, the company's Articles of Association frequently contain provisions with regard to the appointment of secretary as in Table A, Regulation 99.

In the case of a public company, s.286 provides that the directors must take all reasonable steps to secure that the secretary of the company is a person who appears to them to have the requisite knowledge and experience to discharge the functions of secretary of the company and who also meets other requirements laid down in the section. To preserve the position of secretaries of companies holding office on the date when the provisions requiring public companies to have qualified secretaries were brought in by the Companies Act 1980, now consolidated in the Companies Act 1985, s.286, the secretary may be a person who on 22 December 1980 held the office of secretary or assistant or deputy secretary of the company. Other persons qualified to be secretary of a public company under these provisions include the following:

1. A barrister, advocate or solicitor, called or admitted in any part of the United Kingdom.
2. A member of various professional bodies, including the Institute of Chartered Secretaries and Administrators, and members of various accountancy bodies.
3. A person who is a member of any other professional body who appears to the directors to be capable of discharging the functions of the secretary.
4. Persons who, for at least three of the five years immediately preceding his appointment as secretary, held the office of secretary of another company other than a private company.

The duties of the secretary are not specified in detail in the Act but at various places in the Act the secretary is named as one of the persons who may sign prescribed forms on behalf of the company, make statutory declarations and sign the annual return. The secretary is an officer of the company as defined by s.744 and consequently may incur personal responsibility for not complying with requirements of the Act affecting the company. Although in this chapter the statutory matters for which the secretary is particularly responsible are mentioned, many of the other subjects covered in this handbook affect the responsibilities of the secretary. In the field of share registration, however, the company may have appointed its own registrar as a company official or appointed outside service registrars, in which case the responsibilities of secretary in the field of share registration would be delegated to such person or firm.

In view of the fact that the Act and most Articles of Association do not specifically define the powers of a secretary, the position of secretary has been considered by the courts at various times. In the nineteenth century the secretary was considered as a mere servant or clerk without much authority but a case in the Court of Appeal in 1971 (*Panorama Developments (Guildford)* v. *Fidelis Furnishing Fabrics*) decided that the secretary is the chief administrative officer of the company and, with regard to matters affecting the administration of the company, had ostensible authority to make contracts on behalf of the company. Although matters falling within this administrative function are not anywhere explicitly defined, this authority would often extend to matters affecting contracts relating to the employment of staff, the company's premises, data processing and other office machinery, printing and stationery requirements and company cars. If the secretary is responsible for data processing his responsibilities will be governed by the Data Protection Act 1984, especially if he is the person appointed Data Protection Coordinator for the company. However, the secretary's responsibilities would not normally extend to negotiating trading contracts, e.g. sale or purchase of goods and materials or production machinery, which are matters affecting the company's business operations and are the responsibility of other managers. At the same time in many companies he may be the appropriate person to sign contracts relating to such matters on behalf of the company.

Appointment

In the case of the incorporation of a new company, the person named as secretary on Companies Form No. G10 'Statement of first directors and secretary and intended situation of registered office' which is delivered to the Registrar of Companies with the Memorandum and Articles of Association for registration is, on incorporation of the company, deemed to have been appointed as the first secretary of the company (ss.10 and 13). Companies Form No. G10 is signed by the subscribers or by agents on behalf of the subscribers of the Memorandum and it contains a form of consent to be signed by the person named as secretary in addition to the forms of consent to be signed by the first directors of the company. In this case no other formality is required for the appointment of the first secretary of the company other than entering his name in the Register of Directors and Secretaries.

Appointments of secretaries subsequent to incorporation would be made by the directors in accordance with the provisions of the Articles of Association (Table A, Regulation 99). When a new secretary is appointed, the following action should be taken:

1. In the case of an important listed company, it may be appropriate to notify The Stock Exchange, since this could come within the requirement to notify The Stock Exchange of any change in the holding of an executive office (Continuing Obligations, para. 42.1); it would also be appropriate in this case to issue a press release of the appointment.

2. The particulars relating to the new secretary must be entered in the company's Register of Directors and Secretaries and notified to the Registrar of Companies on Companies Form No. G288 'Notice of change of directors or secretaries or in their particulars' within 14 days of the appointment.

3. If the secretary is an authorised signatory on the company's bank account, notification of the change of secretary and a copy of his specimen signature should be sent to the bank.
4. If thought to be appropriate, announcement of the new appointment should be made to the company's staff, suppliers and customers.
5. If it is the company's custom to have service contracts between it and its senior executives, a formal service contract should be drawn up for the secretary for signature by the company and by the secretary.
6. If the company has in force an insurance policy covering officers of the company against liabilities they may incur in carrying out their duties the insurance company should be notified of the appointment of the new secretary (s.310 as amended by CA 1989 s.137).
7. In the case of a listed company, the new secretary should be supplied with the company's rules governing transactions in its securities complying with the terms of The Stock Exchange's *Model Code for Securities Transactions by Directors of Listed Companies*. Although the *Model Code* relates to dealings by directors of listed companies, it is good practice for a company's in-house rules to be drafted so as to include senior executives, like the secretary, who may be in possession of unpublished or price-sensitive information in relation to the securities of the company.

General requirements as to statutory registers

The Act requires that every company keep the following registers or books, and it is the secretary's primary responsibility to see that they are properly maintained and kept up to date:

1. Register of Members (ss.352 and 353).
2. Register of Charges (s.411 inserted by CA 1989 s.101).
3. Books containing minutes of companies' and directors' meetings (s.382).
4. Accounting records (ss.221–2 inserted by CA 1989 s.2).
5. Register of Directors and Secretaries (ss.288–90 as amended by CA 1989 Schedule 19, paras. 2 and 3, and CA 1989 Schedule 24).
6. Register of Directors' Interests in Shares and Debentures of the Company (ss.325 and 326 and Schedule 13, Part IV, as amended by CA 1989 Schedule 24).
7. If the company is a public company, a Register of Interests in Voting Shares (s.211).

The Act does not require that a register of debenture holders be kept and consequently this is not, strictly speaking, a statutory book. However, if such a register is kept, the Act lays down requirements with regard to its maintenance and inspection (ss.190 and 191).

There are particular requirements with regard to the place where the various statutory registers or books are to be kept and where they may be inspected. The general position is as follows:

1. The Register of Directors and Secretaries and the Register of Charges must be kept at the registered office of the company.
2. The Register of Members must be kept either at the company's registered office or at some other place within the country of registration (i.e. England and Wales or Scotland) where the work of making up the Register takes place. Where the Register of Members is not at all times kept at the company's registered office the Registrar of Companies must be informed of the place where it is kept within 14 days on Companies Form No. G353 'Notice of place where register of members is kept or of any change in that place' (s.353(2)–(4)).
3. The Register of Directors' Interests in Shares and Debentures of the Company must be kept either at the company's registered office or at the place where the Register of Members is kept. If this Register is not at all times kept at the registered office, the Registrar of Companies must be informed of the place where it is kept within 14 days on Companies Form No. G325 'Notice of place where register of directors' interests in shares etc. is kept or of any change in that place' (Schedule 13, Part IV).
4. The Register of Interests in Voting Shares must be kept at the same place as the Register of Directors' Interests (s.211(8)).
5. If a register of debenture holders is kept, similar provisions apply as in the case of the Register of Members, except that if the Register is not kept at the registered office of the company, the Registrar of Companies must be informed of the place where it is kept on Companies Form No. G190 'Notice of place where a register of holders of debentures or a duplicate is kept or of any change in that place' (s.190).

The statutory books and registers may be kept in the form of a combined register, either a bound book or in loose-leaf form. The statutory registers (including a register of debenture holders if one is kept) and other records may also now be kept on computer or in other non-legible form provided that adequate precautions are taken against falsification and that they are capable of being reproduced in legible form for inspection (ss.722 and 723). The detailed requirements relating to registers and records kept in non-legible form are contained in The Companies (Registers and Other Records) Regulations 1985 (SI 1985/724). Special forms are prescribed for notifying the Registrar of Companies of the place where registers kept in non-legible form may be inspected in legible form. These are:

1. Companies Form No. G190a 'Notice of place for inspection of a register of holders of debentures which is kept in a non-legible form, or of any change in that place'.
2. Companies Form No. G325a 'Notice of place for inspection of a register of directors' interests in shares etc. which is kept in a non-legible form, or of any change in that place'.
3. Companies Form No. G353a 'Notice of place for inspection of a register of members which is kept in a non-legible form, or of any change in that place'.
4. Companies Form No. G362a 'Notice of place for inspection of an overseas branch register which is kept in a non-legible form, or of any change in that place'.

Register of charges

The provisions described in this section apply to the registration of company charges with respect to companies registered in Great Britain (CA 1989 s.92). A Register of Charges should be kept by every company, even if there are no charges to be entered in the Register, since persons having the right to inspect the Register will wish to know whether or not the company has any charges specifically affecting the property of the company or any floating charges on the undertaking or on any of its property (s.411 inserted by s.101 CA 1989). The Register must contain particulars of all charges on any property of the company and not just those requiring registration with the Registrar of Companies. Section 411 inserted by CA 1989 s.101 also includes an obligation on companies to keep copies of instruments creating charges and this also applies whether or not particulars of the charge are required to be delivered to the Registrar for registration. The Register must be open to inspection by any creditor or member of the company without fee and to inspection by any other person on payment of such fee as may be prescribed (s.412 inserted by CA 1989 s.101). The Register of Charges kept by the company should not be confused with the Register to be kept by the Registrar of Companies under s.397 inserted by CA 1989 s.94 relating to particulars of charges sent to the Registrar of Companies under the provisions of ss.395–401 inserted by CA 1989 ss.93–6.

Register of Directors and Secretaries

The following points of practice arise in connection with completing this Register:

1. There is no need to show former names if the names have not been

used for 20 years or more, and the maiden name of a married woman need not be shown (s.289(2) as substituted by CA 1989 Schedule 19 para. 2(4)).

2. If a person is a director of a number of companies, his occupation may be shown as 'director of companies', but if he is a director only of the company to which the Register relates, his occupation should be described as 'none' unless he has a business occupation such as 'marketing manager'.

3. The date of birth of every director must be included whether or not the company is subject to s.293 relating to the appointment of directors who have attained the age of 70, notwithstanding that the company may have excluded or modified the operation of the section by its Articles (s.289(1) as amended by CA 1989 Schedule 19, para. 2(2)(b)).

4. Other directorships must include past directorships held during the previous five years as well as current directorships, but directorships of dormant companies, as defined by s.250(3) inserted by CA 1989 s.14, and directorships in companies treated as grouped with the company keeping the Register, need not be included (s.289(3) and (4)).

5. Changes in the directors or secretaries or in their particulars must be notified to the Registrar of Companies within 14 days of the change on Companies Form No. G288. The form incorporates a form of consent to be signed by a new director or a new secretary.

6. The Register must be open to inspection at reasonable times without charge to any member of the company or subject to payment of the prescribed fee to any other person (s.288(3) as amended by CA 1989 Schedule 24).

Register of Directors' Interests in Shares and Debentures

This Register is prepared from notices given to the company by the directors in accordance with s.324 and no entry in the Register should be made without such a notice; but the company should enter interests arising when it grants to a director rights to subscribe for shares or debentures in the company (s.325). The director must notify the company within five days of his becoming interested in shares or debentures of the company. Only three days are allowed for the company to make the entry in the Register from the date of the receipt of the notice by the company from the director or the grant of a right by the company.

While under s.325(3) and (4) a director is not required to give particulars regarding the grant to him by the company of rights to subscribe for shares or debentures in the company or the exercise of such rights, he is required to notify the grant of similar rights by the company to his spouse or infant children, and the exercise by them of such rights, within five days of the occurrence (s.328(3)–(5)). In the case of a rights issue it is helpful if the director himself notifies the company of the grant to him of the rights to acquire shares and, in any event, he is required by s.324(2)(c) to notify the company if he should sell his rights. In reckoning the periods of days mentioned in this and the preceding paragraph, Saturdays, Sundays and bank holidays are excluded. Detailed rules for the interpretation of ss.324–8 are contained in Schedule 13.

The Register must be open to inspection on similar terms to those applicable to the Register of Directors and Secretaries as in item (6) above (s.325(5) and Schedule 13, Part IV, para. 25, as amended by CA 1989 Schedule 24). Copies of the Register may also be obtained on payment of the prescribed fee (Schedule 13, Part IV, para. 26).

In the case of a person who is a director of a holding company and of one or more of its subsidiaries (not being wholly owned subsidiaries), he is required to give notice to each company within the group of which he is a director, which will result in the Registers of Directors' Interests of each company in the group containing similar information. There is accordingly an exemption in the case of notifications of interests in the holding company's shares to, and the contents of the Register of Directors' Interests of, a company which is the wholly owned subsidiary company of which the person is a director as well as being a director of the holding company. Here it is sufficient for the interests to be recorded only in the holding company's Register of Directors' Interests. Moreover, any shares held by a director in a subsidiary held by him as a bare nominee of the holding company need not be notified (s.324(6) and Schedule 3, Part I, para. 10).

Register of Interests in Voting Shares

Part VI of the Act as amended by CA 1989 s.134 deals with the disclosure of interests in voting shares of public companies. A public company is required to keep a Register of Interests in Voting Shares, even though there may be no entries falling to be made in the Register at any particular time (s.211). No entries may be made in the Register except on the authority of a notification from the person concerned made to the company, which must be made to the company within two days after the day on which the obligation arises (s.202(1), 202(4) and 206(8) as amended by CA 1989 s.134(3)), even though the company may notice that in its Register of Members there are balances exceeding the prescribed percentage, giving rise to the obligation to make the notification, i.e. 3 per cent or more of the relevant share capital (s.199(2) as amended by CA 1989 s.134(2)). The notification must give the identity of each registered holder to which the notification relates and the number of shares comprised in the notifiable interest (s.202(3) as substituted by CA 1989 s.134(4)).

Having received the notification, the company must make the entry in the Register of Interests in Voting Shares within three days (s.211). However, under the provisions of s.212, the company, by notice in writing, may require a person who it believes to be interested in the company's relevant share capital within the preceding three years to give details of the ownership of the company's relevant share capital. The information so obtained must be entered into a separate part of the Register of Interests in Voting Shares (s.213). Where an entry relates to the termination of an interest or has been superseded by a later entry made under s.211, the entry may be removed from the Register 6 years after it was made (s.217).

For the purpose of this Register, relevant share capital means the issued share capital carrying rights to vote in all circumstances at general meetings, referred to in this chapter for brevity as 'voting shares'.

Under the provisions of s.210A inserted by CA 1989 s.134(5), the Secretary of State may by regulations alter the definition of relevant share capital, the percentage giving rise to a notifiable interest and the period within which the disclosure must be made.

If a notification should be sent by a person to the company under an obligation imposed by any of the provisions of Part VI of the Act to the effect that another person is interested in the voting shares of the company, the company must inform that other person within 15 days of the entry in the Register relating to him made as a result of the receipt of that information, advising him that he may apply to have it removed if the information is incorrect (s.217(2) and (3)).

As mentioned above, notifications of interests in voting shares must be made within two days from the date on which the obligation arises, excluding Saturdays, Sundays and bank holidays. The circumstances giving rise to a notification are as follows:

1. Where the person first becomes interested in at least 3 per cent of the voting shares, not previously having had such an interest.
2. Where, having held 3 per cent or more, there is a decrease in the amount of his interest so that it is reduced below the 3 per cent level.
3. Where, having an interest in 3 per cent or more which has been notified to the company, a person's interest increases or decreases but remains interested in at least 3 per cent of the voting shares where the change in the percentage interest rounded down to the nearest whole number changes by one whole number. However, where the

nominal value of the voting shares is greater after the event than it was before, the percentage interest is calculated in both cases by reference to the larger amount. This covers the position where a rights issue of shares is taken up and where no notification would otherwise fall to be made, since on taking up the rights the percentage of the relevant share capital held would remain the same (s.200).

Interests in shares which have to be notified are detailed in s.208 but are subject to the exceptions contained in s.209 and in SI 1982/677 and SI 1988/706. The interests of a person's spouse, infant children or stepchildren should be notified to the company and notification should also be made by a person who has one-third or more control of a company which is itself interested in the shares concerned. There are complex provisions in ss.204 and 205 requiring the aggregation of interests of persons acting together ('concert parties'). In simple terms, aggregation is required where there is any agreement or arrangement between persons acquiring voting shares in a public company. Under s.206, the parties to such an agreement are required to notify each other of any acquisitions or disposals of shares concerned.

The information to be included in notifications given to a company under the provisions requiring notification of interests in voting shares is specified in s.202 and is as follows:

1. The share capital to which the interest relates.
2. The number of voting shares in which the person was interested at the time the obligation to notify arose, unless the notification is to the effect that the person has ceased to be interested in 3 per cent or more of the voting shares.
3. Particulars of the identity of each registered holder of shares to which the notification relates and the number of shares held by each such registered holder. This information is not necessary, however, if the notification is to the effect that the person concerned no longer has an interest in 3 per cent or more of the voting shares.

In the case of a listed company, particulars of any information notified to the company under the above provisions must be sent to The Stock Exchange without delay (Continuing Obligations, para. 16(a)).

Requisition of information regarding interests in voting shares

A public company has power under s.212 to require any person whom it knows or has reason to believe is or was at any time in the previous three years to have been interested in the relevant share capital of the company (i.e. voting shares) to supply information to the company as specified in the section. The information includes the identity of the persons interested in the voting shares in question and information as to whether such persons were parties to the agreement to which ss.204 and 205 relate (i.e. 'concert parties').

It should be noted that the request for information under s.212 may be made in relation to any shareholding and that there is no requirement for the shareholding concerned to be 3 per cent or more of the company's voting shares. Any information so obtained must be kept in a separate part of the Register of Interests in Voting Shares.

Members holding not less than one-tenth of the paid up capital of the company, giving the right to vote at general meetings of the company, may require the company to exercise its powers under the provisions of s.212 (ss.214 and 215). A report of the information received must be prepared and the members of the company requisitioning the company to make the investigation must be notified that the information is available for inspection at the company's registered office. Copies of the report must also be supplied on request.

Failure to give information to the company under s.212 by any persons may result in heavy penalties (s.216). It is of interest to companies to be aware of the identity of persons who hold significant holdings of voting shares in the company under the cloak of nominee names, since this may be the prelude to a take-over bid for the company. Consequently, with a view to enforcing compliance with requests for information, some companies include provisions in their Articles of Association to disenfranchise the shares comprised in such holdings (i.e. withhold the dividends and exclude voting rights). The Stock Exchange has no objection to such disenfranchisement of the voting shares of listed companies provided that a reasonable time is allowed for compliance, i.e. 28 days (Yellow Book, Section 9, Chapter 1, para. 14).

Register of debenture holders

It has already been mentioned that keeping a register of debenture holders is not a requirement of the Act although, if such a register is kept, there are various statutory requirements to be followed (s.190). If there is just one single debenture, an entry could be made in the company's Register of Charges which would obviate the need for keeping a separate register of debenture holders. It is, however, convenient to keep a register of debenture holders where a series of debentures is issued.

Directors' service contracts

Copies of directors' service contracts (or a memorandum of the terms if the contract is not in writing) which are not teminable by the company without payment of compensation within 12 months must be made available for inspection without charge by any member of the company (s.318). The copies or memoranda must be kept at the company's registered office, the place where the Register of Members is kept if other than at the registered office or at the company's principal place of business provided that it is situated in that part of Great Britain in which the company is registered (s.318). If the copies or memoranda are not kept at the registered office, the Registrar of Companies must be informed of the place where they are kept on Companies Form No. G318 'Notice of place where copies of directors' service contracts and any memoranda are kept or of any change in that place'.

There is no requirement to keep a copy of a contract or a memorandum of the terms of a contract if the director is required to work wholly or mainly outside the United Kingdom, although there must be kept a memorandum for inspection to the effect that such a contract exists, the name of the director concerned and its duration. This must be kept at the same place as the copies of contracts or memoranda relating to employment in the United Kingdom are kept.

There are special requirements imposed in the case of listed companies to the effect that copies of directors' service contracts must be available for the inspection by any person from the date of posting of the notice of the Annual General Meeting until the date of the meeting. They must also be made available for inspection at the place of the meeting, and for at least 15 minutes prior to the meeting and during the meeting itself. The notice of the Annual General Meeting must state that the directors' service contracts are available for inspection in compliance with this requirement (Continuing Obligations, para. 43).

Annual return

This is probably the most important companies form with which the company secretary has to deal during the course of the company's financial year. The specified form is Companies Form No. A363 'Annual return of a company' and the obligation on companies to make an annual return is imposed by ss.363–5 inserted by CA 1989 s.139. The return is made up to a date 12 months after the previous return (or 12 months after incorporation) although a company may choose to make it up to an earlier date. The annual return must be filed with the Registrar of Companies within 28 days of the return date together with a fee of £20.

A new style annual return form will be brought into use in 1991 following the enactment of the Companies Act 1989. Although longer, it is a greatly simplified form compared with the previous one. It has been designed as a 'shuttle' document in that the form with information pre-printed on it as on record in the Companies Registration Office is sent to companies about two weeks before it is due. The information contained in the form may then be verified by a tick in the appropriate box or amended as required. This system will also help to remind companies of the need to submit an annual return. The form must be signed either by a director or by the secretary. There is authority in s.365 inserted by CA 1989 s.139 for the Secretary of State by regulation to vary the contents of the annual return.

The directors are required by s.242(1) inserted by CA 1989 s.11 to deliver to the Registrar of Companies a copy of the accounts for the year, with the auditors' report, and a copy of the directors' report. Some companies find it convenient to file these documents with the annual return but there is no legal requirement to do this.

If practicable, in the case of public companies, it may be desirable to send the accounts, auditors' report and directors' report to the Registrar of Companies on the day that they are posted to shareholders since they would then be available for inspection on the company's file at the Companies Registration Office as soon as they are ready instead of having to wait until the annual return is submitted if it is not due to be sent until a later date.

However, companies which find it convenient to send the accounts, etc., with the annual return, may now change the date on which they submit their annual return to an earlier date so as to reduce the time gap between the availability of the accounts, etc., and the date of submission of the annual return. A company may inform the Companies Registration Office that it wishes to submit its annual return on an earlier date than the date on which it would normally be due and a 'shuttle' form will be sent to the company for completion. The annual return includes particulars of the members of the company and of their holdings, although there is a concession under s.364A(6) inserted by CA 1989 s.139 which allows the filing of changes in membership only if full details have been given for either of the two last years. The list would thus include only the particulars of persons who have become members, have ceased to be members or whose holdings or stock or shares have changed.

In the case of large public companies, however, where the list of members is produced by computer or other mechanised means, it is usually found more convenient to lodge a full list of members with the annual return each year. A full list would certainly be needed if the company has made a rights issue or capitalisation issue within the preceding year, and it is also convenient if there has been a large number of transfers of shares registered during the year.

The principal contents of the annual return are as follows:

1. The address of the company's registered office.
2. The address where the Register of Members and, if applicable, the Register of Debenture Holders, is kept, if these registers are not kept at the company's registered office.
3. The type of company and its principal business activities.
4. The name and address of the company secretary.
5. The name and address of every director giving nationality, date of birth, business occupation and other directorships as recorded in the company's Register of Directors and Secretaries. It should be noted, therefore, that this includes directorships held within the preceding five years.
6. If the company has a share capital, the total number of issued shares of the company of each class at the date to which the return is made and the aggregate nominal value of those shares or, where the company has converted any of its shares into stock, the aggregate amount of the stock issued.
7. The names and addresses of members of the company and the number of shares held by each member (or the amount of stock) of each class held by each member at the date of the return and the names and addresses of persons who have ceased to be members since the date of the last return. The return must also give the number of shares transferred by each member or by persons who have ceased to be members but note the concession under s.364A(6) inserted by CA 1989 s.139 mentioned above.
8. If the company has an overseas branch register the names and addresses of members need only include the details received at the company's registered office up to the date of the return (s.364A(7) inserted by CA 1989 s.139).
9. If the company is a private company and it has elected to dispense with laying accounts before a general meeting under s.252 inserted by CA 1989 s.16 and/or has elected to dispense with holding an Annual General Meeting under s.366A inserted by CA 1989 s.115(2), a statement of that fact by a tick in the appropriate box (s.364(1)(i) inserted by CA 1989 s.139).

With regard to (4) and (5) above, the Registrar of Companies is in the process of creating a computerised register of company directors and secretaries (Directors Register) which will facilitate the insertion of the required statutory information about directors and secretaries which has to be included in the shuttle document. The Register is being created by the extraction of data from annual returns, notifications of changes in director and secretary and incorporation documents sent to the Registrar.

It should be noted that s.365 inserted by CA 1989 s.139 gives power to the Secretary of State to make further provisions with regard to the content of the annual return which are likely to be made at the time that the new style annual return is introduced in 1991.

The following practical points usually arise in connection with the completion of the annual return although it is possible that the regulations mentioned in the previous paragraph may give more specific guidance which may alter or vary what is stated below:

1. Summary of share capital:
    (a) the current position must be given with regard to the nominal value of the company's share capital of each class taken up, ignoring cancelled shares. No distinction need be shown between shares taken up by payment wholly in cash, for a consideration other than cash or the extent to partly paid shares are paid up;
    (b) since the annual return deals only with the nominal value of the share capital taken up, no details of any premium obtained on the issue of shares should be included. The information given relates to nominal value of the shares only.
2. Particulars of indebtedness (which had to be shown on the old annual return form) do not have to be shown on the new annual return form.
4. Past and present members:
    (a) where shares have been converted into stock, the amount of stock held and transferred should be shown;
    (b) itemised particulars of transfers of shares transferred need be shown only against the name of the transferor   but see below regarding a customary concession allowed by the Registrar of Companies;
    (c) it is not necessary to show separately any shares acquired by members during the period to which the annual return relates under a rights or capitalisation issue – only the total number of shares held by the member at the date of the return need be shown;
    (d) it is convenient to arrange issues of shares, e.g. in the case of a rights issue or a capitalisation issue, so that the period of renunciation has expired at the date on which the annual return has to be made. If it is not possible to arrange things in this way, however, the new shares must be included in the summary of the share capital but the list of members will need to be specially annotated to show details of the basis of allotments or provisional allotments in the case of a rights issue and stating that

the period of renunciation in respect of the shares allotted or provisionally allotted does not expire until (date);

(e) the annual return form may be used to notify details of a director or secretary and the form includes a space for signatures consenting to act as director or secretary. This does not obviate the need to notify the Registrar of Companies of changes in directors or secretary within 14 days of the event in accordance with s.288 on Companies Form No. G288.

It has been the custom of the Registrar of Companies to accept a return for registration that does not comply with the usual strict requirements, but if any complaint is made by a person making a search of the company's file at the Companies Registration Office, the Registrar may require an amended return to be submitted. However, the following relaxations of the strict requirements may be allowed by the Registrar although some of these could also be altered or varied when the regulations governing the use of the new style annual return form are published:

1. Statement of the number of stock units instead of the total amount of stock. This is, in any event, more appropriate since the stock units may be regarded as being synonymous with shares.
2. Separate alphabetical sections for past and present members without any index.
3. Where shares have been transferred by one person on a number of occasions since the previous annual return, the aggregate may be shown against his name with the word 'various' in the space for date of transfer instead of the details of each transfer being shown separately. This concession is, of course, irrelevant if the company submits a full list of its members each year with the annual return.
4. The omission of past members and the number of shares previously held by them where, since the date of the last annual return, the class of shares concerned has been cancelled under a scheme arrangement, with an appropriate note made on the annual return to this effect.
5. Omission of past members whose shares were acquired under a takeover, with an appropriate note being included.

Companies Forms

Copies of the various Companies Forms now in use as a result of the consolidation of the former separate Companies Acts into the Companies Act 1985 are contained in SI 1985/854, The Companies (Forms) Regulations 1985 as amended by SI 1986/2097, SI 1987/752 and SI 1988/

1359. The amendments made to the forms were principally required because of the Insolvency Act 1986 and the Financial Services Act 1986. It should also be noted that SI 1985/724, The Companies (Registers and Other Records) Regulations 1985, contain copies of the forms relating to places where Registers not kept in legible form may be inspected in legible form.

There is a convenient arrangement with regard to the numbering of forms, since the numbers of the various Companies Forms correspond with the appropriate section number of the Act or the CA 1989, under which the obligation to lodge the form arises. Further regulations concerning company forms are expected to be published in consequence of changes required following the enactment of the Companies Act 1989 as some renumbering of forms will be necessary on account of some section numbers being changed by the CA 1989.

Agenda

The company secretary is responsible for preparing the agenda for board and company meetings. The agenda lists the items of business to be transacted at the meeting and the order in which they are to be transacted. It is a useful document in that it prevents any items of business being overlooked and when circulated to persons expected to attend the meeting, gives them an opportunity to consider the matters which are to come up for discussion and form some opinion about them before the meeting takes place.

It is desirable that the order of items on the agenda follow a logical sequence and it is also helpful, where formal resolutions are to be passed, to include the wording of the resolutions in the agenda so that the chairman will not have to read them out to the meeting.

In the case of board meetings, there are a number of recurring matters which come up for consideration by the board at certain times of the year. The secretary should keep a careful note of these to ensure that they are not overlooked when the time for that meeting comes round again. He should also maintain a file of letters and documents which support various items on the agenda, to have available at the board meeting in case it is necessary to refer to them.

It is useful to prepare a special copy of the agenda for the chairman, with a wide margin in order that he may note the decision reached and perhaps also any points in the discussion which he considers should be recorded in the minutes. Copies of the agenda for the board meeting should be circulated to all directors with supporting papers as required whenever possible.

The approved minutes signed by the chairman are the only permanent and authentic record of the proceedings. Consequently, copies of the agenda containing any notes made by the chairman or secretary and any summaries of discussion prepared by the secretary at the meeting should be destroyed, since keeping such records might cause complications if any dispute arose regarding a decision taken by the board. Such notes should be kept, however, until after the minutes have been approved, although the prudent company secretary may decide to keep such notes privately for a somewhat longer period in case any query should arise at subsequent board meetings over, say, the next few months.

Minutes

Minute writing is an art, i.e. deciding when merely to record the decision reached or to narrate some of the arguments leading up to the decision. Whenever possible minutes should consist only of a record of the business transacted at the meeting and of the decisions reached. Only in special circumstances should the discussion leading to decisions be summarised in the minutes. It is undesirable to record in the minutes the views expressed by a particular member of the board by name, unless he is dissenting from the decision reached and wishes his dissension to be recorded in the minutes. Some minutes narrate an event occurring at the meeting (called 'minutes of narration') and some minutes include the text of formal resolutions which have been passed at the meeting ('minutes of resolution'). An example of a minute of narration at a board meeting would be:

The question of replacing the company's computer was discussed and it was decided that the proposed purchase of .... should proceed with a view to the installation of the new computer as soon as possible.

.... dissented from this decision and asked that his dissent be recorded in the minutes.

Minutes of narration are unlikely at Annual General Meetings since the business normally consists of formal resolutions to be passed by the meeting.

An example of a minute of resolution at a board meeting is as follows:

It was resolved that the report of the directors, the chairman's statement and the audited accounts for the year ended .... 19...., including the final dividend of .... p per share recommended therein (making a total dividend of .... p per share for the year) be approved and that, subject to approval by the company in general meeting, such dividend be paid on .... 19...., to shareholders registered at the close of business on .... 19....

An example of a minute of resolution at an Annual General Meeting is as follows:

It was resolved that the report of the directors and the audited accounts for the year ended .... 19...., now laid before the meeting, be received and that a final dividend of .... p per share recommended therein be declared payable on 19...., to holders of ordinary shares registered at the close of business on .... 19.....

It is usual for the chairman formally to propose the resolutions to be passed at an Annual General Meeting (except a resolution regarding his own re-appointment as a director following retirement by rotation) and for another member of the board to second the resolution. It is not necessary for the names of the proposer and seconder to be included in the minutes of the Annual General Meeting, although some companies may wish to do this.

Since the minutes constitute a permanent record of the proceedings at board and general meetings they should be framed in a clear, concise form and free of ambiguity. It is important to include all dates and figures so that nothing is left ill defined.

When the minutes have been signed by the chairman of the meeting, either at the meeting at which the business was transacted or by the chairman of the next meeting, they constitute evidence of the proceedings. When the minutes have been signed in this way, the meeting is deemed to have been duly convened and held and that the proceedings recorded therein were duly transacted, unless the contrary can be proved (s.382). The signed minutes are prima facie evidence of the proceedings but they can be set aside by the Court if inaccuracies should be established.

There is no legal provision requiring board minutes to be read at a subsequent meeting and, indeed, there is no need to seek formal approval of them before they are signed. Even so it is good company secretarial practice to circulate the minutes to members of the board in draft so that they may have the opportunity to comment; any agreed alterations may be made to the draft minutes before the approved version comes up for signature by the chairman at the next following board meeting. If any alteration is made to the draft minutes as a result of a comment received from a director, the chairman should mention this fact at the next board meeting when he signs the altered minutes. The minutes of the board meeting at which the minutes are signed (assuming there has been no alteration) should merely record the fact that:

The chairman signed the minutes of the board meeting dated ....

It is not appropriate to record that the minutes were confirmed and signed, since the decisions taken at a board meeting do not require to be confirmed at a following board meeting. It is useful for the minutes to be numbered serially, which facilitates reference to previous minutes or resolutions if this should be necessary. For example, if an alteration is made to the minutes circulated to directors prior to signature, the minute of the next following board meeting at which the minutes are signed could read:

The minutes of the board meeting held on .... subject to the replacement in minute no..... of the sentence '...............................' by the sentence '........................' were signed by the chairman.

Once the minutes have been signed they should not, of course, be altered; if any subsequent amendments are needed this should be dealt with by an amending minute or an amending resolution at a subsequent meeting.

The minutes of general meetings are normally signed by the chairman shortly after the meeting.

Minute books

There are no statutory requirements regarding the location of minute books, except in relation to minutes of general meetings held after 1 November 1929, which must be kept at the registered office.

The type of minute book kept by the company will depend on the size and procedures of the company concerned. In the case of private companies they may be kept in bound books, either hand written or typed on sheets of paper pasted into the bound book with the pages serially numbered. As mentioned above, it is a good idea for the minutes to be numbered consecutively from number 1 upwards throughout the book, so that in minute book number 1 the minutes would be numbered 1.1, etc., and in the next minute book they would be numbered minute 2.1, etc.

The larger public companies, however, generally use loose-leaf minute books with a locking device, the key to which should be kept by the company secretary and a duplicate lodged with the company's bank. Here again, it is recommended that the pages be serially numbered and the minutes numbered consecutively. Some companies also maintain an index at the back of the minute book giving reference to the items covered by the minutes but it is a matter for discretion of the secretary as to whether the time spent in indexing the minutes will serve any useful purpose.

Minutes of general meetings should be kept separate from board minutes since members have a right to inspect the minutes of general meetings but not of board meetings.

The seal

Section 130 of CA 1989 deals with company contracts and the execution of documents by companies in England and Wales and inserted a new section 36A in the Act which provides that a company need not have a common seal. Whether or not a company has a seal, however, the following provisions apply with regard to the execution of documents:

1. Any document signed by a director and the secretary of the company, or by two directors of the company, and using a form of words in the document denoting that it is executed by the company has the same effect as if the document were executed under the company's common seal.
2. A document executed in this way which is intended to be a deed and which makes that fact clear in the document, has effect upon delivery of the document to be a deed unless the contrary intention is proved.
3. In favour of a purchaser a document shall be deemed to have been duly executed by the company if it purports to be signed by a director and the secretary of the company, or by two directors of the company, and where it is made clear on the face of the document that the persons signing it intend it to be a deed, the document will be delivered upon its being executed.

A purchaser is a person who in good faith for valuable consideration acquires an interest in property including a lessee or mortgage.

(Note: The above provisions do not apply to Scotland and Scottish companies. Detailed provisions with regard to the execution of documents by Scottish companies, which also need not have a common seal, are contained in s.36B inserted by CA 1989 s.130(3).)

If a contract is entered into on behalf of a company by a person as agent for a company before the company has been formed, then, subject to any agreement to the contrary, the contract has effect as one entered into by the person purporting to act as agent for the company and he is personally liable on the contract (s.36C inserted by CA 1989 s.130(4)).

It is probably unlikely that in the immediate future many existing companies will decide to take advantage of the above provisions and dispense with having a common seal, although some newly formed companies may do so. Consequently, it is necessary to consider the company secretarial requirements where a common seal exists.

It is usual for a company which has a common seal for it to be kept by the secretary, who will maintain a record of all documents to which the seal has been affixed. In the case of infrequent use of the seal, specific reference to the document sealed may be made in the minutes of the board meeting authorising the sealing. If the seal is used frequently, however, the particulars of the documents sealed should be entered in a seal book to be produced at each board meeting, at which an appropriate confirmatory resolution will be passed. It is quite common for modern forms of Articles of Association (e.g. Table A, Regulation 101) not to require the physical presence of the director and secretary or a second director when the seal is affixed to a document. It is also quite common for large companies to pass a board resolution delegating authority for the use of the seal to various officers of the company. Other persons may be designated 'authorised signatories' to sign documents to which the seal has been affixed. An Article in the form of Table A, Regulation 101, would include the necessary authority for the board to do this. If this procedure is followed, there is no need for the sealings to be confirmed by the directors at a board meeting, although a record of all documents sealed should be kept in a seal book.

Securities seal

Authority is given under s.40 as amended by CA 1989 Schedule 17, para. 3, for a company which has a common seal to have an official seal, which is a facsimile of the common seal with the addition on its face of the word 'Securities' and which can be used to seal certificates relating to the securities of the company. This is particularly useful where the company has appointed an outside service registrar so that the company may keep the use of its common seal, if it has one, under its own control. The provision for companies to have a securities seal came into force on 12 February 1979. Companies incorporated before that date may adopt and use a securities seal notwithstanding the contents of their Articles of Association or of any trust deed securing debenture stock specifying sealing in any other way. Moreover, any provision in those documents requiring documents relating to the securities to be signed do not apply if the certificates are sealed with the securities seal (CP s.11).

Official seal for use abroad

Subject to permission being contained in the Articles, a company which has a common seal transacting business abroad may have one or more official seals for use in the overseas countries where it transacts business (s.39 as amended by CA 1989 Schedule 17, para. 2). In order that such seals may be validly used a company which has a common seal must appoint in writing under its common seal the person or persons in the territory concerned who will affix the official seal to documents in that country. An official seal for use abroad is a facsimile of the common seal with the addition on its face of the name of the country in which it is to be used.

Instead of having a seal for use abroad, however, a company may appoint an attorney in any place outside the United Kingdom to execute deeds on its behalf in that country. If the company has a common seal, the appointment of the attorney would be made by a document under seal (s.38). Articles of Association (e.g. Table A, Regulation 71) usually provide that the company's powers in this connection may be exercised by the directors.

Authentication of documents

Another duty of the secretary (or a director or other authorised officer of the company) is to authenticate by his signature any document or proceeding which is required to be authenticated by the company (s.41 as amended by CA 1989 Schedule 17, para. 4).

The secretary is frequently asked to provide certified copies of documents, resolutions, minutes, etc., and he will usually do this by signing on the document or at the foot of a paper containing a copy of the resolution or minute as follows:

Certified to be a true copy

....

Secretary

Compliance duties of company secretary

It is the general duty of the company secretary to ensure compliance by his company with the provisions of the Companies Acts and the company's Memorandum and Articles of Association. However, company secretaries of groups and companies engaged in financial services, e.g. banking, insurance, Stock Exchange dealing, investment fund and unit trust management, etc., have a special compliance role to fulfil. They are usually required as part of their duties to act as the compliance officer for the group or company in relation to compliance with the provisions of the Financial Service Act 1986 (FSA), the rules and regulations of the Securities and Investments Board (SIB) and the self-regulating organisations (SROs), TSA, FIMBRA, AFBD, IMRO and LAUTRO (see chapter 13 on the securities industry).

The secretary is responsible for meeting the requirements for membership of SIB and of the relevant SRO or SROs as well as the provisions of the FSA and legislation affecting such companies as in the case of banks and insurance companies. In the case of a large financial services group, the day-to-day compliance functions would normally be the responsibility of particular managers engaged in the financial businesses carried on by the group but in this case the group company secretary would usually act as the co-ordinator of their functions as the group compliance officer.

Retention of documents

The secretary is often responsible to exercise control over the company's policy regarding the filing and retention of documents. The period of time for which documents should be retained by the company obviously depends on the nature of the document concerned, and the Institute's booklet *A Short Guide to the Retention of Records*, published in 1989, contains a comprehensive list giving suggested retention periods for a large number of documents, including company records, share registration and TALISMAN documents. A more detailed guide, also published in 1989, *How to Manage your Records*, is available from ICSA Publishing Ltd.

One area in which the company or its registrars receive a substantial quantity of documents is in the field of share registration, e.g. instruments of transfer, dividend mandates and change of address notifications. Accordingly, many public companies have adopted an article in their Articles of Association specifying detailed retention periods for these types of documents.

Microfilming

A considerable amount of space may be saved by a company where documents it wishes to retain for reference purposes are either put on to microfilm or microfiche. It is necessary to ensure that the documents filmed are properly authenticated and certified in order to be admissible in evidence; some guidance on procedures that could be followed in this connection are contained in the book *How to Manage your Records* referred to above. There is also a British Standard on this subject, No. 6498 of 1984, *Guide to the Preparation of Microfilm and other Microforms that may be Required as Evidence*.

Computer records

Information may, of course, be retained on a company's computer but here the situation is more difficult because it is easier to alter computer produced records than in the case of a roll of microfilm which has authentication certificates both at the beginning and at the end of the roll.

There is the further problem of computer malfunction and breakdowns. Clearly, however, it is possible to take some precautions so as to improve the likelihood of information retrieved from the computer being admissible as evidence and it should also be borne in mind that computer based records will become more usual in future, microfilming now being regarded as somewhat out of date. There is some helpful guidance on the subject of retaining records on computer in the book *How to Manage your Records*.

British Standards No. 6498 does not cover computer records and although it is understood that one is in preparation it will be some time before it is published. In relation to records of the company kept or processed by computer it is also necessary for the secretary to ensure compliance with the Data Protection Act 1984, as it is a criminal offence to operate unregistered computer data systems.

CHAPTER 11

Meetings

The meetings of directors and committees

In this chapter the procedure and practice of meetings will be considered, but no attempt is made to govern the question of the law of meetings generally. There is a wide range of law on this subject; consequently, reference should be made to specific treatises on this subject when required.

The procedure for the conduct of meetings of directors, i.e. board meetings, is included in Table A. Companies which have special Articles usually model their Articles concerning directors' meetings on the Table A provisions. Board meetings do not have to be held at fixed intervals and are usually convened from time to time as the directors may think fit; this is especially so in the case of private companies. In the case of public companies, however, it is likely that the board meetings will be held regularly, e.g. once a month, and it would be quite common for an annual timetable of dates of meetings convenient both to the executive and non-executive directors to be drawn up and approved by the board in order that the directors may mark their diaries accordingly. Large companies will also usually have an executive committee, composed of executive directors, which may meet between board meetings on a regular basis, quite often a fixed day every week.

If meetings are not held on fixed dates the chairman will usually instruct the secretary to call a meeting, but under Table A and most companies' Articles any director may summon a board meeting. Where a meeting is convened in this way, there is no length of notice laid down but 7 days would probably be a suitable period of notice. In the case of meetings which are held regularly in accordance with a fixed timetable it would still be appropriate to issue reminders to the directors about the meeting, sending a copy of the agenda for the meeting at the same time. Although Table A, Regulation 88, provides that it is not necessary to give notice of a meeting to a director absent from the United Kingdom, it would of course

235

be appropriate to send notice to a director who resides permanently outside the United Kingdom, in which case the third sentence of Regulation 88 should be omitted from companies' Articles.

Board meetings are in the nature of general discussion meetings and usually proceed on an informal basis, the chairman taking the general view of the meeting to be incorporated in the minutes of the meeting as the decision of the board, either in narrative form or, when appropriate, as a formal resolution. If, however, the views of directors are fairly evenly balanced on the pros and cons of a particular course of action, it would be appropriate to put the matter formally to a vote.

Quorum

The quorum for board meetings, unless the directors otherwise decide, is fixed by Table A, Regulation 89, as two directors. If the company had only two directors and one were to resign or die, Table A, Regulation 90, provides that the sole continuing director may appoint another director. He should do this formally in writing by signing a suitable document, which should be inserted in the company's directors' minute book. A sole director has no other powers other than to appoint another director, except that he may alternatively call a general meeting of the company at which another director or directors could be appointed.

Chairman

Table A, Regulation 91, permits the directors to appoint one of their number to be chairman of the board; in addition, some Articles provide for the appointment of deputy chairmen and vice-chairmen. A person appointed chairman of the board would also usually take the chair at general meetings of the company and would be regarded as chairman of the company, although there is no actual provision for such an appointment.

Appointment of committees

Table A, Regulation 72, provides for directors to delegate their powers to committees with such powers as the board may decide. The proceedings of committees would follow those which apply to the board as a whole (Table A, Regulation 72). Anything done at a meeting of directors is valid, notwithstanding that it may subsequently be discovered that there was a defect in the appointment of one or more of them, but in certain circumstances it may also be desirable that their action should be validated by the company in general meeting.

Resolutions in writing

It is sometimes necessary for the directors to make a decision urgently and Table A, Regulation 93, provides that a resolution signed by all the directors entitled to attend a board meeting is as valid and effectual as if passed at a duly constituted board meeting. Such a resolution could be passed around the directors for them each to sign if they were all located fairly near to each other but if this were not the case, a separate copy of the resolution could be sent to each director for his signature. The document or documents signed by the directors should be inserted in the directors' minute book.

Preparations for a board meeting

Prior to the board meeting, the secretary should undertake the following steps:

1. Send a notice to each director giving time, date and place of meeting with a copy of agenda and supporting papers.
2. If any of the company's managers are to attend the whole or part of the meeting, e.g. the chief accountant, he should also be advised and sent a copy of the agenda and supporting papers. If he is to attend for only part of the meeting, he should be sent only the papers for those particular items for which he will be present.
3. If it is proposed to declare or recommend a dividend at the meeting and the company is a listed company, The Stock Exchange should be advised of the date of the meeting (Continuing Obligations, para. 6).
4. The secretary should ensure that he has a few spare copies of the agenda and supporting papers to take to the meeting.
5. In preparing the agenda for the meeting, the secretary must consider those items which come up on a regularly recurring basis, e.g. half-yearly staff report, and will remind the appropriate department, in this case the personnel department, to have the report ready in time for circulation with the agenda. Other departments of the company will be similarly concerned with reports which they are required to submit to the board from time to time. Reference should also be made to the corresponding board meeting held at the same time last year as a check on items which normally come up for consideration at that meeting. Matters on which no decision was reached at a previous meeting or which were deferred from a previous meeting will have to be included in the agenda as well.

    Sometimes the supporting papers will incorporate a formal resolution which the board is to be asked to pass. This will also save time when the minutes of the meeting are prepared.

6. Just before the meeting, arrangements should be made to ensure that everything necessary for the meeting is ready in the boardroom, not forgetting the irritation which may be caused to the chairman if he finds that the boardroom clock is incorrect! It is also usual to have a copy of the company's Memorandum and Articles and of the Companies Acts in the boardroom in case reference to them is required. In addition, in the case of a listed company, the Register of Directors' Share and Debenture Interests should be available in the boardroom for inspection by any director if required.

Duties of the secretary at the board meeting

1. For incorporation in the minutes, take a note of those directors present and report any apologies for absence.
2. Ensure that a quorum is present and if any item is to come up in which a director has an interest, ensure that there will still be an independent, disinterested quorum to deal with that matter.
3. Take notes during the course of the meeting on any action decided upon by the board and of its decisions reached. The minutes should not be a verbatim record of everything that is said and, indeed, if they were this could cause complications.
4. It is usual to note in the minutes the arrival of any director after the proceedings have started or the departure of a director before the meeting has ended.
5. The chairman may ask the secretary to advise on any point of procedure regarding the conduct of the business of the meeting but it would be appropriate for the secretary to intervene (unless, of course, he is himself a director) only if the board were proposing to do something which was unlawful or contrary to the company's Memorandum and Articles.
6. If a manager is to be called in for discussion of a specific item, ensure that he is standing by and ready to be called when that item is reached on the agenda.
7. If any confidential papers are left behind on the board table by the directors, these should be collected by the secretary before the staff comes in to clear the room generally.

Duties of the secretary after the board meeting

1. If the company has made a decision with regard to the payment of a dividend on the company's ordinary shares and the company is listed on The Stock Exchange, the Exchange should be advised immediately by telephone or telex. If necessary, The Stock Exchange should

also be advised of any decision to make an issue of shares or debentures or to postpone the payment of a preference dividend or of interest. Similarly, The Stock Exchange should be advised if the board meeting has at the same time approved the half-yearly or preliminary results for the financial year (Continuing Obligations, paras. 7 and 8).

2. The company's managers should be notified of any action which the board require them to take, probably by sending a memorandum or letter to the managers concerned.

3. Make a note of any item which has been deferred for future consideration to ensure that it is not overlooked.

4. If the directors have asked for a report on a specific subject to be prepared for their next meeting, ensure that the manager responsible for preparing it is notified.

5. Prepare the minutes of the meeting, showing the names of the directors present, those whose apologies were noted, and the arrival and departure of any director who was not present at the beginning or at the end of the meeting. It is useful to obtain the chairman's copy of the agenda after the meeting so as to observe any remarks that he may have made on his copy, although this should not be relied upon as the chairman may take his copy away with him in order to check on the minutes that the secretary prepares!

6. The procedure to be followed in preparing the minutes will vary from company to company but probably the most convenient procedure is to send a copy of the draft minutes to every director present with a request that he send in, or telephone, any comments by a given date, following which the minutes can be prepared in their final form for signature at the subsequent board meeting. A copy of the minutes for information should be sent to any director who was not present at the board meeting.

7. If any director should make a comment with regard to the wording of a particular minute, the amendment should be agreed with the chairman, who would then mention at the subsequent board meeting before signing the minutes that, for example, a certain sentence had been amended. Since the chairman has agreed the amendment, it is unlikely that any director present at the subsequent board meeting would object to the alteration.

8. It is not desirable in board minutes to include the individual expressions of opinion of any particular director, although it would be appropriate, at the request of a director, to record in the minutes that he had dissented from a decision taken by the board as a whole.

Agenda and minutes

The matters to be discussed at a board meeting will naturally be dependent on the nature of the company's business, the size of the board, and whether the board has an executive committee to deal with routine matters as delegated to it.

It is desirable to number minutes and resolutions serially in order to facilitate reference to any particular minute if it should subsequently be necessary. This often arises in the case of the approval by the board of authorised cheque signatories, when it will be convenient in the future to refer to the previous minute by its number and refer to the deletion or addition of certain names.

The Institute's manual contains numerous precedents for the agenda and minutes of board meetings.

General meetings

In the case of general meetings of a company it is necessary to comply with statutory procedures and obligations as laid down in the Act and CA 1989 as well as with the provisions of the company's Articles, which will often be modelled on those contained in Table A, Regulations 36–63. These regulations cover the convening of general meetings, notice of general meetings, proceedings to be followed at general meetings and the votes of members, including provisions for proxies to be given in the case of members not able or not wishing to attend.

There are three main types of general meetings. These are as follows:

1. Annual General Meeting.
2. Extraordinary General Meeting.
3. A class meeting of the holders of a particular class of the company's capital.

Section 366 provides that every company must hold an Annual General Meeting in each calendar year and that not more than 15 months may elapse between the date of one Annual General Meeting and the next.

The first Annual General Meeting must be held within 18 months of the incorporation of the company. Subsequent Annual General Meetings, however, must not be postponed beyond the end of a calendar year or 15 months from the date of the preceding Annual General Meeting, whichever occurs first. A possible problem arises where, because of a change in the company's accounting reference period or because of some other problem in the preparation of the annual accounts, it may not be possible to have the accounts ready for submission by the last date on which the Annual General Meeting must be held. In this case the meeting must nevertheless be held and then adjourned to a date at which the accounts can be presented.

Section 366A inserted by CA 1989 s.115 provides that a private company may by an elective resolution (s.379A inserted by CA 1989 s.116) elect to dispense with the holding of an Annual General Meeting.

Convening the Annual General Meeting

Usually the directors convene the Annual General Meeting (Table A, Regulations 36 and 37) but if they fail to do so within the time limits stipulated, the Department of Trade and Industry has authority to call, or direct the calling of, the meeting on the application of any member (s.367). Under s.371, the Court also has power to order a general meeting (including an Annual General Meeting) and may direct the manner in which it should be held and conducted. If the Articles do not contain provisions with regard to the convening of the Annual General Meeting, under s.370(3) two or more members holding not less than one-tenth of the issued share capital may call a general meeting (including the Annual General Meeting). It is more likely that a general meeting convened under the direction of the Court will be an Extraordinary General Meeting rather than the Annual General Meeting.

Business at Annual General Meetings

The following is the routine business of an Annual General Meeting:

1. Receiving the report and accounts laid before the meeting as required by s.241 inserted by CA 1989 s.11.
2. The declaration of a dividend.
3. The election of directors. (This will include both the election of directors who have been appointed since the last Annual General Meeting, as normally required by companies' Articles, and the re-election of directors who have retired by rotation under the Articles.)
4. The reappointment, and determining the remuneration, of the auditors.

Apart from the routine business above, other business may also be undertaken at the Annual General Meeting, e.g. as follows:

1. Ordinary Resolutions to increase the company's capital.
2. Special Resolutions for any required alterations to the company's Articles.
3. Authority to the directors to issue capital as required by s.80.
4. Authority for the directors to disapply pre-emption rights under the Act (s.89).

5. Where it is company practice, and there is provision in the company's Articles, to authorise the directors to offer shareholders the right to receive new ordinary shares instead of cash for all or part of any dividend.

The other business mentioned above used to be described as 'special' business but Table A no longer makes a distinction between special business and ordinary business; hence, the suggested use of the terms routine business and other business.

Notice of Annual General Meetings

There is a common law requirement that notices of general meetings should indicate the nature of the business to be transacted. However, in the case of company meetings the detailed items to be transacted at the meeting as set out above are given in the notice of meeting; in the case of business other than routine business to be transacted, it would be quite usual to include the text of any resolutions to be proposed, the notice being accompanied by an explanatory letter from the chairman.

Convening Extraordinary General Meetings

Subject to the Articles, Extraordinary General Meetings may be convened at any time in order to transact business which must be dealt with before the next Annual General Meeting. The directors may convene an Extraordinary General Meeting under authority contained in the Articles (Table A, Regulations 36 and 37); or under s.368 the directors may be required to call the meeting by a requisition of the members, and if the directors fail to do so, the shareholders requisitioning the general meeting may do so themselves. If there are insufficient directors in the United Kingdom to form a quorum, Table A, Regulation 37, authorises any one director to convene an Extraordinary General Meeting; this authority could be useful if some of the directors died or resigned at the same time. The power of the Court under s.371 to convene an Extraordinary General Meeting also applies.

Business at Extraordinary General Meetings

The only business which may be transacted is that which is specified in the notice convening the meeting. The type of resolutions to be passed, i.e. Ordinary Resolutions or Special Resolutions, will be those as required by the Act, CA 1989 or by the company's Articles. Examples of business which may be transacted at Extraordinary General Meetings are to amend the Memorandum, adopt new Articles, amendments to employees' share schemes because of changes in legislation, etc.

Requisitioned meetings

The convening of an Extraordinary General Meeting on the requisition of members of the company is governed by s.368 of the Act as amended by CA 1989 Schedule 19, para. 9. Reference should be made to this section for the detailed requirements as to the proportion of members who may make the requisition and the responsibilities of the directors in convening the Extraordinary General Meeting on its receipt.

Class meetings

As the name implies, class meetings are meetings of holders of a certain class of the company's capital and are held in accordance with the Articles of the company or conditions which attach to the securities concerned. Class meetings are required whenever the rights of the holders of the class are to be varied because of some action proposed by the company. Such variations may relate to a change in the voting rights attaching to the class or to changes proposed in a reorganisation of the company's capital.

It is usually convenient to discuss variation of class rights proposals with institutional investors through the appropriate investment protection committee to ensure their support and the presence of a quorum at the meeting.

Notice of general meetings

Section 369 specifies the minimum periods of notice required for general meetings and these periods of notice cannot be reduced by the company's Articles, although the minimum periods can be extended. It is 21 days for Annual General Meetings.

In all cases, the period of notice is expressed as clear days' notice. This means that the day on which the notice is served (or is deemed to be served) and the day on which the meeting is to be held are excluded from the period of notice. The date on which the notice is deemed to be served varies with different companies' Articles but Table A, Regulation 115, provides that a notice sent by post is deemed to be served 48 hours after posting. An example will make the position clear. If the company wishes to hold its Annual General Meeting on 25 May (May is a fairly common date for companies whose accounting periods end on 31 December), the latest date for posting the notice of meeting would be 1 May as the notice would be deemed to be served on 3 May and the 21 days counted from 4 May would expire on 24 May.

Entitlement to notice of general meetings

Table A and most companies' Articles provide that notice is to be given to every member except to a member whose registered address is outside the United Kingdom, in which case notice need only be given when the member has notified the company of an address within the United Kingdom for the service of notices. In addition, Table A, Regulation 116, provides that executors or administrators of a deceased member or the trustee of a bankrupt member must also be given notice, even though they may not have the right to vote at the meeting. By s.387(1) the auditors have a statutory right to receive notices of general meetings.

Holders of preference shares or non-voting shares will not be entitled to receive notice of general meetings unless, because of some event, they are entitled to vote at them. In practice, however, and especially in the case of listed companies, notice would usually be sent to every holder of shares or debentures whether or not the registered address of the holder is in the United Kingdom and irrespective of whether the securities he holds entitle him to vote at the Annual General Meeting. This is because under s.240, every member and holder of debentures must be sent a copy of the report and accounts, and the notice of meeting is usually incorporated in this document. It would, however, be usual to include an explanatory note at the foot of the notice of meeting stating that, e.g. the notice is sent for information only to debenture holders who are not entitled to attend and vote at the Annual General Meeting. In the case of a class meeting, on the other hand, only the holders of the shares of the class would be entitled to notice. There is provision in most companies' Articles (e.g. Table A, Regulation 39) affording protection to the company in the case of accidental omission to give notice to any person entitled to receive it.

Content of notices

The notice must set out the time, place and date of the meeting, the nature of the business to be transacted or a detailed agenda, including the resolutions to be passed in the case of business other than routine business. Since it would be normal for the directors to instruct the secretary to convene the general meeting, the notice would be signed by the secretary by order of the board. In the case of a company listed on The Stock Exchange, the provisions of the Continuing Obligations, para. 37, must be followed in regard to proxies, i.e. every member must be given the opportunity to vote for and against every resolution included in the notice (colloquially called a 'two-way proxy'). In order to facilitate this, therefore, it is necessary for the various resolutions in the notice of meeting to be numbered so that these numbers may be included on the proxy form with boxes for the member to tick either for or against the resolution. Section 372 requires that in every notice calling a meeting of the company, a statement must appear with reasonable prominence that the member entitled to attend and vote is entitled to appoint a proxy (or one or more proxies in the case of a public company) to attend and vote instead of him, and that a proxy need not be a member of the company. It is also required by that section that any provision in the company's Articles requiring proxies to be lodged more than 48 hours before the meeting is invalid.

It should be noted that under s.372, although a member of a public company may appoint one or more proxies, a member of a private company may only appoint one proxy to attend on the same occasion.

The Continuing Obligations, para. 43(b), provides that in the case of companies listed on The Stock Exchange the notice of an Annual General Meeting of a listed company must include a note that directors' service contracts with the company or with any of its subsidiaries are available for inspection at the registered office of the company from the date of the notice of the meeting and at the Annual General Meeting until its conclusion, or that there are no such contracts. It has been mentioned that the business to be conducted at the Annual General Meeting is the routine business usually set out in the company's Articles and any other business of which notice is included in the notice of the meeting. Some companies include a phrase 'to transact any other ordinary business of the company' or similar words to that effect. It is not correct to include such a phrase in the notice of the Annual General Meeting since it obviously does not have any effect. Precedents for wording of notices of Annual General Meetings of both public and private companies, and of an Extraordinary General Meeting of a public company, are given in the Institute's manual.

Agreement to short notice of meeting

There is a useful concession under s.369 where it is not possible to give the minimum period of notice required by subsections (1) and (2) of that section or by the Articles. Advantage of the concession, however, can in practice usually be taken only by companies with a small number of members, and it is a good idea for the agreement to short notice to be in writing so that there is no doubt that the meeting was validly called. It should be noted particularly that the provision does not allow the complete dispensation of notice.

The number of members required validly to give a consent to short notice is defined in s.369(3) and (4). In the case of an Annual General Meeting the form of consent must be signed by all the members entitled to attend and vote at it. This is the reason why the concession is only useful in the case of small companies. The form of consent to short notice for an Annual General Meeting sometimes includes agreement to accept the company's report and accounts, even though they were not sent to members not less than 21 days before the date of the meeting, as required by s.238 inserted by CA 1989 s.10. In the case of an Extraordinary General Meeting, s.369(4) provides that the requisite majority is a majority in number of the members together holding not less than 95 per cent of the share capital of the company having a right to attend and vote at the meeting. Thus, if in the case of a company with 100 shares, one member held 97 of the shares and three other members held one share each, the one member with more than 95 per cent of the share capital could not hold the meeting at short notice because he would not constitute a majority in number. This provision affords protection to minority members holding less than 5 per cent of the shares.

The requisite majority in s.369(4) also applies in the case of a meeting (other than an Annual General Meeting) at which a Special Resolution is to be proposed. Section 238(4) inserted by CA 1989 s.10 provides that the accounts may be regarded as duly sent notwithstanding that less than 21 days' notice has been given if all the members entitled to attend and vote at the meeting agree. This provision will enable a company with a small number of shareholders to pass the accounts at a board meeting and follow this immediately with the Annual General Meeting, all the members having signed a form of consent to short notice incorporating acceptance of the report and accounts.

Although not legally required it may be advisable to obtain from the company's auditors a letter of non-objection to the short notice to avoid any possible objection on procedural grounds since notice of all general meetings must be sent to the auditors under s.387(1) which gives them the right to attend all such meetings.

Quorum at general meetings

This is usually stipulated in the Articles; Table A, Regulation 40, provides that two members present in person or by proxy may constitute a quorum. Companies' Articles usually make provision for the procedure to be adopted in the event of a quorum not being present. Table A also covers this in Regulation 41.

Chairman at general meetings

If the company's Articles follow Table A, Regulations 42 and 43, the chairman of the board would preside at general meetings. If the chairman were not present, then some other director (e.g. a deputy chairman or vice-chairman if there were one) could take the chair but in the absence of any director, one of the members present shall take the chair.

Adjournment of general meetings

Although the chairman may adjourn the meeting without the consent of the members if there is disorder, the power to adjourn a meeting usually rests with the members attending, who must give their consent. In fact, the adjournment of a general meeting is unusual, although it could occur if the accounts were not ready for submission to the Annual General Meeting but it was necessary for the meeting to be held because of the time limits laid down in s.366. Table A, Regulation 45, provides that no business at an adjourned meeting shall be transacted other than that which could have been transacted at the original meeting. If the meeting is adjourned for more than 14 days, however, fresh notice of at least 7 days, specifying the business to be transacted, must be given. When a resolution is passed at an adjourned meeting, it is deemed to have been passed on the date of the adjourned meeting rather than the date on which the original meeting was adjourned.

It sometimes becomes necessary to postpone or cancel a meeting after the notice of meeting has been sent out. In this case the correct procedure is to hold the meeting at the scheduled time and place and for a resolution to be passed adjourning the meeting to a later date. A circular could be sent to shareholders explaining the reasons for the postponement so that they do not waste their time in attending a purely formal meeting. A similar procedure should be followed when it is necessary to change the venue of a meeting.

Types of resolutions which may be passed at general meetings

These are as follows:

1. An Ordinary Resolution which may, in certain circumstances, require special notice to have been given.
2. An Extraordinary Resolution.
3. A Special Resolution.

A simple majority of those present and voting is all that is required in order to pass an Ordinary Resolution. The practical effect of this should be considered. If there are 12 members entitled to vote present at a meeting, the resolution would be passed if 7 voted in favour and 5 against. The resolution would also be passed if 9 of the 12 members abstained from voting, and of the 3 who did actually vote, 2 voted in favour of the resolution and 1 against.

All the items of routine business at an Annual General Meeting may be passed by an Ordinary Resolution, together with other business which the Act permits to be passed by an Ordinary Resolution. Examples of this other type of business would be the following:

1. Alterations to the share capital under s.121.
2. A capitalisation of profits (Table A, Regulation 110).
3. The grant of authority for the allotment of securities (s.80).
4. A resolution to wind-up the company under s.572(1)(*a*), i.e. when the period fixed for the duration of the company by the Articles has expired or an event occurs whereby the Articles provide that the company is to be dissolved.
5. Subject to provision in the Articles, a resolution authorising the directors to offer shareholders the right to elect to receive new ordinary shares for the whole or part of a cash dividend.

(Note: A resolution under s.95 to disapply pre-emption rights under s.89, which is often passed at Annual General Meetings in association with the resolution under (3) above, must be a Special Resolution.)

Extraordinary Resolutions

Extraordinary Resolutions are defined by s.378(1). If it is intended to propose an Extraordinary Resolution at a meeting it is essential that the notice of the meeting specifies this. To be proposed at an Annual General Meeting, at least 21 clear days' notice must be given (s.369(1)(*a*)). On the other hand, if it is to be proposed at an Extraordinary General Meeting, 14 clear days' notice (7 for an unlimited company) is sufficient (s.369(1)(*b*)).

In order to pass an Extraordinary Resolution, a three-fourths majority is required of those present and voting in person or by proxy. The practical effect of this is that if 12 members are present and all vote, 9 or more votes in favour would carry the resolution as an Extraordinary Resolution. Also, if 8 abstained from voting, and of the 4 who voted 3 voted in favour and 1 against, the resolution would also be carried as an Extraordinary Resolution. Except in the case of class meetings Extraordinary Resolutions do not occur very often since the Act only specifies this type of resolution for certain purposes, e.g., in connection with a creditors' voluntary winding-up. However, care should be taken to follow the company's Articles, which may specify that some business may be transacted only by Extraordinary Resolution.

Special Resolutions

The majority required to pass a Special Resolution is the same as that required for an Extraordinary Resolution (s.378(2)). It is essential that the notice of meeting states that it is intended to propose a resolution as a Special Resolution. Section 378(2) stipulates that at least 21 clear days' notice must be given, and this applies irrespective of whether the resolution is to be proposed at an Annual General Meeting or an Extraordinary General Meeting. The type of business which must be dealt with by a Special Resolution is specified in the Act, CA 1989 and/or the company's Articles, some examples being: alteration of the Memorandum of Articles (ss.4 and 9); change of name (s.28); disapplication of pre-emption rights (s.95); and reduction of capital (s.135).

Special notice

This must not be confused with Special Resolutions. Section 379 specifies what constitutes special notice where the Act and CA 1989 require special notice to be given to the company of certain resolutions required by these Acts to be subject to special notice. Special notice is required for the following resolutions but the resolutions themselves will be Ordinary Resolutions:

1. Under s.388, resolutions:
   (a) to appoint an auditor other than a retiring auditor;
   (b) to fill a casual vacancy in the office of auditor;
   (c) to reappoint as auditor a retiring auditor appointed by the directors to fill a casual vacancy;
   (d) To remove an auditor before the expiration of his term of office.
2. Under s.303, resolutions:
   (a) to remove a director before the expiration of his period of office;
   (b) to appoint somebody in place of the director so removed at the meeting at which he is removed.
3. A resolution to appoint or reappoint a director, subject to s.293, who has reached the age limit stipulated in the Act or the Articles (s.293(5)).

One or more members may give the special notice to the company irrespective of the number of the shares they hold. By s.379 the company is required to give notice of the resolutions to all members in the notice of meeting or, if not practicable, by advertisement in a newspaper not less than 21 days before the meeting.

Circulation of members' resolutions and statements

The procedure under which members may propose resolutions at general meetings of the company and circulate a statement to the members regarding the subject of the resolution is laid down in ss.376 and 377. These rights are rarely exercised in practice, and reference should be made to these sections and to the Institute's manual if a company secretary should be faced with a requisition from members to propose a resolution at a general meeting.

Registration of resolutions with the Registrar of Companies

Various resolutions are required to be filed with the Registrar of Companies and these are specified in s.380. These are mainly Special Resolutions and Extraordinary Resolutions, but there are also others as specified in the section.

In addition, the following resolutions have to be registered with the Registrar of Companies:

1. To increase the authorised capital (s.123(3)).
2. To authorise the allotment of securities (s.80(8)).
3. To make a market purchase of the company's own shares (s.166(7)).

Arrangements for Annual General Meetings

The following paragraphs briefly describe the action which should be taken by the company secretary before, during and after general meetings of public companies with shares listed on The Stock Exchange. In the case of an Annual General Meeting, the business to be discussed will be routine business as set out on page 241. It is also quite common practice to include the following as routine business at an Annual General Meeting of a company:

1. To pass an Ordinary Resolution to give the board authority under s.80 of the Act to allot securities up to a maximum nominal amount during the period from the passing of the resolution to the conclusion of the company's next Annual General Meeting.
2. To pass a Special Resolution under s.95 of the Act to allot equity securities up to a certain aggregate nominal amount, to expire at the conclusion of the company's next Annual General Meeting after the passing of the Resolution, as if s.89 of the Act requiring such securities to be allotted to shareholders on a pre-emptive basis did not apply to the company.

The authorities mentioned in (1) and (2) above can alternatively be provided for in the company's Articles but, in this case, any changes becoming necessary in the amounts of capital covered by the authorities would have to be made by the more cumbersome procedure of altering the company's Articles.

It is also routine business for companies with the appropriate provision in their Articles for an Ordinary Resolution to be passed giving authority to the directors to offer shareholders the option to receive the whole or any part of their dividends in new ordinary shares rather than in cash.

In addition, of course, there may be some items of non-routine business (e.g. alteration of Articles), and these should be described in a separate circular letter to members dispatched with the notice of the meeting.

The venue for the meeting will probably have been fixed several months in advance, the date of the Annual General Meeting having been included in the programme of board meetings for the year and previously approved by the directors. In practice, few shareholders attend Annual General Meetings if the company is doing well, and quite often it will be sufficient to hold the meeting in the company's boardroom. However, in the case of large public companies with many thousands of shareholders, it is necessary to book a special hall for the meeting.

It is quite common for the report and accounts to incorporate the notice of the meeting as well as the chairman's statement. Three proof copies of the booklet containing the notice of meeting and the accounts should have the balance sheet signed by a director and the chairman's signature on his statement. The secretary would sign the notice of meeting and the report of the directors on behalf of the board, although in some cases it is a director who signs the directors' report. The signatures of the auditors to their report would also be obtained on these three proof copies.

Another copy of the report and accounts with the names of the signatories and dates printed in would then be sent to the company's printers for a final proof prior to running off the bulk supply for dispatch to shareholders. The company's registrar (either the company's own in-house registrar or a firm of service registrars) should be advised of the amount of the recommended dividend in order that he may prepare the dividend warrants for dispatch to shareholders following approval at the Annual General Meeting. The company should also arrange with its bankers for a dividend account to be opened in which the money required to pay the dividend will be placed. Proxy forms will also have been prepared to be dispatched with the report and accounts to shareholders. These can be either separate cards inserted in the booklet or a tear-out page in the booklet.

The report and accounts will normally be sent to shareholders by the company's printers; consequently they should be instructed as to the date on which posting should take place and whether the document is to be sent by first class or second class post.

The names of the signatories on the bulk printed supply should be printed in exactly the same way as the original signatures on the three signed copies, e.g. 'Albert Smith' if signed in that way and not 'A. Smith'. One of the three signed copies of the report and accounts booklet will be placed in the company's directors' board minute book, one signed copy will be retained by the company's auditors and the third signed copy sent to the Registrar of Companies in accordance with s.236 inserted by CA 1989 s.9 which requires the auditors' report sent to the Registrar to state the names of the auditors and to be signed by them. The signed copy of the report and accounts for the Registrar of Companies could be sent to him either at the same time that these are dispatched to members or at a later date within the time allowed by s.242 and s.244 inserted by CA 1989 s.11.

In the case of listed companies copies of the directors' service contracts of more than one year's duration must be kept available for inspection at the company's registered office from the day of posting the notice of the Annual General Meeting and also at the meeting until its conclusion (Continuing Obligations, para. 43 (a)).

It would be usual also to invite the company's solicitor to attend the Annual General Meeting and, of course, the company's auditors are entitled to attend under s.387.

Arrangements should be made so that the forms of proxy returned by shareholders are checked against the Register of Members and a report made available for the board on the result of the proxy count following the latest time at which proxies may be received by the company (usually 48 hours prior to the time of the meeting). It should be considered whether or not ballot papers should be prepared for use at the Annual General Meeting in case a poll may be demanded. It might be prudent to do this if many proxy cards have been returned with votes against the resolutions.

If the chairman is going to make supplementary remarks at the meeting additional to those contained in his statement in the report and accounts, copies should be ready to hand to give to the company's press agents at the meeting and also to be sent simultaneously to The Stock Exchange if the company is listed. In this connection regard should be paid to the FSA s.57 and to the guidance note issued by the Department of Trade and Industry dated July 1988 on the application of FSA s.57 to companies listed on The Stock Exchange.

A copy of the Register of Members should be available at the Annual General Meeting. This should not be in the meeting room itself but in a room adjacent to it. This is required in case it is necessary for persons attending the Meeting to be identified, though obviously in the case of a large company this is not practicable.

Attendance sheets should be provided on which shareholders

attending the meeting can sign their names. Attendance sheets should also be prepared for the press, proxies and representatives of companies which are shareholders attending the meeting under authority of s.375.

There should also be available for inspection at the Annual General Meeting copies of the directors' service contracts, and the Register of Directors' Share and Debenture Interests (Schedule 13, Part IV, para. 29).

An order of proceedings will have been prepared setting out the various resolutions to be passed at the meeting and giving the names of those who are proposing and seconding. Although it is quite in order for the directors to propose and second resolutions for the routine business (other than for a director to propose or second himself for re-election as a director) it is usually considered good practice for a shareholder from the floor to propose the resolution to reappoint the auditors and authorise the directors to determine their remuneration.

At the meeting itself the secretary should first check that a quorum is present and then be ready to read the notice of meeting unless it is agreed with the consent of the meeting that this may be taken as read, since it will have been included in the report and accounts sent to all members. The Act, as amended by CA 1989, no longer requires that the auditors' report be read out to the meeting but when it is laid before the meeting it must cover the accounts laid before the meeting and state the names of the auditors (ss.235–6 inserted by CA 1989 s.9). It will, of course, have been included in the booklet containing the report and accounts. Further, the copy of the auditors' report which is delivered to the Registrar of Companies must also state the names of the auditors and be signed manually by them (s.236(3) inserted by CA 1989 s.9).

The secretary will assist the chairman in counting the votes (if necessary) on a show of hands. This would not normally be necessary except perhaps in the case of a Special Resolution, where there might be some doubt as to whether the necessary three-quarters majority of those attending and voting was achieved. A proxy (not himself a member of the company) should not be permitted to ask a question or make an observation since he has no right to speak at a meeting of a public company. At his discretion, however, the chairman may permit a proxy to speak or ask a question. The secretary would be involved if a poll were to be demanded on any resolution, to be taken either at the meeting or after the meeting. Assuming that the dividend is duly declared at the meeting, the necessary arrangements may be put in hand for its payment. The actual payment date will usually be some weeks after the meeting, but in the case of companies that like to pay the dividend as soon as it is passed, the cheques and tax vouchers for the mandated dividends will have been sent to the head offices of banks some days before so that the banks may be authorised to put the payment of the dividend into operation immediately after the meeting.

The minutes of the meeting should be prepared but it would not always be necessary for these to be sent out in draft to the directors for comments since they will cover only routine business or such other business as may have been specified in the notice convening the meeting. If any Special Resolution has been passed at the meeting, a copy signed by the chairman of the meeting must be sent to the Registrar of Companies within 15 days of the meeting.

Receiving report and accounts
It is not appropriate for the minutes of an Annual General Meeting to state that: 'The report and accounts for the year ended .... were received and adopted'. Section 241(1) inserted by CA 1989 s.11 makes no provision for the report and accounts to be adopted by the meeting. All that is legally required is that the accounts be laid before the meeting, so that the appropriate minute would be more correct if it stated: 'The report of the directors and audited accounts for the year ended .... were 'laid before the meeting' (or 'were received').

Declaration of dividend
It is usual for this to be included in the resolution to receive the directors' report and accounts. Since the recommended dividend is part of the accounts, if the accounts are received by the meeting, it would not be possible to alter the dividend by a separate resolution and therefore there is no point in making the declaration of dividend a separate resolution.

Resolution in writing
In the case of a company with only a small number of shareholders which has adopted Table A Articles, it may be convenient to take advantage of the provisions of Table A, Regulation 53, enabling a company to transact the business of a general meeting by resolutions in writing signed by all the members entitled to receive notice and to vote at the meeting. The resolutions could be on a single sheet of paper sent round to all the shareholders to sign if they are located near to each other or the resolutions could be typed on separate sheets of paper to be sent to each shareholder separately for signature. It would be good practice to insert the paper or the separate papers signed by the shareholders in the general meeting minute book.

Under section 381A inserted by CA 1989 s.113 a private company may pass certain members' resolutions by a written document or documents signed by or on behalf of all the members without a meeting or any previous notice who at the date of the resolution would be entitled to attend and vote at a meeting. A record of the resolutions (and of the signatures) must be entered in the company's general meeting minute book. Such written resolutions may not be used to remove a director or auditor before the expiry of his period of office. A copy of any proposed written resolution must be sent to the company's auditors who must notify the company that the resolution does not affect them as auditors or, if it does, that it need not be considered at a general meeting of the company (s.381B inserted by CA 1989 s.113).

Voting at general meetings

Initially the resolution will be put to the meeting for members to vote on a show of hands. If a resolution is defeated on a show of hands and the chairman is aware that he has a substantial proxy vote in favour of the resolution, he will demand a poll. On a show of hands, every member personally present and entitled to vote has one vote only irrespective of the number of shares he holds. On a poll, however, the number of shares held determines the number of votes the member may cast. In the event of an equality of votes, most companies' Articles (including Table A, Regulation 50) gives the chairman a casting vote. On the declaration by the chairman of whether the resolution has been carried or lost and an entry made in the minute book to that effect, the validity of the resolution cannot be questioned and it is unnecessary to insert in the minute book the number of members voting for or against the resolution. However, before declaring that a Special or an Extraordinary Resolution has been passed, it is necessary to ensure that there has been the requisite majority for passing such a resolution.

Demand for a poll

The rules governing the demanding of a poll will be laid down in the company's Articles or in Table A if the company has adopted Table A as its Articles. The provisions of s.373 must be considered, however, when drafting a company's Articles covering voting on a poll, since by that section certain provisions are rendered void.

Regulation 46 of Table A provides that a poll may be demanded by the following:

1. The chairman.
2. At least two members having the right to vote at the meeting.
3. A member or members representing not less than one-tenth of the total voting rights of all the members having the right to vote at the meeting.

4. A member or members holding shares conferring a right to vote at the meeting, being shares on which an aggregate sum has been paid up equal to not less than one-tenth of the total sum paid up on all the shares conferring that right.

In order for a demand for a poll to be valid, it must be called for before or immediately on the declaration by the chairman of the result of the vote on a show of hands.

Before the meeting the following action will have been taken:

1. Prepare a report of the proxies lodged in favour of the chairman, indicating the numbers for the resolution, against the resolution and those who leave it to the discretion of the chairman as to which way he votes.
2. Prepare a separate list of proxies given in favour of persons other than the chairman.
3. Consider the way in which the meeting is likely to go and whether or not there is likely to be a poll demanded.
4. Elect the scrutineers, who will be called upon if a poll should be necessary. Since the company's auditors normally attend the Annual General Meeting, as is their right, it would be quite appropriate for the auditors to act as the scrutineers.
5. Ballot papers should be prepared.
6. An announcement should be drafted for the chairman, which he can read out if a poll is demanded, to inform members of the date and time for the taking of the poll and the procedure to be followed.

Action when poll is demanded
It may be appropriate for the chairman to suggest that since he holds proxies overwhelmingly in favour of the resolution, the person or persons requesting the poll may decide to withdraw their demand.

If the demand for a poll is not withdrawn, however, the validity of the demand should be checked by confirming that those who have demanded it are, in fact, shareholders or, for example, if the member demanding it is a single member, that he holds not less than one-tenth of the total voting rights. It would be for the scrutineers to check on the validity of the demand for the poll.

If the scrutineers advise that the poll has not been properly demanded, the chairman would make a statement to this effect and the meeting would proceed to its next business after having put the matter on which the poll was requested to the vote by a show of hands (if this had not already been done at the time the poll was demanded).

If the demand for the poll is valid and is not withdrawn, the chairman would advise the meeting to this effect. If he did not advise the meeting as to the proxy position when the poll was first demanded, he could now do so. Assuming the poll is still not withdrawn, the chairman would read his statement announcing the time for holding of the poll, e.g. either immediately, at the conclusion of the meeting or at a later date. It would be the usual practice for the poll to be held at the end of the meeting and for it to be kept open for one hour. The meeting would then proceed to its next business until the conclusion of the business of the Annual General Meeting.

At the end of the Annual General Meeting the chairman would declare the meeting closed and then inform the members as to the procedure for the conduct of the poll. He would explain that those who have appointed a proxy need not complete a ballot paper unless they wished to alter their vote.

Stewards would then distribute ballot papers to those present, which would be collected by staff after completion by the shareholders and handed to the scrutineers.

The scrutineers, especially if they are the company's auditors, will no doubt have their own instructions with regard to the checking of the ballot papers, verification of the holdings, and preparation of a report and final certificate of the result of the poll which would be handed to the chairman. The result of the poll would then be notified to The Stock Exchange, in the case of a listed company, and to the press.

Corporate shareholders

A shareholder which is a corporate body may be represented at a company meeting by a person appointed as its representative by a resolution of the corporate body's directors under s.375. This is not the same thing as a proxy since a corporation representative is entitled both to speak at the meeting and to vote either on a show of hands or on a poll. It is usual for the appointed representative to bring a certified copy of his company's board minute appointing him, to be produced on entering the meeting, and it would be usual for such representatives to sign a separate attendance list.

The general position of proxies

Under s.372 an individual or corporate member of a public company may appoint one or more proxies to attend and vote at one particular meeting only, but proxies have no other right. A proxy need not be a member of the company. A proxy may not speak at a general meeting (except at a meeting of a private company) and also may not vote on a show of hands. He may vote only on a poll.

It is a requirement for listed companies on The Stock Exchange to send two-way proxy forms with the notice of the meeting, but this is not obligatory in the case of public companies not listed on The Stock Exchange and also private companies. However, the notice of meeting of a public company should in all cases state the right of the shareholder to appoint one or more proxies (s.372). In the case of public companies not listed on The Stock Exchange and also in the case of private companies, it is not obligatory to send proxy forms with notices of meetings. Consequently, this would only be done if some controversy were expected at the meeting. Where proxy forms are issued, however, they must be issued to all members of the company and not just to those who favour the board (s.372(6)). The company may accept proxy forms lodged at the last minute provided that they are in an appropriate form. The legal restriction is that it is unlawful for a company to require proxies to be lodged with the company *more* than 48 hours prior to the time of the meeting (s.372(5)).

Two-way proxies
It is necessary for companies listed on The Stock Exchange to issue 'two-way' proxy forms (Continuing Obligations, para. 37). A two-way proxy is one which includes provision for members to indicate which way they wish the proxy to cast their votes in the event of a poll being demanded and it must cover all the resolutions on the notice of meeting. The form must also state that if it is returned without any indication as to how the proxy shall vote on any resolution, the proxy may exercise his discretion as to how he votes or whether he will abstain from voting. Further, the form should not restrict the shareholder to appointing the chairman or a director to be his proxy. It must include the provision for the shareholder to appoint a proxy of his own choice. Corporate shareholders will usually be satisfied with the appointment of a proxy, and will usually send along a corporation representative under s.375 only if they wish the representative to make some comment at the meeting and also to be eligible to vote on a show of hands.

Form and dispatch of proxy forms
The requirement of The Stock Exchange for the issue of two-way proxies does involve companies in additional work and is often regarded as a chore, especially in the case of an Annual General Meeting when the business of the meeting is concerned only with the usual routine matters and is consequently not likely to be controversial. In the case of other business to be conducted at the meeting, however, the indications from the proxies will show whether or not there is likely to be any disagreement on the other business. The chairman will thus know in advance whether

he should demand a poll in the event of a motion on other business being defeated on a show of hands, if the majority of proxies lodged with the company are in favour of the resolution.

It is usual for proxy forms to be in the form of prepaid postcards; if there are to be a number of meetings following the Annual General Meeting, e.g. an Extraordinary General Meeting or a meeting of any particular class of the shareholders, the proxy cards for those meetings are usually of a different colour so as to facilitate sorting.

Table A, Regulation 62, and most companies' Articles require that proxies must be lodged at the company's office not less than 48 hours before a meeting. However, it is permissible for Articles to provide for a shorter period but not a longer period (s.372(5)). It is also usual for Articles to permit proxies to be lodged between an original meeting and an adjourned meeting. However, this can be done only if it is specifically provided for in the Articles.

The address to which proxies are to be returned may be the company's office, which in most companies' Articles and in Table A is defined as the registered office of the company, or to some other place which may be specified in the notice convening the meeting. Thus, if the share registration work of the company is carried out by a service registrar at a place other than the registered office of the company, the proxies may be sent to the address of the registrar.

With regard to the wording of the proxy form, in addition to providing numbered boxes for each resolution so that the shareholder may indicate with a tick in each box whether he votes for or against a resolution, it is useful to include a phrase 'on any other business arising at the meeting (including any motion to amend a resolution or to adjourn the meeting) the proxy will act at his/her discretion'. The absence of such a sentence may be taken to preclude the proxy from voting on an amended resolution or on a resolution whether or not to adjourn the meeting. Also, it would give a proxy power to vote on any matter which may arise in connection with the procedure of the meeting.

Evaluation of proxies

As the proxy cards are received by the company or its registrar from shareholders, they should be sorted, scrutinised to see that they have been properly completed and then a running total kept of the votes for and against each resolution – counting in among those voting for the resolutions those who have not indicated how they wish their vote to be cast and have left it to the discretion of the proxy who, if he is the chairman of the company, will obviously vote in favour of the resolutions.

It should be noted that shareholders may limit their proxies to only part of their holdings and that, except in the case of private companies, they can appoint more than one proxy, each proxy appointed covering separate parts of their shareholding. Sorting of the proxy cards will be determined in the light of experience. The awkward ones are those where the proxy is to vote in favour of some resolutions and against others.

The proxy card should be signed personally by shareholders who are individuals. In the case of a corporate shareholder the proxy card must be completed in accordance with the company's Articles, i.e. under seal if the company has a seal, or the company's board may have passed a resolution appointing named persons in the company to sign proxy cards on the company's behalf. In this case, the authority under which it is signed should be lodged with the proxy card if not already registered with the company. In the case of joint holdings, most Articles, including Table A, Regulation 55, provide for the voting rights to be exercised by the first-named holder in the account (the 'senior') and he or she would normally sign the proxy form on behalf of all the joint holders. Unless the Articles so provide it is not necessary for signatures on proxy forms to be witnessed. Incorrectly completed proxy forms must be rejected, but if there is time and if the shareholding is substantial so that it is worthwhile to have the proxy, it should be returned to the holder for amendment. A proxy may be revoked by the lodgement of a subsequent appointment if it is received by the company in time prior to the meeting. A proxy would lapse if the person who gave it were to die prior to the meeting provided notice of the death were received by the time proxies have to be received by the company (i.e. usually 48 hours prior to the meeting).

At the meeting
It should be noted that a shareholder who has appointed a proxy may still attend the meeting and vote in person and his attendance and vote at the meeting would act as a revocation of his proxy appointment. The right of a person appointing a proxy to attend and vote at a meeting would be conditional upon this not being prohibited by the Articles, but such a provision would be exceptional.

CHAPTER 12

Auditors

Section 384 inserted by CA 1989 s.119 requires every company to appoint an auditor whose primary function is to report on the company's statutory accounts prepared in accordance with s.226 inserted by CA 1989 s.4 – individual company accounts – and s.227 inserted by CA 1989 s.5 – group accounts; these sections require the directors of each such company to prepare a profit and loss account and balance sheet in respect of each financial year of the company (s.235 inserted by CA 1989 s.9). Dormant companies may by Special Resolution exempt themselves from appointing auditors in certain cases (s.250 inserted by CA 1989 s.14 and s.388A inserted by CA 1989 s.119). Apart from the basic duty to report on all annual accounts of a company to be laid before the company in general meeting, the auditors' report, auditors are responsible for the following additional matters:

1. Including in their report particulars relating to directors' emoluments, employees' emoluments, substantial contracts with directors and loans to directors if these are not disclosed according to the statutory requirements in the company's accounts (s.237(4) inserted by CA 1989 s.9 and Schedule 6 as amended by CA 1989 Schedule 4).
2. Stating in their report that the information given in the directors' report is inconsistent with the corresponding accounts if they consider this to be the case (s.235(3) inserted by CA 1989 s.9).
3. Making and/or reporting on expert valuations of assets where shares have been allotted either as fully paid or partly paid up by a non-cash consideration if appointed as valuer for the purpose (s.108).
4. Auditing interim accounts where it is desired to pay a dividend and the dividend cannot be justified by reference to the company's last accounts (ss.270 and 271).
5. Issuing a written statement concerning the company's balance sheet to accompany an application by a private company for re-registration as a public company (s.43(3)).

6. Preparing a report to accompany the directors' statutory declaration required where a private company gives financial assistance for the acquisition of its own shares (ss.155 and 156(4)).
7. Preparing a similar statement where a private company purchases its own shares out of capital (s.173(5)).

It should be noted that the copy of the auditors' report sent to the Registrar of Companies must be manually signed

Eligibility for appointment

The law regarding eligibility for appointment as company auditor under s.384 has been considerably strengthened by CA 1989 ss.24–54.

A person to be appointed auditor of a company must be a member of a recognised supervisory body and be eligible for appointment under the rules of that body (CA 1989 ss.25 and 30). An individual or a firm may be appointed company auditor; the term 'firm' includes a body corporate or a partnership.

Some other persons holding an 'appropriate qualification' may also be eligible for appointment under the provisions of CA 1989 s.31. These are persons qualified for appointment under the provisions of s.389 (which is repealed by CA 1989) immediately before 1 January 1990 and immediately before the commencement of the CA 1989 s.25 provisions on eligibility for appointment. Persons with overseas qualifications who meet the educational requirements laid down in CA 1989 s.33 are also eligible.

Persons who are officers or employees of a company or the partners or employees of such persons, are specifically disqualified from being the auditor of the company (CA 1989 s.27) on the grounds of lack of independence.

In the case of the appointment of a partnership in England and Wales, the appointment is (unless a contrary intention appears) an appointment of the partnership as such and not of the partners (CA 1989 s.26). Section 26 CA 1989 also contains special rules which apply where a partnership in England and Wales ceases and another partnership succeeds to the practice involving changes in the partners. It will be recalled that, unlike the case in England and Wales, Scottish partnerships have corporate status and any changes in the partnership would not affect the continuation of the appointment as a corporate body has perpetual status.

Under CA 1989 s.28 an auditor who becomes ineligible for appointment during his term of office must vacate his office and forthwith notify the company in writing and under CA 1989 s.29 the Secretary of State may direct a company to engage a person eligible for appointment as auditor to carry out a second audit for any part of the period during which the company had an auditor ineligible for appointment to that office.

Under CA 1989 s.35 the Secretary of State may make regulations requiring the keeping of a register of individuals and firms eligible for appointment as company auditor and individuals holding an appropriate qualification responsible for company audit work on behalf of such firms. The regulations may make provision for the register of auditors to be open to inspection by members of the public. Supervisory bodies are also required to make information available to the public regarding their members who are eligible for appointment as company auditor (CA 1989 s.36).

Appointment of first auditor

The first auditor would be appointed by the directors who would hold office until the end of the first general meeting at which accounts are laid before the company. If the directors do not make an appointment, however, the company in general meeting may make the appointment (s.385 inserted by CA 1989 s.119).

Periodic appointment

The company is required to appoint or reappoint an auditor at each general meeting at which accounts are laid before the company, to hold office from the conclusion of the meeting until the conclusion of the next meeting at which accounts are laid before the company (s.385 *ibid.*). This usually takes place at the company's Annual General Meeting. If it is desired to appoint a person as auditor other than the retiring auditor, special formalities must be followed.

Should a company fail to make an appointment of auditor the Secretary of State for Trade and Industry is empowered to fill the vacancy. There is an obligation on the company to inform the Secretary of State within one week of the general meeting at which accounts are laid that no appointment has been made and that consequently his powers under s.387 inserted by CA 1989 s.119 have become exercisable.

The directors, or the company in general meeting, have power under s.388 inserted by CA 1989 s.119 to fill a casual vacancy in the office of auditor.

Remuneration

Where auditors have been appointed by the directors, either as the first auditors of the company or to fill a casual vacancy, their remuneration may be determined by the directors. The Secretary of State would determine the remuneration of the auditors if they were appointed by him (s.390A inserted by CA 1989 s.121).

Except in the above special cases the remuneration of the auditors appointed by the company in general meeting is determined by the company in general meeting or in such manner as the general meeting may determine (s.390A *ibid.*). It is the usual practice for companies to pass a resolution at the Annual General Meeting giving authority to the directors to determine the remuneration of the auditors at the same time as the meeting approves the appointment or reappointment of the auditors. This overcomes the difficulty of trying to estimate in advance what the auditors' remuneration for the year might be. It would be appropriate for a shareholder other than a director to propose this resolution.

The amount of the auditors' remuneration must be stated in the annual accounts (s.390A *ibid.*).

Auditor ceasing to hold office

Section 394 inserted by CA 1989 s.123 provides that where for any reason, e.g. removal, resignation or not being reappointed at a general meeting, an auditor ceases to hold office he shall deposit with the company at its registered office a statement of any circumstances connected with his ceasing to hold office which he considers should be brought to the attention of members or creditors of the company or that there are no such circumstances.

In the case of resignation the statement must be deposited with the notice of resignation; in the case of failure to seek reappointment the statement must be deposited not less than 14 days before the end of the time allowed for next appointing auditors; in any other case the statement shall be deposited not later than the end of 14 days beginning with the date on which the auditor ceases to hold office (s.394 *ibid.*).

If the statement is of circumstances which should be brought to the notice of members or creditors a copy of the notice and statement must be sent within 14 days of the deposit to every person entitled to be sent copies of the company's report and accounts or the company may apply to the Court to relieve it from its obligation to circulate the auditor's statement if it considers that the auditor is using the statement to secure needless publicity of defamatory matter.

Resignation of auditors

Under s.392 inserted by CA 1989 s.122 an auditor may resign his office by giving notice in writing to that effect at the registered office of the company. In doing so, he must deposit with the company a statement required by s.394 *ibid.* and the notice of resignation will not be effective unless it is accompanied by such a statement.

Notice of the resignation must be sent to the Registrar of Companies within 14 days.

A resigning auditor whose notice of resignation is accompanied by a statement which he considers should be brought to the attention of members and creditors of the company may lodge with his notice of resignation a requisition calling on the directors to convene an Extraordinary General Meeting of the company to consider the explanation of the circumstances connected with his resignation which must be convened within 21 days of the deposit of the requisition to be held on a date not more than 28 days from the date of convening the meeting (s.392A inserted by CA 1989 s.122). In addition, the auditor's statement must be sent to the members of the company with the notice of the meeting, or if it is received too late for this to be done, the auditor may require that the statement be read out at the meeting. However, the statement need not be sent out if on the application of either the company or any other person claiming to be aggrieved the Court is of the opinion that the provisions are being used by the auditor to secure needless publicity for defamatory matter.

Removal or non-reappointment of auditors

A company may wish to change its auditor and the best way to do this without causing aggravation is for the directors to try to persuade the existing auditor to resign his office voluntarily. The directors could then fill the resultant vacancy as a casual vacancy. The auditor might not be prepared to do this, however, and in this case the matter could be left until the next general meeting of the company at which accounts are laid before the company, usually the Annual General Meeting, when the auditor's appointment would automatically cease at the end of that meeting and the company could appoint a new auditor in his place.

However, the need to change the auditor may be more urgent and it would then be necessary to convene an Extraordinary General Meeting of the company in order to pass an Ordinary Resolution to remove the auditor before the expiration of his current period of office (s.391 inserted by CA 1989 s.122). When the Ordinary Resolution has been passed, notice must be given to the Registrar of Companies within 14 days on the prescribed form. The new auditor to fill the vacancy could be appointed by the directors, or by the company at the general meeting at which the old auditor was removed; the latter would be the normal practice.

Rights of auditors who are removed or not reappointed

There are special formalities which have to be followed where a resolution is to be proposed at a general meeting for removing an auditor before the expiration of his term of office or for appointing as auditor a person other than a retiring auditor.

These formalities are as follows:

1. Special notice must be given to the company of the proposed resolution.
2. Copies of the special notice must be sent forthwith by the company to the person proposed to be removed as auditor, to be appointed as auditor and to the retiring auditor, as the case may be.
3. The auditor proposed to be removed or not reappointed may make representations in writing to the company on the proposed resolution and may ask the company to circulate these to members of the company.
4. The company must comply with that request, unless it is too late to do so, and include in the notice of meeting a note to the effect that such representations have been made and send a copy of the representations to every member of the company to whom notice of the meeting is sent.
5. If the representations are received too late to be circulated to the members of the company the auditor concerned may request that they be read out at the meeting.
6. The auditor proposed to be removed or not reappointed is also entitled to receive notice of, and to attend and speak at, the general meeting at which the resolution for his removal or non-reappointment is to be considered.
7. The representations need not be sent out or be read at the meeting if on the application of either the company or any other person claiming to be aggrieved the Court is satisfied that the rights conferred on the auditor proposed to be removed or not reappointed are being abused to secure needless publicity of defamatory matter (s.391A inserted by CA 1989 s.122).

Rights of auditors in the exercise of their duties

An auditor of a company enjoys certain statutory rights to information in connection with the exercise of his duties. These are as follows:

1. A right of access at all times to the company's books, accounts and vouchers and to require from the company's officers such information and explanations as the auditor thinks necessary for the performance of his duties (s.389A(1) inserted by CA 1989 s.120).

2. The auditor is entitled to attend any general meeting of the company and to receive all notices and other communications relating to any general meeting. He may also speak on any part of the business of the meeting which concerns him as auditor (s.390 inserted by CA 1989 s.120).

3. It is the duty of subsidiary undertakings incorporated in Great Britain and their auditors to give the auditors of the parent company such information and explanation as those auditors may reasonably require for the purposes of their duties as auditors of the parent company (s.389A(3) inserted by CA 1989 s.120).

4. A parent company, having a subsidiary undertaking which is not a body incorporated in Great Britain shall, if its auditors require, take all such steps as are reasonably open to it to obtain from the subsidiary such information and explanations as its auditors may reasonably require (s.389A(4) inserted by CA 1989 s.120).

It is an offence (punishable by fine and/or imprisonment) for an officer of the company, in conveying information and explanations required by the company's auditors, knowingly or recklessly to make a statement which is misleading, false or deceptive in a material particular (s.389A(2) inserted by CA 1989 s.120).

Private companies

A private company may by an elective resolution, passed in accordance with the provisions of s.379A inserted by CA 1989 s.116, elect to dispense with the obligation to appoint auditors annually and when such an election is in force the company's auditors are deemed to be reappointed for each succeeding financial year until a resolution is passed exempting the company from appointing auditors as a dormant company under s.250 inserted by CA 1989 s.14 or a resolution is passed under s.393 inserted by CA 1989 s.122 terminating the appointment of auditors not appointed annually.

Dormant companies

A dormant company, as defined by s.250(3) inserted by CA 1989 s.14, may pass a Special Resolution exempting itself from the obligation to appoint auditors; the detailed conditions of the exemption are contained in s.250 inserted by CA 1989 s.14 and s.388A inserted by CA 1989 s.119. Such a resolution may not be passed by a public company, a banking or insurance company or an authorised person under the FSA. The Special Resolution is passed at a general meeting at which its accounts are laid before the company or, in the case of a newly incorporated company, passed before the first such general meeting if the company has been dormant since its formation. The company must have had no significant accounting transactions as defined in s.250(3) inserted by CA 1989 s.14 since the end of its previous financial year or, in the case of a newly incorporated company, from the time of its formation.

The grant of the exemption does not relieve the company of its obligation to lay accounts at a general meeting but if it is a small or medium-sized company it is entitled to the exemptions contained in ss.246–7 inserted by CA 1989 s.13 and CA 1989 Schedule 6. These exemptions are not available, however, to a public company, a banking or insurance company or an authorised person under the FSA. It should be noted that CA 1989 Schedule 6 replaces Schedule 8 of the Companies Act 1985. Since the accounts of dormant companies need not be audited, there is no auditors' report to be annexed to the accounts. Also, with effect from the accounting reference period in which the Special Resolution not to appoint auditors is passed, the company may be eligible for the small or medium-sized company accounts exemptions notwithstanding that it would not be eligible for the exemption as a member of a group of companies which is ineligible to deliver modified accounts (ss.246–7 inserted by CA 1989 s.13 and CA 1989 Schedule 6). During the continuation of the exemption every copy of the balance sheet delivered to the Registrar of Companies must bear a statement immediately above the signature of the director that the company was dormant within the meaning of s.250(3) inserted by CA 1989 s.14, throughout the financial year ended ....

If the company should cease to be dormant and, therefore, no longer eligible for the exemption, the obligation to appoint auditors applies again immediately. The directors may make the necessary appointment but, if they do not do so, the appointment may be made by the company in general meeting.

The Institute's manual contains various precedents in connection with the appointment, resignation and removal of auditors, as well as the full wording of the statement to appear above the signature of the director on the balance sheet of a dormant company.

CHAPTER 13

The securities industry

In this chapter the work of the securities industry, and particularly The Stock Exchange, is considered, with the exception of the methods by which securities may be brought to The Stock Exchange and the admission of securities to listing, which are considered in Chapter 3, and take-overs and mergers, which are dealt with in Chapter 14.

The Stock Exchange

In the United Kingdom there is one unified stock exchange which is governed by the Council of The Stock Exchange and which has extensive rules and regulations binding the activities of members of the Exchange and governing the requirements for the securities of companies and corporations to be dealt in on The Stock Exchange.

The Stock Exchange started its life as the London Stock Exchange; its origins begin in a coffee shop in the City of London in 1773 where people met to buy and sell securities. They subsequently formed themselves into an organised group out of which the London Stock Exchange developed a system for the control of its activities with its own exclusive rules. Other smaller exchanges were established in the major industrial cities of Great Britain and Ireland so as to provide a marketplace in which the stocks and shares of local industries could be dealt in. In order to achieve a degree of uniformity, these smaller exchanges subsequently organised themselves into a Federation of Stock Exchanges in Great Britain and Ireland governed by a single code of rules and regulations similar to those of the London Stock Exchange. In March 1973 the various exchanges in the Federation joined with London in order to become one single organisation known as The Stock Exchange. The trading floors at Birmingham, Liverpool, Glasgow and Dublin, however, still function separately for small local companies but the trading floor of The Stock Exchange in London is now not in use (except to the limited exception for the traded options market) since the market for buying and selling securities functions electronically through The Stock Exchange Automated Quotations system (SEAQ) on which the prices of stocks and shares are shown on screens in dealers' offices. Although most stockbrokers are London based, there are firms of stockbrokers in leading towns and cities all over the United Kingdom and members of these provincial firms may deal for clients either in London or, in the case of small local companies, on the local trading floors mentioned above. These firms are linked electronically to the central market in London for dealings in securities which are listed on The Stock Exchange, or traded on the Unlisted Securities Market (see pp.58–60) or, until the end of 1990, on the Third Market (see p.60), so that The London Stock Exchange operates nationwide. The full name of The Stock Exchange is now The International Stock Exchange of the United Kingdom and the Republic of Ireland (ISE).

The Stock Exchange is a market for buying and selling shares, debentures and loan stocks in companies whose securities are listed on The Stock Exchange (or quoted on the Unlisted Securities Market or, until the end of 1990 on the Third Market) similar to other markets, e.g. just as a cattle market is a market for buying and selling cattle which are brought to the market for sale, except that investors wishing to buy or sell companies' securities are brought together not directly but through the stockbrokers and market makers who hold stocks and shares of the various companies. In addition to being a market for dealings in stocks and shares of companies, The Stock Exchange is a market for the buying and selling of government securities, i.e. gilt edged stocks, as well as the stocks of various public corporations such as municipal authorities (corporation loans), Commonwealth and overseas government issues, etc.

The former requirement for Stock Exchange firms to act only in one capacity, i.e. as broker or jobber, was terminated with effect from the 'Big Bang' on 27 October 1986. At the same time minimum commissions were abolished. All dealings on The Stock Exchange are conducted in accordance with the Rules, Regulations and usages of The Stock Exchange and the conduct of business rules of the Securities and Investments Board (or a self-regulating organisation) as required by the FSA.

Brokers, broker/dealers and market makers

There are still, however, usually two parties involved in effecting deals on The Stock Exchange, the broker and the market maker. When the broker buys or sells stock or shares from or to a market maker he acts as agent for his client but he may also act as a principal if he himself makes a market in the stock or shares concerned, i.e. he is then a broker/dealer. Although

Stock Exchange firms may now act as broker/dealers, some firms like to specialise as market makers, i.e. as jobbers, or merely to act as brokers, i.e. buying and selling stocks and shares as agents for their clients. Market makers may specialise in certain types of shares, e.g. retailing or oil and exploration, etc., and they must register with The Stock Exchange those securities in which they are willing to deal and undertake to offer to buy or sell such securities at a named price in respect of a marketable quantity.

Brokers and broker/dealers are organised into firms on The Stock Exchange although most are now limited companies. Outsiders could previously only buy into stockbroking firms up to 29.9 per cent ownership but since 1 March 1986, 100 per cent ownership became possible. As a result many brokers are now subsidiary companies of other companies which may be banks or other major financial institutions either British or foreign registered. Brokers act as agents for their clients, who give them instructions to buy or sell securities on The Stock Exchange. They may also offer other services to their clients, such as the supervision or management of investment portfolios. They are remunerated by commission chargeable according to the size of the transaction. The Stock Exchange no longer specifies rates of minimum commission and thus there is a wide variety of commission structures among the various firms of brokers.

Market makers

Market makers are also organised into firms on The Stock Exchange, many also being limited companies. The function of the market maker is to make a market in the stocks and shares in which he deals and he will have available at any one time a quantity of the stocks and shares in which he makes a market, i.e. his 'book'. If he has only very limited quantities of a share available, he is said to be 'short' of the stock, whereas if he has a large amount of the shares of a company on his book he is said to be 'long' of the stock. A market maker is remunerated by the difference between the price at which he buys and the price at which he sells, known as the 'market makers' turn'.

It should be noted that non-members of The Stock Exchange may deal direct with market makers without the interposition of a broker/dealer.

The prices of stocks and shares on The Stock Exchange are determined by the normal rules of supply and demand, i.e. if more people are buying than selling, the price of the shares will increase, whereas if more people are wanting to sell than to buy, the price of the shares will decrease. The market maker does not make a commission charge like the broker but is remunerated, as noted above, by the difference between the two prices at which he will sell stock to a broker, and will buy stock from a broker. As an example, the market maker may quote the shares of the XYZ company at 180–190p i.e. a spread of 10p. The lower price of 180p is the 'bid price', i.e. the price at which he will buy a reasonable market quantity of the shares, and the higher price of 190p is the 'offer price', i.e. the price at which he will offer a reasonable market quantity of shares for sale. Half the difference between the two prices, i.e. 185p, is called the 'middle price' and is the price which is shown in the national newspapers' City pages.

The spread between the bid and offer prices varies according to the price and nature of the stock concerned. In the case of a medium-priced stock which is frequently dealt in, like Boots or Marks & Spencer, there will probably be just a small gap between the bid and offer prices, the market maker making his profit from the high turnover in the shares of such companies. In the case of smaller companies, however, the spread between the two prices will be wider because the market maker will only occasionally receive orders to buy or sell the shares of such companies; the wider spread gives him a higher margin of profit on deals in such shares. This affords him some protection since, if he were to buy shares of such a company which is infrequently dealt in, and take them on his book, he would have no idea as to how long it would be before someone came along to offer to buy those shares back from him and, in the meantime, he would have arrangements in force to finance his book. The spread between the bid and offer prices will be greater in the case of a higher-priced stock, e.g. shares in a price range of between 500p and 1,000p, the amount of the spread again depending on the frequency of activity in the stock.

Each days's dealings on The Stock Exchange and the spread of prices are recorded in *The Stock Exchange Daily Official List* (SEDOL) or, if there should have been no dealings in a particular stock on the day in question, the List will contain particulars of the last transaction carried out.

Mechanics of dealing on The Stock Exchange

A member of the public wishing to deal, i.e. the principal, gives his order to his stockbroker, who will act as his agent, and who will consult his SEAQ screen to ascertain the buying and selling prices of the various market makers who deal in the security concerned. The information regarding SEAQ quotations is provided on the screen terminals in the offices of stockbrokers by subscription to The Stock Exchange's electronic information service called TOPIC – Teletext Output of Price Information by Computer. SEAQ's full name is The Stock Exchange Automated Quotations System. The broker will accept the price most favourable to his client, i.e. the lowest price if buying or the highest price if selling as indicated on the screen. The investor may give specific instructions to his broker that he is not to buy above or sell below a given price, i.e. he may impose a 'limit' on his order. Pages on brokers' TOPIC screen terminals show the SEAQ mid-price of every company's shares by sectors, e.g. retail, chemicals, etc., giving mid-market price trends.

Other pages give an alphabetical index of companies' shares and by bringing up the appropriate page for a company on to the screen the broker can see the initials of all the market makers in that company's shares giving their bid and offer prices. A large company may have as many as 15–20 market makers in its shares but small companies will have only a few. The best quotes for a sell or buy order are highlighted in a yellow band along the top of the screen with the initials of the market makers willing to deal at these prices, e.g. WARB BZW 359–361 UBS. The screen will also show above the yellow band the volume of the company's shares so far traded during the day, the opening price (i.e. the previous day's closing price) and the prices at which previous bargains during the day were transacted.

If the broker is content to accept the prices indicated in the yellow band, he will telephone the market maker concerned and put his order through, sometimes perhaps asking the market maker if he can make a closer price than quoted in which case the market maker may quote a slightly more favourable bid price if he is short of the shares and wishes to take more on to his book or a slightly more favourable offer price if he has a lot of the shares on his book and wishes to dispose of some of them. The market maker must report the bargain to The Stock Exchange within three minutes so that the SEAQ screen price for the company's shares may be updated and the number for the volume of shares traded altered. In the case of a large bargain, however, the market maker is allowed to defer reporting the price of the bargain until the following day so that other market makers may not take advantage of the information to the detriment of the market maker concerned.

Also shown on the screen giving the quotes of the various market makers for a company's shares is an indication alongside the initials of each market maker of the size of bargains he is willing to transact at the prices quoted, e.g. $5,000 \times 5,000$, i.e. willing to buy or sell 5,000 shares at those prices; occasionally one may see '1L $\times$ 1L', which means the market maker is willing to do a large bargain of 100,000 each way. The '$\times$' indicates that the market maker will not deal under The Stock Exchange Automated Execution Facility (SAEF) but if $5,000 + 5,000$ is shown alongside a market maker's initials this means that he is willing to make a bargain under SAEF for a purchase by a broker; or if $5,000 - 5,000$ is shown this means that he will make a bargain under SAEF for a sale by a broker. However, it should be noted that bargains under SAEF are limited to 1,000 shares.

Using SAEF costs brokers money and for these reasons some brokers use one of the other automatic execution facilities offered by market makers with whom they have frequent dealings, e.g. BEST operated by Kleinwort Benson or TRADE operated by Barclays de Zoete Wedd under which bargains for more than 1,000 shares may be transacted. In these cases no telephoning to the market maker is required as the broker only has to press the appropriate keys on a keyboard, i.e. SELL or BUY, the name of the company, the number of shares, the broker's name or reference and on pressing the ENTER key the transaction is completed.

Bargains are checked by The Stock Exchange Centre (which operates the TALISMAN settlement system) each evening for nightly validation of bargains on the basis of information of bargains done supplied to the Centre by member firms either on magnetic tape or by data entry on the firms' terminals. The Centre matches the bargains, i.e. for every buyer there must be a seller, and if all is in order the bargains are validated for settlement. Unmatched bargains which cannot be validated are put aside for validation on the next day.

A SEAQ trigger page shows the mid-price movements during the day of the 100 shares included in *The Financial Times* Stock Exchange 100 Share Index, a green figure indicating no change since the opening, a blue figure indicating that the price shown is higher than the previous price shown and a red figure that the price shown is lower than the previous price shown. This page also shows the latest value of the FT–SE 100 Index itself.

There is also another page which lists the companies which have made announcements during the day concerning results or other matters, e.g. a re organisation, and by calling up the appropriate page the broker can read the text of the announcement.

The above description is of course, only a summary of the facilities which are available on the electronic dealing system and also only applies to the more important stocks and shares traded, called alpha stocks. The information given on the TOPIC screen relating to beta and gamma stocks is naturally less extensive. In particular it should be pointed out that a report (the Elwes report) was published by the ISE in March 1990 entitled 'Report of the Special Committee on Market Development'. Although at the time of preparation of this handbook consultations on the report were still proceeding, most of its recommendations, which will alter the mechanism for trading in UK equities, are likely to be implemented. The following principal changes may be expected to occur:

1. The introduction of a green strip on SEAQ screens (in addition to the yellow strip mentioned above) which will display the best bid and

offer prices in SAEF size without disclosing the names of the market makers unless they wish it.

2. The abandonment of the present method of classifying securities (alpha, beta, etc.) and replacing it by a normal market size (NMS) for each security calculated by reference to a formula based on average daily turnover (in money terms) over the preceding 12 months, thereby avoiding the stigma attached to non-alpha securities.

3. If experiments are successful and a business case can be made out, the introduction of a Central Limit Order Service (CLOSE) which will facilitate the execution of small bargains and bargains for odd lots of shares at better prices and also enhance the authenticity of the SEAQ price because CLOSE will show orders from investors willing to deal at a specific price, i.e. CLOSE will institute an order driven trading system grafted on to the traditional quote driven trading system in UK equities.

4. There will be a change in the size of bargains which must be reported immediately for on-line trade publication so as to increase the on-line publication of bargains in the most liquid securities to a higher level than at present.

5. There is likely to be a redesign of The Stock Exchange Daily Official List.

When the broker has dealt he will issue a contract note to the investor which gives the number and description of the securities bought or sold, the date of the transaction, the price and the total consideration payable or receivable, the stockbroker's commission which became free of VAT on 1 January 1990, plus transfer stamp duty if buying shares or loan stock convertible into shares, to be added to or deducted from the total consideration. However, under the 1990 Budget proposals transfer stamp duty will be abolished when TAURUS is implemented, probably towards the end of 1991. The contract note also states the date of settlement, i.e. the date on which the purchaser must pay for the securities bought or the day on which he may expect payment for the securities which he has sold. A note as to whether the broker acted as agent, i.e. he bought or sold the shares through a market maker, or as principal, i.e. he bought or sold the shares for his own book, will also appear on the contract note. The contract note may also give the time of dealing or state that this information is available on request in case the client has some query about the price paid or received.

If the investor has sold securities he must deliver the relevant share certificate(s) to his broker and sign a TALISMAN sold transfer form. The settlement takes place following the end of The Stock Exchange account. The year is divided into dealing and settlement periods, usually two weeks but occasionally, at the time of public holidays, three weeks. Under TAURUS (see Chapter 5) there may be a move away from the two-week account system and the introduction of a rolling account system under which deals would be settled within five working days.

Sometimes the settlement, instead of being on the account day following the end of a Stock Exchange account, is for cash. This usually arises in connection with the sale of new issues of shares. Shares in a new issue bought for cash are subject to the government *ad valorem* 0.5 per cent stamp duty in this case known as stamp duty reserve tax. This tax will also be abolished on the implementation of TAURUS.

The new issue may comprise a fully paid allotment letter in the case of a new security which has been the subject of an offer for sale, an introduction or a placing; or it may be a renounceable scrip issue certificate issued to an existing shareholder by way of a capitalisation of reserves; or it may be a nil paid or fully paid allotment letter in the case of a rights issue. A person selling a new issue would renounce his entitlement to the security by signing a form of renunciation on the back of the renounceable allotment letter or renounceable certificate and send this to his broker to enable him to complete the deal. The broker would charge commission in the usual way.

It is not necessary to buy and sell shares through a stockbroker direct. An investor may instruct his bank, and some building societies, to buy and sell securities on his behalf and the order will be passed on to a broker. The services provided by banks and building societies are being expanded continually to provide small investors with a convenient and easy to use dealing service at a reasonable cost. There are also some in-store share shops run by stockbrokers or authorised dealers.

The functions of stockbrokers, broker/dealers and market makers described above, are mainly used in the buying and selling of stocks and shares which are officially listed on The Stock Exchange but their functions operate in a similar manner in the case of dealings in shares which are unlisted on what is known as the Unlisted Securities Market (USM) or on the Third Market (see pp.58–60). However, the Third Market will cease to exist at the end of 1990. So far as dealing is concerned the only real difference is that, on the contract note issued by the broker to his client giving the details of the purchase or sale of shares of a company traded on the USM or the Third Market, it will be stated that 'This security is not officially listed on The Stock Exchange'. Dealings in USM and in Third Market securities are recorded in the USM appendix and the Third Market appendix, respectively, of *The Stock Exchange Daily Official List*.

As noted above, the dealing system currently in use is The Stock Exchange Automated Quotations System (SEAQ) which is owned and operated by the Exchange and for the use of which brokers have to pay fees. SEAQ International is used for trading in American Depositary Receipts (ADRs), which represent shares of large UK companies deposited with American banks. Transactions are effected by access to SEAQ terminals in brokers' offices. Some purchases and sales of small lots of shares (up to 1,000) may be executed through SAEF (Stock Exchange Automated Execution Facility). International deals may be executed through SEQUEL by an on line electronic trading matching service.

Rule 535 dealings

Other dealings may also take place in the shares of certain companies on The Stock Exchange which are neither officially listed nor quoted on the USM. Securities may be dealt in under specified bargains between members of The Stock Exchange with the prior approval of The Council of The Stock Exchange under Stock Exchange Rules. There are now few securities dealt in under this rule since many of the companies have sought and obtained a quotation on the USM or on the Third Market, although the latter will cease to exist at the end of 1990. Companies whose securities are at present traded on the Third Market will either move up to the USM or have their securities traded under Rule 535.2. There are two principal categories of companies whose securities are dealt in under Rule 535 as described below.

Rule 535.2
Specific bargains may be made with prior approval of The Council of The Stock Exchange in the securities of public companies or corporate bodies which are not listed on The Stock Exchange, dealt in on the USM or on the Third Market. When the Third Market is phased out in 1990 and is merged with the USM, the shares of companies which do not join the USM or obtain full listing will have to be dealt in under Rule 535.2. The securities likely to be dealt in under Rule 535.2 are those of small developing companies, often operating in the United Kingdom on a local basis, prior to their growth into a company which could apply for a quote on the USM or a listing on The Stock Exchange. No new companies will be admitted to the Third Market in 1990, which will cease to exist at the end of that year. The facility accordingly affords to holders the opportunity of dealing in the securities of such companies at commercial prices. The dealings which take place under this rule are quoted in a special list in *The Stock Exchange Daily Official List* (SEDOL).

Rule 535.4(a)
Dealings under this rule cover securities where the principal market for

dealing is outside the United Kingdom and Eire and which have not been granted a quotation or listing in London. Transactions under this rule are not recorded in SEDOL. In 1989 when Euro-Disneyland shares were being traded in Paris prior to the commencement of official dealings in London, dealings were able to take place in London under Rule 535.4(a).

Over-the-counter market

The securities of some companies which could not normally be bought or sold on The Stock Exchange were previously purchased from, or sold by, specialist companies who acted as market makers in the securities of the companies concerned in what was known as the over-the-counter market (OTC). OTC firms also acted as an agency for bringing together those wishing to sell unquoted securities and those wishing to buy them, i.e. matching bargains.

The Financial Services Act 1986, which was introduced because of the need for investor protection, the launch of the USM and the Third Market on which the shares of smaller companies could be quoted, reduced the activities of the OTC traders.

Authorised stock and share dealers

No person may carry on investment business in the United Kingdom unless he is an 'authorised person', authorised either directly by the Securities and Investments Board (SIB), the Department of Trade and Industry (DTI) under section 25 of the FSA or is authorised by virtue of membership of a self-regulating organisation under section 7 of the FSA. They may undertake transactions in all types of securities, i.e. those listed on The Stock Exchange, those quoted on the USM and some unquoted companies on a matched bargain basis. Authorised stock and share dealers are expected to conform to a code of conduct in their dealings with the public but The Stock Exchange has no control over their activities.

There are, however, many dealers authorised to carry on investment business through their membership of The Financial Intermediaries, Managers and Brokers' Regulatory Association (FIMBRA), which is a self-regulating organisation under the FSA with its own code of conduct. It is an important organisation from the point of view of investor protection and is recognised as a self-regulating organisation by the Secretary of State for Trade and Industry under FSA s.9. FIMBRA is responsible for exercising disciplinary control over its members and consequently they need not be individually licensed by SIB or the DTI. Investors who are clients of members of FIMBRA may also be protected if the firm has a professional indemnity policy. A compulsory professional indemnity insurance scheme to which all FIMBRA members would have to belong and which would pay out awards made by an investment referee has not so far been implemented because of opposition from firms who have already taken out their own insurance. However, because of the very tight disciplinary control which FIMBRA exercises over the activities of its members, the public is strongly advised to deal only with FIMBRA members.

Overseas stock exchanges

The larger foreign stock exchanges, such as Wall Street and Tokyo, use the trading post system of dealing. The floors of these stock exchanges resemble a market place where there are various designated places on the floor at which people meet in order to transact dealings in the securities of particular types of company. The deal is effected by agreement between the two persons concerned, i.e. someone who wishes to sell and someone who wishes to buy, and when the transaction has been completed, the price at which the deal took place and the name of the security will be posted on an indicator as a guide to other people who may be contemplating a transaction in the security concerned.

However, instead of going for a listing on the New York Stock Exchange on Wall Street, or on one of the other traditional American stock exchanges, many companies go for the alternative of a listing on NASDAQ, the National Association of Securities Dealers Automated Quotations system, a screen based market which is one of America's fastest growing stock markets. The electronic technology of NASDAQ provided the model for London's SEAQ system. Of course, many NASDAQ companies also have a listing on the New York Stock Exchange. In the case of British companies listing on NASDAQ is through the issue of American Depositary Receipts.

In most of the other foreign stock exchanges, however, the call over system is used. These smaller exchanges or country exchanges may be found in towns spread over a wide area in the country concerned. Under the call over system an official of the exchange, who may be the chairman, will call out the names of the securities in which transactions may be effected together with the current ruling price at the time in question. This will usually be done a number of times each day. As the name of each security is called out any seller of the security concerned will make himself known thus giving buyers the opportunity to make a purchase if they consider the price satisfactory. As a result of this call over buyers and sellers of securities are put in touch with each other; they can then meet in order to effect a transaction. The price agreed at the transaction may, of course, be different from the call over price and in this case there will be an adjustment in the price announced at the next call over.

Options

In the normal type of transaction effected on The Stock Exchange, as soon as the bargain is struck by the broker indicating his acceptance of the price quoted by a market maker on the SEAQ screen, the seller of the shares loses all his entitlement to them and they become the property of the buyer. The latter is then entitled to all the rights and dividends attaching to the shares which may be announced after the time the transaction is effected between the stockbroker and the market maker notwithstanding that there will inevitably be some delay before the shares become registered in his name in the Register of Members of the company.

It is, however, possible to effect transactions in options to buy or sell shares on The Stock Exchange which may be 'unquoted options' or 'traded options'. Options may be bought or sold on The Stock Exchange in a similar way to the shares themselves.

Unquoted options

An investor, by giving money to a seller of an option, obtains a right to buy the specified number of shares over some future period which may last up to three months, at an agreed price which will be close to the current market price at the time the option is obtained. This option is known as a 'call' option, which means that for a given amount of money the option holder is able to take an interest in a greater number of shares than he could if he were to purchase them outright in the normal way. He would take out a call option if he felt that the price was going to rise during the period in question, so that when the price had risen to what he would regard as a favourable level he could exercise the option by calling for the shares, sell them and make a profit.

If, on the other hand, the investor feels that the price of a share is going to fall over the period of the option he may buy a 'put' option for a stated number of shares. This gives him the option of selling those shares, at the current ruling price on the market at the time he acquired the option, at some future date when he would expect the price to have fallen. He would then exercise the option at a time he considered appropriate and make a profit on the transaction. If he is undecided as to which way the market will move in a particular share he can buy a 'put and call' option which gives him the right to buy or sell the shares during the period of the option at the current ruling price at the time of acquiring the option.

Option prices vary according to the nature of the share concerned, i.e. whether it is one which is traded in on a regular basis or whether it is traded in at irregular intervals, in which case the price may tend to be volatile and more expensive. Of course, if the movement in the market does not go the way in which the investor expects he can abandon his option and all he then loses is the purchase price that he paid for his put or call options. Options may be exercised over most of the securities which are traded on The Stock Exchange, and prices of options on leading shares are quoted in *The Financial Times*.

Traded options

In this case there must be an established market in the traded options for the shares of the company concerned. Consequently, there are far fewer securities on The Stock Exchange in which traded options may be taken out, although their number is growing all the time. A traded option is different from the normal type of option described above in that the option itself, whether it be a call option or a put option, can be bought and sold on The Stock Exchange just as in the case of the shares themselves. As a result if the investors sees that the option he has purchased is moving against him, i.e. the price of the shares concerned is not going up in the case of a call option or not going down in the case of a put option, he can cut his loss by selling the traded option on the market so that he does not lose the whole amount that he paid for the option in the first place. The traded options market has its own market makers who operate from a pitch on the floor of The Stock Exchange.

The Stock Exchange Daily Official List has a traded options section which contains the quotations for prices of traded options, which are also quoted daily in *The Financial Times*.

The traded options market occupies a corner of The Stock Exchange's old trading floor in London left vacant when share trading went electronic under SEAQ. There is the possibility that the London International Financial Futures Exchange (LIFFE) may later take up some of the other space.

Services provided by bankers for the securities industry

As indicated in the chapters of this handbook devoted to public issues, share registration, dividends, and acquisitions and mergers, bankers have a significant role to play in the securities market. Although considered in more detail elsewhere in the handbook, it may be useful to give a brief summary of these services.

Clearing bankers

Clearing bankers will aid the smooth running of the securities industry in the following ways:

1. The distribution of dividends and interest payments through the bulk distribution system.

2. Acting as registrar for companies which do not undertake their share registration work in house or employ a firm of service registrars. Most of the clearing bankers provide share registration services but there are also numerous independent firms who also provide such services. Some firms of accountants also provide share registration services as part of their service to their clients, sometimes combined with a company secretarial service.

3. Rights issues and capitalisation issues. The clearing bankers often act for companies as receiving bankers in connection with a rights issue, which relieves companies of the work involved in connection with the receipt of payments from shareholders on taking up their rights under a rights issue. The bankers would also provide a service in issuing split allotment letters when renounced letters of allotment in a rights issue are sent in by stockbrokers for splitting; this arises when investors have sold some or all of their rights on the market. The latter function would also arise in the case of a company making a capitalisation issue by way of the issue of renounceable share certificates, when some shareholders may be expected to sell some or all of the new shares on The Stock Exchange through their stockbrokers, who will send in the renounced share certificates for splitting. Split allotment letters and split renounceable certificates will be required by stockbrokers in order to make up bargains of various sizes.

4. New issues. The new issues departments of the clearing banks will also act for companies making a public issue of securities, and will deal with the receipt of the application forms accompanied by the application money and the dispatch of the fully paid allotment letters to those who are allotted shares. Following this, there would also be a period during which the clearing bank would provide a service in issuing split letters of allotment since some of the successful applicants for the shares may decide to sell them on the market, especially if they start trading at a premium, and brokers acting for the sellers may require split allotment letters in order to make up bargains of various sizes.

5. Calls on partly paid shares. Companies may appoint a bank to send call notices to shareholders, to receive the calls paid and produce a statement of calls remaining unpaid.

Merchant bankers

All the important merchant bankers are members of the British Merchant Banking and Securities Houses Association. The main service they give to companies is in connection with advice on corporate financial matters in the particular fields of obtaining a quotation for the securities of companies coming to the market for the first time, either by way of offers for sale at a fixed price or offers for sale at a minimum tender price, and in connection with advice on take-overs and mergers. In any take-over of one company by another, each company invariably appoints a merchant bank to act as its adviser during the course of the take-over and some take-overs, as can be seen from advertisements appearing from time to time in the press, may become quite acrimonius. The tactics to be followed by either the acquiring company or the target company require very skilful consideration by those with experience in this field.

The merchant banks also act for companies wishing to arrange finance overseas, e.g. Eurobonds.

Some merchant banks also offer share registration services and will also deal with rights issues, capitalisation issues and new issues in a similar way to the clearing banks.

The Stock Exchange Yellow Book

The secretaries of public listed companies will be very concerned with the content of the Yellow Book, published under the authority of The Council of The Stock Exchange entitled *Admission of Securities to Listing*. This is a loose-leaf book, a new edition of which appeared in November 1984 and which is kept up to date by amendment slips; at the time of writing this handbook seven of these have been issued, dated May and August 1985, August 1986, January, March and September 1987 and April 1989 respectively. The parts of the Yellow Book with which company secretaries are most likely to be concerned, once the shares of the company have been admitted to listing, are the Continuing Obligations for Companies set out in Section 5, Chapter 2, requirements with regard to acquisitions and realisations set out in Section 6, Chapter 1, and take-overs and mergers set out in Section 6, Chapter 2.

Before coming to the market, however, Sections 1, 2, 3, 4, and 9 will be the principal areas of concern. These particular sections of the Yellow Book deal with the following matters:

1. Section 1: this is a general introduction to the admission of securities to listing, including the basic conditions to be fulfilled by an applicant and the methods of issue.

2. Section 2: this deals with the application for listing procedure, including the documents to be lodged and the arrangements made for publicity.
3. Section 3: this is a most important section since it deals with the contents of the listing particulars or the equivalent offering documents and specifies all the information which must be included in the listing particulars, arrangements for their approval and the responsibilities of those who prepare them. The Stock Exchange listing particulars are considerably more extensive than the requirements for a prospectus under ss.64–71 and Schedule 3 of the Act.
4. Section 4: this sets out the detailed requirements for accountants' reports which have to be included in the listing particulars of companies seeking listing on The Stock Exchange.
5. Section 9: this lays down certain provisions which a company being listed on The Stock Exchange must include in its Articles of Association. These provisions are principally concerned with the Articles covering such matters as transfer and registration of securities, definitive certificates for securities, payment of dividends, directors, accounts, notices, voting rights, proxies and untraceable members.

Other sections of the Yellow Book cover matters met with less frequently in practice such as Section 7, Eurocurrency securities; Section 8, foreign companies; and Section 10, individual classes of issuer, such as property companies in Chapter 1, mineral companies in Chapter 2, investment trusts and investment companies in Chapter 3 and unit trusts in Chapter 4.

It should be noted that The Stock Exchange's listing requirements are expected to change at the end of 1990 when the Third Market (p.60) is merged with the USM (pp.58–60) following the implementation of EC directives on listing requirements.

Unlisted Securities

The Stock Exchange publishes a separate booklet containing requirements for the quotation of securities on the Unlisted Securities Market. The requirements here are not so widespread, with a consequent saving in cost to the companies seeking a USM quotation. Companies on the USM do not have to comply with the Continuing Obligations in the Yellow Book but they have to sign a general undertaking on broadly similar terms.

The Third Market

Although there will be dealings on the Third Market during 1990 for

Stock Exchange Company News Service   285

those companies who are at the end of 1989 already quoted on that market, such dealings will cease at the end of 1990 when the companies will either have to move up to a full listing on The Stock Exchange or a quotation on the USM, failing which the securities of the companies concerned will be dealt with under Stock Exchange Rule No. 532.2.

Stock Exchange Company News Service

Companies listed on The Stock Exchange or traded on The Stock Exchange Unlisted Securities Market are required to submit information to The Stock Exchange from time to time under the Continuing Obligations for Companies as set out in Section 5, Chapter 2 of the Yellow Book, or to comply with the undertaking given by companies on entry to the USM. The information covers such things as dividend announcements, the release of preliminary figures and interim statements, changes in company directorate and notifiable changes in company shareholdings.

Such information is needed to ensure a fair and well-informed market in the securities of the companies concerned. The information is sent by companies to The Stock Exchange Company Announcements Office.

In order to ensure the dissemination of the content of company announcements in a rapid but controlled manner, The Stock Exchange has developed a Company News Service (CNS). The objects of CNS are as follows:

1. To receive company announcements from the issuer.
2. To prepare and release documents electronically.
3. To disseminate the announcements.

CNS operates from 8.30 a.m. to 6.00 p.m. every day The Stock Exchange is open and company information is issued throughout this period. Companies may send announcements to The Stock Exchange by hand or by post in hard copy paper form but, under CNS, they are able to issue announcements to The Stock Exchange by electronic means, e.g. telex, Telecom Gold, teletext or by direct computer links. The electronic communication facilities are available 24 hours a day. Companies which use the services of public relations firms or other agencies to make announcements are also accommodated under CNS subject to precisely laid down procedures being adopted and adhered to, both by the company and the appointed firm or agency. On receipt of the news it is disseminated on the Exchange's TOPIC computer service, although there is talk that the Exchange may share its company news service with other news agencies.

Although The Stock Exchange prefers companies to use an electronic method of communicating announcements, the facility of sending information in paper form continues for those companies wishing to adhere to the traditional method or where it may not be feasible for them to adopt an electronic means.

At the time of preparation of this handbook The Stock Exchange is developing a replacement for CNS which will probably be called a Regulatory News Service under which companies will be encouraged to announce important results and other price sensitive information as early as possible following the opening of the TOPIC service.

The Financial Services Act

Considerable changes have been made within the securities industry following the enactment of the Financial Services Act 1986 (FSA) which repealed the Prevention of Fraud (Investments) Act 1958, the provisions of which afforded what were regarded as inadequate protection for investors. In the description which follows references to chapters, schedules and section numbers refer to those of the FSA.

The FSA continues the existing system of self-regulation by City organisations and markets rather than statutory controls on the lines of the Securities and Exchange Commission in New York. Under the Act, the Secretary of State for Trade and Industry may authorise and regulate investment business, but he has exercised his powers under Section 114 and made an order delegating his functions to a designated agency known as the Securities and Investments Board Limited (SIB). The SIB supervises a number of self-regulating organisations (SROs) each controlling specific classes of investment business. There can also be recognised investment exchanges (RIEs), the most important example of which is The International Stock Exchange formed by the merger of The Stock Exchange and the International Securities Regulatory Association, recognised professional bodies (RPBs) like the Institute of Chartered Accountants and recognised clearing houses (RCHs), i.e. firms which provide clearing services for the transaction of investment business.

The Act continues the existing system of self-regulation by City organisations and markets rather than statutory controls on the lines of the Securities and Exchange Commission in New York. CA 1989 ss.192–206 amends the FSA to provide for the Secretary of State to issue statements of principle regarding the conduct and financial standing of persons authorised to carry on investment business, basic rules of SIB applicable to all SROs and codes of practice about the statements of principle and basic rules. Apart from the basic rules SRO rules do not have to be equivalent to the SIB's rules provided that they afford an adequate level of investor protection. SROs' rules also have to take into account the cost of compliance which has been criticised in the past. These changes provide a more flexible framework for the control of investment business. Disciplinary action can be taken against failure to comply with a statement of principle.

It is a criminal offence, punishable by fines or imprisonment, to carry on investment business unless exempted or authorised under the provisions of the FSA. In order to carry on investment business in the United Kingdom a person must be an authorised person under Chapter III or be an exempted person under Chapter IV. Investments are defined in s.1(1) and Part I of Schedule 1 and include the following:

1. Shares and stock in the capital of a company.
2. Debentures, which include debenture stock, loan stock, bonds and certificates of deposit.
3. Government securities and securities issued by a local or public authority.
4. Warrants and other instruments enabling the holder to subscribe for shares, debentures or Government and public securities.
5. Certificates which confer rights in respect of investments included in (1), (2), (3) and (4) above.
6. Units in a collective investment scheme such as a unit trust.
7. Options relating to any investment mentioned in Schedule 1.
8. Future contracts.
9. Contracts for differences.
10. Long-term insurance contracts.
11. Rights and interests in anything which is an investment mentioned in Schedule 1, Part I.

Investment business is defined in s.1(2) and Schedule 1, Part II, and includes the following:

1. Dealing in investments, i.e. buying, selling, subscribing for or underwriting investments whether as principal or agent.
2. Arranging deals in investments, i.e. making, offering or agreeing to make arrangements for another person to buy, sell or subscribe for a particular investment.
3. Managing investments.
4. The giving of investment advice.
5. Establishing collective investment schemes, including acting as a trustee of an authorised unit trust.

However, Schedule 1, Part III excludes the following transactions from the definition of investment business:

1. Dealing in investments as a principal by a person who does not hold

himself out as willing to deal for members of the public on a regular basis at prices determined generally, i.e. not acting as a trader.

2. Transactions between companies of the same group.
3. Transactions by companies or trustees in connection with an employees' share scheme.
4. Transactions by trustees and personal representatives unless they hold themselves out as offering services for remuneration as dealers in investments, investment managers or providing investment advice.
5. Investment advice given in a newspaper, magazine or other periodical publication.

Self-regulating organisations

The SIB supervises a number of self-regulating organisations (SROs), as follows:

1. The Securities Association (TSA) controlling dealers in securities.
2. The Financial Intermediaries, Managers and Brokers Regulatory Association (FIMBRA), controlling independent financial advisers.
3. The Association of Futures Brokers and Dealers (AFBD) controlling commodity dealers.
4. The Investment Management Regulatory Organisation (IMRO) controlling investment managers.
5. The Life Assurance and Unit Trust Regulatory Organisation (LAUTRO), controlling life assurance and unit trust salesmen.

The provisions governing application for, and withdrawal of, recognition as a SRO are contained in ss 7–21, s.13 being as amended by CA 1989 Schedule 24. A SRO is a body which regulates the carrying on of investment business by enforcing rules which are binding on its members. Although these sections refer to the Secretary of State in dealing with these matters, as noted above, his functions in this respect are exercised by the agency designated by the Secretary of State, i.e. the SIB. Each SRO is required to have rules for the conduct of investment business which meet the requirements laid down in the Act, including powers to admit, expel and discipline its members. The SIB has powers to direct a change in the rules of an SRO after consultation with the SRO in question – which may become necessary if something goes wrong. The requirements for recognition as a SRO are contained in Schedule 2, the principal ones being as follows:

1. Its members must be 'fit and proper persons'.
2. Its rules and practices relating to the admission and expulsion of

members and the exercise of its disciplinary control over members must be fair and reasonable.

3. Its rules must afford protection to investors which fulfil the requirements for the conduct of investment business contained in Chapter V.
4. There must be adequate arrangements and resources for the effective monitoring and enforcement of its rules.
5. Membership of its governing body must be such as to secure a proper balance between the interests of its members and those of the public.
6. It must have effective arrangements for the investigation of complaints against the organisation or any of its members.
7. It must provide high standards of integrity and fair dealing in the conduct of investment business.

Recognised professional bodies

The members of a recognised professional body are authorised persons under the FSA for the conduct of investment business. The body must have statutory status, i.e. it must regulate the practice of a profession in the exercise of statutory powers or be recognised for a statutory purpose by the government or be a specified body under certain enactments. It has to meet certain conditions as to the certification of persons entitled to carry on investment business but otherwise the requirements for recognition as an RPB, which are laid down in Schedule 3, are on broadly similar lines to those for recognition as a RIE (see below).

Recognised investment exchanges

Provisions governing recognised investment exchanges (RIEs) are contained in ss.36–41 of Chapter IV which deals with exempted persons. Apart from the RIEs the principal other categories of exempted persons are the Bank of England and members of Lloyds. A RIE is an exempted person as respects anything it does which constitutes investment business. The status of RIE is granted by SIB under power delegated by the Secretary of State to any body corporate or unincorporated association which meets the requirements for recognition set out in Schedule 4. The principal requirements are that a RIE must have the following:

1. Adequate financial resources for the proper performance of its functions.
2. Rules and practices which provide that its business is conducted in a manner affording proper protection for investors, such as:
   (a) limiting dealings to investments which have a proper market;

(b) requiring issuers of investments to afford investors proper information concerning their current value;

(c) having either its own arrangements for ensuring the proper performance of transactions effected on the RIE or ensuring that their performance will be provided by the services of a recognised clearing house;

(d) having arrangements for the recording of transactions effected on the RIE.

3. Adequate arrangements for monitoring and enforcing compliance with its rules and any clearing arrangements it makes.

4. Arrangements for the investigation of complaints.

5. The ability to promote and maintain high standards of integrity and fair dealing in carrying out investment business and willingness to cooperate by sharing information with the Secretary of State or any authority having responsibility for the supervision of investment business.

Clearing houses

A recognised clearing house (RCH) is an exempted person as respects anything done by it in its capacity as a person providing clearing services for the transaction of investment business. Its function is to provide clearing services for the transaction of investment business. A RIE may make arrangements with a RCH for clearing services in respect of business effected on the RIE. The status of RCH is granted by SIB under power delegated by the Secretary of State to any body corporate or unincorporated association meeting the requirements for recognition specified in ss.38–9. Its rules and guidance notes must be approved and, in particular, as provided by ss.(4) of s.39, a RCH must have the following:

1. Financial resources sufficient for the proper performance of its functions.

2. Adequate arrangements and resources for the effective monitoring and enforcement of compliance with its rules or for the monitoring to be carried out by any other body or person able and willing to perform it.

3. The ability to provide clearing services enabling a RIE to make arrangements with it to satisfy the requirements of Schedule 4.

4. The ability to comply with the duties corresponding to those imposed in the case of a RIE by Schedule 4, para. 5 in promoting and maintaining high standards of integrity and fair dealing.

The Financial Services Tribunal

The provisions regarding the constitution and functions of the Financial Services Tribunal (FST) are in ss.96–101 and Schedule 6.

The FST consists of a panel of not fewer than 10 persons nominated by the Secretary of State with legal qualifications or with experience to deal with matters arising under the FSA. When a case is referred to the FST the Secretary of State nominates three persons from the panel to deal with it, the person nominated as chairman being a member of the panel with legal qualifications and the other two being persons with recent experience relevant to the case under consideration.

The functions of the FST is to determine disputes which may arise between the Secretary of State, or the Securities and Investments Board in the case of powers delegated to the Board by the Secretary of State, regarding any adverse decisions which have been made affecting a body or person, e.g. recognition as a SRO or any of its members. Under s.97 the aggrieved body or person may appeal to the FST within 28 days of the service of the following:

1. A notice of refusal, termination or suspension of recognition as an authorised person.
2. A direction that an individual is not a fit and proper person to be employed in connection with investment business.
3. The publication of a statement concerning a person's misconduct.
4. An intervention by the Secretary of State in relation to any authorised person.

CHAPTER 14

Mergers and acquisitions

The object of a take-over transaction is the acquisition by a company of the whole or a majority of the share capital of another company. The consideration for the acquisition may be the issue of shares or other securities in the acquiring company, the payment of cash, or some combination of these two. The following are the main types of take-over transaction:

1. A formal agreement may be made with the shareholders in the company being acquired but obviously this method is practicable only where there are a small number of shareholders involved.
2. Arrangements may be made to purchase, either by private agreement or on The Stock Exchange, blocks of shares in a company in order to build up a sizable holding which could form the basis on which to launch a bid for the remainder of the share capital. It is necessary, however, to have regard to the provisions of *The City Code on Take-overs and Mergers* and *The Rules Governing Substantial Acquisitions of Shares*, compliance with both of which is supervised by The Panel on Take-overs and Mergers.
3. The acquiring company may make a public offer to the shareholders of the company to be acquired by sending documents to its shareholders making an offer to acquire their shares on stated terms.
4. A take-over may be effected under a scheme of arrangement made under the provisions of ss.425–7, although this does involve more complicated procedures.

Companies claiming that they are interested in launching an offer for a company but which do not do so within a reasonable time may face restrictions.

Right from the preliminaries of a take-over, however, it is necessary to ensure compliance with the rules contained in *The City Code on Take-overs and Mergers*, which apply to both listed and unlisted companies and to certain classes of private companies, e.g. private companies whose equity shares have been listed on The Stock Exchange during the 10 years prior to the announcement of an offer or whose equity share dealings have been regularly advertised in a newspaper for at least 6 months in the 10 years prior to the offer, although there is a degree of flexibility in this matter.

The Code is issued by The Panel on Take-overs and Mergers; the latest version was published in January 1988 and has been amended by Releases Numbers 1, 2, 3 and 4 dated 27 October 1988, 27 April 1989, 30 August 1989 and 17 January 1990, respectively. Copies of the Code may be obtained from the Secretary of the Panel, which is responsible for the administration of the Code. Companies are encouraged to consult the Panel on a confidential basis in the event of any difficulty in interpreting the rules.

The company should take professional advice at the earliest possible moment if it is informed that it is to be the subject of a take-over bid. The principal requirements of the Code are as follows:

1. The offer should first be put to the board of the company to be acquired or to its advisers, disclosing the identity of the company making the offer. The company making the offer is referred to as the 'offeror' company and the company which is to be acquired is known as the 'offeree' company.

2. Independent advice on the offer must be obtained by the offeree company, the substance of which should be made known to its shareholders.

3. On receipt of the offer, the offeree company's board should publish a press notice or circular giving details of the offer, a copy of which should be sent to its shareholders. A circular or press notice should also be published if the offeree company should be informed that the offeror company is merely considering the making of an offer. In these circumstances in some cases it may be advisable to request The Stock Exchange to suspend dealings in the shares of the proposed offeree company.

4. Obviously, it is necessary that absolute secrecy should be kept in the period before the announcement of an offer.

5. The offeror company may request particulars of the shareholders of the offeree company and these should be provided promptly.

6. In order that shareholders are in possession of all the facts so as to make an informed judgement on the merits of an offer, any documents addressed to them must be prepared with the same standards required for a prospectus under the Act.

7. Directors, in advising their shareholders, must have regard to the interests of shareholders taken as a whole, together with those of employees and creditors.

8. The Code lays down detailed provisions regarding the content of announcements regarding take-over offers; the offer documents and copies of announcements and documents must be sent to the Panel simultaneously with their dispatch to shareholders and, in the case of listed companies, to The Stock Exchange.
9. It is desirable that the offeree company or its registrars ensure the prompt registration of transfers so that new shareholders may have the opportunity of considering and acting on the offer if they wish.
10. When the offer has been announced the offeror company should take special care with regard to any further acquisitions of shares in the offeree company since, if any such acquisitions take place at a price higher that the offer price, this could result in an obligation for it to make a corresponding increase in the offer price to be made available to all shareholders.

The rules of the *City Code* do not have the force of law but non-compliance with them would adversely affect the position of, and the facilities available to, companies and their advisers concerned with the offer.

Regard should be paid to the provisions of the ss.55–77 of the Fair Trading Act 1973 affecting take-overs and mergers referred to the Monopolies and Mergers Commission. The Companies Act 1989 introduced some new provisions into the FSA relating to take-overs and mergers making possible a less expensive and more rapid clearance of proposed mergers whilst retaining existing safeguards and in some cases improving them. The new FTA provisions are as follows:

1. A company may give voluntary pre-notification of an intended merger in which case if the merger is not referred to the Monopolies and Mergers Commission within the period allowed for consideration following the pre-notification, it cannot be referred if effected within the following 6 months. The existence of the proposal must be made public. The Secretary of State may make regulations as to the manner in which the pre-notification advice is to be given and the information to be provided (FTA ss.75A–F inserted by CA 1989 s.146).
2. Instead of making a merger reference to the Commission the Secretary of State may accept from the parties concerned legally binding undertakings for the disposal of any part of a merged business or other specified action which he considers appropriate to remedy or prevent effects of the proposed merger adverse to the public interest. Any such undertakings accepted for this purpose and advice given by the Director General of Fair Trading (DGFT) must be published unless the Secretary of State is satisfied that publication

would not be in the public interest or could seriously affect the private affairs of an individual or interests of a body corporate in which case he can exclude from publication such information as may be necessary to prevent this. The DGFT is responsible for reviewing the carrying out of undertakings and the Secretary of State may take action if an undertaking is not fulfilled (FTA ss.75G–K inserted by CA 1989 s.147). Any person may also bring civil proceedings in respect of the failure or likely failure to carry out an undertaking (FTA s.93A inserted by CA 1989 s.148).

3. When a merger has been referred to the Commission the parties are prohibited, for the duration of the enquiry, from acquiring shares in any of the other parties without the consent of the Secretary of State until either the reference is withdrawn or the Commission has made its report (FTA s.75(4A–M) inserted by CA 1989 s.149).

4. In order to prevent control of a company passing to another company in the course of two or more transactions within a two-year period, the Secretary of State or the Commission may for the purpose of a merger reference treat the transactions as having occurred simultaneously on the date that the last transaction occurred (FTA s.66A) inserted by CA 1989 s.150).

5. The Secretary of State may by regulations prescribe fees to be paid where there is to be an investigation by the Commission (CA 1989 s.152).

6. Any person who furnishes to the Secretary of State, the Commission or the DGFT any information which he knows to be false or misleading in connection with a merger is guilty of an offence (FTA s.93B inserted by CA 1989 s.151).

Substantial acquisitions

A company contemplating the take-over of another company may launch a 'dawn raid' on its target company's shares where a substantial shareholding may be acquired in listed companies at prices not previously publicised. There is a code to be followed by a company intending to launch a 'dawn raid' entitled *The Rules Governing Substantial Acquisitions of Shares* (SARs), the latest edition of which was also published in January 1988 and amended by Releases Numbers 1, 2, 3 and 4 dated 27 October 1988, 27 April 1989, 30 August 1989 and 17 January 1990 respectively. These rules regulate acquisitions which would result in holdings or rights over shares amounting to between 15 per cent and 30 per cent of the company's voting rights. The *City Code* takes care of acquisitions amounting to 30 per cent or more of the voting rights. The SARs are administered by the executive of The Panel on Take-overs and

Mergers. Their object is to restrict the speed by which a person (which would include persons acting together) will increase their holdings or rights in shares amounting to an aggregate between 15 per cent and 30 per cent of the company's voting rights. They do not apply, however, in the case where a company has announced a firm intention to make an offer for the shares of another company, in which case the rules of *The City Code on Take-overs and Mergers* apply.

The Company Announcements Office of the Quotations Department of The Stock Exchange must be informed by 12 noon on the dealing day following the acquisition of shares or rights over shares if, as a result of the acquisition, a person (including persons acting by agreement or understanding with him) comes to hold shares representing 15 per cent or more of the voting rights of a company or, if the holding already represents 15 per cent or more, the acquisition has increased it to beyond that figure.

The SARs provide that acquisitions of voting shares in companies resident in the United Kingdom or rights over such shares made through The Stock Exchange within any period of 7 calendar days which: (a) amount to 10 per cent or more of the company's voting rights; (b) would take the prospective purchaser's holding (including his existing holding) to 15 per cent or more but less than 30 per cent of the voting rights; or (c) involve shares from more than a single shareholder, may, unless previously announced, be made only by a tender offer published by a paid advertisement in two national newspapers under which all shareholders would be treated on equal terms. The tender may be at a fixed price or at a maximum price. The advertisement should be cleared with the Quotations Department of The Stock Exchange if the tender offer is made through The Stock Exchange, and otherwise with the Panel. The advertisement must include the information set out in Rule 4.2 of the SARs including the name of the buyer and the date and time of closing of the tender offer. The result of the tender offer must be announced by 9.30 a.m. on the business day following the close of the tender.

It should be noted, however, that the SARs are very complex and if it is thought that acquisitions by a company are likely to bring it within the scope of the SARs, then it is important that professional advice should be taken at an early stage.

Agreements with individual members

This is a simple way of effecting a transfer of ownership of a company. It can be effected merely by the exchange of the consideration for duly executed transfers with the share certificates. Usually, however, a formal agreement is entered into between the parties, which should be drawn up with legal advice. The agreement would need to cover such matters as full details of the shares to be acquired and the consideration to be paid for them with a time for completion, and setting out who will be responsible for paying legal costs duty and any other related expenses. Usually warranties are also required to be given by the directors of the offeree company containing financial information about the offeree company, the title to its property, pending litigation, etc., including any changes affecting the company which may have occurred since the date of the last balance sheet.

The following procedural points arise in connection with the take-over of a company by agreement with individual members:

1. The purchase and sale agreement must be carefully drawn up with legal advice to ensure that the interests of both parties to the agreement are adequately protected.
2. The final agreement will then be executed and formally exchanged between the parties and a date set for completion of the exchange of shares for the agreed consideration.
3. At the time of completion the executed transfers, accompanied by the share certificates, are exchanged for the consideration. If any new shares have been issued as part of the consideration, the renounceable certificates for the new shares should be handed over with the forms of renunciation on the renounceable certificates duly signed.
4. The Registrar of Companies should be informed of any changes in director or secretary on Companies Form No. G288 'Notice of change of directors or secretaries or in their particulars' and of any change in the registered office address, to be notified on Companies Form No. G287 'Notice of change in situation of registered office'. A return of allotments should also be submitted to the Registrar of Companies covering the allotments of shares which have been made on Companies Form No. G88(2) (Revised 1988) 'Return of allotments of shares'. If there has been a capitalisation issue, particulars of the contract on Companies Form No. G88(3) 'Particulars of a contract relating to shares allotted as fully or partly paid up otherwise than in cash' should also be sent to the Registrar of Companies.
5. Entries should then be made in the various statutory registers, e.g. the Register of Members, reflecting the registration of any share transfers, and in the Register of Directors and Secretaries. The share transfers should, of course, be properly stamped or be duly certified as being exempt from stamp duty. However, this will not be necessary when, under the 1990 Budget proposals, transfer stamp duty is abolished on the implementation of TAURUS, probably towards the end of 1991.

6. Announcements should be made to The Stock Exchange, the press, the company's customers and its employees. If the offeree company is to become a wholly owned subsidiary of the offeror company, it is necessary to ensure that at least one share in the offeree company is transferred to a nominee of the offeror company in order that the offeree company may have at least two members to ensure compliance with s.24.

Purchases in the market

Arrangements may be made whereby a company obtains a significant proportion of the shares in another company by purchases of the company's shares on The Stock Exchange. Fewer formalities are involved with this type of transaction, but care should be taken to ensure compliance with the rules of *The City Code on Take-overs and Mergers* and *The Rules Governing Substantial Acquisition of Shares*. It is also important to remember that when the holding reaches 3 per cent or more of nominal value of the company's capital, notice must be given to the company within two days as required by ss.199–210 as amended by CA 1989 s.134, and the company receiving the notification is required to inform The Stock Exchange.

In the initial stages, in order to preserve confidentiality, the acquisitions may be made through a nominee or nominees, but when calculating the level of holding giving rise to an obligation to notify the company, i.e. 3 per cent, it should be remembered that purchases by persons acting in concert with the acquiring company must be included in the total and there is an obligation for such persons to keep each other informed to ensure compliance with the notification requirements. It should also be remembered that the acquisition of certain levels of shareholdings may give rise to an obligation to make a general offer for all the shares of the company which could also affect the price of the shares. At the time of writing this handbook, the position is that under Rule 11 of the *City Code* a bidder who had bought just 10 per cent of its victim, either during the bid or in the previous year, would have to offer cash terms matching the best price paid.

Public offers

This is the usual form of take-over, which receives wide publicity in the press, often accompanied by acrimonious advertisements by the offeror and offeree companies.

A public offer is where a take-over offer is made to all the shareholders of a company to acquire all or a proportion of their holdings in the offeree company, either for cash or for shares and/or other securities in the offeror company. Public offers involve many more procedural steps than do take-overs by agreement with individual members or by purchases on The Stock Exchange. It will be necessary to ensure strict compliance with the *City Code*, the FSA and, in the case of a listed company, with the requirements of The Stock Exchange as set out in the Yellow Book, Section 6, Chapter 2. In order to ensure compliance with the requirements of the FSA, the offer documents will usually be sent direct to the shareholders of the offeree company by the merchant bank authorised under that Act.

The secretaries and directors of both the offeror and offeree companies, however, will be closely involved in the preparation of the draft documentation, which will require approval by the respective companies' boards.

Offer documentation for a public offer

Although the issuing house and the companies' solicitors will undertake most of the work in preparing the offer documents, the directors of the two companies concerned take legal responsibility for the accuracy of the documents. The secretary of the offeror company will be particularly concerned with the following matters:

1. It is likely that either the offeror or offeree company, and usually both companies, will be listed companies on The Stock Exchange; consequently, the documentation must comply with the Yellow Book, Section 6, Chapter 2, and be submitted to the Quotations Department for approval.
2. If it is considered that there is a possibility of the offer being referred to the Monopolies and Mergers Commission, the document should state that the offer will lapse if there is such a reference.
3. It often happens that an increase in the share capital of the offeror company is required so that the company has sufficient capital for the issue of shares in connection with the offer. Consequently, it may be necessary to call an Extraordinary General Meeting of the company to approve the increase in capital, the appropriate documents being submitted to The Stock Exchange for approval if the company is a listed company. If the shares to be issued in connection with the offer are to be listed on The Stock Exchange, the offer documentation should also include the listing particulars contained in the Yellow Book, Section 3.

The following practical matters arise in connection with a take-over by a public offer:

1. The document which the shareholder must sign must constitute a transfer of the securities being acquired to the offeror company.
2. Unless contrary instructions are given, any existing dividend mandates applicable to the shares in the offeree company will be applied to the shares in the offeror company being issued in exchange.
3. The form of acceptance and transfer would be designed so that it can be used as a working form, with relevant boxes for various steps in the processing to be filled in as they are completed.
4. Acceptances will need to be made in respect of holdings registered in the name of SEPON Limited since the securities of all listed companies are now dealt with under the TALISMAN settlement system. Consequently, it will be necessary to state in the offer documents that a transfer executed by SEPON Limited or by any other person, endorsed by The Stock Exchange, to the effect that TALISMAN transfers are in course of registration to that person, may be considered by the offeror company or its receiving bank as a valid acceptance of the offer.
5. Envelopes for the offer documents, with reply paid envelopes for the return of forms of acceptance and transfer with the share certificates, should be prepared to be sent to the shareholders in the offeree company.
6. Envelopes should also be prepared for any circular letter to be sent to the offeror company's own shareholders, either to explain the reasons for the offer or in connection with the convening of an Extraordinary General Meeting to approve any necessary increase in capital.
7. Since events in take-over battles sometimes move fairly swiftly, it will be prudent to have further sets of envelope labels, both to the offeror company's shareholders and to the offeree company's shareholders, in case further circulars are to be issued, e.g. perhaps following an improvement in the terms of the offer.

Acceptances of a public offer

Many shareholders, including most institutional shareholders, will not accept the offer until the final few days before the closing date. The office of the offeror company, or its registrar's office or the receiving banker's office, should be organised so that it can deal effectively with the last rush of acceptances. The Panel on Take-overs and Mergers requires stringent procedures to be followed to avoid possible double counting of acceptances and purchases of the same shareholding. The following action should be taken on receipt of the acceptances:

1. Check that the form of acceptance and transfer has been properly completed, with relevant share certificate(s), against the copy of the Register of Members of the offeree company.
2. Usually acceptance forms may be accepted even though not accompanied by the relevant share certificate(s) but such acceptances, although they may be treated as valid, should be set to one side so that they may be completed when the accompanying share certificate(s) is/are sent in.
3. Acceptances may also be certificated in the case of recent purchases and share certificates have not yet been prepared.

If a shareholder has lost his certificate(s), it will be necessary to issue an indemnity in order that a duplicate certificate may be prepared to support the acceptance. Also, if forms of acceptance have been signed by a personal representative or a power of attorney, it will be necessary to ensure that the appropriate documents have been duly registered and, if not, to request their submission.

During the period of the offer the offeree company should notify the offeror company of transfers received for registration in order that the offer documents may be sent out to these new shareholders and the copy of the Register of Members of the offeree company updated. A reminder may be published in the press just before the final date for the acceptance of the offer, sometimes accompanied by a warning that if there is a cash alternative to the offer in shares, the period for which it remains available for acceptance is subject to the underwriting arrangements. If no underwriting is involved, however, it may be extended indefinitely subject to the offer being declared unconditional by the sixtieth day after the posting of the offer.

Action following the first closing date of a public offer

Totals of the complete and incomplete acceptances will be calculated and the board of the offeror company will then consider whether the level of acceptances is such that it may declare the bid to be unconditional or whether it will extend it for a further period. If the level of acceptances is small, the offeror company may decide to extend the period for acceptances and, perhaps, improve the terms of the offer.

The *Receiving Agents' Code of Practice* issued by The Panel on Take-overs and Mergers sets out the procedure which must be closely followed to avoid double counting of acceptances and purchases of the same shareholding. There is thus a need for close cooperation between the receiving agents and the company's registrars.

Once the offer has been declared unconditional, however, it is necessary to prepare the consideration documents, i.e. the definitive certificates for shares and/or other securities in the offeror company to be issued in exchange for shares in the offeree company, and to draw cheques for those who have accepted a cash alternative. A committee of the board of the offeror company should be established in order to make the allotments of the consideration securities. It would be usual for the consideration to be sent out 21 days after the closing date or 21 days after the date on which valid acceptances are received by the offeror company or its agents. Also, upon an offer becoming unconditional options under SAYE and other employee share schemes may become excercisable.

Arrangements should be made to obtain a listing of the securities issued if the company has increased its capital in order to implement the offer.

Transfers to offeror company

The transfer which is executed by or on behalf of the offeror company (i.e. the company making the take-over offer) covering the shares in respect of which duly executed forms of acceptance and transfer have been received in order to put these shares into the name of the offeror company is known as an 'omnibus transfer'. It is used in conjunction with the individual forms of acceptance and transfer for each separate accepting shareholder. The use of the omnibus transfer is obviously more convenient than dealing separately with the many individual forms of acceptance and transfer each of which has been signed by each accepting shareholder and each of which would have to be duly stamped by the Inland Revenue before registration. The omnibus transfer itself has, of course, to be duly stamped by the Inland Revenue in the usual way and, in order that this may be assessed, there is attached to the omnibus transfer a schedule giving details of the forms of acceptance in respect of which the offer has been accepted. This is necessary because the Inland Revenue calculates separately the amount of stamp duly applicable in respect of each holding transferred and these amounts are then aggregated to ascertain the amount of stamp duty payable on the omnibus transfer. However, this will not be necessary when, under the 1990 Budget proposals, transfer stamp duty is abolished on the implementation of TAURUS, probably towards the end of 1991. The completed forms of acceptance and transfer, together with the covering share certificates, and the duly stamped omnibus transfer, are lodged with the offeree company.

Compulsory acquisition

Compulsory acquisition is dealt with in sections 428–430A–F of the Act as inserted by the FSA Schedule 12. These new sections, replacing the old sections 428–430 of the Act, are designed to protect the rights of the minority to resist compulsory acquisition if they have reasonable grounds to do so and to ensure that they are treated no less fairly than shareholders who have accepted the offer. In the description of compulsory acquisition which follows the section numbers refer to those contained in FSA Schedule 12.

Section 429 provides a procedure for the offeror company to acquire compulsorily certain non-assented minority shareholdings. If the offeror company has by virtue of acceptances to the offer acquired or contracted to acquire not less than nine-tenths in value of the shares to which the offer relates it may give notice to the holder of any shares that it has not so acquired, or contracted to acquire, that it desires to acquire his shares. Shares already held by the offeror company, i.e. registered in its name at the date the offer was made, including any shares contracted to be acquired but not registered in the offeror company's name at that date, are excluded from calculating the nine-tenths minimum. However, shares the holders of which are subject to a contract for no consideration to accept the offer after it is made are not excluded (s.428). Shares acquired by the offeror company by market purchases or private agreement subsequent to the date of making the offer, may also count towards the nine-tenths minimum subject to the price paid for the shares not exceeding the value of the offer or revised offer.

The nine-tenths minimum as above must be satisfied within four months from the date of making the offer but the offeror company must give notice of compulsory acquisition to shareholders who have not accepted the offer within two months after it has acquired the nine-tenths minimum (s.429(3)). The latter requirement speeds up the process of giving notice of compulsory acquisition to the non-assenting shareholders. The notice to a non-assenting shareholder must be given on Companies Form No. 429(4) 'Notice to non-assenting shareholders' that it desires to acquire his shares. A copy of the notice with a statutory declaration on Companies Form No. 429dec 'Statutory declaration relating to a notice to non-assenting shareholders' confirming that the conditions for giving the notice are satisfied must be sent to the offeree company.

Section 430 deals with the effects of giving a notice under s.429, the principal ones being as follows:

1. Where the offeror company has given a choice of consideration which may be taken by the offeree company's shareholders for their shares a non-assenting shareholder must be given the same alternatives as shareholders who have accepted the offer even if some of these may have lapsed but the offeror may stipulate in the s.429

notice the terms which will apply in the event that the non-assenting shareholder does not respond to the notice within the 6 weeks allowed to him from the date of the notice in which to give the offeror company notice of his choice of consideration. This provision prevents dissentients from blocking the compulsory acquisition.

2. At the end of 6 weeks from the date of the compulsory acquisition notice, the compulsory acquisition is effected by the offeror company sending to the offeree company a copy of the notice together with a form of transfer for each dissentient shareholder covering his shares in the offeree company which have not been assented to the offer, accompanied by a share certificate for the total number of consideration shares in the offeror company for the non-assenting shareholders if the consideration is shares in the offeror company, or a cheque for the total cash for the non-assenting shareholders if the consideration is in cash, each such transfer being executed by a person appointed by the offeror company on behalf of the shareholders concerned (s.430). These transfers will then be registered by the offeree company thereby putting the dissentients' shares in the offeree company into the name of the offeror company. The shares in the offeror company received as consideration will be held by the offeree company on trust for the former shareholders. Any cash consideration should be held in a separate interest-bearing bank account.

3. The offeree company is required to hold the consideration for the non-assenting shareholders for a period of 12 years at the end of which, providing that it has at intervals during that period made reasonable enquiries to trace the non-assenting shareholders, shares in the offeror company received as consideration may be sold and the proceeds, together with any consideration received in cash being held in the bank account, shall be paid into Court. Similar action would be taken on the winding-up of the offeree company. The company's costs in making the enquiries may be recovered from such proceeds or money held in the separate bank account.

The right of a minority (i.e. non-assenting) shareholder to be bought out by the offeror company is provided by section 430A. When the offeror company has in pursuance of a take-over offer acquired by acceptances not less than nine-tenths in value of all the shares in issue of the offeree company (including any shares which it has otherwise acquired or contracted to acquire since the date of the offer), the holder of any shares who has not accepted the offer may send a written communication to the offeror company requiring it to acquire his shares. The offeror company must within one month of have acquired nine-tenths of all the shares send a notice to any shareholders who have not assented to the offer informing them of their right to be bought out and they they may within three months of the notice require the offeror company to acquire their shares. The notice is sent on Companies Form No. 430A 'Notice to non-assenting shareholders'. Section 430B provides that where the terms of the offer give a choice of consideration which may be taken by the offeree company's shareholders for their shares the notice under s.430A to the non-assenting shareholder must give particulars of the choices available and which choice of consideration is to apply if the shareholder does not indicate a choice when requiring the offeror company to acquire his shares.

It should be noted that terms of take-over offers often provide that where there is a choice of consideration between shares in the offeror company or a sum in cash for each share in the offeree company, the underwriting arrangements stipulate that the cash offer is only open for a certain period at the end of which the consideration may be taken only in shares. However, in the case of compulsory acquisition under s.429 and whether or not any time limit was applicable to any of the terms of the offer, e.g. a cash offer, the offeror is bound to pay cash for the non-assenting shareholder's shares or if the choice chosen is shares and the offeror company is no longer able to provide these, the consideration paid to the non-assenting shareholder must consist of an amount of cash which at the date of the compulsory acquisition notice under s.429 is equivalent to the chosen consideration (s.430(4)). In the case of the exercise of shareholders' rights to be bought out under s.430A the same provisions regarding a cash offer apply, but where the offeror company is no longer able to provide the share alternative the amount of cash payable shall be equivalent to the chosen consideration as at the date that the non-assenting shareholder requires the offeror company to acquire his shares (s.430B(4)).

It will be seen, therefore, that the window for the cash offer is re-opened for the dissentient shareholders to take the cash offer should they so desire. Care must be taken to ensure that the notices are correctly sent, e.g. by recorded delivery if the shareholder's registered address is in the United Kingdom or by air mail if the shareholder's registered address is outside the United Kingdom.

Where the offeror company gives notice of compulsory acquisition under s.429, the Court may on the application of a non-assenting shareholder within 6 weeks of the date of the s.429 notice order that the offeror shall not be entitled to acquire his shares or that the shares shall be acquired on terms different from those of the offer (s.430C(1)). In the case of the exercise of the rights of a non-assenting shareholder under s.430A, on the application of either the shareholder or the offeror, the

Court may order such terms as it thinks fit on which the offeror is entitled and bound to acquire the shares.

Compulsory acquisition under s.429 may be impossible where a company has numerous untraceable shareholders. Under subsection (5) of s.430(C) where a take-over has not been accepted to the extent necessary to effect compulsory acquisition under s.429, the Court may, on the application of the offeror company, authorise the company to proceed to give s.429 compulsory acquisition notices to shareholders who have not accepted the offer if it is satisfied that the offeror company has taken all reasonable steps to trace the shareholders concerned and if the total of the shares assented to the offer added to the total of the shares held by the untraceable shareholders amounts to not less than the minimum required to implement the s.429 compulsory acquisition procedure.

The consideration held by the offeree company on trust for the dissenting shareholders may subsequently be claimed by them on surrender of the documents of title to shares in the offeree company or giving an indemnity if they can no longer be found. Quite often the claim will be made by the executors of a deceased non-assenting shareholder's estate who, in winding up the affairs, find that the deceased held shares in the offeree company and who because of age, inadvertence, or change of address, had not accepted the offer. When a claim is received, any cash will be paid out, or, if the consideration is in the form of shares in the offeror company, the offeree company will execute a transfer in the name of the entitled holder and send this to the offeror company, accompanied by the share certificate for shares in the offeror company being held by the offeree company, for registration. The offeror company will prepare a share certificate in the holder's name and send a balance certificate in the name of the offeree company for the shares in the offeror company still to be claimed. Although a subsidiary company may not hold shares in its holding company, this is excused in the special circumstances by the provisions of s.23. The remaining sections of Schedule 12, ss.430D, 430E and 430F deal respectively with joint offers, the position of associates and offers for convertible securities which are treated as though they were shares.

Stamp duty exemptions

Take-overs (and schemes of arrangements – see below) are sometimes arranged in such a way that there is exemption from stamp duty on the transfer of shares to the offeree company. The arrangements under which this may be effected are extremely complicated and the position was altered considerably by the provisions of the Finance Act 1986 in respect of instruments executed on and after 25 March 1986. More detail on these exemptions is given in the Institute's manual but it is important that professional advice should be obtained if the take-over offer is to be effected by a method which will mitigate liability to stamp duty. However, the need for such arrangements will cease to exist when transfer stamp duty is abolished under the 1990 Budget proposals on the implementation of TAURUS, probably towards the end of 1991.

Schemes of arrangement

A take-over of one company by another may be effected by a liquidation under the provisions of IA s.110 or a scheme of arrangement under the provisions of ss.425–7. These arrangements are, however, more complicated than the forms of take-over described above and involve the incorporation of a new holding company to take over both the offeree and the offeror companies in order to merge their operations. Alternatively, the offeror company may acquire the undertaking of the offeree company for cash. Schemes of arrangement may be useful where it is desired to acquire 100 per cent of the offeree company but, because of the nature of the business, it would not be possible to obtain the required 90 per cent level of acceptances which would enable the offeror company to effect compulsory acquisition under the procedures previously described. The approval of the Court is required and consequently the legal advisers of both companies will be involved in settling the necessary documentation. Also, certain schemes of arrangement have to meet the stringent requirements imposed by s.427A and Schedule 15A of the Act inserted by the Companies (Mergers and Divisions) Regulations 1987 SI 1987/ 1991 implementing the EC third company law directive.

Reconstruction by liquidation

A take-over by means of a reconstruction is effected by winding up the offeree company. This effects the sale of the company's assets to another company in exchange for shares in that company, which are then distributed to the shareholders of the offeree company in proportion to their holdings. Reconstruction by liquidation and sale of the offeree company's assets is appropriate only in cases where the continued existence of the offeree company is not desired. The liquidation is effected as a members' or creditors' voluntary winding-up and the detailed provisions governing procedure are laid down in IA s.110. In view of the many technical and fiscal complications which may arise it is advisable to involve the legal and taxation advisers of the companies concerned.

Reconstruction may be suitable where there is to be a reduction of capital combined with the provision of fresh capital for a new company by the members of the reconstructed company. For example, a company with an adverse balance on its profit and loss account but with good prospects could be wound up and its assets sold to a new company (after paying off creditors) in exchange for partly paid shares in the new company allotted to members of the old company in proportion to their existing holdings. The calling up of the unpaid liability on the new shares would provide working capital for the future operations of the business. In the case of a public company it would be usual for the provision of new capital to be underwritten in case there are dissentients to the scheme for reconstruction or other assenting shareholders failing to pay up the calls on the partly paid shares. However, the total holdings of the dissentients should not exceed an agreed percentage because under IA s.111(2) the underwriters would have to buy out the interests of the dissentients in order that the scheme could be implemented. A dissentient is a member of the transferor company who did not vote in favour of the Special Resolution to wind up the company who notifies the liquidator that he should either abstain from carrying the resolution into effect or to purchase his interest at an agreed price.

It is desirable that resolutions for approving a reconstruction under IA s.110 be submitted to two meetings, the first meeting to approve the reconstruction and the second meeting to put the company into liquidation. If both resolutions were passed at the same meeting, the company would still have to be wound up even if the level of dissentients made the implementation of the scheme of reconstruction impracticable.

The procedural steps for a reconstruction are as follows:

1. A board meeting of the company to be liquidated would be convened for the following purposes:
   (a) to make the necessary declaration of solvency;
   (b) to settle the draft agreement to be entered into by the liquidator for the sale of the company to the new company;
   (c) Memorandum and Articles of the new company to be approved;
   (d) to approve that the draft underwriting contract be executed by the liquidator or for the company to execute with adoption by the liquidator later;
   (e) to approve the circular letter to the shareholders informing them of the reasons for the proposed reconstruction and the terms;
   (f) to approve the notice of Extraordinary General Meeting and form of proxy which must be a two-way proxy in the case of listed companies.

(If the company to be liquidated is a listed company, the company's brokers should be consulted to ensure compliance with the requirements of The Stock Exchange.)

2. Special Resolutions for reconstruction and liquidation will be passed at the Extraordinary General Meeting.

3. The business of the offeree company (i.e. the old company) is continued by the liquidator from the date of the resolution to wind up to the date when the business is acquired by the new company.

4. When the sale agreement has been executed the liquidator transfers the assets to the new company, ensuring that he retains sufficient assets to pay off the creditors of the old company unless they have agreed that liability for these debts may be transferred to the new company by means of a novation agreement. He should also retain assets to purchase the interests of any dissenting shareholders, and to pay the expenses of the liquidation and his own remuneration.

5. A letter is sent to shareholders giving details of their rights to shares in the newly formed company, which will be issued in exchange for their shares in the old company on receipt of their share certificates. As noted above, the shares in the new company would be offered as partly-paid shares in proportion to shareholders' existing holdings in the old company; the additional capital would then be called up and thus provide working capital for the future operation of the business by the new company.

6. The liquidator would continue to complete the liquidation of the old company in accordance with the usual procedure as described in Chapter 16. On completion of the liquidation, it would be usual for the liquidator to execute a conveyance transferring all the residual property of the old company to the new company.

CHAPTER 15

Administrators, receiverships and voluntary arrangements

Administration orders

Administrators

The Insolvency Act 1986 provides a procedure under which a Court may make an administration order if a company is in financial difficulties. The management of the company is then placed in the hands of an administrator. However, before making the order, the Court must be satisfied that the company is unable, or likely to be unable, to pay its debts. There is a definition of inability to pay debts in IA s.123. The order would result in the following:

1. The company's survival as a going concern in whole or in part.
2. An approved composition in satisfaction of the company's debts or its affairs becoming subject to a scheme of arrangement.
3. A compromise arrangement being sanctioned under s.425.
4. The realisation of the company's assets in a more advantageous way than would be effected by a winding-up.

Qualification and remuneration of administrators

Administrators must be licensed insolvency practitioners (IA s.388(1)(a)). Any person acting as an administrator who is not so qualified is liable to imprisonment or to a fine, or both (IA s.389). His remuneration may be determined by the creditors' committee (IR Rule 2.47(3)) but where there is no committee or it does not determine the remuneration, it may be determined by a Resolution of a meeting of creditors or, if still not determined, the administrator may apply to the Court.

Inability to pay debts

The IA s.123 provides that a company is deemed to be unable to pay its debts in the following circumstances:

1. Failure to pay a debt exceeding £750 for three months after a request for payment is made in the prescribed form.
2. Execution issued on a judgement in England and Wales which has not been satisfied in whole or in part.
3. The Court being satisfied that the company is unable to pay its debts as they fall due.
4. The Court being satisfied that the value of the company's assets is less than the amount of its liabilities.
5. In Scotland, a charge for payment on an extract decree, or an extract registered bond, or an extract registered process, has expired without payment.
6. In Northern Ireland a certificate of unenforceability has been granted in respect of a judgement.

Application for administration order

The application is made by way of a petition to the Court on IR Form No. 2.1 (as amended by The Insolvency (Amendment) Rules 1987) 'Petition for an Administration Order' supported by an affidavit with contents as stated in the IR Rule 2.3 (IR Rule 2.1(1)). The petition may be presented by the company itself, its directors, creditors or by any combination of these (IA s.9(1)).

Any person who has appointed, or who is entitled to appoint, an administrative receiver must be given notice of the petition. A petition, once presented, cannot be withdrawn except by leave of the Court (IA s.9(2)). If there is an administrative receiver in office, the petition will be dismissed unless the person on whose behalf the receiver is acting gives his consent.

Effects of petition for an administration order

The following may not take place during the period beginning with the presentation of the petition and ending with the making of an order or the dismissal of the petition by the Court:

1. No resolution may be passed or order made for the winding-up of the company although a petition to wind up the company may be presented.
2. No steps may be taken to enforce any security over the company's property or to repossess goods in the company's possession under a hire purchase agreement without leave of the Court.
3. No other proceedings and no execution or other legal process may be commenced or continued, or distress levied against the company or its property, without leave of the Court (IA s.10).

Effects of administration order

Following the making of an administration order and whilst it remains in force:

1. Any petition for the winding-up of the company shall be dismissed and no resolution may be passed to wind up the company.
2. Any administrative receiver of the company shall vacate office and no administrative receiver may be appointed.
3. No other steps may be taken to enforce any security over the company's property or to repossess goods in the company's possession, except with the consent of the administrator or leave of the Court.
4. The consent of the administrator or the leave of the Court is required to commence or continue any other legal processes against the company.

Powers and duties of administrator

The administrator of a company may do all such things as may be necessary for the management of the affairs, business and property of the company as well as the specific powers listed in the IA Schedule 1 (IA s.14(1)(*a*)). The more important of the things he may do are as follows:

1. Remove and appoint directors and call meetings of members and creditors of the company (IA s.14(2)).
2. Deal with property of the company subject to a floating charge as if it were not charged without the consent of the Court (IA s.15(1)). The proceeds of the property disposed of under this power become subject to the floating charge with the same priority as the original security (IA s.15(4)).
3. Deal with any other charged property or goods subject to a hire purchase agreement with the consent of the Court (IA s.15(2)).
4. Give notice of his appointment to interested parties specified in the IR Rule 2.10 (in particular to the Registrar of Companies on IR Form No. 2.7 'Administration order') and advertise it in the *London Gazette* (or the *Edinburgh Gazette* if appropriate) and appropriate newspapers.
5. Take control or custody of all property of the company to which the company appears to be entitled (IA s.17(1)).
6. Request the officers of the company (or other persons specified in the IA s.22(3)) to submit a statement of affairs on IR Form No. 2.9 'Statement of Affairs' which includes an affidavit to be sworn by the officers or other persons submitting the statement of affairs. This statement of affairs must be submitted within 21 days of the administrator's request.

Administrator's proposals

Within two months after the end of every 6 months from the date of his appointment, and within two months after he ceases to act, the administrator must send to the Court, to the Registrar of Companies and to each member of the creditors' committee, accounts of the receipts and payments of the company.

The administrator is required within three months of the making of the order to submit to the Registrar of Companies, all members and all creditors of the company, details of his proposals for achieving the purposes specified in the order. These have to be submitted to a meeting of the creditors on IR Form No. 2.11 'Notice of Creditors' Meeting in Administration Proceedings', the meeting being summoned at not less than 14 days' notice (IA s.23). The notice convening the meeting must also be published in the *London Gazette* or the *Edinburgh Gazette* and in the same newspapers in which the administration order was published.

The meeting of creditors has to decide whether to approve the administrator's proposals either in their original or, with the consent of the administrator, in a modified form (IA s.24). The Court, the Registrar of Companies and the creditors must be informed of the results of the meeting on IR Form No. 2.12 'Report of Meeting of Creditors'. The administrator may wish to make substantial alterations to proposals which have already been approved and in this case the same procedure must be followed as in the case of the original proposals although notice need not be given to the Registrar of Companies.

Where the Court does not approve the proposals, it may discharge the administration order in which case an office copy of the order must be sent to the Registrar of Companies within 14 days (IA s.24(6)). Instead of discharging the administration order the Court may make a further order (IA s.24(5)).

If at the meeting of creditors the proposals are approved (with or without modification) the meeting may establish a creditors' committee to assist the administrator in discharging his functions to bring the proposals into effect. Under the IA s.27 the Court may make an order giving relief if an application is made to the Court by any creditor or member of the company who considers that the administrator is acting in a manner prejudicial to his interests. Such an order will not, however, prejudice or prevent the implementation of any composition or scheme already approved or any compromise or arrangement sanctioned under s.425. If the application to the Court by any creditor or member who feels that the administrator is acting in a manner prejudicial to him is made more than 28 days after approval of the administrator's proposals, the Court's order will not prejudice or prevent their implementation.

Release of administrator

The Court may by order remove an administrator from office or he may resign his office by giving notice to the Court. Also, he vacates office if he ceases to be a qualified insolvency practitioner, if he dies or when the administration order is discharged (IA s.20)).

Receiverships

The law governing receiverships is considerable and in a practical handbook on company secretarial practice it is appropriate to consider only general matters affecting the appointment and procedures to be followed when a receiver is appointed. Consequently, reference should be made to appropriate books on the subject, and expert legal advice sought if necessary.

Definition

An administrative receiver is a receiver or manager of the whole (or substantially the whole) of the company's property. He would normally be appointed by or on behalf of the holders of debentures of the company secured by a floating charge but may also be appointed by the Court. In the case of a fixed charge, the person appointed would be known merely as a receiver since he has no power to manage the business of the company like an administrative receiver under a floating charge who may also be appointed as manager.

Any reference in the Companies Act 1985 or in the Insolvency Act 1986 to a receiver or manager of the property of a company, or to a receiver of it, includes a receiver or manager of part only of that property and a receiver of the income only from the property or part of it (IA s.29(1)(a)).

The legislation relating to receivers in England and Wales is contained in s.196 (as substituted by IA Schedule 13, Part I), ss.403 and 405, IA ss.28–49 and s.72, and the IR Rules 3.1–3.35. The law relating to receivers in Scotland is different and will be found in ss.462–6 as amended by CA 1989 s.140 and Schedule 24, and in IA ss.50–72 also amended by Schedule 24. The description which follows deals with the position in England and Wales. The position in regard to Scotland is described later in this chapter.

Qualification and remuneration

Under the IA s.388, only a licensed insolvency practitioner may act as an administrative receiver of a floating charge and any person acting as such who is not so qualified is liable to imprisonment or to a fine, or both (IA s.389). There are detailed provisions governing who may be regarded as a fit and proper person and as to the education, practical training and experience, for appointment as a licensed insolvency practitioner which are contained in the IA ss.390–8, e.g. a person who is adjudged bankrupt or who is subject to a disqualification order under the CDDA is not qualified to act as an insolvency practitioner.

In the case of receivers appointed under a fixed charge, it is desirable to appoint as receiver only professionally competent persons because of the administrative and legal tasks involved. It should be noted that in the case of both types of receiver a corporate body may not be appointed as a receiver (IA s.30).

It is usual for debentures to specify the maximum rate of remuneration for the receiver or that it shall be agreed between the receiver and the debenture holder. If the receiver is appointed by the Court, the receiver's remuneration will be determined by the Court. Also, a liquidator of a company may apply to the Court to determine the receiver's remuneration (IA s.36).

Appointment by the Court

Appointments by the Court are usually made on the application of a mortgagee or debenture holder in the following circumstances:

1. Where repayment of principal and/or interest is in arrears.
2. When the security has become crystallised into a specific charge by the making up of a winding-up order or passing a resolution to wind-up.
3. Where the security of the mortgagee or the debenture holder is in jeopardy.

A receiver may be appointed by the Court on the application either of a contributory (i.e. a person liable to contribute to the assets of the company in the event of its being wound-up) or of the company. The Court will sometimes appoint a receiver and manager on a short-term basis if the directors, because of a dispute between them, are not fulfilling their functions of management and pending a general meeting where there has been no governing body. However, the Court will not appoint a receiver if winding-up would be more appropriate.

Appointment by debenture holders

A deed of appointment of receiver is executed, which constitutes his authority to act. This usually arises in the following circumstances:

1. Failure to pay the principal and/or interest in accordance with the terms of the debenture.

2. Where a borrowing limit has been exceeded and has not been reduced within a specified period.
3. Some other provision of the debenture or trust deed being breached.

In the case of a fixed charge, the receiver has no power to manage the business; in a case of a floating charge, and if the debenture permits, the receiver may be appointed manager. A receiver appointed under a fixed charge may only call in the assets and realise them in the interests of the debenture holders, whereas a receiver appointed under a floating charge may manage the business of the company if the charge is on the goodwill or business of the company. Bank debentures usually provide for a fixed charge on such assets as interests in land, and for a floating charge on the general undertaking of the company.

Procedure on appointment

Acceptance of the appointment as an administrative receiver must be made before the end of the next business day following receipt of the notice of appointment, be advertised in the *London Gazette* and published in an appropriate newspaper (IA s.46 and IR Rules 3.1 and 3.2 as amended by The Insolvency (Amendment) Rules 1987).

The following are the matters which the receiver or manager should attend to following his appointment:

1. Examine the deed of appointment and a copy of the debenture (or trust deed) in order to consider the validity both of the debenture and of his appointment.
2. Verify that the appointment has been registered with the Registrar of Companies within 7 days on Companies Form No. 405(1) 'Notice of appointment of receiver or manager' (s.405(1)).
3. Take possession of the assets charged.
4. Check that insurance is in force and adequate.
5. Notify the appointment to the company's bankers and open an account in the name of the receiver or manager, as appropriate.
6. Consider the position of employees, whether they should be dismissed or retained.
7. Check arrangements for the receipt and dispatch of goods and collect the book debts.
8. Ensure that all invoices, statements etc., are endorsed 'Administrative Receiver' and that letters are signed 'For and on behalf of .... Limited/PLC, Administrative Receiver'; refer only to 'Receiver' if appropriate (IA s.39).
9. Consider the position of current contracts, where they should be completed or whether the business should be disposed of in whole or in part and the mode of disposal.

10. Make sure that the company's books are written up to the commencement of the receivership.

11. Inform all creditors within 28 days (IA s.46) and customers of his appointment and, in particular, notify judgement creditors, persons who have issued writs against the company, and their solicitors, if known. The position of other secured creditors, hire purchase agreements and claims by landlords should also be considered.

12. Keep his own records and books of accounts of his receivership (IR Rule 3.32).

13. Where an administrative receiver is appointed, the directors must prepare a statement of affairs verified by affidavit on IR Form No. 3.2 'Statement of Affairs' to be submitted by the directors to the receiver within 21 days.

14. Within three months of his appointment (or such longer period as the Court may allow) the receiver must send to the Registrar of Companies, to any trustees for secured creditors and to all such creditors of which he is aware, a report giving details of the following matters:
    (a) the events leading to his appointment;
    (b) the disposal or proposed disposal of any property and the continuation or proposed continuation of the business;
    (c) the amounts of principal and interest payable to the debenture holders who appointed him and the amounts due to preferential creditors;
    (d) the amount likely to be available for payment to other creditors (IA s.48).

The report need not include any information the disclosure of which could affect the performance of the administrative receiver's functions (IA s.48(6)). The report should also be sent to unsecured creditors or be published in the same newspaper in which notice of his appointment was advertised (IA s.48).

Employees

An appointment of a receiver by the Court is generally considered to terminate employees' contracts of employment. An appointment by debenture holders does not, however, automatically sever employment contracts. It may do so if the receiver sells the business or if there are new terms and conditions of employment inconsistent with the previous contracts. If the receiver becomes personally liable on contracts of employment he must fulfil the obligations of the employer. It is important, therefore, for him to ensure that there are sufficient funds or indemnities available to him before he allows circumstances to develop in which he may be held liable. On the termination of employment the receiver becomes the employer's representative under the Employment Protection (Consolidation) Act 1978 and is thus responsible for dealing with employees' claims.

Powers, liabilities and responsibilities

An administrative receiver has the powers which the debenture holders have conferred on him which are deemed to include the 23 powers listed in IA Schedule 1 (IA s.42). On application to the Court he may seek authority to dispose of any of the company's property as if it were uncharged (IA s.43(1)).

The IA s.43(5) provides that the administrative receiver is deemed to be the company's agent until the commencement of liquidation and, unless the contract provides otherwise, is personally liable on any contract entered into by him in carrying out his functions although he is normally entitled to indemnity out of the assets of the company. However, if the administrative receiver enters into contracts without authority, his liability is unlimited with no right of indemnity.

Records and returns

It is obviously important that the receiver should maintain full and proper records and accounts since under the provisions of IA s.38 and IR Rule 3.32, he is required to send to the Registrar of Companies, to the company concerned, to the person by whom he was appointed and, where there is a creditors' committee, to each member of the committee, an abstract of his receipts and payments on IR Form No. 3.6 'Receiver or Manager or Administrative Receiver's Abstract of Receipts and Payments' (IA s.38). The IR Rule 3.32 provides that the accounts must be sent within two months after the end of 12 months from the date of his appointment, and of every subsequent period of 12 months and within two months after he ceases to act as administrative receiver. The Court may, on the administrative receiver's application, extend the period of two months.

Taxation implications

Tax on any income arising during the receivership, e.g. from trading profits, deposit interest and capital gains, is usually considered to be assessable on the company and is not a charge on the receiver. If the assessment relates to a period after liquidation, it is an expense in the liquidation but is otherwise merely a claim against the company.

Priority in distribution of funds

1. The proceeds realised from specific assets charged under a fixed charge must be used first to meet the costs of realisation, then the receiver's remuneration and then the claims of the debenture holders. If there is then any surplus remaining, the excess is to be distributed in accordance with the priorities for floating charges as in (2) below.

2. The priorities for distribution of funds arising from a floating charge are as follows:
   (a) cost of realisations;
   (b) other outgoings and costs of the receivership;
   (c) the receiver's remuneration;
   (d) preferential creditors, e.g. PAYE and National Insurance contributions, taxes, employees' arrears of salary or wages, etc;
   (e) interest due under the debenture subject to the debenture's terms;
   (f) principal sum secured by the debenture;
   (g) surplus to the company or liquidator if appointed.

Vacation of office

The IA s.45 provides that an administrative receiver may only be removed from office by order of the Court although he may resign and, indeed, he must vacate his office if he ceases to be qualified as an insolvency practitioner.

On vacating office any remuneration and expenses and any indemnity to which the receiver is entitled, shall be paid out of the property of the company in his custody or under his control in priority to any security held by the person by or on whose behalf he was appointed.

The receiver should attend to the following matters on the termination of his receivership:

1. Send a notice in the prescribed form of ceasing to act as receiver or manager to the Registrar of Companies within 14 days of vacating office (IA s.45(4)).

2. If the company is in liquidation he must also notify the liquidator and the members of the creditors' committee if there is one (IR Rule 3.35 as amended by The Insolvency (Amendment) Rules 1987.

3. File a final abstract of receipts and payments within two months of the termination of the receivership with the Registrar of Companies on IR Form No. 3.6 'Receiver or Manager or Administrative Receiver's Abstract of Receipts and Payments'.

4. Ensure that a director of the company or the company's secretary has filed with the Registrar of Companies in the prescribed form for registration a memorandum to the effect that any charge on the company's property has ceased to affect the company's property.
5. The receiver should return the books and documents no longer required to the company or to the liquidator if the company is being wound-up.

Receivers in Scotland

A holder of a fixed charge over Scottish property has no power to appoint a receiver. Sections 462–6 as amended by CA 1989 s.140 and Schedule 24 and IA ss.50–72 also amended by Schedule 24 contain the law concerning floating charges and receivers in Scotland:

1. The holder of a floating charge created after 27 October 1961 may appoint a receiver in the following circumstances:
   (a) under the provisions of the instrument creating the charge;
   (b) to the extent that the instrument creating the charge does not otherwise provide, on the occurrence of the following events:
      (i) on the expiry of 21 days after making a demand for payment without payment having been made;
      (ii) on the expiry of a period of two months during the whole of which interest due and payable has been in arrears;
      (iii) on the making of a winding-up order or the passing of a resolution to wind up the company; and
      (iv) on the appointment of a receiver in respect of any other floating charge.
2. The holder of the floating charge may alternatively apply to the Court to appoint a receiver under IA s.51(2) in the following circumstances:
   (a) on the occurrence of any of the events in item 1(b) above; or
   (b) if the Court is satisfied that the position of the holder of the charge is likely to be prejudiced if no appointment is made (IA s.52).
3. It is not essential that the instrument creating the charge should give express power for a receiver to be appointed by the Court.
4. The powers of the receiver are specified in IA Schedule 2 (IA s.55); he may exercise these in so far as they are not inconsistent with the instrument creating the charge. The list contained in the section is very detailed, but the receiver is given full powers to take possession of the company's property and to take any action in connection therewith to enable him properly to exercise his powers of receiver.
5. It should be noted, however, that the powers in IA Schedule 2 are

subject to the rights of any person who has effectually executed diligence on any part of the property of the company prior to the receiver's appointment (IA s.55(3)). The powers of a receiver appointed by the holder of a floating charge are suspended to the extent that another receiver is appointed having precedence over him (IA s.56(4)).

(Note: Diligence is a process which may be instituted under Scots law to attach goods or property.)

6. The receiver may continue contracts entered into prior to his appointment without personal liability (IA s.57(4)). However, he is personally liable on contracts which he himself enters into in performing his functions unless the contract otherwise provides and on any contract of employment adopted by him in carrying out those functions (IA s.57(2)). A receiver personally liable under the IA s.57(2) may be indemnified out of the property in respect of which he was appointed (IA s.57(3)).

7. The remuneration of the receiver is determined by agreement with the holder of the charge or, if there is no such agreement, by the Auditor of the Court of Session on application of the receiver (IA s.58).

8. Other matters relating to receivers in Scotland are similar to those applicable in England, e.g. as follows:

   (a) notification to the Registrar of Companies of the appointment, on IR Form No. 1(Scot) 'Notice of appointment of a Receiver by the holder of a Floating Charge' (IA s.53(1) or IR Form No. 2 (Scot) 'Notice of appointment of a Receiver by the Court (IA s.54(3));

   (b) notification of ceasing to act as receiver to the Registrar of Companies on IR Form No. 3(Scot) 'Notice of the Receiver ceasing to act or of his removal' (IA s.62(5));

   (c) notification of appointment to be sent forthwith to the company on IR Form No. 4(Scot) 'Notice of appointment of Receiver' (IA s.65(1)(a)). The creditors must also be informed within 28 days unless the Court otherwise directs;

   (d) an inclusion on all communications of the statement that a receiver has been appointed (IA s.64(1));

   (e) preparation, submission and filing of statements of affairs on IR Form No. 5(Scot) 'Statement of Affairs' (IA s.66(1)), and submission of reports to the Registrar of Companies, the holder of a floating charge, trustees for secured creditors and unsecured creditors as required by IA s.67;

   (f) submission of a report to the Registrar of Companies, the holder of the floating charge by virtue of which he was appointed,

trustees for secured creditors and all unsecured creditors of the company giving the details listed in (14) on p.317 (IA s.67);
(g) the termination and release procedure for receivers is also similar to that obtaining in England (IA s.62).

Company voluntary arrangements

A voluntary arrangement is where an administrator, a liquidator (or where the company is not subject to an administration order or is in liquidation) the directors propose to the company and its creditors a composition in satisfaction of its debts or a scheme of arrangement of its affairs (IA s.1). However, the rights of preferential creditors cannot be affected without their concurrence (IA s.4(4)). The voluntary arrangement is implemented by a licensed insolvency practitioner who acts as nominee for the purpose of the implementation of the arrangement (IA s.1(2)).

Procedure for voluntary arrangements

The procedure varies according to whether the nominee is or is not the administrator or liquidator. If he is not the administrator, the following procedure should be followed:

1. The directors to prepare a proposal for the intended nominee, of which he is given formal notice, on which he will report to the Court within 28 days of its receipt if he agrees to act which is signified by his endorsing the notice (IA s.2; IR Rules 1.3 and 1.4).
2. Within 21 days after delivery of the proposals to the nominee, or such longer time as he may allow, the directors to deliver a statement of affairs of the company in the prescribed form (IR Rule 1.5).
3. In reporting to the Court the nominee gives his opinion whether meetings of the company and its creditors should be called and, if so, when and where the meetings should be held.
4. Unless the Court directs otherwise, the nominee summons the meetings, giving at least 14 days' notice, which must be held not less than 14 days nor more than 28 days of filing the nominee's report with the Court (IA s.3(1); IR Rule 1.9).

Where the nominee is the administrator or liquidator he may summon the meetings of the company and its creditors directly without application to the Court, giving at least 14 days' notice (IA s.3(2); IR Rule 1.11).

Procedure and effects of meetings

The following points arise in connection with the meetings of the company and its creditors:

1. The notices calling the meetings must include:
   (a) the proposals;
   (b) the statement of affairs;
   (c) the nominee's comments.
2. The creditors at their meeting must approve the voluntary arrangement by a majority in excess of three-quarters in value of the creditors present in person or by proxy.
3. The members of the company at their meeting must approve the voluntary arrangement by a majority in excess of one-half of the members present in person or by proxy (IR Rules 1.19 and 1.20 as amended by the Insolvency (Amendment) Rules 1987).
4. Either meeting may alter the voluntary arrangement by changing the nominee provided that the person is a licensed insolvency practitioner (IA s.4(2)).
5. The votes of some creditors must be left out of account as specified in IR Rule 1.19(3) and a creditors' resolution is invalid if those voting against it include more than one-half in value of such creditors (IR Rule 1.19(4)).
6. Approval at the meetings of the voluntary arrangement by both the creditors and the company binds every person who had notice of, and was entitled to vote at, either of the meetings.
7. The company may already be in the process of being wound-up or be subject to an administration order and, in this case, the Court may stay the winding-up proceedings or discharge the administration order so as to facilitate the voluntary arrangement (IA s.5).
8. The voluntary arrangement approved at the meetings may be challenged on application to the Court by any of the following:
   (a) a person entitled to vote at either meeting;
   (b) the nominee or any person appointed to replace him;
   (c) the administrator or liquidator (IA s.6).

Implementation of voluntary arrangement

The person who implements the approved voluntary arrangement, who may be the nominee (or another licensed insolvency practitioner who has replaced him) is known as the supervisor (IA s.7(2)).

The supervisor would see to the following matters:

1. Take possession of the company's assets (IR Rule 1.23) to implement

the arrangement subject to any administrator's or liquidator's costs first being met out of those assets.

2. Ensure that the chairmen of the meetings of the creditors and of the company have filed with the Court reports of the meetings. This should be done within four days of the meetings being held. Copies of the relevant report should also be sent to each person who was sent notice of the meetings (IR Rule 1.24(3), (4)).

3. Send forthwith a copy of the chairmen's reports to the Registrar of Companies if the voluntary arrangement has been approved (IR Rule 1.24(5)).

4. Keep accounts and records of all his dealings including records of all receipts and payments of money (IR Rule 1.26).

5. Submit within two months of the end of each 12 months beginning with the date of his appointment an account of receipts and payments to:
   (a) the Court;
   (b) the Registrar of Companies;
   (c) the company;
   (d) all creditors bound by the arrangement;
   (e) members of the company bound by the arrangement;
   (f) the auditors of the company if it is not in liquidation.

Remuneration, expenses and completion of the voluntary arrangement

The following fees, costs, charges and expenses may be incurred in connection with the voluntary arrangement:

1. Disbursements by the nominee prior to approval of the arrangement and agreed remuneration for his services.

2. Disbursements sanctioned by the terms of the arrangement or which would be payable in an administration or winding-up.

The supervisor shall send a notice that the voluntary arrangement has been fully implemented within 28 days of its final completion (or within such extended time as an application to the Court may be allowed) to:

1. The Registrar of Companies.
2. The Court.
3. All creditors and members of the company who are bound by it.

With this notice the supervisor should send a report summarising all receipts and payments and explaining any difference in the implementation compared with the approved proposals (IR Rule 1.29).

CHAPTER 16

Winding-up

The amount of law on the subject of winding-up is considerable and was substantially amended with effect from 29 December 1986 when the Insolvency Act 1986 came into force. In view of the complexity of the subject the company secretary faced with a situation in which the company may not be able to pay its debts as they fall due would be strongly advised to seek specialist advice. Some special provisions have been introduced into the law of insolvency by CA 1989 regarding the operations of financial markets which are noted at the end of this chapter.

The statute law is principally contained in ss.73–229 of the Insolvency Act 1986, the Company Directors' Disqualification Act 1986 and in other Acts, Rules and Regulations which are referred to in Chapter 15 of the Institute's manual.

Methods of winding-up

There are three methods of winding-up. These are as follows:

1. Members' voluntary winding-up.
2. Creditors' voluntary winding-up.
3. Winding-up by the Court.

Members' voluntary winding-up

For this to be available the directors must resolve within the five weeks immediately preceding the resolution to wind-up that, having made full enquiry, they are of the opinion that the company will be able to pay its debts in full with interest at the official rate within a period not exceeding 12 months from the commencement of the winding-up (IA ss.89 and 90). If a director makes this declaration without reasonable grounds and the debts and interest are not paid within the specified period, he is liable to fine or imprisonment or both and the burden of proof of innocence is on the director (IA s.89(4)).

The resolution to wind-up will appoint a liquidator and if during the course of the liquidation he should form the opinion that the company could not pay its liabilities in full within the stipulated time, he should call a meeting of creditors within 28 days of his becoming aware of the company's insolvency. At least 7 days' notice of the meeting should be given which must be published in the *London Gazette* or the *Edinburgh Gazette*, as appropriate, and advertised in two newspapers in the locality where the company principally conducts business. Before the meeting the liquidator must supply creditors with information concerning the affairs of the company.

Creditors' voluntary winding-up

This occurs where a declaration of solvency by the directors cannot be made, in which case the company may be wound-up as a creditors' voluntary winding-up. A meeting of the creditors must be called and held within 14 days after the meeting of the members of the company at which a resolution to wind-up is passed (IA s.98). The liquidation commences at the time of passing the resolution to wind-up (IA s.86).

Winding-up by the Court

A company may be wound-up by the Court if:

1. The company so resolves by Special Resolution.
2. A judgement creditor or a creditor petitions the Court where an amount in excess of £750 has not been paid following written demand for payment (IA s.123).
3. It is just and equitable for the company to be wound-up.
4. The company failing to comply with certain statutory requirements, e.g. the minimum number of members (IA ss.122 and 124).

The most usual ground for a petition to the Court is the inability of the company to pay its debts. A contributory, the Official Receiver, the Secretary of State, the Bank of England and the Attorney General may present a petition under various statutory provisions even if the company is solvent.

Members' voluntary winding-up: initial procedures

1. The company's board resolve to make a declaration of solvency, which must embody a statement of assets and liabilities and be made within five weeks immediately before the passing of the resolution to wind-up. The declaration has to be filed with the Registrar of

Companies within 15 days of the passing of the resolution to wind-up (IA ss.89 and 90).

2. The board will also authorise the calling of an Extraordinary General Meeting at which a Special Resolution to wind-up will be considered. An Ordinary Resolution will suffice if the period for the life of the company has expired or the occurrence of an event on the happening of which the Articles provide that the company should be wound-up (IA s.84).

3. If the resolution is passed, it is necessary to appoint a liquidator. This may be done by an Ordinary Resolution of the company, although notice of the proposed appointment would usually be given.

4. The resolution passed by the company in general meeting to wind-up, signed by the chairman of the meeting, should be published in the *London Gazette* or the *Edinburgh Gazette*, as appropriate, within 14 days of its being passed (IA s.85). The resolution and all documents for publication in the *Gazette* must be authenticated by a solicitor or a member of an established body of accountants or secretaries. The resolution to wind-up must also be filed within 15 days with the Registrar of Companies (s.380 and IA s.84).

5. The liquidator must himself within 14 days of his appointment publish in the *Gazette* and deliver to the Registrar for registration a notice of his appointment on Companies Form No. 600 'Notice of appointment of liquidator voluntary winding-up (members or creditors)'.

6. IR Rule 4.148A, as amended by The Insolvency (Amendment) Rules 1987, provides for the liquidator's remuneration.

The subsequent procedure is similar to that for a creditors' voluntary winding-up set out below, except that meetings of, and notices to, creditors are not required.

Creditors' voluntary winding-up: initial procedures

1. A meeting of the board will authorise the calling of an Extraordinary General Meeting to consider an Extraordinary Resolution that the company, by reason of its liabilities, cannot continue and that it is advisable to wind-up (IA s.84(1)(c)).

2. A meeting of the creditors should be called by the company to be held within 14 days of the members' meeting to consider the resolution to wind-up (IA s.98). At least 7 days' notice of the meeting must be given to the creditors. Notice of the creditors' meeting should be advertised in the appropriate *Gazette* and two local newspapers (IA s.98(1)(b)(c)).

3. The notice must be given either:

    (a) the name and address of the insolvency practitioner who will give such information to the creditors before the meeting takes place as they may reasonably require; or

    (b) a place in the principal area of business of the company where a list of names and addresses of the company's creditors will be available for inspection without charge.

4.   The creditors' meeting will be presided over by one of the directors who should prepare a statement of affairs in the prescribed form verified by affidavit to be laid before the creditors' meeting.

5.   At the Extraordinary General Meeting an Extraordinary Resolution is passed to wind-up and an Ordinary Resolution is passed to nominate the liquidator.

6.   At the creditor's meeting, which must be attended by the liquidator, the directors may answer questions put to them by the creditors concerning the administration of the company, although there is no legal requirement for them to do so.

7.   The creditors either endorse the members' nomination of a liquidator or appoint some other person of their own choice. If the creditors nominate a different person as liquidator he will be the liquidator. Otherwise, the members' nominee continues as liquidator. However, within 7 days of the nomination of a liquidator by the creditors, any member or creditor of the company may apply to the Court for an order that the members' nomination shall remain liquidator instead of, or jointly with, the creditors' nomination, or that some other person be appointed liquidator (IA s.100).

8.   On the appointment of a liquidator all the powers of the directors cease.

9.   The creditors have the power to appoint a liquidation committee which may sanction the continuation of some of the directors' powers (IA ss.100 and 101).

10.   The remuneration of the liquidator is fixed by the liquidation committee or, if there is no committee, by the creditors.

11.   Upon his appointment, the liquidator should immediately see to the following matters:

    (a) if not already done, arrange for the redirection of mail;

    (b) if thought necessary, change the registered office address;

    (c) take over all books and records of the company;

    (d) make a formal report to each creditor enclosing a copy of the directors' statement of affairs, and a copy of any statement made by the directors at the creditors' meeting. Creditors must be informed of the liquidator's appointment and invited to forward a statement of their claims;

    (e) advertise for claims at the appropriate time;

(f) inform the appropriate sheriffs and bailiffs of the winding-up resolution and of the appointment of the liquidator;

(g) take into protective custody the company's assets and ensure that there is adequate insurance cover;

(h) open in the name of the liquidator separate bank accounts; any sums not immediately required should be transferred into a deposit account in the liquidator's name or in other suitable interest-bearing security;

(i) it may be desirable for the liquidator to issue a disclaimer of onerous property or contracts;

(j) the position of secured creditors should be considered and if necessary discussed and negotiated with them;

(k) consider the position of any landlords, particularly any distress warrants;

(l) consider the most appropriate way of disposing of the company's assets and discuss this with appointed agents;

(m) make a demand for the company's outstanding book debts and consider the position as to work in progress;

(n) any pending or future litigation outstanding against the company should be considered and discussed with the company's solicitors.

Winding-up by the Court: initial procedures

1. When the Court makes its winding-up order, the Official Receiver becomes the liquidator (IA s.136(2)).
2. The Official Receiver may require officers of the company or other persons as specified in the IA s.131(3) to prepare, swear and submit a statement of affairs within 21 days (IA s.131).
3. Separate meetings of creditors and contributories may be summoned by the Official Receiver at his discretion to choose some other person to be liquidator of the company (IA s.136(4)). Contributories are defined by the IA s.79 but are usually synonymous with the term 'members'. The Official Receiver remains liquidator if another person is not appointed. The Official Receiver must summon a meeting to choose another liquidator if one-quarter in value of the creditors requisition him to do so on IR Form No. 4.21 'Request by creditor(s) for a meeting of the company's creditors [and contributories]' in accordance with the IA s.136(5)(c) and IR Rule 4.57.
4. The Court may make any appointment or Order to give effect to the wishes of the meetings or make any other Order that it may think fit.
5. The creditors and contributories may nominate as liquidator any person who is qualified to act as an insolvency practitioner (IA s.139)

and in the absence of a nomination by the creditors the contributories' nominee (if any) will be the liquidator.

6. At any time the Official Receiver may apply to the Secretary of State for the appointment of a liquidator in his place. Any such liquidator must send notice of his appointment to the creditors and also advertise the appointment as the Court may direct (IA s.137(3)(4)).

The liquidator should deal with the following matters:

1. Take over responsibility for the assets of the company, together with its books and records.
2. Take other necessary steps to protect and realise the assets, as indicated above in the case of a creditors' voluntary winding-up.
3. Disclaim any onerous property or unprofitable contracts (IA s.178 and IR Rules 4.187–94).
4. The winding-up Order halts any proceedings against the company except by leave of the Court (IA s.130(2)).
5. Provide the Official Receiver with information, access to books or such other assistance as he may reasonably require.

Qualifications of liquidators

A liquidator must be a person who is qualified to act as an insolvency practitioner (IA s.388). They are also required to fulfil certain bonding requirements. The Secretary of State may give authority to act as an insolvency practitioner or authorise another competent authority to do so (IA s.392).

Duties and powers of liquidators

The IA ss.165–70 and Schedule 4 specify the duties and powers of a liquidator. The principal ones are as follows:

1. To realise the company's assets to the best advantage, to determine the claims against the company and to distribute the funds realised, after payment of costs, to the creditors and contributories, in accordance with the priorities laid down by law.
2. The liquidator has considerable powers, although the exercise of some of them requires specific sanctions. Full details are given in the IA Schedule 4. No sanction is necessary in respect of the following matters:
   (a) to sell the company's assets and transfer title on behalf of the company;
   (b) to execute deeds, receipts and documents and affix the company's seal, if it has one, where necessary;

(c) to prove, rank and claim in bankruptcy or insolvency;
(d) to draw, accept and endorse bills of exchange or promissory notes in the name, and on behalf, of the company;
(e) to raise money on security of the company's assets;
(f) to take out letters of administration to the estate of a deceased contributory;
(g) to appoint agents, although in practice sanction of any liquidation committee is usually sought;
(h) to exercise the Court's power to settle a list of contributories;
(i) to convene general meetings of the company to obtain its sanction by Special or Extraordinary Resolution or for any purpose he may think fit (IA s.165(4)).

3. In the case of a winding-up by the Court, but not in the case of a voluntary winding-up, the liquidator requires sanction in order to do the following things:
(a) bring or defend actions or other legal proceedings;
(b) carry on the business for beneficial winding-up.

4. Sanction is required in all cases to:
(a) pay any class of creditor in full;
(b) make any compromise or arrangement with creditors or contributories;
(c) make any compromise affecting the assets or winding-up of the company, take security for the discharge of any debt and give a discharge in respect of it.

5. Sanction for the matters in (4) above is usually sought from the liquidation committee in a winding-up by the Court except for matters which are reserved to the Court. If there is no liquidation committee the Secretary of State may exercise its functions except where they are exercised by the Official Receiver (IA s.141(4)(5) and IR Rule 4.172).

6. In the case of a creditors' voluntary winding-up the liquidation committee's sanction for the matters in (4) above is usually sought or, if there is no such committee, it is sought from the creditors.

The acts of a liquidation committee will be valid notwithstanding any defect in the appointment or qualifications of members of the committee (IR Rule 4.172A as amended by The Insolvency (Amendment) Rules 1987).

Liquidators' records and their audit

The administrative and financial records to be kept by a liquidator are specified in The Insolvency Regulations 1986 (SI 1986/1994) and vary according to whether the winding-up is by the Court or is a voluntary winding-up.

Winding-up by the Court

The following records must be kept, and action taken, by the responsible insolvency practitioner:

1. Prepare and keep separate financial records in respect of each insolvency and enter day to day all receipts and payments made by him (Regulation 9).
2. Keep separate records if a business is carried on (Regulation 10).
3. Submit a certified account to the Department of Trade and Industry for audit annually (Regulation 12) and within 14 days of vacating office (Regulation 12(6)).
4. Keep records of minutes of meetings and other matters required to give an accurate record of the administration (Regulation 8).
5. Retain the financial records under (1) above and the administrative records under (4) above for 6 years following vacation of office (Insolvency (Amendment) Regulations 1987 (Regulation 10A)).
6. All money received in the course of carrying out his functions must be paid without deduction into the insolvency services account kept by the Secretary of State with the Bank of England (Regulation 4), although the insolvency practitioner may apply to the Secretary of State for authority to open a local bank account when carrying on the business of an insolvency.
7. Obtain authority of the Official Receiver to sell, destroy or otherwise dispose of books, papers and other records of the company during or on vacating office.

Voluntary winding-up

The following records must be kept, and action taken, by the liquidator:

1. Prepare and keep such financial records as the liquidation committee, or if there is no committee, as the creditors direct and enter day to day all receipts and payments made by him (Regulation 27(1)).
2. Keep the business and administrative records required by Regulations 10 and 8 as in (2) and (4) above under winding-up by the Court (Regulations 26 and 28).
3. Retain financial records under (1) and business records under (2) for a period of 6 years following vacation of office (Insolvency (Amendment) Regulations 1987 (Regulation 28A).
4. Submit a statement of his receipts and payments to the Registrar of

Companies covering the first 12 months' period of the liquidation within 30 days of the end of the first year and thereafter for every 6 months' period (IA s.192 and IR Rule 4.223) as amended by The Insolvency (Amendment) Rules 1987 on IR Form No. 4.68 'Liquidator's statement of receipts and payments'.

5. Submit records kept under (1) above to the liquidation committee, or if there is no committee, to the creditors (Regulation 27(2)).
6. After the expiry of one year from the company's dissolution the liquidator may destroy or otherwise dispose of books, papers and other records of the company (Regulation 32).

Directors

A report must be made forthwith to the Secretary of State under Section 7(3) of the CDDA if in the winding-up proceedings it appears to a liquidator or to the Official Receiver that the conduct of a director of the company is such as to render him unfit to the concerned in the management of a limited company. Under the provisions of the Insolvent Companies (Reports on Conduct of Directors) No. 2 Rules 1986, a return must be submitted to the Secretary of State within 6 months of the liquidator's or Official Receiver's appointment stating whether or not there is any such knowledge of the conduct of director(s) or if the conduct return will be delayed beyond that date. If subsequent to the conduct return, further information about the conduct of director(s) should come to notice, a further return must be submitted. Appropriate forms for making these returns are annexed to the Rules mentioned above, which also apply to administrative receivers and administrators.

The matters determining the unfitness of directors are set out in the CDDA Schedule 1.

A Court of summary jurisdiction may impose a disqualification order for a maximum of 5 years, or in the case of superior Courts, 15 years.

Investigations, preferences, fraud and criminal offences

The liquidator must investigate the records of the company to establish whether any of the following have occurred:

1. Transactions at an undervalue and preferences (IA s.238).
2. Floating charges created in favour of a connected person within two years of the commencement of the liquidation or within one year if created in favour of any other person or created between the time of presentation of a petition for an administration order and the making of the Order (IA s.245).
3. Fraudulent trading (s.458 and IA ss.213 and 215).

4. Wrongful trading (IA ss.214 and 215).
5. Any misfeasance by any director or manager (IA s.212).
6. Failure to register any charge under ss.395–8.
7. Audited and management accounts.

Under the IA s.218(4) the liquidator has a statutory duty in a voluntary winding-up to report any fraud or criminal act he discovers to the Director of Public Prosecutions.

Employees

The employees' contracts of employment are terminated by the winding-up order of the Court. In a voluntary winding-up the subsequent failure by the liquidator to maintain the terms of the employment terminates the employment.

The liquidator acts as the employer's representative so far as claims are concerned under the Employment Protection (Consolidation) Act 1978.

The employer's representative, with certain limits, is provided with funds from the Department of Employment to meet the claims of employees, which he then distributes to the employees concerned. The claims of the employees against the insolvent company paid in this way are then assigned to the Department of Employment, which may claim in the liquidation of the company. The Department of Employment will also probably claim any sums which have been paid for redundancy.

Tax implications of liquidation

A separate record should be kept of tax liabilities incurred by the liquidator during the course of the liquidation, these being part of the costs of the liquidation as distinct from tax liabilities arising up to the date of commencement of the winding-up, which would be the subject of a claim in the liquidation. Any value added tax arising would be treated similarly.

Determination of creditors' claims

In a winding-up by the Court creditors must submit their claims in writing on IR Form No. 4.25 'Proof of Debt – General Form' (IR Rule 4.73).

In the case of voluntary liquidations the liquidator may require a creditor to submit his claim in writing but no specific form is provided for this.

If the liquidator rejects a claim in whole or in part he must give his reasons in writing to the creditor. A creditor has 21 days to require the matter to be put before the Court if he is dissatisfied with the liquidator's decision (IR Rule 4.83).

Distributions and release

Voluntary winding-up

After payment of relevant fixed charges, the order of priority for payment is roughly as follows:

1. Costs of the winding-up.
2. Preferential claims. Details of these are in the IA Schedule 6, but the principal categories are as follows:
   (a) PAYE deductions and National Insurance contributions relating to 12 months prior to the relevant date;
   (b) VAT relating to 6 months prior to the relevant date;
   (c) employees' unpaid salary or wages for four months prior to the relevant date limited to the amount fixed by delegated legislation;
   (d) employees' accrued holiday remuneration;
   (e) sums paid by third parties on behalf of the company to discharge debts which would have been preferential had the third parties not paid them and which remain outstanding to such third parties.
   (Note: The relevant date applicable to the above is defined in the IA s.387, but it usually means the date of appointment of the liquidator, or if no liquidator has been appointed, the date of the winding-up order.)
3. Creditors who have a floating charge (IA s.175(2)(b)).
4. Admitted ordinary unsecured creditors.

After payment of the above claims any surplus should be paid to contributories (i.e. the members) (IA s.107). Any unclaimed funds should be paid into the insolvency services account at the Bank of England (Regulation 16).

Upon completion of a creditors' voluntary winding-up the liquidator should call general meetings of the contributories on IR Form No. 4.23 'Notice to Contributories of Meeting of Contributories' and of the creditors on IR Form No. 4.22 'Notice to Creditors of Meetings of Creditors' to lay an account of his administration before the meetings and to give explanations. At least 28 days' notice of the meetings must be given which must also be published in the appropriate *Gazette* at least one month beforehand (IA s.106(2)).

Within one week of the meetings being held he should file a copy of the accounts and a return of the holding of the meetings with the Registrar of Companies. Three months after the registration of the return with the Registrar of Companies, the company is deemed to be dissolved (IA s.201(2)).

Similar provisions to the above apply in the case of a members' voluntary winding-up except that meetings of creditors are not called.

Winding-up by the Court

1. The order of distribution is generally the same as in the case of a voluntary winding-up.
2. Upon completion of the winding-up, the liquidator should attend to the following matters:
   (a) summon a final general meeting of the creditors, giving at least 28 days' notice, on IR Form No. 4.22 to receive his report on the winding-up and to determine whether he should be released as liquidator (IA s.146). If the Court so orders the meeting must be advertised;
   (b) give notice to the Court and the Registrar of Companies that a meeting has been held under the IA s.146 and the decision of the meeting. If the creditors have not objected to the liquidator's release he vacates office and his release is effective from that time;
   (c) if the final meeting resolves against the release of the liquidator, the liquidator must apply to the Secretary of State to determine the outcome;
   (d) if there should be no quorum at the final meeting, it is deemed to have been held without the liquidator being released who must, therefore, report the matter to the Court (IR Rule 4.125(5)).

Dissolution without liquidation

A company may apply to the Registrar of Companies to be struck off the Register. This is an alternative to formal liquidation by the members, creditors or the Court, and is a simpler and more convenient method of dissolving a company which is not trading and has no assets or liabilities, i.e. a defunct company. A company may become defunct if it was formed to carry on any business which did not come to fruition or if the business for which the company was formed has ended and it is left with neither assets nor liabilities.

The full procedure and the steps to the taken in the case of a company applying to the Registrar of Companies to be struck off the Register are described in s.652.

Winding-up in Scotland

Certain provisions relating to winding-up are peculiar to Scottish law and are described in various sections of the IA. These are ss.120–1, 122(2), 142, 157, 161–2, 169, 185, 193, 198–9, 204 and 243.

It should be noted that floating charges in Scotland are dealt with in the Companies Act 1985, ss.462–6 as amended by CA 1989 s.140 and CA 1989 Schedule 24.

Financial markets and insolvency

The provisions of CA 1989 ss.154–91 and Schedules 21 and 22 are designed to prevent or minimise the effects on the financial markets arising from the insolvency of a market participant, mainly recognised investment exchanges (RIEs) and recognised clearing houses (RCHs). RIEs and RCHs are required to establish default rules complying with CA 1989 Schedule 21 which will be applicable in the event of a member of an exchange or clearing house defaulting, i.e. appearing to be unable to meet his obligations in respect of one or more market contracts.

Provision is made so that action taken in accordance with the rules cannot be challenged in the Court under insolvency law, which if strictly applied could lead to consequences causing a general market collapse. However, the exemptions from, and modifications of, insolvency law introduced by the CA 1989 provisions are limited to the extent necessary to deal with the specific problem of operations in financial markets.

The new provisions, however, make significant changes in regards to the powers of administrators and receivers to deal with property which is subject to a market charge as defined by CA 1989 s.173 granted to members of RIEs and RCHs as security for debts and liabilities arising in connection with the settlement of market contracts (CA 1989 s.175). Other provisions of insolvency law, such as the power to disclaim onerous property, the Court's power to order recission of contracts, transactions at an undervalue, preferences or transactions defrauding creditors, etc., do no apply to market contracts or to a contract effected by a RIE or RCH for the purpose of realising property provided as margin in relation to market contracts (CA 1989 s.164).

Within three months of CA 1989 Part VII coming into force, a RIE, a RCH or a person in whose favour a market charge has been granted, may apply to the Court for an order to put them generally in the position they would have been in had the new provisions been in force on 22 December 1988, the date on which the Companies Bill, now CA 1989, was first published. The provisions in Schedule 22 will apply in such cases and are somewhat different to those included in Part VII as enacted because

Schedule 22 reproduces certain provisions of Part VII as they appeared in the first draft of the bill.

It should be noted that CA 1989 gives power to the Secretary of State to make provision by regulations for further modifications of insolvency law to be applicable in the case of operations in financial markets.

The subject of the application of insolvency law to financial markets is extremely specialised and is unlikely to affect those concerned with normal commercial companies.

Index

339